MUSIC IN MEDIEVAL AND EARLY MODERN EUROPE

MUSIC IN MEDIEVAL AND EARLY MODERN EUROPE

PATRONAGE, SOURCES AND TEXTS

Edited by

IAIN FENLON

Fellow of King's College, Cambridge

CAMBRIDGE UNIVERSITY PRESS

Cambridge

London   New York   New Rochelle
Sydney   Melbourne

Published by the Press Syndicate of the University of Cambridge
The Pitt Building, Trumpington Street, Cambridge CB2 1RP
32 East 57th Street, New York, NY 10022, USA
296 Beaconsfield Parade, Middle Park, Melbourne 3206, Australia

First published 1981

Printed in the United States of America

British Library Cataloguing in Publication Data
Music in medieval and early modern Europe.
1. Music – History and criticism – Medieval, 400–1500 – Congresses
2. Music – History and criticism – 16th century – Congresses
3. Music, European – History and criticism – Congresses
I. Fenlon, Iain
789'.903   ML172   80-40490
ISBN 0 521 23328 3

ML
172
.M87

CONTENTS

Contents

vi

Contents

ILLUSTRATIONS

Illustrations

PREFACE

THIS volume presents, in revised form, some of the papers read at an international conference on medieval and Renaissance music held at King's College, Cambridge, in the late summer of 1979. The aim of the conference, as first conceived, was simply further reconnaissance, though not in the rather unsystematic fashion which frequently characterises such events. Rather, within certain practical constraints, we hoped to concentrate on a number of broad issues or areas of concern which seemed ripe for detailed exploration. Each of these topics either raised important questions which had exercised musicologists for some time but which seemed ready for re-examination or, conversely, demanded exposure precisely because of their comparative unfamiliarity. The papers dealing with the possible applications of stemmatic techniques to early music sources is an obvious example from the latter category; although filiation theory and technique have been discussed and elaborated for almost a century by literary scholars, it is only within the last two decades that their possibilities for musicological work have been seriously debated, with chant scholarship taking the lead. The present group of papers aims to provide considerable stimulus to the continuation and extension of that debate. Recent interest in the various types of evidence relating to the complex of questions which might be loosely grouped under the heading of 'patronage' has grown to such an extent that it seemed worthwhile to devote two complete sessions of the conference to this issue. The result is two sets of papers, one offering complementary and comparative accounts of various aspects of Church patronage of music in England, France and Italy during the fifteenth century, the other presenting a less heterogeneous exploration of various aspects of the patronage nexus as it operated in a number of Italian centres in the period c. 1450–1550. A fourth group of essays gathers new information about and offers new approaches to a long-established debate, the origins and early

Preface

development of instrumental music both in England and on the continent.

As always with collaborative efforts of this sort, much help has been received from friends, colleagues and well-wishers. Individual authors have acknowledged some of these debts in footnotes, but it would be quite improper if we failed to express our collective gratitude to the staff of the Cambridge University Press, and particularly to Clare Davies-Jones who encouraged this book during its early stages, Rosemary Dooley who has speeded its publication with enthusiasm and forgiven our foibles with patience, and Eric Van Tassel who has given characteristically close readings to all the texts.

IAIN FENLON

King's College
1 March 1980

EDITOR'S NOTE

IN the convention used in this book for naming pitches in a specific octave, each octave is regarded as beginning at C and rising to B. The octaves are designated in ascending order C,–B, C–B c–b c′–b′ c″–b″ etc., with c′ = middle C.

PART I

CHURCH PATRONAGE OF MUSIC IN FIFTEENTH-CENTURY EUROPE

1

OBLIGATION, AGENCY, AND *LAISSEZ-FAIRE*: THE PROMOTION OF POLYPHONIC COMPOSITION FOR THE CHURCH IN FIFTEENTH-CENTURY ENGLAND

ROGER BOWERS

MUSICOLOGY is a study of relatively recent origin, and it does not yet possess a complete critical vocabulary tailored to express its own particular needs. Many of the terms which are used to create a conceptual framework within which to organise appreciation of music history have been borrowed from other disciplines – in particular, from the history of art. Such borrowings have not always been conspicuously fortunate. In music history, for instance, the concept of a 'Renaissance' occurring in the first half of the fifteenth century has by now become so thoroughly absorbed into the collective musicological consciousness that it is difficult to imagine trying to explain the course of music history at that time without recourse to it. Yet it could be argued that the concept of 'The Renaissance' in music obscures and distorts quite as much as it illuminates and explains, and that consequently we would be well advised to abandon it, or at least to use it only with circumspection.

The concept of patronage is in much the same case. It is another borrowing from the history of art; it too is really of only limited applicability to the history of music; and if the term comes to be used indiscriminately, it also will end up by obscuring more than it illuminates. In particular, there are many reasons for hesitating to attach the label 'patronage' to the relationship between fifteenth-century English musicians and the church authorities who employed them. While acknowledging that the Church did a very great deal to encourage and promote music in the later middle ages, I would suggest that the Church did not act as a 'patron' of music in any of the usually accepted senses of the word. Much of the Church's promotion of music was the consequence of obligation, not of patronage; and where some element of true patronage was involved, it usually turns out to have been lay patronage, not Church patronage. Indeed, the whole relationship between the Church and its musicians was quite different from that of patron and client – different in ways which turn out possibly to have had a perceptible significance for both the form and content of fifteenth-century English composition.

In the first place, it is necessary to isolate and identify some of the basic characteristics of the manner in which the conduct of music in the Church was undertaken, in order to clarify the true nature of the avenues open to those seeking to promote and encourage it. As a performing art, there were two distinct sides to the cultivation of music – composition and performance. Church authorities could offer encouragement in both areas – in the first place by providing composers with a livelihood, and in the second by supplying them with the performing medium necessary for their art, the liturgical choir. These two areas are quite separate, and must be dealt with accordingly.

The first area to consider is the provision of the performing medium, and here too there is a fundamental distinction between, on the one hand, the maintenance of the choral force of each church as already established at any given moment and inherited from past generations and, on the other hand, the progressive alteration, expansion and modernisation of that original choral force to enable it to cope with the latest trends in musical composition.

At all the major secular churches, a high proportion of total expenditure was devoted to maintenance of the established choral personnel: the vicars-choral or chaplains, clerks of the second form, and (where possible) choristers, as defined and enumerated by custom, or foundation statute, or act of chapter. In the maintenance and preservation of the choirs, the governing bodies of the major churches were seen as the heirs and trustees of past benefactors. The endowments acquired at the foundation of each church, and those accumulated subsequently, had been earmarked by the donors for specific purposes, and it was the responsibility and duty of every chapter to see that as long as these endowments continued to produce an adequate income, those specified purposes continued to be observed. The maintenance of the choral staff specified for the observance of both the standard liturgy and the paraliturgical services founded by benefactors was the central and most important of these duties.

In this maintenance by the chapter of the basic choral force, there are many grounds for hesitating to describe the consequent performance of the music of the Church as the product of 'patronage'. Genuine patronage incorporates an element of discretion: by definition, a patron selects and chooses to what and to whom he offers his patronage. But the promotion and encouragement of music was not an enterprise in which church authorities were at liberty to decide whether to engage or not. Insofar as each church was obliged to observe the liturgy in the manner which the founders and benefactors specified, it was obliged to cultivate musicians and music. The due performance of the plainsong of the liturgy was wholly obligatory at every ecclesiastical institution sufficiently well staffed to undertake its performance. The promotion of music was one of the things the pre-Reformation Church existed for; no element of choice or discretion entered into it. Thus the ordinary, routine, day-to-day exercise of music by the church authorities cannot legitimately be considered as a consequence of 'patronage'. If such a term is to have any validity and usefulness as an intellectual tool, then its received meaning needs to be adhered to strictly. It was the Church's business to cultivate music, and an institution can hardly be said to have acted as patron to an art-form which in fact it had been founded to promote, and for the cultivation of which it was already endowed to maintain practitioners in full-time employment. In such circumstances, it was the original founders and benefactors who were the patrons; the church authorities were merely their long-term heirs, trustees and agents.

Maintaining the established choral force was one thing, and was the consequence of obligation, not of discretionary patronage.

Coping with those innovations in church music which necessitated actual alterations to the existing choral force was quite another. For there was much more to the promotion of church music in fifteenth-century England than mere maintenance of the status quo. Although the great bulk of each major church's resources was devoted to the preservation of what had already been established, there were occasions when the progress of music could be served only by the church authorities' making available funds and resources above and beyond what was necessary merely to maintain existing forces. This was a continuous process; as soon as one set of needs was satisfied by the adequate provision of extra resources, the rapid pace at which the composers were pushing along the development of music opened up new ones. At the wealthiest churches, the costs of this constant process of modernisation might, with some difficulty, be met from existing resources; but more commonly, either they had to be met from funds specially donated for the purpose by benefactors, or they could not be met at all. Under these circumstances, the adoption of such innovations, though evidently highly desirable, could only be optional, being dependent on the donation of the necessary financial resources.

In respect of the constant job of modernising old-established choirs, there was much that needed to be done in the fifteenth century. In the early part of the century, funds had to be found at many churches to enable the acquisition and employment of singers competent to perform polyphonic music at all, at least as a regular and frequent observance. Also, in order to secure a place in the choir which these expert musicians could occupy, the post of clerk of the second form had to be drastically transformed. In place of the youthful deacon or subdeacon who exhibited aspirations to become a vicar-choral, for whom this post had originally been designed and who had commonly been paid little more than pocket-money, it had to be modified so as to accommodate the career lay-clerk, who needed a full living wage. Some churches created specialist musical appointments, for instance that of organist, and found money for the provision of books of polyphony. Far more expensive than any of these were the jolting changes which had to be made in order to cater for the two big developments of the second half of the century, which together altered many choral establishments almost out of recognition – first, the adoption of choral in addition to solo performance of polyphony, and secondly, the expansion of the compass of composed polyphony to include boys' voices for the first time. At several prominent churches, this latter development involved endowing extra choristerships in order to expand the number of boys to at least the minimum required to sustain the treble part in four- and five-part polyphony; it also involved creating a post for a highly qualified – and highly paid – Instructor of the Choristers. By the last quarter of the century the minimum forces needed to perform composed polyphony involved full teams of both boys and men, requiring groups of adult voices to be added to choirs consisting only of boys and vice versa.[1]

Throughout the century, the governing bodies of most major churches successfully acquired and deployed funds and resources for purposes such as these. However, when this process is examined, it becomes evident that the source of these funds was not the Church itself, but the contemporary generation of benefactors from the secular world. The funds were not generated by the Church itself from its own accumulated wealth; they were donated by benefactors from among the lay and ecclesiastical aristocracy. Even in the cases of benefactions made by bishops and archbishops, it remains difficult to interpret this generosity as patronage of music by the Church. Churchmen at the very top of the hierarchy owed their wealth, and thus their capacity to foster music, not to their mere ecclesiastical rank, but to their position as holders of extensive landed estates. In founding new choral establishments, or re-organising long-established ones, or endowing memorials and votive antiphons, their conduct is quite impossible to distinguish from that of those members of lay society in similarly elevated positions who likewise chose to devote their money to the uses of the Church in these ways. In this respect – as in very many other respects of their public lives – the bishops were acting from motives arising not from their rank as churchmen, but from their estimation in contemporary protocol as mitred earls.

However, although the identity of the lay patron can often be readily discovered, one important factor often difficult to establish is the source of the initiative lying behind his donation. In instances in

[1] These developments in the history of the liturgical choir in England will be discussed in my study *Church and Cathedral Choirs in Late Medieval England* (forthcoming).

which the church authorities themselves perceived a need, and consciously sought a benefactor to offer funds to effect a musical project already appreciated and defined by the chapter, then it might well be possible to discern an instance of true patronage of music by the Church. This would still be partly true in cases in which a benefactor made an unconditional offer of a donation which the chapter, in their wisdom, decided to devote to musical ends. In no instance, however, is such detailed information known to be available – and since the source of the necessary funds did in practice almost invariably originate outside the Church, the suspicion must frequently arise that any deployment of those resources for the furtherance of the institution's musical life was being undertaken by the authorities in consequence of wishes and instructions defined and expressed by the donors, rather than by themselves. If such be the case, then again the church authorities were conducting themselves simply as agents or trustees, and not as self-motivated patrons in any real sense.

Thus the expansion of the musical enterprise of the Church in the fifteenth century did depend on patronage – but in origin it was generally lay patronage, not Church patronage. This is most conspicuously true in the case of choral institutions newly founded during the century. The Church itself did little on its own initiative from its own resources; all the major foundations of the century were created by members of either the lay or the ecclesiastical aristocracy. Several bishops and archbishops were active in this field, but in their provision for music there is absolutely no way in which Bishop Wayneflete's Magdalen College Oxford can be distinguished from King Henry VI's King's College Cambridge, Archbishop Courtney's Maidstone from the Duke of York's Fotheringhay, or Archbishop Chichele's Higham Ferrers from Baron Cromwell's Tattershall.[2] The episcopal foundations were neither more nor less ecclesiastical or musical than those of the lay aristocracy, and no specific patronage of music by the Church can be discerned here.

Only where church authorities themselves found the money to establish a new choir on their own initiative can there be said to have

[2] Information relating to these colleges, drawn from sources too numerous to list here, is presented in Roger Bowers, 'Choral institutions within the English Church, 1340–1500', Ph.D. diss., University of East Anglia, 1975, parts 4, 5 and 6, *passim*.

been genuine Church patronage of music; and instances of this were rare. They were limited to a very few establishments of the most modest kind – the Lady Chapel choirs of the greater Benedictine and Augustinian monasteries. The earliest second-generation choir of this kind was apparently established at Westminster Abbey in 1399, and others followed at intervals right up to the eve of the Dissolutions.[3] These choirs were inexpensive to run since they consisted only of an adult master and a group of boys; since the boys were already being provided for as pupils of the monastery's almonry grammar school, the only new expense was the salary, board and lodging of the master. At the richer monasteries, this expense could be met almost painlessly by splitting the total cost into many small sums, each one met from the account of one of the obedientiaries. At Ely Cathedral Priory, for instance, where the Lady Chapel choir was inaugurated in about 1404, no fewer then eight obedientiaries contributed.[4]

This expedient, however, could be applied only at the few monasteries that were sufficiently rich for any such diversion of their existing funds to be undertaken without prejudice to the customary provision of services. At institutions less well endowed, resort had to be made to the more usual expedient of lay patronage. At Bridlington Priory, for instance, the Lady Chapel choir was created in 1447 as a result of a benefaction from the laity – in this case, on the proceeds of certain exemptions from taxation granted by King Henry VI.[5] In the absence of such external support, however, not even a choir so modest as a Lady Chapel choir could take root. Norwich Cathedral was one of the least rich of the Benedictine cathedral priories, apparently unable to fund such a choir from its own resources. An injection of lay initiative came in 1424 when the bishop, John Wakeryng, appointed one Thomas Wath as *magister*

[3] Herbert F. Westlake, *Westminster Abbey* (London, 1923), p. 346; other examples of choirs of this kind are mentioned in Frank Harrison, *Music in Medieval Britain*, 2nd edn. (London, 1963), pp. 38–44, 185–93.

[4] Cambridge University Library, Archives of the Dean and Chapter of Ely, obedientiary accounts (not yet catalogued): see accounts of Almoner, Cellarer, Granetarius, Warden of Lady Chapel, Precentor, Sacrist, Hostillarius, Steward of Prior's Household. In 1490 the Bishop of Ely, John Alcock, transferred responsibility for paying the cantor from the priory to his own treasury: Cambridge University Library, Archives of the Diocese of Ely, EDR G/2/3, fol. 105.

[5] John Strachey (ed.), *Rotuli parliamentorum; ut et petitiones et placita in parliamento*, 6 vols. (London, 1767–77), v, p. 188; *Calendar of Charter Rolls 1427–1516*, pp. 95–7, 118–20.

scole cantus.[6] However, Wath's name has not been found elsewhere in the cathedral archives, and his appointment seems not to have taken effect; the project apparently proved abortive on Wakeryng's death only a few months later, before he had begun to endow the project with the funds necessary to make it viable. In 1441 Prior John Heverlond began a second initiative; this time, the master, John Scarlet, was paid under the standard expedient of diverting to him small sums from the various obedientiaries.[7] This worked for a time, but eventually it appears to have made demands greater than their limited resources could sustain; in or around 1469 the project foundered and was never revived.[8] In the absence of lay patronage, even so modest a venture as this proved to require more than the church was able (or willing) to provide.

Instances are rare indeed in which the church authorities themselves both perceived a need to improve their provision for music, and took the initiative to meet it by finding the necessary money through juggling their existing resources. Generally speaking, it seems that few initiatives in founding a new choir, or making a major modernisation of an old one, were ever undertaken without external funding by a secular patron. At St George's Chapel, Windsor, for example, the transformation of the post of clerk of the second form so as to accommodate the new phenomenon of the career lay-clerk was undertaken as early as the 1390s;[9] but the college could not at that time afford the necessary corollary, the payment of an increased salary commensurate with the skills of professional singers. Only in 1437 did the chapter make an agreement with the clerks whereby extra sums, at the rate of 26*s* 8*d* or 53*s* 4*d* a year, were added to their basic salary of £4 6*s* 8*d*; two years later a further supplement of 20*s* a year was made available for the clerk who acted as organist.[10] This degree of belated patronage had become possible not through any

---

[6] Norwich and Norfolk Record Office, Archives of the Diocese of Norwich, Register 4 (Book 8) (Register of John Wakeryng), fol. 87.

[7] Appointment, dated 1445: *ibid.*, Register 5 (Book 10) (Register of Thomas Brown), fol. 62. Payments occur on the accounts of the Master of the Cellar, Almoner and Precentor: Norwich and Norfolk Record Office, Archives of the Dean and Chapter of Norwich, account rolls 86–7, 545–60, 918–30.

[8] The story is narrated in fuller detail in Bowers, *op. cit.*, Appendix A7.

[9] Windsor, The Aerary, St George's Chapel, Archives of the Dean and Chapter of Windsor, xv.34,16–24 (accounts of Treasurer, 1393/4–1406/7), *dona et placita*.

[10] *ibid.*, xv.34.38*, 39–41 (accounts of Treasurer, 1437/8–1441/2), *stipendia et vadia officiariorum*.

machinations of the chapter itself, but through grants to the college made at the instance of a lay benefactor, John, Duke of Bedford, in the 1420s and early 1430s.[11]

During the 1470s the choir of St George's was expanded to dimensions suitable for it to undertake choral polyphony; the thirteen vicars-choral, four clerks and six choristers were increased to sixteen, fifteen and thirteen respectively, and the salaries of all the musical personnel were raised.[12] The funds were provided by the college's lay patron, King Edward IV; and it was from him, apparently, that the original initiative came, since the earliest mention of the scheme occurs in his will drawn up in 1475.[13] When an extra chorister was added to the six already maintained at St Mary Newarke College, Leicester, in c. 1500, the endowment was drawn from the property of one of the canons who had recently died, but the initiative for his bequest came from a lay patroness of the college, Margaret, Lady Hungerford.[14] Between 1485 and 1501 a team of seven choristers was added to the collegiate church of Rushworth, Norfolk, through the munificence of its patron, Anne, Lady Wingfield.[15]

There is no space here to multiply examples further. It must suffice to state that in a great many cases in which the authorities of the major churches undertook to modify or modernise their choral forces in the fifteenth century, a little investigation reveals that the necessary funds were not generated by the chapter from their existing wealth, but were supplied by a lay benefactor. In virtually all aspects of the provision and progressive modernisation of the performing medium, therefore, the Church acted as agent, not as patron. The supply of funds came from members of the laity; it is as

[11] A. Kathleen B. Roberts, *St George's Chapel, Windsor Castle: A Study in Early Collegiate Administration* (Windsor, 1947), pp. 26, 70, 150–1.

[12] A fairly full account of the manner in which this expansion of the choral staff was undertaken appears in Bowers, 'Choral Institutions within the English Church', pp. 6036–41.

[13] Samuel Bentley (ed.), *Excerpta historica* (London, 1831), p. 375.

[14] Alexander Hamilton Thompson (ed.), *Visitations in the Diocese of Lincoln, 1517–31*, 3 vols., Publications of the Lincoln Record Society nos. 33, 35, 37 (Lincoln, 1940–7), III, pp. 146, 155, 192, 218; idem, *The History of the Hospital and the New College of the Annunciation of St Mary in the Newarke, Leicester* (Leicester, 1937), pp. 211, 228.

[15] John C. Cox, 'Rushworth College' in William Page (ed.), *Victoria County History of Norfolk*, 2 vols. (London, 1906), II, p. 459.

likely to have been their initiative and instructions, as much as those of the church authorities, that largely directed the manner in which the promotion of their music was undertaken.

The second area in which the Church enjoyed an opportunity to promote music lay in its potential capacity to foster the craft of composition by offering a livelihood to composers. Yet, in respect of the work of the individual musicians also, the circumstances direct that we refrain from applying the term 'patronage' to the relationship between the artist and his paymaster – in this case, between the church authorities and the musicians who composed and performed church music. This relationship was simply not that of patron and client: it was the far more prosaic relationship of employer and employee.

In a patronage relationship, the client is an independent craftsman, beholden to no one particular patron, and at liberty to decline requests for his work if he so pleases; he resides at his own workshop and domestic premises, where he uses his own tools to make goods for his patrons in response to individual orders placed at irregular intervals of time, and paid for singly and separately. The musician in ecclesiastical employment supplied the fruits of his labour on a basis entirely different. The duty of performing the liturgy was not composed of discrete packages which could be parcelled out separately by a patron to his clients; it was an unceasing round, a constant web of worship and praise occupying several hours a day, 365 days a year, such as could be undertaken only by expert practitioners employed full-time for the purpose. The church musician was retained either as a full-time singer, or as a singer and Instructor of the Choristers and director of polyphonic music, in permanent employment. He worked exclusively for a single employer (not for various patrons), at his employer's premises (not his own), in return for an assured and regular salary (not for fees separately negotiated). And as an employee, he was not at liberty to accept or decline work as he pleased; he had to do what was expected of him by his employer.

The first thing which leaps immediately to the attention is the fact that in the particular circumstances under which the Church promoted the exercise of music, performers were employed as performers, but nobody was employed specifically as a composer. Unlike the painter or architect, the composer was not a type of independent craftsman, sought out by patrons to provide the wares they desired. Composition was merely a sideline, pursued by men whose primary occupation was as executant musicians, principally as singers. It was very exceptional indeed for any church musician to be required specifically to undertake composition as part of his contractual duties. The archives of Durham Cathedral Priory supply the only instances known to me. When in 1487 Alexander Bell was appointed cantor and master of the Lady Chapel choir there, his duties included an obligation to compose each year a new Mass in four or five parts in honour of God, St Mary and St Cuthbert.[16]. For his successor Thomas Foderley, appointed in 1496, this requirement was altered to the Mass, or something equivalent to it at the discretion of the prior and the precentor[17] – an unprecedented example of church authorities' seeking power to take an initiative in directing the nature of the music composed for them by an employee. This stipulation was repeated in all the subsequent contracts that were made with Foderley's successors down to the Dissolution.[18] However, examination of the scores of surviving contracts issued at many other churches has failed to yield any similar requirement elsewhere, and it appears that Durham Cathedral was quite exceptional in this respect. As a general rule, it seems that for his employers, any musician's talent for composition was just a windfall – a bonus they were probably glad of when it manifested itself, but one which they had no particular right to expect, and did not normally attempt to demand, of any of their musicians.

In this context, of course, it is important to remember that composed polyphony made only a very subordinate contribution to the performance of the pre-Reformation Latin rite in England. The staple fare of the church service, and of the church musician, was plainsong. Even at the end the of the fifteenth century, there was only

[16] Durham, The Prior's Kitchen, Archives of the Dean and Chapter of Durham, Priory Register V, fol. 3v.

[17] *Ibid.*, fol. 37 (modern pencil foliation); printed in James Raine (ed.), *Historiae Dunelmensis scriptores tres*, Surtees Society XVIII (1839), p. cccxv.

[18] John Tildesley, 1502 (Priory Register V, fol. 70), Robert Porret, 1512 (*ibid.*, fol. 142), Thomas Ashwell, 1513 (*ibid.*, fol. 152, revised version *ibid.*, fol. 153), John Brimley, 1537 (*ibid.*, fol. 261v). The contracts with Tildesley and Ashwell are printed in Raine, *op. cit.*, pp. ccclxxxvi and ccccxiii; the latter is reprinted thence in Harrison, *op. cit.*, pp. 429–30. A short section of a Mass *Sancti Cuthberti* by Ashwell still survives: London, British Library, Add. MS 30520.

one observance at which settings in composed polyphony were regularly deployed on a daily basis, and that was the evening votive antiphon. Otherwise, polyphony was limited almost exclusively to High Mass and Lady Mass on festivals, and to the greater Offices at three times of the year: Holy Week, All Saints-tide, and the period from Christmas to Epiphany. It need cause no surprise, therefore, to learn that the church authorities did not in fact appear to consider that the composition of polyphony fell within those aspects of the life of their institutions which it lay in their province to need to direct. It just did not loom large enough to warrant such attention.

Only the express predilections of certain of their lay patrons may ever have impelled the authorities specifically to ask their musicians to compose particular pieces of music. It is possible that the impetus behind the rise of the polyphonic votive antiphon in the fifteenth century lay to some extent in actual requests from the chapter that compositions in this category be undertaken. Such requests, however, arose not from any wish to act as patrons of music, but rather as a consequence of their role as agents for others: their source lay in the obligations imposed upon the chapters either by the foundation statutes of their churches or by the terms of private benefactions. At Eton College, for instance, it was the founder's wish, expressed in the statutes of *c.* 1453, that each evening all the choristers and their Instructor should gather at the principal image of the Virgin (which stood in the antechapel) to sing 'in the best manner they know' the Marian antiphon *Salve Regina* during Lent, and other antiphons during the rest of the year.[19] This probably explains the existence of settings of this text by composers on the staff of the college such as Robert Wylkynson and John Sutton, eventually preserved in the Eton Choirbook.[20] In 1395 the Dean and Chapter of Salisbury agreed with the bishop, John Waltham, that each day after compline the cathedral choristers should sing the antiphon *Sancta Maria virgo intercede* at the high altar, in recognition of the various benefits which

[19] Statute 30: James Heywood and Thomas Wright (eds.), *The Ancient Laws of the Fifteenth Century for King's College Cambridge, and for the Public School of Eton College* (London, 1850), p. 555. This statute made no provision for the attendance of the clerks, or for the singing of the antiphon in a polyphonic setting; when these practices began is not known.

[20] Frank Harrison (ed.), *The Eton Choirbook*, 3 vols., Musica Britannica 10–12 (London, 1956–61), I, p. 90, and II, p. 1.

them. In the history of music, the parallel procedure is certainly of use – for example in the case of continental secular music of the fourteenth, fifteenth and early sixteenth centuries. For scholars searching for reasons why the vernacular chanson of this period takes the shape and form it does, appreciation of the social, courtly function which this music was composed to serve goes a long way towards explaining its outward shape and content – its social function being to satisfy the particular musical and courtly needs of the composer's aristocratic or royal patron.

However, the patronage nexus was absent from the conditions under which church music was composed in England; and this absence proves to be as eloquent in explaining the prevailing nature and content of the English repertory as is its presence for the nature of continental secular music. The nature of much of the fifteenth-century repertory is, with the possible exception of some settings of votive antiphons, conspicuous for the fact that the existence of the music cannot be explained in terms of its having to satisfy some particular function which the composer's employer required and intended it to serve. For instance, the polyphonic vernacular carol appears to have arisen quite spontaneously, serving no particular ecclesiastical function at all that can now be discerned. No place can be found for it in the celebration of either the Mass or the Office, and its most probable purpose was to serve as home-made after-dinner entertainment of an edifying nature in the Vicars' Hall. Similarly, though no doubt the development of the polyphonic cyclic Mass occurred with the approval and blessing of church authorities, it too served no particular liturgical purpose; certainly it met no needs not already satisfied by the sort of Mass which could be concocted on an *ad hoc* basis from volumes such as the Old Hall Manuscript,[24] composed of discrete movements selected from any that happened to be based on tenors appropriate to the day. Since it cannot be shown to answer any special liturgical or extraliturgical need that could have been perceived by the authorities and communicated by them to the composers,[25] the cyclic Mass seems most likely to have grown spon-

[24] London, British Library, Additional MS 57950; *The Old Hall Manuscript*, ed. A. Hughes and M. Bent, Corpus Mensurabilis Musicae ser. 46, vols. 1–3 (n.p., 1969).
[25] A different point of view has been expressed by Geoffrey Chew, 'The Early Cyclic Mass as an Expression of Royal and Papal Supremacy', *Music and Letters*, 53 (1972), p. 254.

the bishop had conferred upon them.[21] The Gyffard Partbooks preserve a four-part setting of this text by Thomas Knyght, who was Instructor of the Choristers at Salisbury Cathedral between 1529 and 1543.[22] However, these seem to be the only circumstances prevailing at the time under which the church authorities might ever have found themselves impelled to request specific compositions; and they arose not from any role as patron, but from that of agent and trustee of others.

In any event, it is clear that the composer, though not unvalued, was not seen in the contemporary view as a creative artist on the same plane as the painter, architect or poet. Nobody offered the composer patronage; nobody could make a living solely by composition. It was at best no more than a sideline, and the composer's creations were no more than merely transient phenomena. It is well known that books of polyphonic church music in the fifteenth century contained only modern music. There were no classics, no established repertory pieces; when a piece went out of fashion, it was discarded and was not recopied. Not a single piece of church music by Dufay, for instance, is known to have been copied into any manuscript written later than a dozen years after his death. The architect's buildings, the artist's paintings, the poet's verses, the illuminator's miniatures would last for generations; but the church composer wrote music which he himself would have been surprised to hear sung even thirty years later. As a creative artist contributing to the worship of God, his offering was on a level comparable with that of the parish ladies who arrange the flowers on Christmas Eve – a genuine contribution to the overall effect, pretty while it lasts, but not destined for more than immediate use, and therefore of only limited value and esteem. Thus these characteristics removed composition from consideration as a major art-form comparable with painting or illumination, the practitioners of which were considered to merit sufficiently generous patronage to enable them to engage in

[21] Salisbury, Diocesan Record Office, Archives of the Dean and Chapter of Salisbury, charter without reference in box marked 'Vicars Choral'; also Chapter Reg. Holmes, fol. 3v.
[22] London, British Library, Add. MSS 17802–5, fols. 236, 233v, 226, 215 respectively. For an inventory see Roger W. Bray, 'British Museum Add. MSS 17802–5 (The Gyffard Part-Books): An Index and Commentary', *R.M.A. Research Chronicle*, 7 (1969), pp. 31–50.

their art full time. Composition was simply in a different, and very minor, league.

Therefore, in the fifteenth century there were many separate factors at work whose effects coalesced to cause the craft of composition to be considered, in contemporary estimation, as of too little significance on its own to merit patronage. On the whole, it seems that even the broad details of the practice of composition were something which the church authorities simply did not regard as needing their direction. Had it been otherwise, provisions such as those specified in the Durham Cathedral Priory contracts would surely be encountered more frequently. Numerous indications appear in the cathedral archives to show that the monks of Durham took unusual care for the standard, and concern for the content, of their music.[23] The absence elsewhere of such contractual requirements to compose is consistent only with a prevailing absence of such particular expectations at other major churches. Although all the responsibility for the conduct of music in a great church properly devolved on the chapter in general, and on the precentor in particular, as far as polyphonic music was concerned it seems clear that, so long as necessary decorum, dignity and good taste were observed, composers and performers were simply left to get on with their job as they were best able to do, with neither direction nor interference from the authorities. The attitude of the authorities was not one of intrusive, patronly concern, but rather of benign abstention.

Accordingly, so far as the craft of composition was concerned, it was the prevailing absence of any relationship recognisable as that of patronage that mainly characterised the English fifteenth century. This conspicuous absence draws attention to the relationship which

[23] Roger Bowers, 'The Inauguration of the Song Schools at Durham in the Early Fifteenth Century', forthcoming. Starting with the appointment of Thomas Foderley in 1496, all the cantors were contractually obliged, at the request of the precentor, to look over the music to be sung beforehand ('tenebitur eciam, ad vocacionem precentoris ... pro cantibus previdendis, tociens quociens ad hoc premunitus fuerit') (references as in notes 17 and 18 above). Throughout a very extensive examination of English archival sources, I have never encountered any other instance of a requirement that some formal rehearsal of the music be undertaken. In 1426/7 the prior and convent of Durham elevated the parish church of Hemingbrough, Yorkshire, to collegiate status, with a choral staff of six vicars-choral and four clerks; this represents the only example known to me of a new choral institution founded entirely on the initiative, and at the expense, of an ecclesiastical rather than a lay patron. See Richard Barrie Dobson, *Durham Priory 1400–1450* (Cambridge, 1973), 156–62.

existed in its stead – that relationship between the comp employer which could be described less as that of patroi than as one of plain *laissez-faire*. This phenomenon may in fac of some positive significance for the manner in which the m Church developed at that time, since appreciation of this fe. mits an observer to perceive some possible insights into the d nature and content of the English fifteenth-century repert

This arises because the absence of the patronage nexus seen to have had at least one unexpectedly positive conseque the craft of composition. Paradoxically, perhaps, the prev absence in England of any individual recognisable as a p conspired to give church composers a degree of artistic freedoi exceeding that enjoyed by most other creative artists. The comp did not depend on patronage in the way that most other artists He did not survive on fees and commissions: he was already assu of a livelihood as an executant musician in the Church. Nor was constrained by the principal feature of the working of a norm patronage relationship, the need to please the patron. Secular art di have to satisfy its patron – and a human patron was very close to hand and correspondingly hard to please, and well placed directly to influence the manner in which his clients undertook his commissions. Church music had only to satisfy the Almighty – and a divine patron was not in a good position to communicate his wishes in any detail. So the manner in which composers and performers of polyphonic music were left to go about their business as best they could meant, in fact, that they were being left with a quite unusual degree of initiative and artistic freedom.

In circumstances in which it is genuinely applicable, the main value of the concept of 'patronage' to historians of the arts lies in its capacity to supply reasons why any particular art-form took the shape and nature which it did at any given time. In the history of art, the creation by scholars of the concept of 'patronage' has supplied them with an additional intellectual dimension whereby a more satisfactory and better-informed understanding of their subject can be hammered out. This is achieved by creating the opportunity to incorporate into their studies a consideration of the wants and predilections of a class of people who did not actually paint the pictures, but who did pay the bill for the finished goods, and who therefore exercised a considerable influence over what went into

taneously, as a result only of the composers' urge to glorify God by writing the best and most expansive music they could – and to exploit the much-improved standards of performance produced by the upheavals of the period *c*. 1385–1425. It appears, therefore, that the church authorities' willingness to accept whatever the composers chose to write, in the benign absence of direction or interference from external influences such as patrons, constituted at least one of the factors encouraging the rise of these two important forms.

The prevailing absence of the types of stimulus supplied elsewhere by the workings of the patronage system may also have had a negative effect on the variety of forms of composition practised in England. Indirectly, it may help to explain some of the conspicuous omissions that occur in the corpus of English music, as compared with that of the continent. This applies to two important forms. One was the commemorative motet. Written to texts celebrating weddings, births, other conspicuous family occasions, peace treaties, dedications of churches and so on, such works were clearly products of the patronage system. The second was the vernacular courtly song, written to delight the members of princely and aristocratic courts. On the continent, most items in these classes were produced by chapel musicians in the direct employment of the secular aristocracy; indeed these two forms have in common the facts that both emanated exclusively from the households of the aristocracy and that both were virtually, or entirely, ignored by English composers.

In England, the prevailing spirit of piety and devotion appears to have drawn the attention of composers predominantly, if not exclusively, in the direction of sacred music, both liturgical and devotional. They seem to have felt no impulsion to write music to other sorts of text, and the aristocratic employers of those working in household chapels evidently abstained from pressing them to do so. This curious circumstance may be explained by remembering that the private chapels established in aristocratic households were modelled directly on the choirs of the greater churches, especially those of the major collegiate establishments. It has already been suggested that in England during the fifteenth century the authorities at the major churches, in a spirit of benign abstention, left their composers to follow their own motivation and artistic inspiration. So it would be wholly consistent to propose that when the aristocratic employers of church musicians adopted for their household chapels the choral constitutions and practices in force at the greater secular churches, they adopted also the relationship prevailing there between the church authorities and the composers on their staffs. That is, aristocratic employers thought fit to observe in their relationship with their chapel composers only the same properties as did the chapters of collegiate churches with theirs – and thus, like them, refrained from making any attempt to suggest or specify to their composers what they should compose.

In England, therefore, the composers' taste for devotional and liturgical music could be indulged in an environment which allowed it to flourish to the virtual exclusion of all else. It certainly appears that aristocratic employers did not expect their chapel musicians to write celebratory motets, and in the absence of any such direction, such items simply did not get written. The same circumstances will explain the virtually complete absence of the English vernacular courtly song. The chapel musicians appear to have felt no inner impulsion to write such songs; and following the example set by the greater churches, their employers declined to press them otherwise.

Thus it seems that, both directly and indirectly, the prevailing absence of the patronage relationship had a significant effect on the forms of composition cultivated in England. It is unlikely to be mere coincidence that the two items so conspicuously absent from the English repertory have in common the fact that both require an initiative from a musician's employer to stimulate their composition – an initiative which, in the absence of a true patronage relationship, failed to materialise. Meanwhile, as has been seen, two of the most characteristic achievements of the English fifteenth century – the cyclic Mass and the vernacular polyphonic carol – seem to have been allowed to take their particular shape, at least to some degree, as a direct consequence of that atmosphere of artistic enterprise and freedom that was stimulated by the absence of patronly direction from the composers' employers.

At all levels, it seems, employers of musicians abstained from cultivating the somewhat intrusive type of patronage nexus favoured on the continent. Instead, the devout piety of the period, coupled with contemporaries' prevailing appreciation of the composers' work as merely functional and transient, coalesced to promote in its place a spirit of *laissez-faire*, which was moderated only by the occasional requirement that the Church see that its composers fulfil such musical obligations as had been imposed by their lay patrons. Principally, the Church promoted and encouraged music by supplying composers with their performing medium, and in this respect, it proved as alert and responsive to composers' needs as the generosity of its lay patrons allowed it to be. As to the content of their composition, the spirit of benign abstention appears to have prevailed; and in producing both gains and losses, it certainly seems to have helped to impart to the insular fifteenth-century repertory some of its distinctive character.

2

CHURCH PATRONAGE OF MUSIC IN FIFTEENTH-CENTURY ITALY

Giulio Cattin

THE many forms of music in fifteenth-century Italy may be summarised under three main headings: first, people, not only Church dignitaries as patrons of musicians or as addressees of compositions, but also composers working within ecclesiastical institutions; secondly, events, namely special religious occasions (or at least occasions connected with religious events) that resulted in musical compositions being written or performed; and thirdly, ecclesiastical institutions expressly established to foster musical activity or to encourage its development. This essay deals with these three aspects not separately but together, and chronologically. However, what follows may easily be placed in one of these three categories for the sake of methodological clarity.

The major trends in the history of fifteenth-century Italian music are well established. It is enough to say here that the late manifestations of the Ars Nova continued into the first decades of the century together with the fruitful symbiosis of French and local tradition in northern Italy, particularly in the Veneto. But the middle decades of the century seem to have been a period of inactivity, at least as far as polyphonic composition by Italian composers is concerned, until native composition started again in the last decades of the century. At first this resurgence of interest was confined to *popolareggiante* church and secular music; later it encompassed learned polyphony as well. There is no need to dwell on the important part played by northern singers and composers in the evolution of Italian musical taste and practice. Quite often, as we shall see later, they were the examples for Italian emulation. But first let us consider the Church's attitude towards patronage of music as characterised by Pirrotta.[1]

[1] Nino Pirrotta, 'Music and Cultural Tendencies in Fifteenth-Century Italy', *Journal of the American Musicological Society*, 19 (1966), pp. 127–61.

Pirrotta was not entirely negative when dealing with the attitudes of the Italian Church towards music, but neither did he credit the Church with a leading and active role. Taking his cue from Josquin's difficult career after his arrival in Milan, Pirrotta maintained that 'his example dramatically raises the question of the degree to which the atmosphere of the Italian courts and towns . . . was actually favorable to the artistic development of a young composer of polyphonic music'. To be fair, Pirrotta is not referring directly to churches here, but the context allows the application of his statement to churches as well. But without playing down the soundness of Pirrotta's point of view, which is well supported and correct in principle, I do believe that some events and trends suggest a more varied picture of attitudes towards music on the part of churchmen and the Church.

Liturgical services in fifteenth-century cathedrals and other main churches were conducted with care and propriety, if not sumptuously. Clearly they were essentially clerical and private, following a tradition which had begun in previous centuries and which perhaps reached its highest point in the fifteenth. On one side was the clergy with its ceremonies, rites and chant in an incomprehensible language, on the other the *plebs fidelium* with its devotions and saints, its confraternities and organised *artes*. The so-called Gregorian chant was usually performed by the *chorarii* and by the *mansionarii* attached to the cathedral chapter, and sometimes by the canons themselves.[2] This fact is sufficiently demonstrated by innumerable choir books, illuminated with various degrees of elaboration, which were copied in the fifteenth century and which now comprise the bulk of surviving books in chapter archives and libraries. Furthermore, there is evidence enough of the widespread application of *biscantare* treatment to the traditional monody, at least in some parts of solemn services; examples of the *cantus planus binatim* or *contrapunctus planus* have been discovered in increasing numbers in the last few years and are the subject of many scholarly reports.[3] The *binatim* chant, and,

---

[2] The traditional posts of *cantor* and *praecentor* were still occasionally filled in chapters, but they had only administrative and representative functions (see Pirrotta, *op. cit.*).

[3] For information about Italian music sources see Kurt von Fischer and Max Lütolf, *Handschriften mit mehrstimmiger Musik des 14., 15. und 16. Jahrhunderts*, RISM B/IV 3–4 (Munich and Duisburg, 1972); also Agostino Ziino, 'Polifonia "arcaica" e "retrospettiva" in Italia centrale: nuove testimonianze', *Acta Musicologica*, 50

even more, monodic performances were the Church's traditional musical inheritance which it continued to practice and to encourage during the fifteenth century, and the *mansionarii* and the *chorarii* were trained for it by following a practical apprenticeship that enabled them to become performers. Quite often the cathedral itself managed a grammar and chant school according to traditional methods. Particularly able children were admitted to these schools, and their educational curriculum lasted some years during which they assisted their seniors in the choir, to which (if they were aiming at a Church career) they were admitted as full members after their voices had broken. This procedure was not the only one followed in Italy; indeed, it is characteristic of the fifteenth-century Italian Church that similar schools were established where they were lacking, existing ones were enlarged and strengthened with better organisation, and their continuation and vitality were ensured by providing sources of income for the *magistri in grammatica* and *in cantu* (quite often *beneficia* or *prebendae*) as well as scholarships which allowed the *pueri* to live and study.

Confirmation of the encouragement given to these schools comes from the example of the institution of St Mark's school in Venice in 1403 for *octo pueri veneti originarii*, the source of patronage in this case being the Venetian government since St Mark's basilica was a ducal church.[4] This example could well have influenced Gabriele Condulmer, Pope Eugenius IV (a Venetian by birth), when through Papal directives he established or regulated similar schools in Turin in 1435 (two bulls), in Bologna and Florence in 1436, in Treviso in 1437–8 (two bulls), in Padua and Urbino in 1439, and in Verona in 1440–2 (two bulls).[5] Despite the quite unfavourable traditional

(1978), pp. 193–207. The phenomenon of improvised polyphonic performances has been too little studied. Tinctoris had already explained the meaning of *cantare super librum* in his *Liber de arte contrapuncti* (1477) and had given clear rules as well. From this book one might think of the practice as one which was followed outside Italy too, and in fact evidence is now coming to light from various parts of Europe: see Craig Wright, 'Performance Practices at the Cathedral of Cambrai 1475–1550', *Musical Quarterly*, 64 (1978), pp. 313–22.

[4] A facsimile of the foundation document is published in F. Alberto Gallo (ed.), *Antonii Romani Opera* (Bologna, 1965), p. xiii.

[5] For Turin, cf. G. Borghezio, 'La fondazione del collegio nuovo "Puerorum Innocentium" del duomo di Torino', *Note d'Archivio per la Storia Musicale*, 1 (1924), pp. 251–3; for Florence, cf. Albert Seay, 'The Fifteenth-Century Cappella at Santa Maria del Fiore in Florence', *Journal of the American Musicological Society*, 11 (1958), pp. 46–9; for Bologna, Gaetano Gaspari, 'La musica in S. Petronio. A con-

judgements about Eugenius IV's pontificate, it has to be admitted that he was a diligent organiser and patron of musical and liturgical activity. However, all these examples fall within the usual activity of a Church aiming to ensure the continuity of its decorous liturgical services. This paper aims instead to investigate the beginnings of patronage outside the daily routine of liturgical music, particularly the encouragement given to the cultivation of polyphony.

It is possible to find signs of a more lively interest in polyphony in the Veneto during the early decades of the century. One could mention Johannes Ciconia (referring to him, incidentally, as one person, pending a thorough explanation of 'il giallo Ciconia').[6] In Padua, he was the link between the fourteenth and fifteenth centuries, he conformed to the Venetian tradition of celebratory motets of which, at least in Venice, there had previously been some notable examples. His compositions were addressed to Paduan bishops, including (in chronological order) Stefano da Carrara, Albano Micheli, and Pietro Marcello,[7] to the Abbot of Santa Giustina (Andrea da Carrara), and in particular to Francesco Zabarella, who was to be Archbishop of Florence. Zabarella seems to have been Ciconia's real patron, and to him are addressed two motets, *Ut te per omnes celitum* and *Doctorum principem*. So far, there is not enough documentation to determine the exact musical resources of the Paduan circle,[8] but it is most likely that Ciconia's compositions were

---

tinuazione delle memorie risguardanti la Storia dell'arte musicale in Bologna', in *Musica e musicisti a Bologna* (Bologna, 1969), pp. 114–15 (repr. from *Atti e Memorie della R. Deputazione di Storia Patria per le Provincie della Romagna*, 1st ser., vol. 9 (1870)); for Treviso, cf. G. D'Alessi, *La cappella musicale del Duomo di Treviso* (Vedelago, 1954); for Urbino, Bramante Ligi, 'La cappella musicale del duomo di Urbino', *Note d'Archivio per la Storia Musicale*, 2 (1925), pp. 6–7; for Padua and Verona, see below.

[6] Cf. David Fallows, 'Ciconia padre e figlio', *Rivista Italiana di Musicologia*, 11 (1976), pp. 171–7; S. Clercx-Lejeune, 'Ancora su Johannes Ciconia', *Nuova Rivista Musicale Italiana*, 11 (1977), pp. 573–90; Anne Hallmark, 'Ciconia's Life Re-examined', paper presented to the New England Chapter of the American Musicological Society, 2 March 1979.

[7] Ciconia's motets for bishops are: *O felix templum iubila*, *Albane misse celitus / Albane doctor maxime*, and *Petrum Marcellum venetum / Petre antistes inclite*. It is still not known to whom *O Petre Christi discipule* is addressed. Suzanne Clercx thinks that it could have been composed for the election of Pierre Lupi de Luna (Benedict XIII): cf. Clercx, *Johannes Ciconia* (Brussels, 1960), I, p. 88.

[8] For what has been published see Raffaele Casimiri, *Musica e musicisti nella cattedrale di Padova nei sec. XIV, XV, XVI* (Rome, 1942). These documents have been published in *Note d'Archivio per la Storia Musicale*, 18 (1941) and 19 (1942).

performed in Padua. Turning to Venice, immediate mention should be made of Antonius Romanus, called *magister cantus* in documents dated 1420, who wrote polyphonic compositions for the liturgy and ceremonial music to mark the elections of two doges in 1414 and 1423.[9] Strictly speaking, the categorisation of these two compositions as commemorative music for secular events is misleading, because of the ambivalent status of St Mark's *cappella*. Remaining in Venice and the Veneto, mention should also be made of evidence both from archives and from attributions in a series of manuscripts which were copied there: Bologna Q 15, Bologna 2216, and Oxford Canonici misc. 213, containing works by well-known composers such as Arnold and Hugo de Lantins.[10] The first wrote some date-able compositions in Venice; the second is the composer of *Tra quante regione*, an epithalamion for Cleofe Malatesta and Teodoro Paleologo written in 1421, and of *Christus vincit*, further evidence of the Venetian symbiosis between religious and political or even military events.[11] And Antonius de Civitate, a Dominican friar from Cividale, wrote *Felix Flos Florentia/Gaude felix Dominice* for Leonardo Dati, elected superior-general of the Dominican order in 1414, *Pie Pater Dominice/O Petre martir inclite/O Thomas lux ecclesiae* in honour of the Dominican saints, and *Sanctus itaque patriarcha Leuntius* in honour of St Leucio, the patron saint of Brindisi and Trani. (The incorrect texting of this motet – 'Leuntius' instead of 'Leucius' – misled Gilbert Reaney into relating it to Vicenza.)[12] It is also known that Bertrand Feragut celebrated the arrival of the Venetian Pietro Emiliani as Bishop of Vicenza in 1409, composing for the occasion the motet *Excelsa civitas Vincencia*, subsequently re-used for Bishop Francesco Malipiero in 1433. Johannes de Limburgia, the patron of Bologna Q 15, took an active part in musical activity in the Veneto, singing the praises of St Leonzio and St Carpoforo, the patron saints

---

[9] See Gallo (ed.), *Antonii Romani Opera*; Gilbert Reaney (ed.), *Early Fifteenth-Century Music, VI*, Corpus Mensurabilis Musicae ser. 11 (n.p., 1977).

[10] Bologna, Civico Museo Bibliografico-Musicale, MS Q 15; Bologna, Biblioteca Universitaria, MS 2216; Oxford, Bodleian Library, MS Canonici misc. 213.

[11] F. A. Gallo, 'Musiche veneziane nel ms. 2216 della Biblioteca Universitaria di Bologna', *Quadrivium*, 6 (1964), pp. 107–27. On the tradition of ceremonial music in Venice see Denis Stevens, 'Ceremonial Music in Medieval Venice', *Musical Times*, 119 (1978), pp. 321–7.

[12] For more accurate information on San Leucio, see G. Cattin, 'Formazione e attività delle cappelle polifoniche nelle cattedrali. La musica nelle città, in *Storia della cultura veneta*, III (Vicenza, in press).

of Vicenza (*Martires Dei incliti*), celebrating Padua (*Gaude felix Padua*), and dedicating the motet *Congruit mortalibus plurima* to the patriarch Giovanni Contarini. Presumably he is also the author of *Salve vere gracialis* in honour of Cardinal Antonio Correr and the composer of other Italian *laude*. Finally, there is Nicholaus Zacharie, who composed the two-voice ballata *Già per gran nobeltà* in honour of Martin V (1417–31), the first Pope after the great schism.

What were the important events in the life of the Church in the first decades of the fifteenth century? There should be no need to emphasise the importance of councils in general, in particular (as far as music is concerned) those of Constance and Basel. In the first place, it is clear that the councils provided a meeting-place for different European musical traditions and for the singers of the *padri conciliari*.[13] But, paradoxically, the schism itself had positive effects on musical activity, since both Popes and antipopes organised their own groups of singers.[14] These circumstances helped give rise to the *musicale collegium*, and to compositions by Zacharias (*Sumite karissimi*), Conradus da Pistoia (*Veri almi pastores/Musicale collegium*), and Bartolomeo da Bologna (*Arte psallentes*), all musicians in the employment of Pietro Filargo, Archbishop of Milan and later Pope Alexander V. It is not necessary to know exactly the name of the patron or the town where the *collegium* was based (Pirrotta suggests Bologna, and Sartori Pavia);[15] it is sufficient here merely to take note of the *collegium*'s existence. French compositions such as Tapissier's

---

[13] For the Council of Constance, see Manfred Schuler, 'Die Musik in Kostanz während des Konzils, 1414–1418', *Acta Musicologica* 38 (1966), pp. 150–68. A general bibliography is also given by Marian Cobin, 'The Compilation of the Aosta Manuscript: A working Hypothesis', in Allan W. Atlas (ed.), *Papers Read at the Dufay Quincentenary Conference, Brooklyn College, December 6–7, 1974* (Brooklyn, 1976), pp. 82–5, where also evidence is reported of E. S. Piccolomini's patronage of the Aosta manuscript.

[14] Mention could be made of the motet *Argi vices Poliphemus / Cum Philemon rebus paucis* in honour of John XXIII (1410–15), which is in the Aosta manuscript. Guillaume de Van ascribed the motet to Nicholaus Zacharie (see G. de Van, 'A Recently Discovered Source of Early Fifteenth-Century Polyphonic Music', *Musica Disciplina*, 2 (1948), pp. 54–7), but in recent researches it has been ascribed to the priest Nicolò da Liegi who was in the Papal chapel (see F. A. Gallo, *Il Medioevo II* (Turin, 1977), pp. 80–1). About the circumstances of the composition of this motet see also Cobin, *op. cit.*, pp. 84–5.

[15] See Ursula Günther, 'Das Manuskript Modena, Biblioteca Estense, α.M.5,24 (*olim* lat. 568 = *Mod*)', *Musica Disciplina*, 24 (1970), pp. 44–5.

Eya dulcis/Vale placens and Johannes Carmen's *Venite adoremus/Salve
sancta eterna Trinitas* refer to the very theme of the schism itself, as does
Hubertus de Salinis's *Gloria*, with its trope *Gloria iubilacio*, copied
into the Franciscan manuscript Marciana ital. IX. 145.[16]

The activities of the Papal *cappella* fall within the scope of this
paper only incidentally. In fact, this institution can be considered
'Italian' neither in a strict legal sense nor, in most cases, from the
point of view of the nationality of its members. Nonetheless, the
effects of the presence of this institution in Italian towns cannot be
ignored. Its efficiency, its cosmopolitanism, and the quality of its
repertory stimulated imitations by courts, towns, and churches,
particularly in the first half of the century when Popes frequently
stayed for some time outside Rome, particularly at Florence and
Bologna. A review of the history of the Papal choir is not needed
here, after Haberl's exploration of the documents and the studies of
the pontificates of Eugenius IV, Pius III and the sixteenth-century
Popes, and the work of Frey, Bragard, Schuler and Sherr.[17] It is
enough to say that the most propitious years were the pontificates of
the more famous humanistic Popes: Eugenius IV, Nicholas V, Pius
II, Paul II, Sixtus IV,[18] and Alexander VI, whose liking for magnifi-
cent liturgical ceremonies is well documented.[19] Among the generations of northern singers who served in the Papal choir, a number

[16] Venice, Biblioteca Nazionale Marciana, MS ital. IX.145. An inventory of this
codex is given in G. Cattin, 'Il manoscritto venet. marc. ital. IX.145', *Quadrivium*, 4
(1960), pp. 1–61. For transcriptions of some melodies in the first section of this
manuscript, see Cattin, *Laudi Quattrocentesche del Cod. Veneto Marc. It. IX.145*
(Bologna, 1958).

[17] H. W. Frey, 'Regesten zur päpstlichen Kapelle unter Leo X. und zu seiner
Privatkapelle', a series of articles in *Die Musikforschung*, 8 and 9 (1955 and 1956).
A.-M. Bragard, 'Détails nouveaux sur les musiciens de la cour du pape Clément
VII', *Revue Belge de Musicologie*, 12 (1958), pp. 5–18. M. Schuler, 'Zur Geschichte
der Kapelle Papst Martins V', *Archiv für Musikwissenschaft*, 25 (1968), pp. 30–45;
idem, 'Zur Geschichte der Kapelle Papst Eugens IV', *Acta Musicologica*, 40 (1968),
pp. 220–7; *idem*, 'Die Kapelle Papst Pius III', *ibid.*, 42 (1970), pp. 225–30. R. J.
Sherr, 'The Papal Chapel ca. 1492–1513 and Its Polyphonic Sources', Ph.D.
diss., Princeton University, 1975.

[18] It should be remembered that it was Sixtus IV who established the Sistine
Chapel. Rome, Archivio della Cappella Sistina, MS 14 was copied for him in
about 1481. José Llorens, *Cappellae Sixtinae Codices musicis notis instructi sive manu
scripti sive praelo excussi* (Vatican City, 1960), pp. 18–20.

[19] It is beyond the scope of this paper to discuss the influence of humanism on these
Popes.

were notable composers.[20] The outstanding example, of course, is Dufay, though he is mentioned here not because of his talent, but rather because of his active participation in major Church events and his musical celebrations of ecclesiastical personalities. Not only did he write for princely weddings (*Vasilissa ergo gaude* for Cleofe Malatesta and Teodoro Paleologo, and *Resveillés vous, et faites chiere lye* for Carlo Malatesta and Vittoria Colonna, Martin V's niece), but he also composed works on the occasion of Papal elections (*Ecclesiae militantis*, for Eugenius IV in 1431), liturgical events (*Balsamus et munda cera*, for the distribution of the wax *Agnus Dei*, perhaps in 1431), the consecration of churches (*Nuper rosarum flores* for Santa Maria del Fiore in Florence, 25 March 1436; *Apostolo glorioso* for Pandolfo Malatesta, Archdeacon of Bologna and newly elected Archbishop of Patrasso, when his cathedral was consecrated in 1426),[21] and Candlemas day (*Fulgens jubar*, with the acrostic 'PETRUS DE CASTELLO'). Other motets were composed on the occasion of the peace treaty between Eugenius IV and Emperor Sigismondo (*Supremum est mortalibus*), and in praise of Niccolò III, Marchese of Ferrara, who mediated peace between Florence, Venice and Milan in 1433 (*C'est bien raison de devoir essaucier*). Dufay also bewailed the fall of Constantinople (*Lamentatio Sancte Matris Ecclesie Constantinopolitane*), celebrated the arrival of an eminent churchman, perhaps Leonardo of Chios, Archbishop of Mitilene (*Seigneur Leon, vous soyes bienvenues*), while a number of liturgical works were composed for particular institutions – such as the *Missa Sancti Jacobi* for San Giacomo Maggiore in Bologna (and not for St Jacques de la Boucherie in Paris, as has been maintained),[22] or the cycle of liturgical hymns for the Papal chapel. The influence of churchmen and Church life on composers, quite apart from strictly liturgical works, was considerable. It is surprising how much importance Dufay attached to some Italian traditions and how he complied with

[20] See also Adriano Cavicchi, 'Appunti sulla prassi esecutiva della musica sacra nella seconda metà del XVI secolo con riferimenti alla musica di Palestrina', in *Atti del Convegno di studi palestriniani (Palestrina 1975)*, ed. F. Luisi (Palestrina, 1977), pp. 300–1.

[21] On the composition of this motet see Alejandro Enrique Planchart, 'Guillaume Dufay's Masses. A View of the Manuscript Traditions', in Atlas (ed.), *Dufay Quincentenary Conference*, p. 57, n. 70.

[22] New evidence for this theory has been given by Planchart's analysis, *ibid.*, pp. 26–33.

certain *topoi*, such as the celebration of St Nicholas with isorhythmic motets (Ciconia: *O virum omnimoda veneratione*; Carmen: *Pontifici decori speculi*; Arnold de Lantins: *Celsa sublimatur victoris*; Dufay: *O gemma lux et speculum*), or of St Anthony of Padua (Ciconia: *O proles Yspaniae*; Johannes de Sarto: *O lux et decor Hispanie*; Dufay: *O proles Yspanie*).[23] Certainly it should be easy to find similar local connections in the work of minor composers as well.

The setting-up and strengthening of cathedral schools has been already mentioned, and clearly the purpose of some of these was not merely the revival of liturgical services with Gregorian chant. Although the presence of singers with a specific role (such as *tenorista* or *basso*) does not prove the existence of a polyphonic *cappella*, it undoubtedly means that performances of polyphonic music took place to an increasing extent in many Italian towns. An illustration is the terms under which Matteo da Perugia was engaged at the cathedral in Milan in 1402:[24]

Quod ipse Magister Matheus cum habitu, videlicet camisia, singulis festis sollemnibus intersit officiis Missarum et Vesperorum eiusdem Ecclesiae una cum dominis Ordinariis, ibique biscantet, chorumque eiusdem Ecclesiae dulcibus melodijs honoret.

His work contained with some vicissitudes, through the patronage of Pietro Filargo, Archbishop of Pavia, until 1416. By that time at least two more *dischantatores* had been engaged. During the following years there were only a few local singers. Bertrand Feragut, a priest from Avignon, was engaged with the title of *musicus* in 1425, but left the following year, with the result that three singers from the city asked to take his place on the grounds that their engagement would have spared the authority the risk of being embarrassed through 'recipiendo advenas et forenses qui ad eorum arbitrium recedunt'. I do not know if similar charges against foreign singers were made elsewhere. Certainly, in a large city such as Milan, where local singers were available, the presence of foreigners was resented, and their habit of leaving as soon as more rewarding conditions were

---

[23] S. Clercx, *Johannes Ciconia*, I, p. 87, had already noted this series of compositions. On Dufay's devotion to St Anthony of Padua and on the place of *O proles Yspanie*, see again Planchart, *op. cit.*, pp. 34–7.

[24] See Claudio Sartori, 'Matteo da Perugia e Bertrand Feragut i due primi maestri di cappella del Duomo di Milano', *Acta Musicologica*, 28 (1956), pp. 12–27; *idem*, 'La cappella del Duomo dalle origini a Franchino Gaffurio', in *Storia di Milano*, IX (Milan, 1961).

offered elsewhere was openly criticised. Nevertheless, the comings and goings of foreign singers are documented throughout Italy, though the fact should not be overemphasised since, even in Milan and certainly elsewhere, local talent could not compete with the skill of French and Flemish singers. One further remark should be made about Milan Cathedral, namely that during this early period *signori* such as the Visconti and the Sforza were taking an interest in it and sometimes imposing their own wishes. The same thing could be said for musical life elsewhere, in Florence, Modena, Naples and so on, where the *signorie* and the Church did not have clearly separated spheres of influence and where the *signori* were involved in the activities and control of cathedral *cappelle*, at least until they established private *cappelle* of their own. Such cooperation between public and ecclesiastical authorities also took place in Florence.[25] As D'Accone's research has shown, at Santa Maria del Fiore, at least two singer–chaplains were among the members of the chapter from the first decades of the fifteenth century,[26] among them Don Paolo *tenorista* (there is some doubt about his identity), Corrado da Pistoia, Ugolino da Orvieto and Nicholaus Zacharie. And the polyphonic *cappella*, in the strict sense of the word, really began to operate in 1438 with a repertory largely influenced by the stay in Florence of the singers of Martin V (1419–20) and of Eugenius IV (1434–6).

Unfortunately such rich documentation is not available for other towns and cities, and research has been made in a rather summary way, if at all. It is also true, as Hay has recently remarked, that many documents have been destroyed or lost.[27] Venice seems to be typical in this respect, since there are many converging clues to suggest that the city was a leading centre of polyphonic music throughout the fifteenth century, despite the lack of documents discovered for St Mark's *cappella*, for example, for the last fifteen years of the century.[28]

[25] Frank A. D'Accone, 'The Singers of San Giovanni in Florence during the 15th Century', *Journal of the American Musicological Society*, 14 (1961), pp. 307–58; *idem*, 'The Musical Chapels at the Florentine Cathedral and Baptistry during the First Half of the 16th Century', *ibid.*, 24 (1971), pp. 1–50.

[26] F. A. D'Accone, 'Music and Musicians at Santa Maria del Fiore in the Early Quattrocento', in *Scritti in onore di Luigi Ronga* (Milan, 1973), pp. 99–126.

[27] Denys Hay, *The Church in Italy in the Fifteenth Century* (Cambridge, 1977).

[28] For a summary view of the Venetian situation, see Cattin, 'Formazione e attività delle cappelle polifoniche'.

But it is known that in 1451 the first Venetian patriarch forbade all secular songs in churches '*praeter mottettos . . . ad laudem Dei et beatae Virginis Mariae*'; and he appointed *cantores*,[29] and these appointments cannot have referred only to monodic singing. For some of the mainland towns that came under Venetian rule at the beginning of the century, both archival documents and musical sources have survived. As far as Treviso is concerned, there is D'Alessi's thorough research, and his study of the history of the cathedral *cappella* has been further clarified by Pesce's biography of Bishop Ludovico Barbo, a stimulating book rich in documentation.[30] For Padua, the main trends in the musical life of the cathedral can be traced through Casimiri's documents; and it should also be noted that, in addition, there are two processionals in the Biblioteca Capitolare there which reflect local liturgical and musical traditions during the fourteenth and fifteenth centuries. These include some compositions presumably by Marchetto, and other songs added in about 1450 and ascribed to Johannes de Quadris in a Petrucci print,[31] while another gathering containing a series of older two-voice liturgical *Lamentazioni* by de Quadris has been found in the Archivio Capitolare in Vicenza.[32] It should be remembered that the Paduan processionals, and the Vicenza gathering reflect liturgical practice rather than a patron's taste, and that from 1431 the cathedral clergy had to learn *cantus figuratus*. Furthermore, by the time Johannes de Limburgia was in Vicenza, the grammar and chant school had been firmly established by a bull of Pius II in 1460.[33] For Verona there are few fifteenth-century documents, but the so-called 'Scuola degli Accoliti' was quite active and trained composers such as Marchetto Cara and

[29] Fabio Fano, *Profilo di una storia della vita musicale in Venezia dalle origini alla vigilia della fioritura rinascimentale* (Bologna, 1975), pp. 44–8.

[30] D'Alessi, *La cappella musicale del Duomo di Treviso*; L. Pesce, *Ludovico Barbo Vescovo di Treviso (1437–1443)*, 2 vols. (Padua, 1969).

[31] Facsimile and transcription by Giuseppe Vecchi, *Uffici drammatici padovani* (Florence, 1954). Petrucci's print is the *Lamentationum Hieremie prophete Liber primus* (Venice, 1506).

[32] G. Cattin, 'Uno sconosciuto codice quattrocentesco dell'Archivio Capitolare di Vicenza e le Lamentazioni di Johannes de Quadris', in *L'Ars Nova Italiana del Trecento*, III (Comune di Certaldo, 1970), pp. 281–304. The edition of de Quadris's works is by Cattin, *Johannis de Quadris Opera* (Bologna, 1972).

[33] A. Gallo and G. Mantese, *Ricerche sulle origini della cappella musicale del Duomo di Vicenza* (Venice and Rome, 1964); G. Mantese, *Storia musicale vicentina* (Vicenza, 1956).

Michele Pesenti around the end of the century.[34] There are more documents about musical activity in Udine and other towns in Friuli,[35] while the results of Pierluigi Petrobelli's announced research into the manuscripts and the *cappella* at Cividale are eagerly awaited.

From the data briefly given here it is clear that institutions founded through the initiative of the Church flourished in northern Italy (the list could also include Brescia and Bergamo),[36] and that the presence there of French and Flemish composers alongside native singers gradually encouraged the latter to adopt a more professional approach and even to develop compositional skills. The question of the number of singers in the main *cappelle* has recently been illuminated by D'Accone with tables including data from Siena, Bologna, Mantua, etc.,[37] though the results could be misleading since only a small number of *cappelle* are drawn upon for these statistics. But in how many places was polyphony performed around the middle of the century? One must be cautious, after the discovery of polyphonic songs copied in about the third and fourth decades of the century into chant manuscripts at Guardiagrele, a small town in the Abruzzi.[38] In any case, there are well-known documents from the second half of the century relating to the cathedrals of Modena (where the singer–priests formed the congre-

---

[34] See E. Paganuzzi's chapters on the medieval and Renaissance periods in the book *La musica a Verona* (Verona, 1976), pp. 3–215. On the 'scuola degli Accoliti' see A. Spagnolo, 'Le scuole accolitali di grammatica e di musica in Verona', *Atti e memorie dell'Accademia d'Agricoltura . . . di Verona*, 4th ser., vol. 5 (1904–5). See also E. Paganuzzi, 'Notizie veronesi su Marco Cara e Michele Pesenti', *Rivista Italiana di Musicologia*, 12 (1977), pp. 7–24.

[35] G. Vale, 'La cappella musicale del Duomo di Udine', *Note d'Archivio per la Storia Musicale*, 7 (1930), pp. 87–201; *idem*, 'Vita musicale nella Chiesa metropolitana di Aquileia (343–1751)', *ibid.*, 9 (1932), pp. 201–16; *idem*, *La 'schola cantorum' del duomo di Gemona e i suoi maestri* (Gemona, 1908).

[36] On musical activity at the Cathedral of Ferrara, where Ugolino da Orvieto was canon after 1430, see Lewis Lockwood, 'Dufay and Ferrara', in Atlas (ed.), *Dufay Quincentenary Conference*, p. 5.

[37] F. A. D'Accone, 'The Performance of Sacred Music in Italy during Josquin's Time, c. 1475–1525', in E. E. Lowinsky and B. J. Blackburn (eds.), *Josquin des Prez – Proceedings of the International Josquin Festival – Conference* (London, 1976), pp. 601–18. Further information in Keith Polk, 'Ensemble Performance in Dufay's Time', in Atlas (ed.), *Dufay Quincentenary Conference*, pp. 61–75.

[38] G. Cattin, O. Mischiati, and A. Ziino, 'Composizioni polifoniche del primo Quattrocento nei libri corali di Guardiagrele', *Rivista Italiana di Musicologia*, 7 (1972), pp. 153–81.

gation of the 'Mensa comune'), Parma, Trento, Fano, Chioggia, Arezzo, and Rieti,[39] and some others. There is no need to continue this list; by the end of the century many cathedrals maintained similar establishments. It is much more interesting to note that, after the standstill in the middle of the century, the first native composers were products of the cathedral schools. The particular case of Verona has already been mentioned. Equally indicative are the careers of the composers of frottole and *laude* printed by Petrucci: for the most part these were priests or laymen who were trained in church schools and subsequently pursued their careers in the ecclesiastical *cappelle* of northern Italy. As for Florence, there are the composers named in Santa Maria del Fiore MS 21,[40] a processional surely used in Florence Cathedral, which preserves works by Bartolomeo degli Organi and Ser Giovanni Serragli,[41] both of whom worked alongside Isaac and perhaps under his guidance.

Alongside the cathedral schools, religious orders also gradually increased their efforts to train composers such as the Servite Alessandro Coppini, who worked at SS. Annunziata in Florence; the Friars Minor established a polyphonic *cappella* in the basilica of St Anthony of Padua in 1480;[42] and a similar institution was founded in Assisi under the direction of Fra Ruffino. The Benedictines were active in the field of music throughout the century, beginning with the so-called 'Paduan fragments' copied by Dom Rolando da Casale,

[39] Gino Roncaglia, *La cappella musicale del duomo di Modena* (Florence, 1957), pp. 11–15 and 285, n. 8. N. Pelicelli, 'Musicisti in Parma nei secoli XV–XVI', *Note d'Archivio per la Storia Musicale*, 8 (1931), pp. 132–42; well-known personalities such as Giorgio Anselmi, Nicola Burzio and others are mentioned there. Trent holds the richest collection of musical documents dating back to the second half of the fifteenth century. For other towns, see R. Paolucci, 'La cappella musicale del duomo di Fano', *Note d'Archivio per la Storia Musicale*, 3 (1926), p. 84; I. Tiozzo, 'Maestri e organisti della cattedrale di Chioggia fino al XVII secolo', *ibid.*, 12 (1935), pp. 284–96; F. Coradini, 'La cappella musicale del duomo di Arezzo dal sec. XV a tutto il secolo XIX', *ibid.*, 14 (1937), pp. 49–56; A. Sacchetti Sassetti, 'La cappella musicale del duomo di Rieti', *ibid.*, 18 (1941), pp. 49–88.

[40] Florence, Archivio Musicale dell'Opera di Santa Maria del Fiore, MS 21. The codex is described in G. Cattin, *Un processionale fiorentino per la settimana santa, Studio liturgico-musicale sul ms. 21 dell'Opera di S. Maria del Fiore* (Bologna, 1975).

[41] F. A. D'Accone, 'Alessandro Coppini and Bartolomeo degli Organi – Two Florentine Composers of the Renaissance', *Analecta Musicologica*, 4 (1967), pp. 38–76; 'Some Neglected Composers in the Florentine Chapels, ca. 1475–1525', *Viator – Medieval and Renaissance Studies*, 1 (1970), pp. 263–88.

[42] Antonio Sartori, *Documenti per la storia della musica al Santo e nel Veneto* (Vicenza, 1977), p. 197.

whose biography has recently been reconstructed,[43] and leading up to the works of Bartolomeo da Bologna.[44] A mostly anonymous repertory had been produced by then and was circulated amongst Benedictine monasteries; traces of it can be found in various manuscripts copied for monasteries of the Benedictine Congregation of Santa Giustina, later called the Cassinese.[45] The well-known manuscript Montecassino 871 was copied at the monastery of Sant'Angelo in Gaeta, or perhaps in some Neapolitan monastery, and reflects the activities of the Aragonese *cappella*.[46] Similarly, the manuscript Cape Town Library, Grey 3.b.12 comes from a Benedictine monastery in northern Italy.[47] As for the Dominicans, it is enough to mention Giordano Pasetto, who copied the manuscript A 17 in the Biblioteca Capitolare in Padua in 1522, a source marking the transition to a new phase of musical culture in the cathedral *cappella*, characterised by a full assimilation of French and Flemish traditions.[48] Other manuscripts testify to this assimilation of the northern polyphonic language, notably the Gaffurius manuscripts in Milan, and other sources in Verona, Treviso, Piacenza, Siena, and Pistoia.

The indications of this new period are everywhere and indisputable, in the activities of composers such as Francesco D'Ana, Spataro or Fogliano, theorist–composers such as Gaffurius (and before him foreigners such as Hothby and Ramos de Pareja) whose career was within the sphere of the Church, and patrons such as Cardinal Ascanio Sforza (though his relationship with Josquin was not

[43] *Ricerche sulla musica a S. Giustina di Padova all'inizio del Quattrocento*, I: G. Cattin, 'Il copista Rolando da Casale. Nuovi frammenti Musicali nell'Archivio di Stato', and II: F. A. Gallo, 'Due "siciliane" del Trecento', both in *Annales Musicologiques*, 7 (1964–77), pp. 17–50.

[44] Adriano Cavicchi, 'Altri documenti su Bartolomeo da Bologna, *Rivista Italiana di Musicologia*, 12 (1976), pp. 178–81.

[45] G. Cattin, 'Tradizione e tendenze innovatrici nella normativa e nella pratica liturgico-musicale della Congregazione di S. Giustina', *Benedictina*, 17 (1970), pp. 254–99; *idem*, 'canti polifonici del repertorio benedettino in uno sconosciuto "Liber quadragesimalis" e in altre fonti italiane dei secoli XV e XVI inc.', *ibid.*, 19 (1972), pp. 445–537.

[46] Montecassino, Archivio Musicale della Badia, MS N 871: transcribed by Isabel Pope and Masakata Kanazawa, *The Musical Manuscript Montecassino 871. A Neapolitan Repertory of Sacred and Secular Music of the Late Fifteenth Century* (Oxford, 1978).

[47] G. Cattin, 'Nuova fonte italiana della polifonia intorno al 1500 (Ms. Cape Town, Grey 3.b.12)', *Acta Musicologica*, 45 (1973), pp. 165–227.

[48] Padua, Biblioteca Capitolare, MS A 17.

perhaps as enlightened as Lowinsky would wish)[49] and Cardinal Ippolito I d'Este[50] who inaugurated the sixteenth-century tradition of Church patronage of music. For this development, the documents and evidence of contacts between the Church and court *cappelle* exceed the scope of a simple essay. Nevertheless, this sketched review would be lacking if it did not mention the *lauda*, that typically Italian composition that flourished within religious movements and institutions. While the *laude* was the natural song of the confraternities of *laudesi* or *disciplinati* during the fourteenth century,[51] it became a more widely used devotional song in the fifteenth. There is evidence of this in the dozens of *laudari* that have survived without music and, more specifically, in fifteenth-century musical documents[52] from Franciscan or Benedictine monasteries. On the one hand the most important of these documents, Marciana ital. IX.145, comes from Venetian Franciscan circles and shows in its two sections the unrefined tradition alongside a tendency much closer to the intonations of Dufay's time.[53] On the other hand the repertory of the Cape Town manuscript comes from the Benedictine tradition and includes some interesting two-voice polyphonic *unica* dateable to the third decade of the century, together with more mature examples from the last years of the century;[54] these have concordances in Perugia G.20 and Florence, Panciatichi 27.[55] Furthermore, in the

[49] E. E. Lowinsky, 'Ascanio Sforza's Life: A Key to Josquin's Biography and an Aid to the Chronology of His Works', in Lowinsky and Blackburn (eds.), *Josquin des Prez – Proceedings*, pp. 31–75.

[50] Lewis Lockwood, 'Music at Ferrara in the Period of Ercole I d'Este', *Studi Musicali*, 1 (1972), pp. 101–31; *idem*, 'Josquin at Ferrara: New Documents and Letters', in Lowinsky and Blackburn (eds.) *Josquin des Prez – Proceedings*, pp. 103–37 (esp. pp. 118–21), including (p. 116) notes on a document concerning Giordano Pasetto from which it can be inferred that the composer was born in 1484.

[51] F. A. D'Accone, 'Le Compagnie dei Laudesi in Firenze durante l'Ars Nova', in *L'Ars Nova Italiana del Trecento*, III (Comune di Certaldo, 1970), pp. 253–80.

[52] In addition to the information given in Knud Jeppesen's classic book *Die mehrstimmige italienische Laude um 1500* (Leipzig and Copenhagen, 1935), the sources are listed by Piero Damilano, 'Fonti musicali della lauda polifonica intorno alla metà del sec. XV', *Collectanea Historiae Musicae*, 3 (1963), pp. 59–89.

[53] On this manuscript, see note 16 above.

[54] Modern edition by G. Cattin, *Italian 'Laude' and Latin 'Unica' from the Ms. Cape Town, Grey 3.b.12*, Corpus Mensurabilis Musicae ser. 76 (1977).

[55] Perugia, Biblioteca Comunale Augusta, MS 431 (G 20): see Allan W. Atlas, 'On the Neapolitan Provenance of the Manuscript Perugia, Biblioteca Comunale Augusta, 431 (G 20)', *Musica Disciplina*, 31 (1977), pp. 45–105. Florence, Biblioteca

rather peripheral region of Friuli, the priest Pietro Capretto composed some *laude* for the Confraternity of Battuti of Pordenone[56] before Petrucci printed his two books of *laude* (1508).

To sum up, a longer view of the period shows both starting points and developments. The former (an abiding concern for chant, the creation or expansion of cathedral song schools, and the continuing use of *biscantare* treatment of Gregorian melodies etc.) and the latter (to mention only one, the revival of polyphony in the work of Italian composers) share a common implication: to a large extent these developments took place within the Church or as an indirect consequence of the Church's actions. Obviously this does not mean that the Church intended or planned such development: there was no organic plan laid down by ecclesiastical authority. Rather, the Church's attitude should be seen as one of healthy pragmatism, a flexibility in adapting to the tendencies and needs of the time. Since the trend was toward polyphony, the Church trained polyphonists and adapted its services to polyphonic music. The fruits of this broadening of the Church's approach proved to be more prolific and more durable than the more isolated, ephemeral musical splendours cultivated in the secular court circles of Italy.

Nazionale Centrale, M S Panciatichi 27, on the other hand, has a northern Italian origin (perhaps Mantuan): see Atlas, *The Cappella Giulia Chansonnier (Rome, Biblioteca Apostolica Vaticana, C.G.XIII.27)*, 2 vols., Musicological Studies 27 (Brooklyn, 1975), I, p. 252.

[56] G. Cattin, 'La laude in ambiente veneto. Le composizioni di Pietro Capretto', to be published in the proceedings of the Convegno Internazionale di Studi held at Castelfranco Veneto in September 1978 to commemorate the fifth centenary of the birth of Giorgione.

3

ANTOINE BRUMEL AND PATRONAGE
AT PARIS[1]

CRAIG WRIGHT

TO appreciate how the practising musician and composer functioned
within the system of musical patronage in northern French cathedrals at the end of the middle ages, one must understand the administrative structure within the cathedral. For no matter what the
creative genius of the composer or the interpretative skills of the
performer, the impulse for novelty and spontaneity was always
tempered by an ecclesiastical hierarchy that looked upon statute and
custom rather than artistic innovation as its touchstone. The
apotheosis of the artistic spirit to the olympian realm of independent
action, free to create apart from the functional demands of a formulaic liturgy or the fashions of a secular court, was still more than
three centuries away. For Antoine Brumel and his contemporaries,
just as later even for Bach and Mozart, the system of Church
patronage was a comparatively secure means of satisfying economic
need, but one under which creative genius and ego often chafed.

The administrative structure at Notre Dame of Paris was typical
of the clerical hierarchy in northern French cathedrals. It was governed by a chapter, a college of fifty-one canons led by a dean, that
usually met thrice weekly to decide the practical business of the
church.[2] The chapter had the right to elect the bishop, though he

---

[1] Research for this communication was supported in part by a grant from the
American Philosophical Society. The author is also indebted to Professor Jeremy
Noble of the State University of New York at Buffalo for his insights into a number
of the issues raised here.

[2] For a more detailed discussion of the chapter of Notre Dame of Paris, see
J. Emmanuel des Graviers, '"Messeigneurs du Chapitre" de l'église de Paris à
l'époque de la guerre de cent ans', *Huitième centenaire de Notre-Dame de Paris (Congrès
des 30 Mai – 3 Juin 1964): Recueil de travaux sur l'histoire de la cathédrale et de l'église de
Paris* (Paris, 1967), pp. 185–222.

played no significant role in the daily operation of the church or in the execution of the divine service. This latter task fell to the chapter. Although canons had gathered around the bishop in pre-Carolingian times, in part to assure the performance of the divine rites, by the twelfth century they had become preoccupied with the considerable business affairs of the church and had engaged surrogates, usually erstwhile choirboys, to execute the liturgy. Except on a few solemn feast days, the canons were rarely to be found in their choir stalls. Only the succentor, who was to supervise the offices, was required by oath to attend regularly the canonical hours and Mass.

Thus the daily performance of the *opus dei*, the continuous round of communal worship, devolved upon a group of lesser clerics – lesser not with regard to their ranking in holy orders, but in terms of patrimony, prestige, and political power. These lower ecclesiastics, the career liturgists as we may call them, were broadly divided into two groups: the beneficed and the unbeneficed clerks. Within this twofold division was an ascending scale of prelation that was distinctly medieval in its rigidly hierarchic structure.

Foremost among the beneficed clerks were the two canons of St Aignan, who traced the establishment of their prebend back to a foundation made by archdeacon Etienne de Garland about 1119.[3] Although they were titularly clerks of the small chapel of St Aignan situated within the close of Notre Dame, their principal duty was to assist with the daily recitation of the hours and Mass within the choir of the cathedral. Unlike the other servants of the choir, the canons of St Aignan were permitted to attend the meetings of the chapter and jointly had the vote of one canon. Similarly, each enjoyed half the daily distributions of a canon and half the annual revenue of one prebend. Canon of St Aignan was the highest position a singer working within the system of patronage at Notre Dame could hope to achieve. A musician was never appointed a full canon at Notre Dame unless, as was true for Philippe de Vitry, Johannes Ockeghem and Antoine de Longeval, his nomination came directly from the king by royal pressure on the bishop or by regalian right, in which case the system of advancement at Notre Dame had been circumvented.

Somewhat less prestigious and lucrative than the position of canon of St Aignan was that of great vicar (*magnus seu perpetuus*

---

[3] B. Guérard, *Cartulaire de l'église Notre Dame de Paris*, vol. IV of *Collection des cartulaires de France*, I (Paris, 1850), pp. 328–9.

vicarius) at Notre Dame. There were two vicars of St Aignan (offices founded in 1297),[4] as well as six others who served as representatives for an abbot or provost of six churches in and around Paris, the monasteries of St Maur des Fossés, St Victor, St Martin des Champs, St Marcel, and St Denis de la Chartre, and the collegiate church of St Germain l'Auxerrois. The vicariate of St Maur des Fossés had been established as early as 868,[5] that of St Victor sometime before 1138.[6] Originally the monastic vicars were appointed by the abbot of their respective communities, but by the fourteenth century the collation to these benefices rested *de facto*, if not *de jure*, with the chapter of Paris. Although the vicars had no income from a prebend, their daily distributions for attendance at Mass, the hours, votive and obit services, and processions in and around the cathedral were the same as those paid a full canon. The chapter required, just as it did of all adult choristers, that each new vicar commit to memory a large portion of the liturgy – the psalter and the *commune sanctorum* of the usage of Paris. The vicars were also to be skilled in singing, specifically in plainchant, as the following two entries in the capitular acts suggest:

14 July 1406. Jean Houssete, having petitioned that he be received as great vicar of St Martin des Champs ... the chapter deputed masters Jean Rolland, canon of Paris, and Denis de Cursone, succentor, to examine him in singing and the other necessary things, [and they] reported, after due examination, that he sings plainsong very well and securely; and having heard this report, the chapter received him. (See the Appendix, Doc. 1)

10 May 1566. Henceforth the great vicars beneficed within the church should be tested by the chapter, or someone designated by them, on their vocal skill and proficiency, at least in plainsong, and only those favourably judged should be admitted. (Doc. 2)

Next in rank to the great vicars of Notre Dame were the ten canons of St Denis du Pas and eight canons of St Jean le Rond. These were clerics nominally assigned to two ancillary churches of Notre Dame, one (St Denis) situated just behind the chevet, to the east of the cathedral, the other (St Jean) next to the north tower. Both churches had existed before the construction of the present cathedral. They made up part of what archeologists have come to term 'un groupe

---

[4] Paris, Archives Nationales (hereafter cited as AN), L 523, no. 4, p. 2.
[5] AN, L 524, no. 1.   [6] AN, L 521, no. 119.

cathédral', a cluster of three or so minor churches or chapels surrounding the mother church[7] – see Figure 1. St Jean le Rond functioned as the baptistery of Notre Dame, possessing the only bap-
tismal font on the Ile de la Cité. It also served as the parish church for
the lay servants who attended to the needs of the canons of Notre
Dame within their claustral homes. The clergy assigned to these two
institutions consisted of four priest canons, three deacon canons, and
three subdeacon canons for St Denis, and two priest canons, three
deacon canons, and three subdeacon canons for St Jean. But, except-
ing the two priest canons of St Jean, these clerics had no parochial

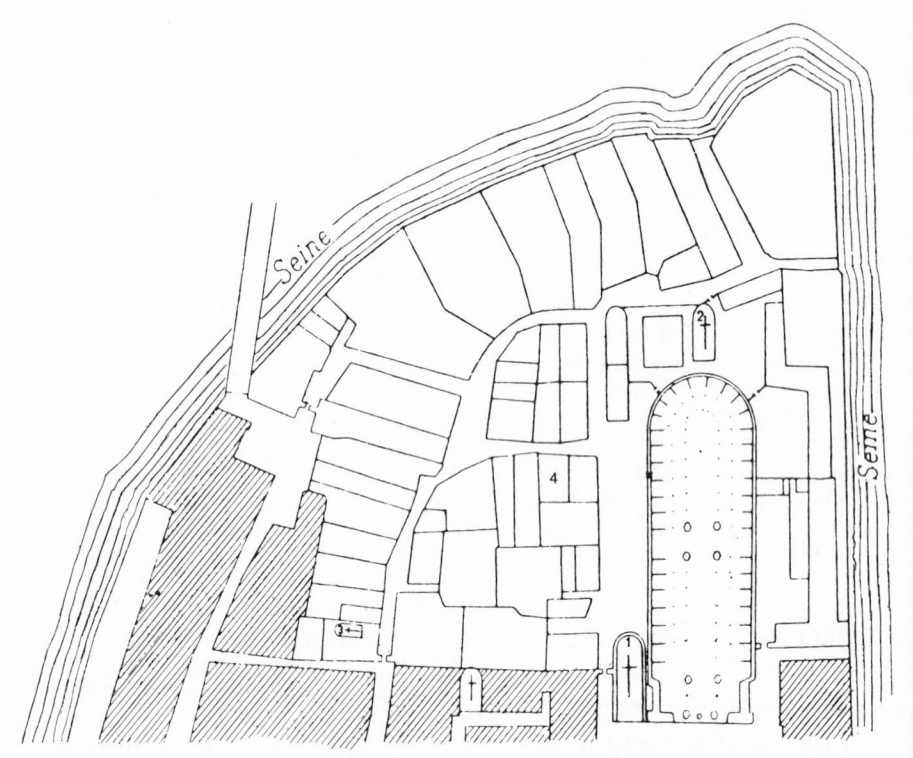

Figure 1. Plan of the close of Notre Dame of Paris (F.-L. Chartier, *L'ancien chapitre de
Notre-Dame de Paris et sa maîtrise* (Paris, 1897), p. 9), showing the collegiate churches
of St Jean le Rond (1) and St Denis du Pas (2), the chapel of St Aignan (3), and the
site of the *maîtrise* in 1455 (4)

[7] See Jean Hubert, 'Les origines de Notre-Dame de Paris', *Huitième centenaire de
Notre-Dame*, pp. 1–22.

duties; their canonicates were sinecures and their sole responsibility was to perform the divine service within the cathedral, singing and psalming with the other choristers. On all but solemn feast-days (when their functions were assumed by the canons of the chapter), they served in weekly rotation as officiants of the liturgy, acting as celebrants, lectors, *rectores chori*, and soloists in antiphonal and responsorial chants. Although the canons of St Denis and St Jean received roughly equal emoluments from their communally held prebends and, after 1404, from daily distributions, a canonicate at St Denis was preferable to one at St Jean because it provided more substantial housing within the close and the most immediate route to the even more lucrative position of great vicar.

The most numerous of the *socii chori* at Notre Dame of Paris were the sixteen unbeneficed clerks. Documents of the twelfth and thirteenth centuries preserved mainly in the cartularies of the church refer to them as *pauperes clerici*,[8] suggesting they were the French equivalent of the English 'poor clerks'. Indeed, they had no income from a prebend, and their daily distributions valued only about half of those assigned the canons of St Denis du Pas and St Jean le Rond. Judging from their frequent truancy, insolence, and incontinence, the unbeneficed clerks, or clerks of matins as they were called, were the least reliable component of the cathedral choir. Many of these young men were still in their teens, having been drawn directly from the ranks of choirboys whose voices had recently broken, or from among former choirboys who had been sent to the University (usually to the Collège de Fortet) at the expense of the chapter. Their position carried no tenure and they were required to resign *en masse* annually at the first capitular meeting after the feast of St John the Baptist, to be reappointed at the pleasure of the chapter. All clerks of matins were expected to be skilled singers, thoroughly familiar with the liturgical usage of Paris. During the second half of the sixteenth century, the more talented among them received instruction on musical instruments, principally keyboard instruments, as the following capitular act attests:

3 February 1571 [n.s.]. The succentor and sire Brunet [canon of St Aignan] should provide the organist of the church with the organ and other musical instruments necessary in the house of the choirboys for the instruction of

[8] See, for example, Guérard, *Cartulaire*, I, p. 396 = AN, L 528A, no. 1; and AN, L 528A, no. 5.

those boys and clerks of matins who are found to be among the more apt at this.[9] (Doc. 3)

Throughout the late middle ages, the statutes of Notre Dame decreed that there be sixteen unbeneficed clerks of matins in the choir of the cathedral. But in point of fact, there were occasionally more than sixteen and frequently fewer, depending on the economic weal of the church. In 1347, for example, there were eighteen clerks of matins, but by 1428, because the Plague and the Hundred Years War had caused the loss or destruction of much revenue-producing land, the number had been reduced to five; and the full complement of clerks was not again attained until the sixteenth century.[10] The six most senior clerks of matins were assigned the position of *machicotus*. Although the meaning of the term has yet to be fully explained,[11] at Paris the *machicoti* functioned as did the canons of St Denis du Pas

[9] The clavichord was undoubtedly among the 'other musical instruments' mentioned here, since instruction on it was provided at other French and English cathedrals at this time (see André Pirro, 'Gilles Mureau, chanoine de Chartres', *Festschrift für Johannes Wolf* (Berlin, 1929), p. 166; Arthur-Emile Prévost, *Histoire de la maîtrise de la cathédrale de Troyes* (Troyes, 1906), p. 116; and Kathleen Edwards, *The English Secular Cathedrals in the Middle Ages*, 2nd edn (Manchester, 1967), p. 174). *Discipuli organici* often received their first lessons on the clavichord because, according to Sebastian Virdung: 'What you learn to play on the clavichord, you can then play easily on the organ' (*Musica getutscht* (Basel, 1511), fol. E); see also Michael Praetorius, *De organographia*, vol. II of *Syntagma musicum* (Wolfenbüttel, 1618), chap. XXXVI.

[10] AN, LL 260, fols. 59–63.

[11] The origin of the word can apparently be traced to the verb *machicolare* (*machecoller*, *machicoler*, or *machicoter*) with the general sense of to ornament or embellish by the addition of figural detail. The noun *machicot* (*machicotus* or *massicotus*) was a title given to functionaries of the choir in churches in Milan, Genoa, Poitiers, Orléans, and Senlis, in addition to the cathedral of Paris. By at least the seventeenth century, however, the word had come to denote in France a professional singer, specifically in the choir of the cathedral of Paris, who embellished and filled in around the given plainsong (see s.v. *machicot*, Gilles Ménage, *Dictionnaire étymologique ou origines de la langue françoise* (Paris, 1694); Antoine Furetière, *Dictionnaire universel contenant généralement tous les françois tant vieux que modernes*, 3rd edn (The Hague and Rotterdam, 1701); Frédéric Godefroy, *Dictionnaire de l'ancienne langue française* (Paris, 1937–8); and *Grand Larousse de la langue française* (Paris, 1971–8)). What remains to be explored is the implication that the presence of trained soloists to embellish the chant at Notre Dame in the seventeenth century seems to signify a long history of vocal ornamentation within the choir, a tradition that likely goes back to the era of Leonin and Perotin. It was the clerks of matins, of course, who sang the organum at Notre Dame. An excellent discussion of the vocal techniques used in the organum of Leonin and Perotin can be found in Edward Roesner, 'The Performance of Parisian Organum', *Early Music*, 7 (1979), pp. 174–89.

CRAIG WRIGHT

and St Jean le Rond, yet without additional remuneration; they acted as hebdomadary deacon and subdeacon lectors, *rectores chori*, and soloists for plainsong and polyphony. *Machicotus* was thus a preparatory position from which a clerk of matins ascended to a benefice. When he joined the choir, an unbeneficed clerk could be of any rank within the hieratic scale – simple tonsured clerk, acolyte, subdeacon, deacon, or priest – but if he were not in sacerdotal orders, he was encouraged to progress rapidly to the priesthood so as to facilitate the execution of the liturgy and his own advancement within the system of beneficial patronage.

Younger than the beneficed clerks, but better maintained, were the choirboys of Notre Dame. Boys had been among the *ministri inferiores* of the church since at least the twelfth century and undoubtedly long before.[12] Initially they seem to have lived singly as the wards of the bishop or individual canons, but by at least 1208 they were grouped communally under the tutelage of a master, specifically a music master (*magister cantus puerorum chori*).' The chapter maintained eight choirboys by 1396, ten by 1489, and increased the number to twelve on 9 February 1551.[13] Much of the income to purchase food, clothing, housing, and instruction for the boys came from *la prébende morte*, so called because the prebendal income had been suppressed from a canon and assigned exclusively to the maintenance of the boys. In 1349 the deadly effects of the Plague (*quod pestilante epidimia insolita*) so reduced revenues that additional support was thought necessary and was secured by the imposition of a small tax on each benefice conferred by the chapter; henceforth canons, chaplains and even curates at the time of their reception had to pay a surcharge for the upkeep of the young choristers.[14] A receiver collected all prebendal revenues and fees and paid them to the master at a fixed annual rate per capita. For the fiscal year 1435–6, for example, master Thomas Hoppinel, a musician who had

[12] A legend of the life of St Marcel (d. 436), ninth Bishop of Paris, relates that a boy aged about ten sang 'quelque Antienne ou Respons' during the liturgical service (Jacques Du Breul, *Les antiquitez de la ville de Paris* (Paris, 1640), p. 490). And Fortunatus mentions how St Germain (d. 576), twentieth Bishop of Paris, officiated in his church: 'Pontificis monitis clerus, plebs psallit, et infans' (quoted in Jean Lebeuf, *Traité historique et pratique sur le chant ecclésiastique* (Paris, 1741), p. 11).
[13] AN, LL 290, fol. 156; and AN, LL 297, fols. 11v and 89.
[14] AN, L 464, no. 56; Guérard, *Cartulaire*, III, p. 428; and Du Breul, *Antiquitez*, p. 19.

previously served in the chapel of the Duke of Burgundy and in that of the English regent Duke John of Bedford,[15] was allocated twenty *livres* for each of eight boys.[16] The amount was still set at twenty *livres* per annum in 1465, but had been raised to thirty-five *livres* by 1533, and to fifty *livres* by 1550.[17] In addition to the eight, ten, or twelve choirboys serving the cathedral, the chapter often would permit one or two other boys to be boarded and educated in the *maîtrise* – the dormitory-school for young choristers – as long as their expenses were paid by an outside party.[18] Thus servitors of the bishop, nephews of canons, and sons of members of parliament and of the bourgeois of Paris vied to become pensioners. The following two entries suggest that selling a musical education could be mildly profitable for the chapter:

28 July 1393. The canons are pleased to allow the master of the boys to admit to the *maîtrise* a certain young boy of a certain burgess of Paris (who wishes to make him a monk of the monastery of St Denis of France) for instruction in singing, provided that he [i.e. the master of the boys] receive a good and sufficient remuneration. (Doc. 4)

6 October 1413. The canons are pleased to admit two boys whom my lord bishop [Gerardus de Monte Acuto] wishes to place with the other choir-boys, provided that they shall be subject to the chapter in all things without contradiction by the bishop, this in view of the fact that the bishop offers for the expenses of these two boys fifty francs annually. (Doc. 5)

Yet, whatever the source of their support, boys were customarily taken for service in the church of Paris at ages six to nine and remained until their voices changed about seven or eight years later. When they were considered for admission, they underwent an audition that usually required them to sing a *Benedicamus domino*. Judge-

15 Hoppinel was a chaplain to John the Fearless, Duke of Burgundy, from 1415 through 1419, and to John, Duke of Bedford, from 1425 through 1430. Craig Wright, *Music at the Court of Burgundy, 1364–1419: A Documentary History* (Henryville, Ottawa, and Binningen, 1979), pp. 99–100 and 106; and AN, LL 256, fol. 86v.
16 AN, LL 297, fol. 2.   17 AN, LL 297, fols. 3, 17, and 89.
18 By 1433 the *maîtrise* had been established in a house situated at the beginning of a street that led directly to the *porte rouge*, the door just to the east of the north transept by which the clergy entered the choir from the close. Undoubtedly because of the ease with which the boys and their master could reach the church – proximity was especially important to attendance at midnight matins – the *maîtrise* of Notre Dame has remained at this location (8 rue Massillon) to the present day; see Figure 1.

ment was rendered by a committee of canons, not by the master of music, according to the candidate's vocal skill and aptitude for music and letters (*super idoneitate vocis et aptitudine ad musicam et litteras*). If the verdict was favourable, the boy received a clerical tonsure by the bishop and the habit of the cathedral of Paris, and was placed in the *maîtrise*. There he was given lessons in Latin grammar, logic, and morals by a master of grammar, and instruction in plainchant, counterpoint, vocal techniques, and liturgical ceremony by the master of music.[19]

In exchange for this education, the choirboys were required to perform manifold services. Within the choir they assisted the officiants, bearing candles, incense and holy water, accompanying readers to the lectern, and conveying instructions from the dean, cantor, succentor, or ruler of the choir to various soloists. They themselves read lessons, chanted versicles, and sang the solo portions of selected responsories and of the Alleluia of the Mass on certain feast days. In chantry chapels outside the choir they recited psalms and orisons and sang Masses and polyphonic motets as memorial services for deceased benefactors of the church. Within the close of Notre Dame, the boys transported holy water to the homes of the canons and occasionally sang secular songs in these same *hôtels*, provided they had the permission of the chapter. Virtually everything they rendered in church had to be committed to memory, and those boys selected to sing the next day had to rehearse their chants with the master or the eldest boy before retiring.

The status of the senior choirboy requires special comment, for even among the *angeli dei* there was a hierarchy of position. The oldest boy, or *spe* as he was called,[20] had exceptional responsibilities and privileges. Besides helping the master of music to prepare the

---

[19] For a general discussion of choirboys at Notre Dame of Paris, see F.-L. Chartier, *L'ancien chapitre de Notre-Dame de Paris et sa maîtrise* (Paris, 1897), chap. II; and A.-M. Yvon, 'La maîtrise de Notre-Dame aux XVIIe et XVIIIe siècles', *Huitième centenaire de Notre-Dame*, pp. 359–99.

[20] The etymology of the word *spe* is even more elusive than *machicotus*. *Spe* is clearly a contraction of *spetus*, in turn from *sepetus* which is a variant of *cepetus*. This may be related to *cepones*, the benches on which boy choristers sat in the choirs of certain monasteries; or conceivably it may derive from *coepi, coeptus*, a beginner (see Charles Du Fresne Ducange, *Glossarium ad scriptores mediae et infimae latinitatis* (Paris, 1733–6), s.vv. *cepeti, cepones*). With regard to *cepetus* and *cepones*, we can only reiterate the words of Ducange: 'Cur autem sic dicantur haud facile est divinare'.

boys, the *spe* also helped to enforce discipline among the young choristers, announced to the chapter when the morni g Mass (*magna missa*) was about to begin, and carried the cross during processions. Unlike the other boys, he was allowed to walk unattended through the church and close, and was supplied with a distinctive vestment. Were he to demonstrate sufficient interest and talent, the *spe* would be given lessons on the organ that was kept in the *maîtrise*:

4 September 1424. It pleases the canons that Denis Martini, *spe* of the church, may learn to play the organ, and they give to him the amount that one Mass will cost in order to learn to play it. (Doc. 6)

13 July 1436. Thomas Hoppinel, master of the choirboys, should be told that Lambertus Meteii, *spe* of the church, petitioned and sought the chapter to give him licence to learn a Mass on the organ existing in the house of said choirboys, and this by master Jacques [le Mol], organist of the church. (Doc. 7)

11 July 1583. It pleased the canons that Abraham [Blondet], the oldest of the choirboys, may continue for the next three months to learn to play the organ, and for this the receiver of said boys is to pay one gold [*écu*] to the master [of the organ] for each of the three months. (Doc. 8)

By the time each boy in his turn had passed out of the *maîtrise*, he had been offered instruction in voice and (often) keyboard instruments, and in plainsong and polyphony. Like the adult choristers, the *spe* was expected to memorise the psalter and the *commune sanctorum*. This feat of memory was a preliminary step to admission to the rank of unbeneficed clerk of matins. Indeed, the *spe* was the principal source of new clerks of matins, as he was already imbued with the liturgical traditions of the cathedral. Usually a vacancy among the clerks of matins was the agent of promotion of the *spe*:

31 March 1393. In place of Jean Constantinus, Herbert Berengarius is made *machicotus*, and he who was the *spe* is made clerk of matins, and the next oldest boy after him, namely Michael Bruneau, is made *spe*. (Doc. 9)

But as the middle ages drew to an end, the chapter increasingly felt compelled to provide the senior boy with a higher education at the University – at first for two or three years, but by the seventeenth century for four years – usually with the stipulation that he continue to frequent the choir on the major feast-days and with the expectation that the young man would pursue his career as a liturgist of the choir when his studies were completed. In sum, the chapter of Paris saw service in the choir as a lifelong occupation, commencing as early as the age of six, and terminating only upon death. And many a modestly talented liturgical singer did enter the church as a choirboy and advance to canon of St Aignan in the course of a career of fifty or sixty years. In this progression a singer might occupy any one of thirteen positions:[21]

canon of St Aignan (2)
vicar of St Aignan (2)
great vicar (6)
priest canon of St Denis du Pas (4)
deacon canon of St Denis du Pas (3)
subdeacon canon of St Denis du Pas (3)
priest canon of St Jean le Rond (2)
deacon canon of St Jean le Rond (3)
subdeacon canon of St Jean le Rond (3)
clerk of matins *machicotus* (6)
clerk of matins (10)
spe (1)
choirboy (7, 9, or 11)

Naturally a vacancy toward the top of the beneficial ladder would generate a nearly complete series of promotions. The wholesale advance occasioned by the death of Clément Mellot, a canon of St Aignan, on 4 August 1454 provides an illustration of the progressive, interlocking nature of the system: on 26 August the chapter installed Radoulph Fourbeur, formerly vicar of St Aignan, as the new canon of St Aignan; Fourbeur in turn was replaced by Jean Loublyer as vicar of St Aignan, Loublyer by Philippe Lenfant as priest canon of St Denis du Pas, Lenfant by Jean Valet as deacon canon of St Denis, Valet by Jean Goizot as subdeacon canon of St Denis, and Goizot by *machicotus* Hugo Pate as subdeacon canon of St Jean le Rond.[22] Besides these seats in the choir of Notre Dame, the chapter of Paris also had collation to more than a hundred chaplainries at the cathedral in addition to a host of canonicates, chaplainries, and curacies at various collegiate and parochial churches throughout the diocese. The canons individually provided to these benefices in rotation (*per rotam*), but were reluctant to confer them upon members of the choir; such supplementary positions, unless absolute

[21] The figure in brackets is the statutory number of incumbents for each post.
[22] AN, LL 117, p. 89.

sinecures, were thought to deter the singers from their principal duty, the perpetual performance of the *opus dei* within the choir of the cathedral.

At the capitular meeting on the morning of 29 November 1497, the canons of Paris voted to dismiss the master of the choirboys, Pierre Croisy, because of his unsatisfactory teaching 'tam in cantu quam in cerimonis et aliis'.[23] This was not a hasty decision, for the chapter had voiced its displeasure with the quality of Croisy's instruction as early as 4 January 1497.[24] To replace him, the canons determined to inquire as to the skills of a singer at Laon who had previously offered his services in this capacity. Six weeks later, on 5 January 1498, the chapter received master Antoine Brumel, priest and canon of the cathedral of Laon, who swore to instruct the boys diligently 'in cantu et bonis moribus' and was installed in the lower row on the dean's (the right) side of the choir (Doc. 10). This act represented a radical departure for the chapter of Paris: in the previous hundred and fifty years, the canons seem invariably to have selected the *magister puerorum chori* from among clergy of the diocese of Paris, and usually from among those already in the habit of the cathedral. Antoine Brumel was the first in a succession of masters to be drawn from the north of Paris, specifically from Picardy and from towns such as Laon, Cambrai, and Noyon. His reception is tangible evidence of a subtle yet important change in attitude on the part of the ruling clergy of the cathedral. From the beginning of the sixteenth century, the canons of Paris began to permit more polyphonic music and newer modes of performance within their church, to select *magistri* who were composers as well as pedagogues, and to encourage the recruitment of better musical personnel by broadening the geographic area of selection beyond the limits of the diocese.

During the first weeks of his tenure, the chapter seems to have been favourably impressed with the vigour with which Antoine Brumel assumed his new position. He immediately dismissed the young choristers' barber and ordered repairs within the *maîtrise*.[25] On 26 February 1498, the canons recognised the 'bonum zelum' with which he instructed the boys 'in arte musice et in bonis moribus' by granting him sixteen additional *écus* to support a

[23] AN, LL 127, fol. xxxij ˅.   [24] AN, LL 126, p. 463.
[25] AN, LL 127, fols. xli, xliiij, and iiij ˣˣ iij.

housemaid and a clerk.[26] At the same time the canons honoured him, acknowledging that he was 'gravis persona presbyter et canonicus ecclesie cathedralis laudunensis'; they declared that he might take a stall in the upper row, between the canon priests and canon deacons of the cathedral, rather than among the lower clergy. Thus, for the funeral service of Charles VIII on 30 April 1498, Brumel may either have remained among the canons in the upper stalls or joined the *socii chori* who had been displaced to the top of the *jubé* (rood screen) whence they chanted the Requiem Mass down into the choir.[27] Undoubtedly the preceptor marched behind his ten charges during the processional entry of the new king when, on 2 July 1498, Louis XII was welcomed to the cathedral 'campanis pulsantibus et organis ludentibus puerisque et alijs de choro *Te deum* cantantibus et jubilantibus'.[28]

As master of the choirboys at Paris, Brumel received a salary that was equal to the wages or daily distributions paid to a clerk of matins. In 1498, these totaled about twenty *livres tournois*.[29] In addition to this sum, he was entitled to one of the twelve shares or *porciones* the chapter allocated to pay the expenses of the *maîtrise* (there was one share for each of ten boys as well as one each for the masters of music and grammar). In 1498, a share likewise brought twenty *livres tournois*.[30] And finally the master earned extraordinary distributions when he and the choirboys sang for the various votive and anniversary services endowed by benefactors of the church.

By the end of the middle ages, votive and anniversary, or obit, services had come to constitute a significant part of the religious rites of collegiate and cathedral churches in France and England.[31] Whereas the eleventh and twelfth centuries saw an increase in the number and wealth of prebends founded at cathedrals, and the

---

[26] AN, LL 127, fol. xliiij; see also André Pirro, 'Dokumente über Antoine Brumel, Louis van Pullaer und Crispin van Stappen', *Zeitschrift für Musikwissenschaft*, 11 (1928–9), p. 350.

[27] AN, LL 127, fol. liii ᵛ; see also A. Mirot and B. Mahieu, 'Cérémonies officielles à Notre-Dame au XVᵉ siècle', *Huitième centenaire de Notre-Dame*, pp. 285–90.

[28] AN, LL 127, fol. lxv.   [29] AN, LL 127, fol. vᵛ.

[30] AN, LL 127, fol. xliiij.

[31] On votive and obit services, see Auguste Molinier, *Les obituaires français au moyen âge* (Paris, 1890), pp. 105–50; H. Leclercq, 'Obituaire', in *Dictionnaire d'archéologie chrétienne et de liturgie*, XII/2 (Paris, 1936), cols. 1834–57; Frank Ll. Harrison, *Music in Medieval Britain* (London, 1958), pp. 77–81; and Edwards, *Secular Cathedrals*, pp. 46–7, 285–6 and 316.

thirteenth and fourteenth centuries recorded sizeable donations to rebuild churches and construct apsidal and ambulatory chapels, the fifteenth and early sixteenth centuries were marked by an astonishing growth in the number and type of commemorative services, most of which were to be celebrated outside the choir at adjacent chapels or altars. Just as the canonical hours and the Mass of the day were supported collectively by the chapter of the church, so many votive and memorial services were instituted and maintained by single donors. Individual patrons provided for antiphons, responds, versicles, collects, motets, and Masses in praise of the Virgin, the Holy Sacrament, the Holy Trinity, a patron saint, or any one of a host of other saints. They also established countless obit services that usually included a vigil, consisting of Vespers and Matins of the Office for the Dead, and the Requiem Mass the next day. Through these foundations, the benefactor – be he bishop, barrister, or baker – sought to recommend his soul, and sometimes those of friends and kinsmen, to his creator. In this way musical patronage was a corollary of the desire for personal salvation.

By the time Antoine Brumel was received at Paris, more than six hundred privately endowed services, whether simple versicle or complete polyphonic Mass, had been established at the cathedral of Paris and registered in the necrology of the church.[32] Naturally the choirboys assisted in a number of these. On Saturdays before the ringing of prime, the master and the boys sang a Mass of Our Lady in the chapel of St George and St Denis, according to the foundation of Bishop Denis du Moulin (d. 1447).[33] Later that day they chanted a Requiem Mass in the chapel of Mary Magdalen in memory of the deceased canon Jean Lupi, as refounded from an earlier endowment in 1427.[34] In recompense for a donation of three hundred *écus* made in 1469, the choirboys also chanted a Requiem each month in the chapel of St Rémi for Guillaume Juvenal des Ursins (d. 1472), Chancellor of France.[35] Similarly, they performed a Mass of St Peter

---

[32] AN, L 523, no. 4 bis, p. 17. Paris, Bibliothèque Nationale, fonds Latin 5185cc, 5658b, and 18361, and Bibliothèque de l'Arsenal, MS 1064, are the four extant Parisian necrologies for the thirteenth through sixteenth centuries. Extracts from these are preserved in AN, LL 290. They are partially printed in Guérard, *Cartulaire*, IV; and Auguste Molinier, *Obituaires de la Province de Sens*, I (Paris, 1902), pp. 91–240.

[33] AN, LL 290, fol. 114v.   [34] AN, LL 290, fol. 33.

[35] Guérard, *Cartulaire*, IV, p. 43.

'alta voce' annually on June 29 at the altar of the Assumption, as canon Pierre Garnier established for his patron saint through a benefaction of half the income derived from the sale of his claustral home in 1488.[36] And Bishop Louis Beaumont (d. 1492) provided thirty *livres* annually for the young choristers to sing the psalm *De profundis* immediately after the *Salve regina* that they were accustomed to chant in the *maîtrise* each night before bed.[37] Of the many foundations requiring the participation of the choirboys, perhaps the most significant for the history of polyphonic music was that made by succentor Pierre Henry, for it generated a motet from the hand of master Antoine Brumel.

On 22 April 1486, the chapter of Paris entered into an agreement with canon and succentor Henry in the following terms:

The chapter accepted the foundation of master Pierre Henry by which he wishes that on the first feast of each month at which all the choirboys are present at Matins the said boys are to kneel before the great altar after Matins and sing the versicle *Ave Maria gratia dei plena per secula*, and afterwards one of the said boys shall say *Requiescant in pace* and the others should respond *Amen*; and in order to maintain this foundation the said master Henry gives and relinquishes to the church a fief situated in the area of Falaise and Aubergenville [27 km north of Versailles] in the domain of the church. (Doc. 11)

By the time of canon Henry's death on 14 May 1501, the versicle *Ave Maria* had come to be sung by the boys in polyphony. The inscription of Henry's foundation recorded in the necrology of the church reads:

14 May: *Ave Maria gratia dei plena per secula* [to be sung] in notated discant by the boys of the choir after matins and following the *Regina celi* on the first Sunday of each month, unless there shall be a [convenient] solemn feast near that Sunday, and there should be a distribution of two deniers to each boy; and at the end of this *Ave* the youngest boy should say in a loud voice *Requiescant in pace* and the chorus *Amen*. By foundation of sire Pierre Henry, succentor. (Doc. 12)

A further reference to this endowment in a capitular act of 20 April 1502 declares that both during his life and thereafter the *Ave Maria* was performed 'in rebus factus' (Doc. 13). There can be no doubt about what the chapter intended by an *Ave Maria* 'cum notulis discantus' or 'in rebus factus', for fortunately the very piece to which the canons referred still exists. At the beginning of a manuscript of

[36] Guérard, *Cartulaire*, IV, p. 162.   [37] Guérard, *Cartulaire*, IV, p. 100.

51

polyphonic chansons and motets preserved in Bologna is a three-voice *Ave Maria* with 'Brumel' given as the author (Figure 2).[38] Positive identification of this piece as the one sung at Notre Dame of Paris can be made on the basis of the text. The Brumel motet sets only the words *Ave Maria gratia dei plena per secula* – exactly those given in the foundation of Pierre Henry – and then repeats them twice. While the salutation *Ave Maria gratia plena Dominus tecum* ... and others related to it were widespread in the late middle ages, the phrase *Ave Maria gratia dei plena per secula* appears at this time to have been a text sung only at Paris.[39] Besides the references to this versicle in the chapter acts and necrology of the cathedral and its setting by Brumel, its only other known appearance before the end of the sixteenth century is in the short three-voice setting by Claudin de Sermisy published in 1534 by the Parisian printer Pierre Attaingnant.[40] Claudin, of course, was not only master of the king's chapel, but had been a choirboy and was later a resident canon at the Sainte Chapelle of Paris, and thus was intimately familiar with the liturgical practice of the cathedral.[41] That Brumel's motet not only was sung at Notre Dame but was sung there by the choirboys can be deduced from the vocal ranges of the three parts. The *superius* (c′ to c″), *altus* (c′ to a′), and *tenor* (g to c″) are all in the same high tessitura, one ideal for boys, but awkward for adult males unless they sang in falsetto. The intricate counterpoint and difficult syncopations evident in Brumel's work suggest the high degree of musical skill required of the young choristers at Notre Dame.

Thus we have at least one tangible example of how a gift of land could ultimately be transformed into a musical creation. The mechanism of metamorphosis was, of course, the system of patron-

[38] Bologna, Civico Museo Bibliografico-Musicale, MS Q 17, fols. 2v–3. The presence of Brumel's *Ave Maria* (composed 1498–1500) in Bologna Q 17 provides a *terminus post quem* of 1500 for this manuscript. The motet is transcribed and edited by Barton Hudson, *Antonii Brumel opera omnia*, Corpus Mensurabilis Musicae ser. 5, vol. v ([Rome], 1972), pp. 6–7.

[39] There is no listing of this text in John R. Bryden and David G. Hughes, *An Index of Gregorian Chant* (Cambridge, Mass., 1969), or in *Analecta hymnica medii aevi* (Leipzig, 1886–1922). Cyr Ulysse Chevalier, *Repertorium hymnologicum* (Louvain, 1892–1921), no. 23602, cites it in a hymnal from Besançon edited 1589.

[40] *Liber tertius: viginti musicales quinque/sex/vel octo vocum motetos habet* (Paris, 1534); ed. Albert Smijers, of *Treize livres de motets*, III (Paris, 1936), pp. 41–2.

[41] Michel Brenet (pseudonym of Marie Bobillier), *Les musiciens de la Sainte-Chapelle du Palais* (Paris, 1910), pp. 49 and 106–7.

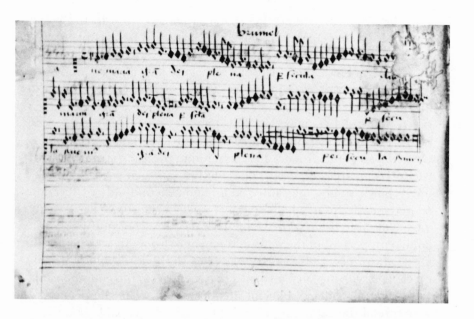

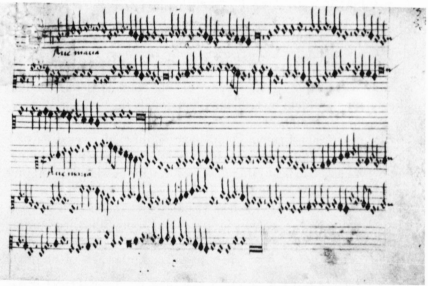

Figure 2. Antoine Brumel, *Ave Maria*: Bologna, Civico Museo Bibliografico-Musicale, MS Q 17, fols. 2v–3

age. But, ironically, the same system that gave rise to the motet seems also to have precipitated the departure of its creator. By the summer of 1500, a rift had developed between Antoine Brumel and the canons of Paris, the causes of which were several. First, and most important, for a period of months the chapter had failed to pay the music master the full amount owed him for the *porciones* of the ten choirboys and two masters. The total revenues accruing to the *officium puerorum chori* in 1500 unexpectedly had fallen short of the twenty *livres* per capita needed to maintain the *maîtrise*, and Brumel was forced to appear before the canons time and again to demand his due.[42] Surprisingly, the cathedral had no general fund or collection of petty cash from which to meet such a shortfall. Like many medieval churches, Notre Dame of Paris was enormously rich in landed property, but the rents and revenues from this were assigned to specific projects, often as stipulated by the donor. While a 'liquidity crisis' involving such a small sum would seem incomprehensible to nearly all modern financial institutions, in 1500 the pecuniary structure of the cathedral of Paris was indeed incapable of quickly generating the seventy-odd *livres* owed to master Brumel; it was tied to a cumbersome system of endowment that provided well for the long-term need, but not for the short-term emergency. The chapter did borrow a sum from the *officium anniversarium* on 23 October, but this had to be repaid quickly so that a deficit would not occur in that account.[43] Finally, on 14 November, the canons determined to alleviate the problem by reducing temporarily the number of choirboys from ten to nine.[44]

Perhaps master Brumel could have endured the vexation of a temporary shortfall occurring within an inflexible system of funding, but he was asked to bear other disappointments as well. The chapter had failed to provide him with a benefice at the cathedral or elsewhere in the diocese. After two and a half years of service, he still had no prebend at Paris to elevate his base salary above that of a humble clerk of matins. That the canons were aware of their negligence in this matter is shown by an entry in the capitular acts of 27 July:

Because there was a question of how to provide for the master of the choirboys, sire [Nicolas] de Haqueville offered to confer upon the master

[42] AN, LL 128, pp. 3, 29, 61, 63 and 66–7.
[43] AN, LL 128, p. 63.
[44] AN, LL 128, p. 71.

the first benefice that will fall vacant when it comes to his turn to collate, as long as said sire Haqueville will not lose his turn.   (Doc.14)

Yet no benefice was forthcoming from this offer, probably because of a lengthy wait before the *rota* of beneficial preferment turned to canon Haqueville. Sometime in the autumn of 1500, Brumel agreed to trade a chaplainry he held in the castle of La Fère, south of Laon,[45] for one of the subdiaconal canonicates of St Denis du Pas at Notre Dame, but by the time this permutation was presented to the chapter on 15 February 1501 the composer had already left the cathedral, and the canons disallowed the exchange (Doc. 15).

Finally, adding to the contention between music master and chapter, there was the question of the selection of choirboys, an issue not so much of patronage but more of prerogatives, artistic judge-ment, and professional self-esteem. Because canons had taken choirboys into their households (*familiae*) centuries before the crea-tion of the position of *magister puerorum chori*, tradition dictated that they, and not the master of music, had the right to audition and grant admission to choirboys as well as all other *ministri inferiores*. In July 1500, Brumel apparently ignored this custom and was twice reprimanded for harbouring a boy whom the chapter had found unfit for service in the church.[46] Then on 14 November, he presented a candidate for admission to the *maîtrise* but was informed, after the boy had sung a *Benedicamus*, that the youngster should compete against another boy previously presented to the chapter, probably a candidate brought forth by one of the canons (Doc. 16). Two days later, on 16 November, Brumel appeared at the morning meeting of the chapter and resigned his post (Doc. 17). And although the canons soon sent a committee to dissuade the master,[47] Brumel was resolute in his decision to leave the cathedral. An inflexible system of endowment, a wheel of beneficial preferment that turned too slowly, and a structure of authority that valued tradition and custom more than professional competence had cumulatively proved insupport-able. Brumel left Paris and eventually made his way to northern Italy.

The ultimate destination of Antoine Brumel was the court of Duke

---

[45] See Auguste Longnon, *Pouillés de la Province de Reims* (Paris, 1907), p. 697; and Paul Joanne, *Dictionnaire géographique et administratif de la France* (Paris, 1894), p. 1465.
[46] AN, LL 128, pp. 3 and 9.
[47] AN, LL 128, p. 76.

Alfonso d'Este of Ferrara, where the mechanism of artistic patronage was strikingly different from that at Notre Dame of Paris. Here revenues were not bound to endowments, and decisions were not made by a college of clerics following statute and custom. Rather, a single patron allocated funds according to practical need and personal pleasure.[48] After some initial bargaining, Duke Alfonso offered Brumel an annual salary of 100 gold ducats, a benefice that would bring the same amount, fifty ducats for his transportation to Ferrara, and a residence when he arrived. Perhaps more important to the ego of a professional musician, the duke personally wrote to the composer entreating him to enter Ferrarese service as *maestro di cappella*.[49] At this secular court, the *maestro* was no longer under the onus of rearing eight or more choirboys; to the contrary, in some ways this was an honorific position, one that allowed the incumbent ample time for musical composition. The real charge of the *maestro* was to enhance the renown of the patron by the mere proximity of a composer of great reputation. Here was a system of patronage altogether more responsive to the professional and psychological requirements of a creative artist than the one Brumel had left behind in Paris and before that in Laon and in Chartres. In the twelfth and thirteenth centuries the centre of artistic patronage in the West shifted from the rural monastery to the urban cathedral, and then in the fifteenth and sixteenth centuries from the Church to the secular state. The career of Antoine Brumel epitomised the latter stage of this transition.

[48] On music at the court of Ferrara, see Lewis Lockwood's studies 'Music at Ferrara in the Period of Ercole I d'Este', *Studi musicali*, 1 (1972), pp. 101–31, and 'Josquin at Ferrara: New Documents and Letters', in Edward E. Lowinsky and Bonnie J. Blackburn (eds.), *Josquin des Prez – Proceedings of the International Josquin Festival–Conference* (London, 1976), pp. 103–37.

[49] The correspondence concerning Brumel's recruitment is published in Edmond Vander Straeten, *La musique aux Pays-Bas avant le XIXᵉ siècle* vi (Brussels, 1882), pp. 95–102. For evidence that Brumel did, in fact, enter Alfonso's service as *maestro di cappella*, see Anne-Marie Bautier-Regnier, 'Jachet de Mantoue (Jacobus Collebaudi) v. 1500–1559', *Revue Belge de Musicologie*, 6 (1952), p. 103. He remained at the Ferrarese court until late 1509 or early 1510 and then sought refuge in Mantua from the difficult political situation that had developed at Ferrara (information kindly supplied me by Professor Lewis Lockwood).

APPENDIX: DOCUMENTS

DOC. 1: 14 JULY 1406

Petito ex parte magistro Johanne Houssete recipi ad magnam vicariam sancti martini de campis . . . domini deputaverunt magistros Johannem Rolland canonicum parisiensis et Dionysium de Cursone succentorem ad ipsum examinandum in cantu et ceteris necessariis qui post examinationem debitam retulerunt ipsum valde bene et secure cantare planum cantum; domini audita ipsorum relatione eum receperunt. (AN, LL 238, fol. 37)

DOC. 2: 10 MAY 1566

A cetero magni vicarii in ecclesia fundati probentur per capitulum aut deputato ab eodem super eorum peritias et vocis idoneitate ac sufficientia, reperti et non alias admittantur ad minus in plano cantu.

(AN, L 525, no. 155)

DOC. 3: 3 FEBRUARY 1571 [N.S.]

Domini succentor et Brunet [canonicus sancti Aniani] vocato organista ecclesie provideant de organis et musicalibus instrumentis in domo puerorum chori necessario habendis pro instructione eorum qui de dictis pueris aut clericis matutinalibus magis idonei ad id reperientur.

(AN, LL 297, fol. 97)

DOC. 4: 28 JULY 1393

Placet dominis quod magister puerorum recipiat in domo sua quemdam parvum puerum cujusdem burgensis parisiensis quem vult facere monachum monasterii sancti dionysii in francia pro docendo ei cantum dummodo habeat bonum pretium et competens. (AN, LL 297, fol. 25)

DOC. 5: 6 OCTOBER 1413

Placet dominis quod duo pueri quos vult ponere dominus episcopus parisiensis sint cum pueris chori ita quod sint omnino subditi ecclesie sicut ceteri et absque quod dominus episcopus possit aliquid reclamare, attento quod dominus episcopus offert pro expensis ipsorum L francos anno quolibet. (AN, LL 297, fol. 25)

DOC. 6: 4 SEPTEMBER 1424

Placet dominis quod Dionysius Martini spe ecclesie adiscat ludere de organis et dant ei quod decustabit una missa ad adiscendum ludere.

(AN, LL 297, fol. 59)

DOC. 7: 13 JULY 1436

Loquatur magistro Thome Hoppinel magistro puerorum chori et audiatur super eo quod Lambertus Meteil spe ecclesie petiit et requisivit sibi dari licentiam per capitulum ut possit addiscere unam missam de organis existentibus in domo dictorum puerorum et hoc per magistrum Jacobum organistam ecclesie parisiensis.   (AN, LL 297, fol. 59)

DOC. 8: 11 JULY 1583

Placuit Abrehamum maximum puerorum chori continuari in discenda arte organica per trimestre et ad id singulis mensibus dicti trimestris magistro tradi unum aureum per manus officiarii dictorum puerorum.

(AN, LL 297, fol. 104v)

DOC. 9: 31 MARCH 1393 [N.S.]

Herbertus Berengarii factus est macicotus loco Johannis Constantini et ille qui erat spe factus est clericus matutinarum et antiquior puerorum post ipsum factus est spe scilicet Michael Bruneau.   (AN, LL 297, fol. 81)

DOC. 10: 5 JANUARY 1498 [N.S.]

Ex deliberatione et conclusione capituli receptus est ad officium magistri cantus puerorum chori exercendum magister Anthonius Brumet presbyter canonicus laudunensis ad relacionem dominorum decanj et cantoris qui fecit juramenta solita videlicet de fideliter exercendo et de instruendo dictos pueros diligente in cantu et bonis moribus juxta ipsius ac dictorum puerorum capacitatem, fuitque eidem datus habitus ecclesie ac fuit installatus in dextera parte chori et data est eidem onus recepte et expense dictorum puerorum sicut habebant Joly et Papot sui predecessores.

(AN, LL 127, fol. xxxvij)

DOC. 11: 22 APRIL 1486

Capitulum acceptavit fundationem magistri Petri Henry per quam vult quod prima die festi cujuslibet mensis quo omnes pueri conveniunt in matutinis, dicti pueri cantent post matutinas ante majus altare ecclesie, genibus flexis hunc versiculum *Ave Maria gratia dei plena per secula*, et postea unus dictorum puerorum dicat *Requiescant in pace*, et alii respondeant *Amen*; et ad manutenendam hujusmodi fundationem dictus Henry dat et dimittet ecclesie unum feudum nobile situm in terra de Falais et Aubergenvilla in dominio ecclesie. (AN, LL 290, fol. 153)

DOC. 12: 14 MAY (ANNUALLY)

Ave Maria gratia dei plena per secula per pueros chori prima dominica cujuslibet mensis, nisi sit festum solemne prope dictam dominicam, post *Regina celi* post matutinas, et debet dici cum notulis discantus, et fit distributio cuilibet de 2 denarios et in fine *Ave* minor puerorum debet dicere alta voce *Requiescant in pace* et chorus *Amen*. Ex fundatione domini Petri Henry succentoris. (AN, LL 290, fol. 49)

DOC. 13: 20 APRIL 1502

Placuit dominis acceptare fundationem per ipsum defunctum (magistrum Petrum Henry) in suo testimento fieri ordinatam, videlicet de cantando per pueros chori prout facere consueverunt vita durante ipsius defuncti prima dominica die cuiuslibet mensis post matutinas *Ave Maria* in rebus factis et *Requiescant in pace*, transportando per dictos executores et heredes feudum per ipsum defunctum propter hoc legatum officio puerorum chori. (AN, LL 128, p. 302)

DOC. 14: 27 JULY 1500

Quia fuit questio qualiter esset providendum magistro puerorum chorj dominus de Haqueville obtulit quod quando erit in suo magno turno primum beneficium quod vacabit in suo turno conferatur eidem magistro puerorum chori proviso quod ipse dominus de Haqueville maneat nichillominus in suo turno. (AN, LL 128, p. 21)

DOC. 15: 15 FEBRUARY 1501 [N.S.]

Magister Michael Celot presbyter procurator et nomine procuratoris domini Johannis Buyer presbyteri canonici subdiaconalis sancti dionysii de passu licteratura fundationis resignavit canonicatum et prebendam subdiaconales ipsius Buyer causa permutationis fiende cum magistro Anthonio Brumel nuper magistro puerorum chorj licenciato ad capellaniam nostre dame in castro de Lafere laudunensis diocesis suplicans huiusmodi resignationem recipi. Super quo deliberatum est et conclusum quod huiusmodi resignacio non admicteretur causis pluribus hic per dominos allegatis. (AN, LL 128, p. 105)

DOC. 16: 14 NOVEMBER 1500

Magister puerorum chorj adduxit unum puerum ut reciperetur in puerum chorj qui cantavit *Benedicamus* et ipso audito ordinatum est quod ipse et alius parvus de quo alias locutum est veniatur ad primum capitulum et magis ydoneus recipietur. (AN, LL 128, p. 71)

DOC. 17: 16 NOVEMBER 1500

Comparuit in capitulo magister Anthonius Brumel magister puerorum chori et officio suo renunciavit ac congedium cepit a dominis. Quo audito fuit ordinatum quod loquatur cum ipso ad sciendum cuius occasione vult recedere. (AN, LL 128, p. 72)

PART II:

SIXTEENTH-CENTURY INSTRUMENTAL MUSIC

4

NOTES (AND TRANSPOSING NOTES) ON THE VIOL IN THE EARLY SIXTEENTH CENTURY

Howard Mayer Brown

AT least one thing seems certain about the conventions of transposition in the first half of the sixteenth century. When the music went too high, German viol-players transposed it down a fourth in order to make it fit more comfortably on their instruments. Their explanation of this practice, I hasten to add, did not involve questions of absolute pitch. Instead, they described the relationship between what a written note was called and its position on the fingerboard of a viol. Thus a G on the middle line of a staff in the soprano clef (g'), for example, indicated to the player of a viol said to be tuned 'in G' – that is, with open strings described as on G c f a d' g' – that he should sound the top string of his instrument, although the actual pitch he produced might have varied from place to place and from time to time, and it might never have corresponded exactly with today's officially accepted standard pitch.[1] The German musicians referred,

[1] Questions of transposition and pitch standards are closely enough related, however, to justify dedicating this study to the memory of a good friend and stimulating colleague, Arthur Mendel, who read it shortly before his death and made many valuable suggestions for its improvement. Professor Mendel's recent study of pitch standards in the sixteenth century and later, 'Pitch in Western Music since 1500. A Re-examination', *Acta musicologica*, 50 (1978), pp. 1–93, which cites earlier studies, characteristically urges extreme caution in making assertions about pitch standards of earlier times.

in other words, to performers' conventions: how players coped with their written parts and how they adapted them to the strengths and limitations of their instruments.

Hans Gerle's *Musica und Tabulatur, auff die Instrument der kleinen und grossen Geygen, auch Lautten* (Nuremberg, 1546), originally published in 1532 and republished and revised several times in the following decade and a half, offers the clearest exposition of the practice of transposition as it affected viol-players.[2] Like so many writers of elementary instruction books published in the sixteenth century, Gerle did little more than set out fingerings for a variety of instruments and supply the beginning student with a few elementary facts about the way they were tuned, held, and played. As the title-page of his treatise states, he introduced the student to the rudiments of playing the lute, the viol, and the rebec.[3] Example 1 reproduces the tunings Gerle preferred for the three sizes of viola da gamba he described.[4] But viols were apparently not tuned in one invariable way in early-sixteenth-century Germany, for Gerle's advice differs significantly from that of Martin Agricola, whose tunings for the five- and six-stringed viols, as given in the 1528 edition of his *Musica instrumentalis deudsch*, are reproduced as Example 2.[5]

---

[2] The 1532 edition, *Musica Teusch, auf die Instrument der grossen und kleinen Geygen, auch Lautten*, is listed and described in Howard Mayer Brown, *Instrumental Music Printed before 1600: A Bibliography* (Cambridge, Mass., 1965), pp. 40–2, as 1532$_2$. It was reprinted in 1537 (Brown 1537$_1$) and revised and augmented in 1546 (Brown 1546$_9$; facs. repr. Minkoff: Geneva, 1977). All references are to the 1546 edition, unless otherwise noted. On Gerle's treatise, see also Alexander Silbiger, 'The First Viol Tutor: Hans Gerle's *Musica Teusch*', *Journal of the Viola da Gamba Society of America*, 6 (1969), pp. 34–48.

For a brief description and translation of all Gerle's treatises, and a transcription into modern notation of all the music he published, see Jane I. Pierce, 'Hans Gerle: Sixteenth-Century Lutenist and Pedagogue', 2 vols., Ph.D. diss., University of North Carolina, 1973.

[3] Gerle called rebecs 'Kleingeigen' or 'klainen Geyglen . . . die kain Bündt haben'. The modern reader might suppose that he referred to violins, if it were not for the fact that he illustrated his remarks with cuts of rebecs (fol. H4 in 1532 edn, fol. K4 in 1546 edn).

[4] After Gerle, *Musica und Tabulatur*, fols. K1^v–K2.

[5] The 1528 and 1529 editions of Agricola's treatise are listed and described in Brown, *Instrumental Music*, p. 27, 1528$_1$ and 1529$_1$. For later editions, see Brown 1530$_1$, 1532$_1$, 1542$_1$, and 1545$_1$. The 1545 edition was completely revised; for example, Agricola did not even mention five- or six-stringed viols there, although he did give tunings for four- and three-stringed instruments. References to the 1528/9 and the 1545 versions are given here after the quasi-facsimile edition in *Publikation älterer praktischer und theoretischer Musikwerke* 20, ed. Robert Eitner

Example 1. Viol tunings after Gerle (1532 and later)

Example 2. Viol tunings after Agricola (1528)

Example 1 suppresses some important information supplied by Gerle. Although he wrote about both five- and six-stringed instruments, the example does not include information about the sixth string, which Gerle indicated was to be tuned in every case a fourth below the fifth string, A, for the bass, D for the tenor/alto, and A for the treble.[6] But whereas six-stringed viols were thus obviously known in early-sixteenth-century Germany, Gerle made it clear that he preferred the five-stringed instrument. He did not consider the sixth string necessary, and he seems not to have considered it desirable.[7] Certainly in his examples of music for four viols, written in tablature, he never once required a player to use his sixth string, nor did he ever ask a player to ascend above first position on the fingerboard.

Gerle's advice about tuning viols not only differs from that of Agricola; it also differs from the tables supplied by the Italian instrumental virtuoso Silvestro Ganassi in his *Regola Rubertina*, published in Venice in two volumes in 1542 and 1543.[8] Ganassi's first

(Leipzig, 1896). The section on *Geigen* with three, four, five, and six strings appears in the 1528/9 edition, pp. 86–100. Tuning tables for viols with five and six strings appear on pp. 90–1. The English translation of Agricola's treatise in William S. Hollaway, 'Martin Agricola's *Musica instrumentalis deudsch*: Translation and Commentary', Ph.D. diss., North Texas State University, 1972, is not altogether reliable.

[6] Gerle, *Musica und Tabulatur*, fol. A4ᵛ.

[7] Gerle, *Musica und Tabulatur*, fol. A2ᵛ: 'Und ist gleich wol an den fünffen gnug'. Moreover, he called the top string of each viol 'die quintsait', which suggests he thought of it as the fifth of five. Unlike Gerle, I have consistently numbered the strings from top to bottom, the highest in pitch as the first, the lowest as the fifth or sixth.

[8] Ganassi's two volumes, *Regola Rubertina* (Venice, 1542) and *Lettione Seconda* (Venice, 1543), are listed and described in Brown, *Instrumental Music*, pp. 66–8, as 1542₂ and 1543₂. They are both published in facsimile by Max Schneider (Leipzig, 1924) and by Forni Editore in 2 vols. (Bologna, 1970), and translated into German

order of tunings, reproduced as Example 3, are those that became standard and are still used by most viol-players today. In comparing the six-stringed viols of Gerle and Ganassi, a disturbing fact emerges: Gerle seems to be writing about viols tuned a fourth lower than those Ganassi wrote about. But the difference is more apparent than real, for Gerle's five-stringed instruments are tuned almost like Ganassi's six-stringed viols, except that the third appears in a different place, and Ganassi's instruments were supplied with an extra string a fourth above the others. Suddenly we are in the realm of metaphysics. Are Gerle's viols tuned a fourth lower than Ganassi's and were they therefore larger? Or are Ganassi's instruments the same as Gerle's but with an added top string? Or are Gerle's instruments best explained by pointing out that they are tuned like Ganassi's except that their third is in a different place?[9]

Example 3. Viol tunings after Ganassi (1542–3)

bass   tenor/alto   treble

and English by Hildemarie Peter (Berlin and Lichterfeld, 1972 (German version) and 1977 (English version)). A second and more literal German translation with extensive commentary appears in Wolfgang Eggers, *Die 'Regola Rubertina' des Silvestro Ganassi, Venedig 1542/43. Eine Gambenschule des 16. Jahrhunderts*, 2 vols. (Kassel, 1974). On Ganassi's treatise, see also Richard D. Bodig, 'Silvestro Ganassi's *Regola Rubertina* – Revelations and Questions', *Journal of the Viola da Gamba Society of America*, 14 (1977), pp. 61–70.

[9] The most extensive discussion of the apparent anomaly between Gerle's and Ganassi's tunings appears in Nicholas Bessaraboff, *Ancient European Musical Instruments* (Boston, 1941), Appendix B: 'Sizes and Tunings of Viols of the Sixteenth and Seventeenth Centuries', pp. 357–73. Bessaraboff, however, confuses the issues in a number of ways, not least by trying to relate the information given in the treatises to absolute pitch standards, and to surviving instruments. It is true that hypotheses about the sizes of viols in the sixteenth century need to be confirmed by surviving instruments, but such an investigation poses so many difficult problems that it requires a separate study. Even if it is clear, for example, what pitch a surviving instrument was supposed to be tuned to, it is difficult to know what that pitch was called by musicians who first played the instrument or, indeed, what range (treble, alto, tenor, bass, and so on) the instrument was said to play in. Questions about the present state of each instrument and the sorts of restorations each has undergone during its history further complicate any attempt to relate surviving instruments to the tuning practices described by the theorists.

For information about surviving sixteenth-century instruments, see Ian Harwood, 'An Introduction to Renaissance Viols', *Early Music*, 2 (1974), pp. 235–46; Laurence C. Witten II, 'Apollo, Orpheus, and David', *Journal of the American Musical Instrument Society*, 1 (1974), pp. 5–55; and Ian Harwood and

HOWARD MAYER BROWN

Whatever the final answers to those questions, Gerle eventually came in his treatise to explain how the player should intabulate vocal music for his instrument. Example 4 (p. 66) shows a scale on the tenor viol in the tablature Gerle used, with the corresponding note names beneath each symbol.[10] The open strings, indicated by the numbers 3, 4, and 5, are circled for the convenience of the reader. A great disadvantage of these five-stringed instruments tuned as Gerle proposed was that much of the music of the early sixteenth century would not comfortably fit on them because the notes on the page appear to go too high if the viols were played only in first position.[11] The top string of the treble can go as high as d″ in first position, and

Martin Edmunds, 'Reconstructing 16th-Century Venetian Viols', *Early Music*, 6 (1978), pp. 519–25.

For a survey of tunings in the sixteenth and seventeenth centuries, see also Gerald R. Hayes, *The Viols and Other Bowed Instruments* (London, 1930; repr. New York, 1969), pp. 8–19. Although Hans Judenkünig published two volumes purporting to include information about *Geigen* – the *Utilis & compendiaria introductio* (Vienna, n.d.; Brown 151?₁) and *Ain schöne kunstliche underweisung* (Vienna, 1523; Brown 1523₂) – he gave information only about the tuning of the six-course lute, in fourths with a third in the middle following the pattern of other writers of the time.

While it is true that in both Gerle's untransposed and transposed tablatures the viol parts stay for the most part on the upper two strings of the instrument, those are actually the second and third strings of six-stringed viols tuned in the manner of Ganassi as shown in Example 3. The statements in Michael Morrow, 'Sixteenth-Century Ensemble Viol Music', *Early Music*, 2 (1974), p. 163, and Howard Mayer Brown, *Sixteenth-Century Instrumentation: The Music for the Florentine Intermedii* (n.p., 1973), pp. 52–3, must be modified accordingly. The latter also gives as Ex. 22 the mnemonic aids a sixteenth-century viol player used to help him transpose his parts to various other pitches and not merely a fourth below written pitch.

[10] On intabulation technique, see Gerle, *Musica und Tabulatur*, fols. H3ᵛ–K2ᵛ, and especially fols. K1–K2ᵛ. The chart of tablature reproduced as Example 4 is adapted from Gerle, *Musica und Tabulatur*, fol. H4ᵛ. He gave two scales with each size of viol, the first for music with a signature of one flat, the second for music without a signature but with flats indicated as alternatives.

[11] In fact, Gerle, *Musica und Tabulatur*, fol. B1ᵛ, explained left-hand fingering on the viol only in terms of the so-called half position, that is, with the index finger reserved for the first fret, the middle finger for the second fret, the ring finger for the third fret, and the little finger for the fourth and all higher frets. On fols. A3–A3ᵛ he described the viols as though five frets were normal, taking the player a fourth above each open string, although he mentioned some viols with seven frets, taking the player a fifth above each open string. Ganassi regularly took his players of consort music up to the seventh fret, and he also discussed shifts of position, high positions and playing above the frets, though presumably only for solo playing. On his fingering instructions, see Ian D. Woodfield, 'Viol Playing Techniques in the Mid-16th Century: A Survey of Ganassi's Fingering Instructions', *Early Music*, 6 (1978), pp. 544–9.

Example 4. Gerle's tablature for the tenor viol

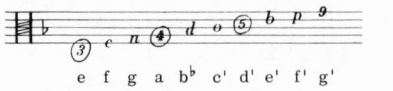

e f g a b♭ c' d' e' f' g'

although a player could reach e″ by extension if his instrument had
seven frets, quite a bit of music goes up to f″ or even g″ or higher.
Similarly, the top string of the tenor viol can go as high as g′ in first
position, and the top string of the bass viol to d′. Gerle himself noted
that much of the music of his time goes higher than that in all
ranges.[12] Therefore, he provided a second table for the intabulator to
use when the music exceeded the limits of the instrument's
capabilities. Example 5 shows one of the scales Gerle wrote for the
tenor viol, using his alternative table. Again, the open strings are
marked by the numbers 3, 4, and 5, but instead of corresponding
with the notes e, a, and d′, they were to be used when the intabulator
saw a, d′, and g′ on the page of music before him. Thus the effect of
using the table is to transpose the music down a fourth. Such a
transposition, then, so far as Gerle is concerned, is simply a practical
way out of a real technical difficulty. And he offered a simple
mechanical solution that should not cause the player who used
tablature the slightest inconvenience.

Example 5. Gerle's tablature for the tenor viol when the music goes too high

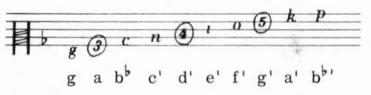

g a b♭ c' d' e' f' g' a' b♭'

It would be good to know how generally Gerle's advice was
followed among German viol-players; but, unfortunately, very little
viol music written in German tablature survives from the sixteenth
century. Johannes Wolf, for example, listed only Gerle's treatise in
his *Handbuch der Notationskunde*, still one of the most useful and
complete sources of information about sixteenth- and seventeenth-

---

[12] Gerle, *Musica und Tabulatur*, fol. J2ᵛ, states that the table reproduced from fol. J3 as
Example 5 was prepared for use 'wan du ein gesang in die Tabulatur setzen wolst,
und er ging so hoch, das du nit so vil bünd auff der Geygen hettest'.
  Like his table for untransposed tablature, that for transposed tablature
includes two scales for each size of viol, the first for music with a signature of one
flat, and the second for music without a signature, but with flats indicated as
alternatives.

century tablatures.[13] There is, however, at least one manuscript of German viol music written in tablature that Wolf did not know, a book of notes on mathematics and music taken by the student Jorg Weltzell in 1523 and 1524, perhaps while he was at the University of Ingolstadt.[14] Weltzell intabulated for viol consort a great many German dances and Lieder by Hofhaimer, Senfl, and their contemporaries. When his versions are compared with those in printed editions and manuscripts containing the vocal versions, it will be seen that some of his Lieder are transcribed at pitch and some a fourth lower. Moreover, he included among his notes tables of German tablature to help him transcribe vocal music for instruments, and these tables reveal not only that Weltzell tuned the various sizes of viol precisely the way Gerle recommended, but also that he had prepared exactly the same sort of shorthand mechanical aid as Gerle so that he could intabulate viol music either at pitch or, when the voices went too high to fit comfortably on the instruments, a fourth lower.[15]

Equally striking confirmation of the soundness and practicality of

[13] See Johannes Wolf, *Handbuch der Notationskunde*, 2 vols. (Leipzig, 1913–19; repr. Hildesheim, 1963), II, p. 39. Agricola, *Musica instrumentalis deudsch*, 1528/9 edn, pp. 104–5, includes a letter tablature (a for a, b for bb, h for b, c for c′, and so on) for all instruments that play a single line.

[14] Munich, Universitätsbibliothek, 4° Cod. MS 718 (hereafter Munich 718) is described and its contents listed in Clytus Gottwald, *Die Musikhandschriften der Universitätsbibliothek München* (Wiesbaden, 1968), pp. 55–62.

[15] The tables, almost the same as those in Gerle's treatise, appear in Munich 718, fols. 98v–99v.

Individual parts for each piece are scattered throughout Munich 718, a manuscript that deserves to be studied more carefully. At least four compositions in it are notated according to the alternative tables that produce music a fourth lower than the staff notation would suggest:

Dich als mich selbst (discantus fol. 90v, tenor fol. 124, bassus fol. 149v; altus omitted). The vocal version is published in a modern edition in *Georg Forster, Frische Teutsche Liedlein (1539–1556). Erster Teil*, ed. Kurt Gudewill, Das Erbe Deutscher Musik 20 (Wolfenbüttel and Zurich, 1964), no. 1, p. 3.

Die Brünnlein die da fliessen, by Ludwig Senfl, although anonymous in Munich 718 (discantus fol. 91, tenor fol. 136, bassus fol. 150; altus omitted). The vocal version is published in a modern edition in Ludwig Senfl, *Sämtliche Werke*, vol. 4: *Deutsche Lieder . . . II. Teil*, ed. Arnold Geering and Wilhelm Altwegg (Wolfenbüttel and Zurich, 1962), p. 40.

Cupido (altus fol. 113, tenor fol. 128, 'Vagannt' fol. 95v; discantus omitted). The vocal version is published in *Das Liederbuch des Arnt von Aich*, ed. Eduard Bernoulli and H. J. Moser (Kassel, 1930), p. 50.

Cum sancto spiritus from Josquin's *Missa de Beata Virgine* (discantus fol. 114v, altus fol. 111, tenor fol. 125v, bassus fol. 148v). The vocal version is published in a

Gerle's advice comes from testing it empirically against a volume of music. Choosing, quite at random, the *Liederbuch* published by Erhard Oeglin in Augsburg in 1512, I found it no surprise that thirty-six of the forty-nine compositions in it fit comfortably on five-stringed viols tuned in the way Gerle recommends, and twelve needed to be transposed a fourth downwards because the ranges of some or all of the voices went beyond the instruments' ranges.[16] Nor did it come as a surprise that most of the twelve that needed to be transposed downwards could readily be identified because the top voice was written in treble clef or the bass part in baritone clef, or both. Obviously, music in a relatively high range is most conveniently printed in relatively high clefs, if leger lines are to be avoided.[17]

If Martin Agricola is to be believed, similar sorts of transpositions were also common practice among German flautists in the early sixteenth century. The demonstration of that claim is properly the subject of a separate study.[18] Suffice it to say here that although Agricola's explanation of the convention is difficult to understand, he seems to maintain that players of the transverse flute performed some music 'at pitch' (more accurately two octaves above written pitch), in spite of the fact that when they did so they had to play in an uncomfortably high part of their range. But many compositions of the period go too high to fit on instruments played in this way, and so Agricola also included in his treatise diagrams for transposing pieces

modern edition in *Werken van Josquin des Prez*, ed. Albert Smijers, *Missen*, no. 16 (Amsterdam, 1952), pp. 137–8.

I am grateful to Mr Hiroyuki Minamino of the University of California, Irvine, for making available to me his transcription of Munich 718.

[16] *Aus sonderer künstlicher Art und mit höchstem Fleiss seind diss Gesangkbücher mit Tenor Discant Bass und Alt corgiert worden* (Augsburg: Erhard Oeglin, 1512), published in a modern edition by Robert Eitner and J. J. Maier in *Publikationen älterer praktischer und theoretischer Musikwerke* 9 (Berlin, 1880). The Lieder that would need to be transposed a fourth lower if played on five-stringed viols are nos. 1, 11, 16, 19, 32, 36, 37, 38, 40, 43, 44, and 45. No. 47 is an exceptional piece written in four bass clefs, and hence is not included in my tabulation. The remaining thirty-six pieces could all be played by viols at written pitch.

[17] Mendel, 'Pitch in Western Music', pp. 58–63, reviews the extensive musicological literature on 'natural' and high clefs ('chiavette') in the later sixteenth century. So far as I know, none of the scholars involved in discussions of 'chiavette' and their significance has pointed out the connection between clef combinations and the transposing conventions of early-sixteenth-century instrumentalists.

[18] See Howard Mayer Brown, 'Notes (and Transposing Notes) on the Transverse Flute in the Early Sixteenth Century' (forthcoming).

down a fifth (which works relatively well for music in sharp keys, even though some of the diatonic notes are chancy or out of tune), and for transposing them down a fourth (which works well for music without a signature and for music with a signature of one flat – that is, for most of the compositions written during the first half of the sixteenth century).

Agricola's advice thus appears to complement Gerle's. Transposition down a fourth enabled players of the viol and the transverse flute to bring most of the music they performed within the compass of their relatively fixed consorts of instruments. Indeed, the practice seems to have been widespread enough to encourage makers of keyboard instruments, especially in Italy, to build virginals that automatically transposed a fourth down. If John Shortridge's hypothesis is correct – and it must be said that it has by no means found general support – then many Italian virginals in the sixteenth century were built in such a way that when the player pressed down what appears to be a C key, what sounded was the note G a fourth lower.[19] His theory presupposes that so many performers regularly

[19] See John Shortridge, 'Italian Harpsichord Building in the 16th and 17th Centuries', *U.S. National Museum Bulletin*, no. 225 (1960), pp. 95–107. Shortridge's conclusions are challenged in Frank Hubbard, *Three Centuries of Harpsichord Making* (Cambridge, Mass., 1965), pp. 40–2, and debated in John Barnes, 'Pitch Variations in Italian Keyboard Instruments', *Galpin Society Journal*, 18 (1965), pp. 110–16; William R. Thomas and J. J. K. Rhodes, 'The String Scales of Italian Keyboard Instruments', *ibid.*, 20 (1967), pp. 48–62; J. H. van der Meer, 'Harpsichord Making and Metallurgy – A Rejoinder', *ibid.*, 21 (1968), 175–8; John Barnes, 'Italian String Scales', *ibid.*, 21 (1968), pp. 179–83; Michael Thomas, Charles W. Strong, W. R. Thomas, and J. J. K. Rhodes, 'Brass Strings on Italian Harpsichords', *ibid.*, 23 (1970), pp. 166–70; Michael Thomas, 'String Gauges of Old Italian Harpsichords', *ibid.*, 24 (1971), pp. 69–78; and Friedemann Hellwig, 'Strings and Stringing: Contemporary Documents', *ibid.*, 29 (1976), pp. 91–104. In an unpublished talk given at the annual meeting of the American Musical Instrument Society in 1979, Professor Stanley Vodraska of Canisius College supported Shortridge's hypothesis using as evidence the surviving music of the period.

Mendel, 'Pitch in Western Music', pp. 48–58 and 63–6, summarises earlier debates about the somewhat more complicated conventions of transposition adopted by organists in the sixteenth century. Adrian le Roy, *Les instructions pour le luth* (1574), ed. Jean Jacquot, Pierre-Yves Sordes and Jean-Michel Vaccaro, 2 vols. (Paris, 1977) instructed his readers about conventions of transposition adopted by lutenists. He set out a system of transposition coordinated with the modes but made necessary in the first place by the limitations of the instrument. In some but by no means all cases he recommended a transposition a fourth down; for example, following his instructions, players of the lute 'in G' would have intabulated vocal music in G-Dorian mode so that it sounded a fourth lower

transposed down a fourth that it was economically feasible to invent a machine that allowed keyboard-players with limited talents at transposition to keep up with their colleagues without the fatigue of using their brains.

Silvestro Ganassi's two volumes on playing the viol – the *Regola Rubertina* of 1542 and its companion *Lettione Seconda* of 1543, the most sophisticated of all sixteenth-century treatises on playing instruments – take up the question of transposition only peripherally, and yet Ganassi's volumes actually seem to confirm Gerle's, Weltzell's, and Agricola's views of sixteenth-century conventions. Much of the first volume of *Regola Rubertina* deals with the ways in which viols in a consort should tune to each other, and how scales on the viol are fingered. Example 3, above, gives the first of four ways in which Ganassi suggested tuning viols, in what has become the standard arrangement, in fourths with a third in the middle, with the tenor viol a fourth higher than the bass and the treble an octave higher than the bass and a fifth higher than the tenor. Ganassi gave, as well, three other arrangements: in the second way of tuning viol consorts, the tenor was a fifth higher than the bass and the treble an octave higher, giving D, A, and d as the lowest open strings on the three sizes. He suggested, too, a third way in which all the viols were tuned a fourth apart, the bass with its lowest string tuned to D, the tenor to G, and the treble to c or – if that were too inconvenient – with all of them raised a tone to produce viols in E, A, and d. Ganassi's fourth tuning arrangement which he calls 'playing a fourth higher' I shall return to presently. Even from this brief glimpse at Ganassi's instructions, though, it should be clear that tuning was, according to him, a variable matter – changing, presumably, according to the opportunities that particular pieces afford for the greatest number of open strings and hence the clearest possible intonation.[20]

For each of the tunings Ganassi proposed, he supplied fingerings

'in D'. But his principal concern – like that of Gerle and Ganassi – was that a given composition should fit comfortably on his instrument; he wished important chords in a mode to be fingered conveniently on the lute, and important notes to fall on open strings.

[20] The first way of tuning viols to one another is set out in *Regola Rubertina*, chaps. 12–14, and the second, third, and fourth ways in chaps. 15–18. Ganassi did not actually explain the reason for the different ways of tuning. In chap. 11, he pointed out that the absolute pitch standard of a viol can be changed by moving the bridge closer to the tailpiece or further away from it, or by changing the thickness of the strings.

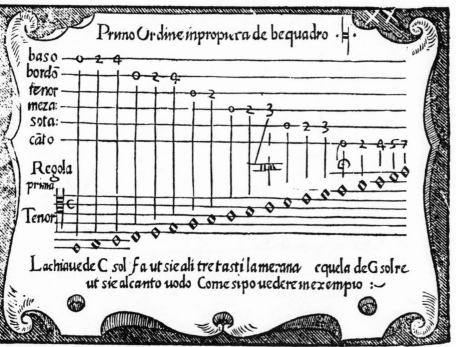

Figure 1. Table for fingering the viol in the natural order: Ganassi, *Regola Rubertina*, p. xx

for each size of instrument, not (as we would) according to the keys in which they play, but according to modes. That is, he presented fingering charts for each instrument in each way of tuning, first for pieces without a key-signature – that is, in untransposed modes – and then with a signature of one flat – that is, once-transposed modes or those like F-Lydian which, exceptionally, include a flat in the signature. In this he followed time-honoured practice. Both Gerle and Agricola, for example, gave their fingering tables for scales with B♮ and with B♭, although they compress and condense the material rather more than Ganassi. And Ganassi added a third table, for twice-transposed pieces, in what he called the order of 'musica ficta' – that is, for pieces with a signature of two flats.[21] Figures 1 and 2 present in facsimile Ganassi's tables for fingering the tenor viol

[21] Giovanni Maria Lanfranco, *Scintille di Musica* (Brescia, 1533) also wrote of a separate and distinct hand of the order of musica ficta, meaning the arrangement of notes in music with a signature of two flats. See Barbara Lee, 'Giovanni Maria Lanfranco's *Scintille di Musica* and Its Relationship to 16th-Century Music Theory', Ph.D. diss., Cornell University, 1961, pp. 102–3.

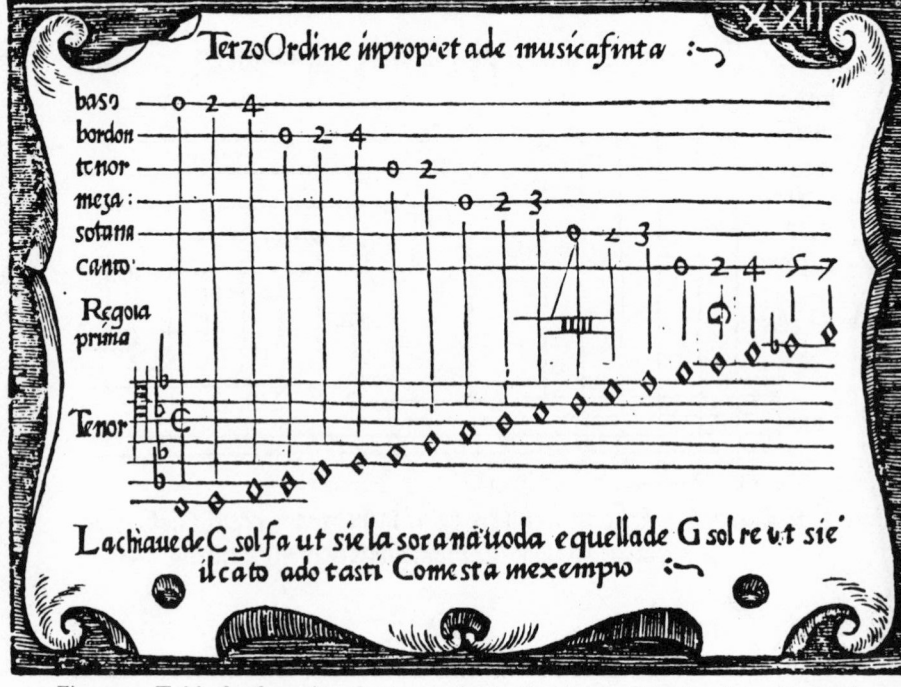

Figure 2. Table for fingering the tenor viol in the order of musica ficta: Ganassi, *Regola Rubertina*, p. xxii

according to the natural order and the ficta order. Ganassi set out the tablature above, using numbers in the Italian fashion (0 = open string; 1, first fret; 2, second fret, and so on), with their equivalents in staff notation beneath. Thus, in the First Order (Figure 1), the open strings (0) on the *basso*, *bordon*, *tenor*, *mezana*, *sotana*, and *canto* strings are clearly labelled as G c f a d′ g′ on the staff notation below. And Ganassi even makes an explicit connection between the staff notation and the tablature by his explanation of clefs at the bottom of the page. In this First Order, for example, he writes that the C clef is on the third fret of the *mezana* ('La chiave de C sol fa ut sie ali tre tasti la mezana') – that is, middle C (c′) is the third fret on the A string – and that the treble clef is on the empty *canto* string ('e quela de G sol re ut sie al canto vodo') – that is, whatever is written as a G above middle C (g′) is to be played on the open top string.

Ganassi seems to indicate that he intended his players to tune their instruments down a whole tone when they played pieces in two flats, for the Third Order of the tenor viol (Figure 2) shows the open strings on F Bb eb g c' f', and again Ganassi makes explicit this interpretation by explaining which clefs go with which notes. A moment's reflection will suggest why Ganassi has set out the material in this way, and even what the musical advantages are. A piece in the Dorian mode has D as its final. Once transposed, with a flat in the signature, the final becomes G a fourth higher. Twice transposed, the same piece appears with two flats and a final of C: a whole tone, as it were, below the original final, D. That is the conventional way of explaining twice-transposed pieces, and, indeed, it is the way Lanfranco adopted. Tuning the instrument a whole tone lower has several advantages to the player: important notes in the mode, for example, c' and g, fall on open strings; the fingering for scale passages is more or less the same as for untransposed or once-transposed pieces, especially with regard to the relationship between scale and final of the mode; and the new tuning preserves whatever temperament the player has set for his instrument by the placement of his frets. Any modern player, though, can immediately appreciate the major disadvantage of such retuning since modern strings will not stay in tune – a disadvantage that Ganassi seemed to ignore in the rest of his treatise. But in any case, it seems likely that Ganassi recommended this procedure in order to ensure that consorts played with a more sonorous sound and, curiously, that they would sound more in tune with one another.[22]

A second serious disadvantage of playing twice-transposed pieces a tone lower, of course, is that the player must learn new fingerings for such pieces. Middle c' on the tenor viol in untransposed or once-transposed pieces would thus sound as the third fret on the A string, whereas a player seeing a middle c' in a twice-transposed piece must sound his open second (*sotana*) string. Ganassi is patently indifferent to absolute pitch. It may be that he intended his Third Order (Figure 2) to be played on normally tuned viols. The effect of that, of course, would be to transpose the twice-transposed pieces up a tone to their untransposed form. Pieces in C-Dorian with a two-flat signature would become untransposed Dorian pieces on D. But if Ganassi intended to suggest that, why did he make an explicit connection between clef and position on the fingerboard?

But it is Ganassi's fourth tuning – again shown here in the form for

[22] Further on tuning according to the order of musica ficta, see Eggers, *Die 'Regola Rubertina'*, II, pp. 234–48.

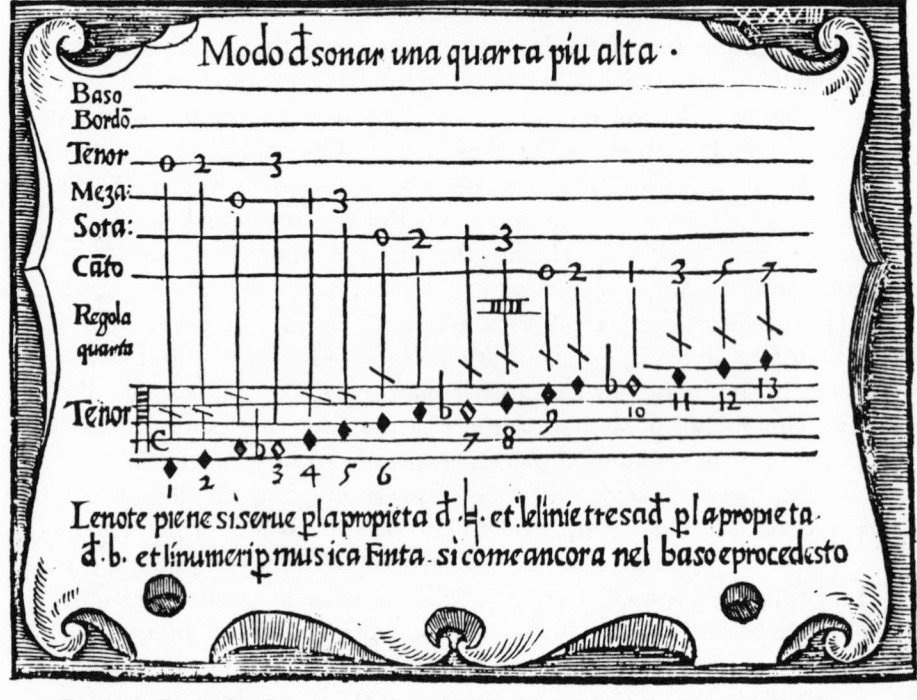

Figure 3. Table for fingering the tenor viol 'a fourth higher': Ganassi, *Regola Rubertina*, p. xxxix

the tenor viol (Figure 3) – which is the most difficult to understand, and which has caused misunderstandings in past writings about Ganassi. Let me quote his explanation of the table in chapter 18 of *Regola Rubertina*, in the translation of Hildemarie Peter:

As most viol players play the viol a fourth higher than was shown in our first rule, I should like to include a fourth rule to instruct you in this mode of playing, and I shall give you examples as I have done for the other rules.[23]

[23] The translation is taken from *Regola Rubertina*, transl. Peter, p. 33. In presenting information about the fourth way of tuning, Ganassi condensed the kind of information found in his earlier tables, incorporating tunings in the orders of B♮ (black notes in the staff notation), B♭ (those notes in the staff notation connnected to the tablature by lines that have a diagonal stroke through them) and musica ficta (numbered notes in the staff notation).

In the original (*Regola Rubertina*, p. xxxvii), the translated passage reads: 'E perche il piu di sonatori si sona le viole una quarta piu alta de la prima regola nostra: però voglio insegnarti il ditto modo & sera per la quarta regola, sappi che ti presento il modo figurato simile a le altre.'

What he lacked in eloquence he might have made up by his table, save that it, too, unfortunately lacks the necessary key to be absolutely positive about its meaning, since he did not relate the tablature to the staff notation by means of a written explanation, as in his earlier tables, of the clefs and their relationship to the frets on the strings. Two explanations immediately offer themselves:

(1) He presented the table in the way Agricola presented his information about flutes and their transpositions,[24] so that in equating tablature with staff notation he supposed that the player retains the same instrument – in this case, a tenor tuned G c f a d' g' – and relates the written notes before him to new places on his fingerboard, so that every time he sees c', for example, he will play the third fret on the next-to-top string. If that string is a d' string, then every time a player sees a written c' he will sound f', a fourth higher. But the implications of this solution are staggering and highly improbable, especially in view of the fact that Ganassi wrote that '*most* viol-players play the viol a fourth higher', for it suggests that most early-sixteenth-century music was – for no very good reason – automatically transposed up a fourth when it was played on viols, and it goes against what we have seen was a well-established practice of transposing down a fourth, when necessary, only such music as went too high to fit on the instruments.

(2) He presented the table in exactly the same way as the others he gave earlier in his book, in which there is a direct relationship between tablature and written pitch, so that one can easily see from looking at the open strings in the tablature (the 'o' signs in Figure 3) that he meant the top four strings of the tenor instrument to be tuned c e a d', and therefore he must have been writing about a tenor instrument whose six strings would be tuned D G c e a d'. That explanation is confirmed by a remark he made at the end of his first volume, to the effect that this Fourth Order of tuning, so called, is not in fact a new tuning (it is exactly like the First Order) but that it is a way of changing the position of the clefs.[25] And, moreover, as Wolfgang Eggers points out in his excellent German translation of the treatise, Ganassi also explicitly declared that this Fourth Order

---

[24] See Brown, 'Notes (and Transposing Notes) on the Transverse Flute'.
[25] *Regola Rubertina*, p. xxxxix 'la quarta regola non è variata ne lo accordo suo: ma bene il loco delle chiave come hai veduto essere una quarta piu alta di quello che è nella prima regola'.

of tuning refers not to six-stringed viols but to five-stringed viols.[26] Therefore, what Ganassi seems to be writing about is a five-stringed tenor viol tuned G c e a d' – that is, precisely the sort of instrument Gerle described in his *Musica und Tabulatur* of 1532.[27]

To explain such instruments as 'playing a fourth higher' seems at the very least to be misleading, and there is a certain irony in the fact that Gerle's tunings, which at first sight appear to be for viols tuned a fourth lower than 'normal', could have been characterised by Ganassi as enabling players to perform a fourth higher. But there is some logic in conceiving tenor parts on a five-stringed instrument tuned like a D-bass without its bottom string as being played a fourth higher than usual, and, in any case, no other interpretation satisfactorily accounts for Ganassi's description of the practice.

He may, in fact, have been making an historical statement, if national boundaries can be safely ignored. The viol was introduced into Italy from Spain at the end of the fifteenth century and modified to become the instrument we know.[28] From Italy it presumably moved to Germany early in the sixteenth century, for Virdung already described the instrument there in 1512, albeit he pictured *Grossgeigen* without bridges.[29] Perhaps, then, the German musicians Jorg Weltzell (in 1523/4) and Hans Gerle (in Nuremberg in 1532) explained the earliest tunings of the viols with five strings – a procedure subject to some modifications, though, as Martin Agricola and Ganassi instruct us. Possibly the sixth string became a regular addition to the instrument in Italy during the first two or three decades of the sixteenth century. It is first documented by

---

[26] See Eggers, *Die 'Regola Rubertina'*, II, pp. 249–55.

[27] Again, like Gerle, Ganassi's bass viol in this way of tuning sounds its open strings on D G B e a, and the treble on g b e a (with the bottom string presumably tuned to d). See *Regola Rubertina*, pp. xxxviii and xxxx.

[28] On the origins of the viol in Spain and its migration to Italy, see Ian D. Woodfield, 'The Origins of the Viol', Ph.D. diss., University of London, 1977, and also Woodfield, 'The Early History of the Viol', *Proceedings of the Royal Musical Association*, 103 (1976–7), pp. 141–57.

[29] Sebastian Virdung, *Musica getutscht* (Basel, 1511; facs. edns by Leo Schrade (Kassel, 1931), and by Klaus Wolfgang Niemöller (Kassel, 1970)), fol. B2. Gerle, too, showed *Grossgeigen* without bridges (see *Musica und Tabulatur*, fol. A4). Whereas musicologists have traditionally interpreted these illustrations as simple mistakes, it may be that late-fifteenth- and early-sixteenth-century viols only gradually came to have separate bridges; Woodfield points out that similar Spanish instruments of the fifteenth century were not supplied with them, and they may have been added to the instrument only after it had migrated to Italy.

Lanfranco in 1533[30] and then by Ganassi, as a standard practice, in 1542 and 1543. But the sixth string was not a fourth below the lowest string, as the early German experiments with the instrument had suggested was appropriate, but rather a fourth higher than the previous top string. In saying that most performers play a fourth higher, then, Ganassi may have been implying that most older or old-fashioned players still used five-stringed instruments that were rapidly becoming obsolete, at least in Italy.

Although Ganassi did not say so, these instruments a fourth higher, which most viol-players played, did not go as high in first position as much of the music of the early sixteenth century requires. If players were to adopt the five-stringed viols of Ganassi's Fourth Order, they would also need regularly to apply Gerle's rules for transposing music down a fourth, in order that they might include in their repertory all of the music they wished to play. The inconvenience of playing some music at written pitch and some transposed down a fourth may have suggested to players and instrument-makers that an additional string was necessary, and it may even explain why the sixth string, when it finally became standard in Italy in the 1530s and 1540s, extended the range upwards rather than downwards.

Such a conjecture is not completely fanciful, for Ganassi did give instructions for transposition in his explanation of how to tune and play viols with only four strings.[31] Often, he wrote, the top two strings of a viol break; therefore, players should know how to cope with viols with only four strings, and he recommended tuning them as in Example 6. This is presumably another notional tuning, and

Example 6. Tunings for four-stringed viols, after Ganassi (1542–3)

bass   tenor/alto   treble

such viols may actually have sounded somewhat higher – as high as the string tension would allow in order that the sound not be muddy. In any case, Ganassi realised that with such tunings players would not be able to perform all the music they might wish, since some of it went too high for them to play in comfort, especially (he wrote) when

[30] See Lee, 'Lanfranco's *Scintille*', pp. 259–60.
[31] *Lettione Seconda*, chap. 25. Chap. 26 explains how to tune viols with only three strings.

the range of the music is indicated by treble, mezzo-soprano, and tenor clefs. In that case, he suggested, the player should simply substitute another set of clefs – soprano, tenor, and bass – and the music would then fall within the compass of the instruments, though it would be transposed a notional fifth lower than written. Example 7 illustrates Ganassi's recommendation; a G major scale played with the first set of clefs will become a C major scale played with the second set of clefs. High clefs, far from being a secret and arcane language of the composer, were merely an inconvenience which needed to be overcome by instrumentalists in the early sixteenth century.

Example 7. Ganassi's method of transposing down a fifth

Although Ganassi's way of playing the viols a fourth higher has nothing to do with transposition (as he himself wrote), he did in fact discuss the subject with specific reference to tuning viols, and mentioned the subject in several other passages in the treatise. But it is merely practical advice about how and why musicians should transpose. It reveals Ganassi's casual attitude towards absolute pitch, and it is a relatively soothing way to end this essay, already over-full of confusing paradoxes and treacherous thickets. Ganassi wrote that he himself always followed the example of Gombert when the composer and chapel master was conducting a choir.[32] When they came to a piece where the disposition of extreme voices was awkward – for example, when the sopranos went too high or the basses too low – Gombert always adopted the general principle that one should either rewrite the parts, at which he was very expert, or pitch the piece so that the lowest notes of the bass are just audible. Gombert would advise, according to Ganassi, that it is better to pitch the instruments a tone too low than a semitone too high. But in any case, govern the absolute pitch by the pitch level of the bass part – the part which is, after all the fundamental voice of the music.

[32] Ganassi reported Gombert's practice in *Regola Rubertina*, chap. 11. Mendel, 'Pitch in Western Music', pp. 58–66, reviews the extensive modern literature on transposing sacred choral music. See also Peter Phillips, 'Performance Practice in 16th-Century English Choral Music', *Early Music*, 6 (1978), pp. 195–9.

5

SONGS WITHOUT WORDS BY JOSQUIN
AND HIS CONTEMPORARIES

WARWICK EDWARDS

THE received view of the early development of instrumental music in
the Renaissance, as portrayed in most modern reference books, may
be broadly summarised as follows. In the fifteenth century the scene
was dominated by keyboard compositions preserved in a series of
manuscript tablatures of German provenance, including notably the
Ileborgh tablature of 1448 and the Buxheim organ book of the 1460s.
The tradition continued into the sixteenth century, for example with
the first printed volume of keyboard music by Arnolt Schlick in 1512.
Keyboard music was also cultivated in Italy, and by the sixteenth
century was perhaps more advanced than that of Germany, though
we lack sources until Antico's publication of frottola arrangements
in 1517. Italy was also rich in music for the lute, several publications
appearing in 1507 and the years immediately following. Most of these
keyboard and lute compositions are idiomatic arrangements of what
was originally vocal music, but we also find compositions presumably written especially for the instruments concerned, such as
preludes, fantasias and, in fifteenth-century German organ manuscripts, cantus-firmus settings for liturgical use.

Although of considerable historical interest, these repertories are
perhaps not altogether rewarding. The minority of pieces written
especially for keyboard and lute are rather slight in stature, and the
adaptations of vocal part-music, although of outstanding importance for the light they shed on contemporary performance practice,
are mainly the work of second-rate arrangers. And this suggests a
further reservation about the early Renaissance instrumental repertory as described in textbooks: in spite of its considerable extent, in
its own time it failed to attract the attention of any of the major
composers of the day. Of course the predominant concern of such
composers was with vocal music. However, it is equally certain that

a small but significant concern of some important composers was with a type of music not usually discussed in reference books until well into the sixteenth century – music for instrumental ensemble. If it is dealt with in respect of the late fifteenth century it forms a rather vague appendage to the discussion of certain individual composers, especially Josquin, Isaac, Agricola and Obrecht.[1]

The reason for the reticence of modern writers on this subject is not difficult to find. It is the thorny problem of deciding what is and what is not instrumental. At first sight the problem does not seem to arise with keyboard and lute music since the notational form of the repertories neatly places the subject within bounds. Part-music, on the other hand, is usually found in staff notation regardless of whether it is destined for vocal or instrumental performance. One can, of course, proceed on the assumption (admittedly a large one) that items not underlaid with words in particular sources were intended for instrumental performance. For example, the three hundred or so wordless pieces in Petrucci's *Odhecaton* series may well form such an instrumental repertory even though many of them originated as vocal works.[2] Taken on its own this perfectly valid line of inquiry leads to what might be called a socio-historical approach to the development of Renaissance instrumental ensemble music.

However, any serious critical examination of the music itself (whether it be for keyboard, lute or ensemble) has to come to terms sooner or later with the fact that some compositions are simply transcriptions or adornments of vocal part-music, whereas others were conceived from the start without words, presumably as instrumental music.[3] There are many traps for the unwary here, the chief

---

[1] To be sure, some specialist studies have addressed themselves to this topic, most recently Dietrich Kämper, *Studien zur instrumentalen Ensemblemusik des 16. Jahrhunderts in Italien*, Analecta Musicologica 10 (Cologne and Vienna, 1970); transl. as *La musica strumentale nel rinascimento* (Rome, 1976). References in my notes are to the German edn.

[2] Maurice Cauchie, 'L'Odhecaton, recueil de musique instrumentale', *Revue de Musicologie*, 6 (1925), pp. 148–56, and 'A propos des trois recueils instrumentaux de la série de l'Odhecaton', *ibid.*, 9 (1928), pp. 64–7. For a more wide-ranging consideration of the implications for performance of texting practices in the sources see Louise Litterick, 'Performing Franco-Netherlandish Secular Music of the Late 15th Century: Texted and Untexted Parts in the Sources', *Early Music*, 8 (1980), pp. 474–85, and 'On Italian Instrumental Music in the Late Fifteenth Century', in this volume.

[3] Cf. the introductory comments in my article 'The Instrumental Music of *Henry VIII's Manuscript*', *The Consort*, 34 (1978), pp. 274–82.

of which is to be beguiled by melodic and rhythmic idioms whose
apparent instrumental characteristics merely reflect anachronistic
modern assumptions about the nature of instrumental music. It is
often stated that most vocal music of the period could be performed
instrumentally.[4] Seldom observed, yet perhaps equally valid, is the
converse: there is very little instrumental part-music that could not
on occasion be sung.[5] The point is worth stressing since a lot of sterile
debate during the last fifty years has gone into discussing the vocality
or otherwise of individual lines of medieval and Renaissance
polyphony, and has produced no conclusions.[6] In fact one of the
main premises underlying this paper is that few pieces can be safely
pronounced vocal or instrumental on purely internal analysis.
Instead one must look for *traditions* which are particularly closely
associated with wordless compositions; and within the limits of this
brief introduction to the subject I shall try to point to some such
traditions which could repay more systematic investigation.

One of the least problematic approaches to the subject is through
those numerous wordless compositions which are built around a
literal quotation of a voice or voices from an already existing
polyphonic piece, usually a chanson. It is difficult to find a succinct
term for this type of cantus firmus, not to be confused with the
quotation of a monophonic melody such as a popular tune. With
some reserve I use here Tinctoris's admittedly problematic expression *res facta*, in the first of the two senses proposed by Ferand:
'a written, not improvised, composition in plain or florid counterpoint'.[7]

One of the chansons employed for such compositions was the
widely circulated mid-fifteenth-century rondeau *Le serviteur hault*

[4] See, for example, Howard Mayer Brown, *Instrumental Music Printed before 1600: A
Bibliography* (Cambridge, Mass., 1965), p. 3.
[5] The German manuscripts Berlin, Staatsbibliothek Preussischer Kulturbesitz,
Mus. 40021, and Leipzig, Universitätsbibliothek, 1494, for example, contain
many Latin contrafacta of pieces which for one reason or another must be
considered instrumental in origin.
[6] The arguments are summed up – and disposed of – in Lloyd Hibberd, 'On
"Instrumental Style" in Early Melody', *Musical Quarterly*, 32 (1946), pp. 107–30;
cf. Kämper, *Studien zur instrumentalen Ensemblemusik*, pp. 5ff.
[7] Ernest T. Ferand, 'What is *Res Facta*?', *Journal of the American Musicological Society*, 10
(1957), pp. 141–50. Cantus firmi consisting of popular melodies fall, one assumes,
into the category of improvised composition since they are not derived from fixed
archetypes – see p. 87 below.

guerdonné.[8] A composition by Isaac,[9] written not later than the 1480s, consists of the top part of this song as cantus firmus with two entirely new lower parts added. Like most of the pieces in its sole source, a late-fifteenth-century Florentine chansonnier,[10] it is notated with the text incipit 'Le serviteur' in all voices, but with no further words. What did Isaac have in mind when he wrote it? Presumably not a resetting of the same poem, for the original melody is now set in augmentation, each perfect breve of the original being occupied by three imperfect breves in the new parts.[11] Instead of being a clearly articulated rondeau-cinquain setting in the classic Burgundian tradition, Isaac's composition has become an essay in motivic construction in which a simple musical idea, stated at the beginning by the middle voice, is ingeniously repeated throughout the piece at different pitches, all against the constriction of a cantus firmus.

Isaac's *Le serviteur* is representative of a sizeable group of compositions from the secular sources of the late fifteenth century which draw on a relatively small circle of existing chansons for their cantus firmi. Besides *Le serviteur* the originals include the rondeaux *Comme femme* possibly by Binchois, *D'ung aultre amer* and *Fors seulement* by Ockeghem, the anonymous *J'ay pris amours*, and Hayne's *De tous biens plaine* – the last-mentioned a veritable *In nomine* of late-fifteenth-century Continental music.[12] The principal composers are Isaac and

---

[8] Published in the *opera dubia* section of *Guglielmi Dufay: Opera omnia*, ed. Heinrich Besseler, Corpus Mensurabilis Musicae ser. 1, vol. vi (Rome, 1964), no. 92. Most writers agree with Besseler in rejecting the ascription to Dufay in a single peripheral source, Montecassino, Biblioteca della Badia, MS N 871.

[9] *Heinrich Isaac: Weltliche Werke*, ed. Johannes Wolf, Denkmäler der Tonkunst in Österreich 28, Jg. xiv[1] (Vienna, 1907), p. 31.

[10] Florence, Biblioteca Nazionale Centrale, MS Banco rari 229; see Anne-Marie Bragard, 'Un manuscrit florentin du Quattrocento: le Magl. xix, 59 (B.R. 229)', *Revue de musicologie*, 52 (1966), pp. 56–72. Howard Mayer Brown, in his forthcoming complete edition of the manuscript, argues that it was compiled in 1490–1.

[11] Wolf, in his edition, was surely mistaken in underlaying the words to the superius editorially and classifying the piece as a chanson.

[12] Related settings of the six chansons are listed as follows: *Petrucci: Harmonice musices Odhecaton A*, ed. Helen Hewitt and Isabel Pope, Mediaeval Academy of America Studies and Documents 5 (Cambridge, Mass., 1942), 'Concordance' nos. 20, 21, 35 (*De tous biens plaine, J'ay pris amours, Le serviteur*); Howard Mayer Brown, *Music in the French Secular Theater* (Cambridge, Mass., 1963), 'Catalogue' nos. 61, 73, 85, 195, 264 (all save *Fors seulement*); Helen Hewitt, '*Fors seulement* and the Cantus Firmus Technique of the Fifteenth Century', in Gustave Reese and Robert J. Snow (eds.), *Essays in Musicology in Honor of Dragan Plamenac* (Pittsburgh, 1969), pp. 91–126 (*Fors seulement*).

Agricola, with Josquin, Ghiselin, Japart and Obrecht contributing smaller quantities, and there is also a considerable number of pieces by lesser and anonymous composers. Unlike Isaac's *Le serviteur*, many of these pieces use a cantus firmus which did *not* bear a text in the original chanson, or which could be made to take words only with considerable awkwardness. This serves to emphasise the observation – made in connection with Isaac's piece, and emerging from study of the repertory as a whole – that these pieces are not resettings of the same words as the original chansons. Nor presumably are they designed for replacement texts now lost, for the titles are almost always those of the original chanson, not those of contrafacta.

But there is another possible vocal use that we must not overlook in a misguided rush to interpret the virtuoso scale figures of Isaac's *Le serviteur* as 'obviously instrumental' in conception: that is, in the by now well-established tradition of *res facta* settings, the Ordinary of the Mass. Fifteenth-century Mass movements were quite commonly detached from their original contexts and circulated without words in the secular sources. Most tend to be of the freely constructed kind, but there are several confirmed instances of *res facta* settings too. However, confusion with the supposedly instrumental *res facta* settings just considered is usually ruled out since in Mass settings composers normally modify the melody, rhythm and structural proportions of the borrowed material rather than quote it literally.[13] Because there are no compelling reasons to suppose that a tradition of non-literal *res facta* quotation existed as an instrumental genre, such isolated wordless pieces of this kind as do turn up have very strong claims to vocal origins, especially as Mass sections.

A promising case is one of Isaac's wordless four-voice settings of *J'ay pris amours*.[14] Suspicions are aroused not only by the fact that the cantus firmus (the superius of the original chanson) is quoted in the top voice in freely modified form (see Example 1),[15] but by the division of both piece and cantus firmus into two separate parts. Moreover, we actually have evidence of a lost Isaac Mass which could well have contained this very pair of movements, say as Kyrie

[13] Edgar H. Sparks, *Cantus Firmus in Mass and Motet 1420–1520* (Berkeley, 1963).
[14] *Weltliche Werke*, p. 78.
[15] An important fact which eluded Gombosi in his analysis of this work, and which vitiates Kämper's arguments that the piece belongs to a certain genre of 'instrumental chanson'. See Otto Gombosi, *Jacob Obrecht: Eine stilkritische Studie* (Leipzig, 1925), pp. 69f, and Kämper, *Studien zur instrumentalen Ensemblemusik*, pp. 70f.

Example 1

A. Anon., *J'ay pris amours* – original superius

B. Isaac, *J'ay pris amours a 4* – superius

I and II. In a letter of 11 March 1490 to Ercole I d'Este of Ferrara a Florentine singer records that Isaac has completed 'una missa supra Jay prins amours' and that he will send it to the Duke shortly.[16] The implied date and place of composition – in Florence just before

[16] Martin Staehelin, *Die Messen Heinrich Isaacs* (Bern, 1977), I, p. 45, and II, pp. 31f.

March 1490 – is entirely consistent with the unique source, a Florentine manuscript which also contains detached sections from another
Isaac Mass, and which was compiled (as Atlas has shown) in the
first half of the 1490s.[17]

Literal quotation of the cantus firmus is, of course, far from
unknown in Mass compositions, especially among composers of the
Josquin generation. Often the cantus firmus is presented literally in
just a single movement, for example the Agnus Dei III. The crucial
point here is that for all their diversity of musical style such movements belong to a quite different tradition from the wordless *res facta*
settings in the secular sources.

But there are some exceptions. For example, amongst the whole
family of eight wordless settings which quote a voice or voices of *Le
serviteur* literally,[18] there is one that belongs to a quite different
stylistic world from the rest. It is found only in the *Odhecaton A*,[19]
attributed to Busnois in the first edition, but anonymous in subsequent ones.[20] The piece stands out because, unlike the other settings,
it retains the borrowed melodies – superius and tenor of the original
chanson – without augmentation, and is thus in triple metre.
Moreover, its style is such that if the words of, for example, the final

[17] Florence, Biblioteca Nazionale Centrale, Magl. XIX.178; see Allan Atlas, *The
Cappella Giulia Chansonnier (Rome, Biblioteca Apostolica Vaticana, C.G.XIII.27)*, 2
vols., Musicological Studies 27 (Brooklyn, 1975–6), 1, p. 247. The manuscript
also includes, under the titles *Amis des que* and *A fortune contrent*, the Christe and
Qui tollis I sections, respectively, of Isaac's *Missa Chargé de deul*.

[18] Of the seven listed by Hewitt and Brown (see note 12, above) one, the setting *a 2*
by Pullois in El Escorial, Real Monasterio, MS IV.a.24 (recorded by Hewitt as
anonymous), is outside the scope of this discussion since its superius consists of a
free paraphrase of the cantus firmus; it is published in *Johannis Pullois: Opera omnia*,
ed. Peter Gülke, Corpus Mensurabilis Musicae ser. 41 (n.p., 1967), p. 45. To the
list may be added: an anonymous setting *a 2* in Perugia, Biblioteca Comunale
Augusta, MS 1013 (M 36), fols. 103v–4, published in *Eustachio Romano: Musica
Duorum*, ed. Hans T. David, H. M. Brown and E. E. Lowinsky, Monuments of
Renaissance Music 6 (Chicago, 1975), pp. 38ff; a setting *a 4* in Augsburg, Staats-
und Stadtbibliothek, MS 142a, fols. 55v–57, anonymous but in a fascicle which
may well be devoted exclusively to music by Agricola – cf. Martin Staehelin,
'Möglichkeiten und praktische Anwendung der Verfasserbestimmung an
anonym überlieferten Kompositionen der Josquin-Zeit', *Tijdschrift van de Vereeniging voor Nederlandsche Muziekgeschiedenis*, 23 (1973), pp. 79–91, on pp. 84f.

[19] Ed. Hewitt, no. 35.

[20] The removal of this and five other attributions after the first printing of the
Odhecaton A raises doubts about authorship, as Hewitt (*Odhecaton*, pp. 7ff) and
others have observed.

Agnus Dei were underlaid, the result would be a movement indistinguishable from a Mass section by one of the Busnois generation. Is this a section from a lost *Missa Le serviteur*?[21] Or is it simply an isolated textless movement – a song without words – but in a style one and the same as that used for Mass composition? Does the search for pieces which 'look instrumental' ignore the possible existence of pieces for instruments which do not set out to exploit in any way the fact that instruments are different from voices?

Another awkward factor is the survival of certain *res facta* Mass sections which contain material every bit as suggestive of instrumental conception as the Isaac *Le serviteur* setting. The three-voice Pleni from Isaac's *Missa Een vrolic wesen*, for example, contains a passage which appears to place it very much in the instrumental *res facta* tradition.[22] The movement as a whole, though, is not really comparable to *Le serviteur* since it lacks the latter's single-minded devotion to motivic construction; its more diffuse structure befits its position as an intermediary section of a larger work. However, the movement serves as a warning that a composer may on occasion adopt the 'instrumental style' for a Mass movement, and that pieces like Isaac's *Le Serviteur* could turn out to be vocal after all.

But could the whole surviving repertory of *res facta* settings be accounted for in this way? If so, then we have lost a sizeable number of Masses, especially on *De tous biens plaine* and *Fors seulement*.[23] Moreover, there are many more songs used for cantus-firmus

[21] Known Mass settings of *Le serviteur* include the following: Faugues *a 4*, published in *Guillaume Faugues: Collected Works*, ed. George C. Schuetze (Brooklyn, 1960), p. 5; anon. *a 3* (Trent, Castello del Buon Consiglio, MS 88, fols. 267v–275v), published in *Sechs Trienter Codices*, III, Denkmäler der Tonkunst in Österreich 38, Jg. xix[1] (Vienna, 1912), 141; De Orto *a 4* (Credo), in Vienna, Österreichische Nationalbibliothek, MS 1783, fols. 197v–201; Agricola *a4*, published in *Alexander Agricola: Opera omnia*, ed. Edward R. Lerner, Corpus Mensurabilis Musicae ser. 22, vol. 1 (n.p., 1961), p. 1.

[22] The passage is quoted in Charles Warren Fox, 'Ein fröhlich Wesen: the Career of a German Song in the Sixteenth Century', *Papers Read by Members of the American Musicological Society . . . 1937* (n.p., n.d.), pp. 56–74, on p. 66. The complete Mass is not yet available in a modern edition; for information see Staehelin, *Die Messen Heinrich Isaacs*, III, pp. 94–9.

[23] Known Masses on *De tous biens plaine* in this period include those by Gafurius, Josquin (Credo only) and Obrecht, and possibly the mysterious *Missa Dubliplen* by Compère which was no. 12 in the lost partbooks, Berlin, former Preussische Staatsbibliothek, Mus. MS 40634. Masses on *Fors seulement* are known by Obrecht and Pipelare (the latter, however, on Pipelare's own setting which is only indirectly related to Ockeghem's chanson – see Hewitt, '*Fors seulement*', pp. 98ff).

Masses than ever appear as the basis for separate movements in the secular sources. There is also the fact that a composer like Agricola left a considerable corpus of *res facta* settings in secular sources, as well as a representative sample of *res facta* and other Masses, but reserved quite separate styles for each of the two types of composition. On the whole it is best to follow the laws of probability, and conclude that no more than a fraction of the sizeable number of compositions like Isaac's *Le serviteur* could have been conceived as sections of Masses and large-scale motets. In other words, most of the *res facta* settings in the secular sources which quote their borrowed material unaltered are 'instrumental' in the broadest sense – they are conceived without words.

The search for instrumental traditions now turns to a much more problematic category of pieces: those compositions which employ a cantus firmus of secular monophonic origin. Such melodies may be broadly described as 'popular' in the sense that they were more or less widely known, at least within their own circles. The description 'popular' need not of course imply that the melodies were necessarily folk-tunes, though they share one quality widely associated both with folk and popular melodies, the capacity for retaining their essential identity in spite of never being quoted in exactly the same form in any two situations.[24] In this feature this class of compositions is sharply distinguished from the *res facta* pieces just discussed where the cantus-firmus quotation is always exact.

In some instances the popular melody is treated as a scaffolding device, and laid out in such a way as to preclude its being sung to the original words. The poem *T'Andernaken op den Rhijn* is preserved in several contemporary sources of popular verse, but its melody is preserved only through a number of cantus-firmus settings of the fifteenth and sixteenth centuries, where it is usually presented in augmented note-values, effectively destroying the rhythmic life it should have as a popular setting of the words.[25] In fact it is more akin to those unmeasured melodies whose long notes served as a basis for *basse danse* improvisations, the most famous of which is called *La*

---

[24] Cf. Howard Mayer Brown, 'The *Chanson rustique*: Popular Elements in the 15th-and 16th-Century Chanson', *Journal of the American Musicological Society*, 12 (1959), pp. 16–26, on pp. 19–20.

[25] For further information on *T'Andernaken* and a summary of settings see my article 'The Instrumental Music of *Henry VIII's Manuscript*', pp. 28off.

Spagna.[26] Probably neither the extant *T'Andernaken* nor *La Spagna* settings represent what professional bands of instrumentalists really improvised, but we may surmise that they preserve in sublimated form some of the techniques one might reasonably expect to find: virtuosic runs of parallel sixths and tenths against the cantus firmus, more or less standardised syncopated formulas, simple sequences especially where the cantus firmus ascends or descends by step for three or more notes, and so on.

Compositions like these can be fairly readily accepted as instrumentally conceived because they belong to a clearly identifiable tradition associated with wordless music. This tradition has some points of contact with the *res facta* instrumental genre in its use of the borrowed melody as structural material to be heard in the background, not projected. But in the vast majority of settings of popular material the melody is treated quite differently. It is in the foreground, clearly framed so as to be immediately recognisable; and it is, above all, singable. Many such settings clearly belong to the world of pure vocal music, especially when, for example, homophonic texture predominates, each part accepting the text comfortably. But then, as now with modern arrangements of hit tunes, one may expect some cases where instrumental use is intended, and others where it is immaterial whether the melody is sung or not. In either event the element of instrumental exploitation will usually be played down, since the main object is to display the tune, not to write 'instrumental music' as such. Again, in determining the likely status of individual pieces it is important to relate them to traditions rather than relying on internal pointers alone. The difficulty here, however, is that there is no single tradition but a multiplicity of different ones. The subject is of such fascinating complexity that it will have to be dealt with at length on a separate occasion.

Meanwhile, there is a third type of song without words to be considered – the freely composed movement. Such pieces offer still more severe problems in trying to decide what is instrumental in conception and what is vocal. Yet historically speaking they should

[26] For lists of *La Spagna* settings see *Compositione di Meser Vincenzo Capirola, Lute-Book*, ed. Otto Gombosi (Neuilly-sur-Seine, 1955), pp. lxiiff, and Frederick Crane, *Materials for the Study of the Fifteenth-Century Basse Danse* (Brooklyn, 1968), pp. 74ff.

have a special significance, bearing in mind the emergence of the freely composed ricercare for instrumental ensemble later in the sixteenth century. Here one must rely more than ever on the elucidation of traditions, and be particularly wary of prejudging what freely composed instrumental movements ought to have been like.

Helen Hewitt was aware of this danger when in the early 1940s she isolated a number of 'instrumental tricinia' from the *Odhecaton A* and elsewhere which differed markedly in style from any known secular song.[27] It is true that some of these compositions were found in certain sources underlaid as Latin motets, but in such an unconvincing way as only to 'confirm the supposition that this music was intended for instruments'. Hewitt characterised such pieces by describing their formal introduction, consisting of a 'head-theme' of striking character often spanning an extensive range. After this, she wrote, the music follows a very free course, but usually features sequential passages, and especially 'a passage in which one voice, in long held notes, recedes into the background while the other two voices play about it in quicker notes, in parallel tenths, or employing imitations'. A good example of such a piece is Josquin's *La Bernardina*,[28] often cited – along with its very similar counterpart by Ghiselin, *La Alfonsina*[29] – as the quintessential early predecessor of the sixteenth-century instrumental fantasia.

Another of Hewitt's 'instrumental tricinia' in the *Odhecaton A* is a piece by Isaac entitled *Benedictus*[30] which has subsequently been identified with the Benedictus section of his four-part *Missa Quant j'ay au cueur*.[31] There can be little doubt that this movement was composed as an integral part of the Mass setting as a whole – motivic links with other sections of the Mass and the widespread use of the

[27] *Odhecaton*, ed. Hewitt, pp. 74ff.

[28] *Werken van Josquin des Prez: Wereldlijke Werken*, vol. II/4, ed. Myroslaw Antonowycz and Willem Elders (Amsterdam, 1965), no. 42.

[29] *Johannes Ghiselin-Verbonnet: Opera omnia*, ed. Clytus Gottwald, Corpus Mensurabilis Musicae ser. 23, vol. IV (n.p., 1968), no. 21.

[30] *Odhecaton*, ed. Hewitt, no. 76.

[31] Martin Just, 'Heinrich Isaacs Motetten in italienischen Quellen', *Analecta Musicologica*, I (1963), pp. 1–19, on pp. 3f. The complete Mass is published after Milan, Archivio della Fabbrica del Duomo, M S 2268 (Kyrie and Agnus Dei after *Misse Jzac*, Venice, 1506) in *Heinrich Isaac: Misse*, ed. Fabio Fano, Archivium Musices Metropolitanum Mediolanense 10 (Milan, 1962), p. 38. For further information see Staehelin, *Die Messen Heinrich Isaacs*, I, pp. 32ff, and III, pp. 76ff.

title 'Benedictus' for the detached movement settle this point.[32] Yet, as I have suggested elsewhere,[33] Hewitt's arguments are not really damaged by this. Because the words to be set are few and Isaac makes no attempt to match textual and musical phrases, the piece is still 'instrumental' in the sense that it was conceived without words. In fact *La Bernardina* and *La Alfonsina* look as if they were written specifically in response to Isaac's *Benedictus*. They can hardly have preceded it since the style of writing is not at all typical of either Josquin or Ghiselin, whereas it fits in perfectly naturally with Isaac at a certain stage in his development. His Masses on *Chargé de deul*[34] and *Comme femme*,[35] for example, include a number of reduced sections for three voices written along similar lines. Some of these too were detached and copied into chansonniers, often with substitute titles.[36] One such piece is the anonymous *Gracias a vos donzella* of the Cappella Giulia and Wolffheim chansonniers, which Atlas argued on grounds of style and context may be by Isaac.[37] It is indeed the Benedictus from Isaac's *Missa Comme femme*, a point which escaped even Martin Staehelin's eagle eye. But none of these movements enjoyed the phenomenal popularity of the *Missa Quant j'ay au cueur* Benedictus, which became one of the most widely circulated pieces of its time[38] and must have influenced many other compositions, both secular and sacred.

In conclusion I should like to return to the idea of *traditions* in European music at the turn of the fifteenth century. In the last twenty years song traditions have been relatively well documented. It is fairly easy to identify a given song with a school of composition, whether the text is preserved or not, and even if the piece happens to

[32] See Atlas, *Cappella Giulia Chansonnier*, I, pp. 126ff.

[33] 'The Instrumental Music of *Henry VIII's Manuscript*', p. 276.

[34] Modern edition after Milan, Archivio della Fabbrica del Duomo, MS 2268 (Kyrie and Agnus Dei II after *Misse Jzac*, Venice, 1506) in *Isaac: Misse*, ed. Fano, p. 74. For further information see Staehelin, *Die Messen Heinrich Isaacs*, I, pp. 30f, and III, pp. 86ff.

[35] No modern edition currently available; for information see Staehelin, *Die Messen Heinrich Isaacs*, I, pp. 31f, and III, pp. 81ff.

[36] See, for example, note 17 above.

[37] Rome, Biblioteca Apostolica Vaticana, Cappella Giulia, MS XIII. 27, (modern) fols. 91v–92; Washington, Library of Congress, MS 2.1 M 6 Case, fols. 95v–96. Atlas, *Cappella Giulia Chansonnier*, I, p. 189.

[38] The most comprehensive list of sources is in Staehelin, *Die Messen Heinrich Isaacs*, I, pp. 33f.

survive only in the guise of a Latin contrafactum. Mass and motet traditions have fared less well, not for lack of scholarly attention, but because vast tracts of the repertory are still not available in modern editions.[39] Nevertheless schools of composition can be identified, and they are quite distinct from those of songwriting, again notwithstanding the existence of secular contrafacta.

My central thesis here is that, when all the song traditions and all the traditions normally associated with sections of the Ordinary of the Mass and other extended sacred works are filtered out, there remains a residue of movements whose styles do not comfortably fit in with any of these traditions, although, in keeping with the flexible aesthetic of the time, such pieces may frequently be borrowed for one type of music or another. The identification and clarification of this neutral territory – still vaguely defined but clearly existing – is a pressing task for students of Renaissance music.

As to what such pieces are for, I am a little wary of calling them 'instrumental'; I prefer the expression 'songs without words' because that seems to epitomise more closely what the aims and objectives of the composers were. Doubtless the music was played on instruments, but Josquin and his contemporaries were concerned less with 'instrumentality' than with writing coherent musical structures which take something other than words as their starting point. The appearance of so many songs without words at the end of the fifteenth century is probably not unconnected with the large number of French-speaking musicians employed at that time in foreign courtly and ecclesiastical establishments where, notwithstanding certain important exceptions, French texts were neither understood nor appreciated. In Italy, for example, where the cultivation of instrumental music appears to have been particularly intense, most Franco-Netherlandish composers were primarily concerned with the production of sacred music. Faced with a demand for secular music (as testified by the many surviving Italian chansonniers), but not for songs in the French tongue, what could be more natural than to explore the possibilities of writing music which is self-sufficient without the words?

Clearly a fuller understanding of this repertory is vitally important

[39] Only a fraction of the sacred works of Isaac and La Rue, for example, is conveniently accessible, although collected editions of both composers are in progress or forthcoming in the series Corpus Mensurabilis Musicae.

for any adequate assessment of the origins and development of sixteenth-century 'instrumental style'. However, one should not be lured by the wealth of later instrumental music, with its apparently more clearly defined boundaries, into thinking that the earlier repertory is of historical interest only. That attitude of mind goes hand in hand with the belief that instrumental music was somehow undergoing a process of 'emancipation' from vocal music around the turn of the century;[40] but what evidence is there to suggest that composers were struggling to do any such thing? Such an assumption carries the implication that instrumental music was 'coming of age' at this time; but since the composition of songs without words at the end of the fifteenth century occupied several of the leading composers of the day, it is difficult to think of instrumental music as being any more experimental than the many other new departures in the field of vocal music that characterise this exciting era of change.

[40] Cf. Kämper, *Studien zur instrumentalen Ensemblemusik*, pp. 1f.

6

INSTRUMENTAL MUSIC, SONGS AND VERSE FROM SIXTEENTH-CENTURY WINCHESTER: BRITISH LIBRARY ADDITIONAL MS 60577

IAIN FENLON

IN recent years, much has been done to develop the view that the spread of education and the growth of literacy in fifteenth-century England induced a much greater reliance by the middle strata of English society upon the written word for social, moral and spiritual guidance, as well as for entertainment and personal communication. As one writer has put it, the redistribution of wealth which fuelled the demand for more widespread schooling made England 'a land in which men felt a sharpening self-consciousness about their social status'.[1] Another analysis of middle-class prosperity and its consequences emphasises the higher standards of domestic comfort enjoyed by classes which had hitherto benefited little from the social system, and notes that the quickening of social aspirations and its attendant anxieties are well revealed by 'the books of etiquette devoured by the new middle classes as they struggled with novel and perplexing social difficulties'.[2] It is no doubt true that these forces inspired the production of courtesy manuals just as they prompted the establishment of new inns of court, responsible for training not only lawyers but also civil servants and administrators, and encouraged the foundation of new colleges at Oxford and Cambridge. But this upward striving is reflected not only in books of etiquette but also in a host of other volumes designed to provide social, moral and spiritual direction as well as recreation. Good examples of manuscripts testifying to the increased reliance on such compilations by

[1] F. R. H. Du Boulay, *An Age of Ambition. English Society in the Late Middle Ages* (London, 1970), p. 61.
[2] A. R. Bridbury, *Economic Growth: England in the Later Middle Ages* (Hassocks, Sussex, 1975).

the middle strata of society are Lincoln Cathedral Library MS 91[3] and British Library Additional MS 31042, both associated with Robert Thornton. Another, slightly later example of the trend is the British Library's recently acquired Additional MS 60577,[4] an anthology most probably put together in the second half of the fifteenth century. Its earliest layers contain Middle English verse and prose, some of it recorded elsewhere but much of it (including the earliest English translation from Petrarch's *Secretum*) apparently unique; it includes sermons, treatises, verse alphabets, medical recipes, astrological notes, and a lapidary – the standard fare of a collection of this type. Additions to the manuscript continued to be made throughout the sixteenth century, and these too are of considerable textual significance. They include a series of songs and instrumental pieces entered, almost certainly, about the mid-century – that is, at a time from which remarkably few English music sources of any kind survive.

Unlike the Thornton manuscripts, the earliest layers of Add. 60577 contain the work of a number of scribes none of whom can be identified as the volume's first owner. But from about 1500, shortly after it received its present binding, the history of the manuscript can be traced through a succession of owners among the Winchester clergy until at least 1560 or so – that is, for the whole period during which further additions continued to be made. This lends Add. 60577 an exceptional interest as a document of taste and as testimony to the growth of literacy, particularly since the circles through which it passed can be charted with some precision. The principal aim of the following discussion is to reconstruct the history and changing function of the manuscript through paleographical and textual evidence, initially since such a characterisation of the social aspects of the book is of interest in itself, but ultimately so that the musical additions can be seen within a social context. That account starts in the second half of the fifteenth century, and continues chronologically until some time in the 1560s.

It should be said at the outset that some possible indications of the

---

[3] *The Thornton Manuscript – Lincoln Cathedral MS. 91*, facs. intr. by D. S. Brewer and A. E. B. Owen, 2nd, rev. edn (London, 1977).

[4] The manuscript came to light as Lot 57 at a sale of manuscripts at Sotheby's in London on 19 June 1979 and was subsequently acquired by the British Library. I am grateful to Dr Daniel Waley, Keeper of Manuscripts, for allowing me to consult Add. 60577 at the earliest possible opportunity.

date and provenance of the earliest layers of the volume cannot yet be successfully interpreted. This is true, for example, of the account on fos. 50–51, beginning 'Clerkys of Oxenforde have determynid', dealing with the appearance of comets. The 'Clerkys' are almost certainly members of the Merton school of astronomy, famed throughout Europe since the fourteenth century;[5] but it is not possible to determine which appearance is described in the text. And, as might be expected, the watermarks in the paper provide an unhelpfully broad range of dates for its manufacture.[6] What is striking is that the only explicable indications of provenance seem to associate the manuscript exclusively with Winchester. The earliest is a reference in the poem on fols. 22v–24, addressed to a Bishop of Winchester, the composition of which can be dated with reasonable precision. From the text itself it seems that the bishop's immediate predecessor had died only a short time before, that a period of unrest had followed as a result of which a number had gone into exile, and that for four years there had been widespread suspicion. The piece goes on to remark on the fine qualities of the new bishop, and notes that his symbol is the lily, though one that is now choked with thorns. These historical, biographical and heraldic details make it highly probable that the poem is addressed to William Wayneflete (c. 1394–1486), Headmaster of Winchester College from 1429 to 1441–2, Provost of Eton during the 1440s, Chancellor of England from 1456 to 1460, founder of both Magdalen Hall and Magdalen College, Oxford, and Bishop of Winchester from 1447 until his death.[7] The biographical details match the recorded activities of Wayneflete during the period immediately following his appointment as bishop in succession to Cardinal Beaufort, the troubles referred to

---

[5] For the Merton school see R. W. T. Gunther, *Early Science in Oxford*, 15 vols. (Oxford, 1920–67), II, pp. 65ff.

[6] Further details of some paleographical aspects of the manuscript are given in the inventory, pp. 111–12 below. The paper used is marked in two ways. The first, of the 'fleur-de-lys' type, is close but not identical to Briquet's number 1541, with recorded examples from the period 1528–55. The second, showing the arms of Troyes, is similar to Briquet 1043. For further details see C. M. Briquet, *Les filigranes. Dictionnaire historique des marques du papier dès leur apparition vers 1282 jusqu'en 1600*, 4 vols. (Paris, 1907).

[7] For further details of Wayneflete's career and interests see R. Chandler, *The Life of William Waynflete, Bishop of Winchester, &c., Collected from Records, Registers, Manuscripts, and Other Authentic Evidences* (London, 1811), and A. B. Emden, *A Biographical Register of the University of Oxford to A.D. 1500*, 3 vols. (Oxford, 1957–9), III, pp. 2001–3.

being the Wars of the Roses. Since the text makes no reference to his disfavour and imprisonment in the Tower after the return of Edward IV to London in April 1471, it was most probably composed before then. Above all, there can be no ambiguity about the poem's reference to Wayneflete's arms, derived from those of Patten (alias Barbour), of 'a field, fusily ermine and sable', on which Wayneflete inserted, upon becoming Provost of Eton, 'on a chief of the second, three lilies slipped argent', these being the arms of the college.[8] Wayneflete retained these bearings after his removal to the see of Winchester, caused them to be engraved on the public seal of Magdalen Hall, and transmitted them to his college.[9]

The rather specialised local interest of this poem already suggests that it was copied in the Winchester area, and elsewhere in the earliest layers of the volume are bidding prayers for a Bishop of Winchester and a number of texts associated with school life. The latter include a Latin–English *vulgaria* (fols. 67–77) containing sentences for translation by schoolboys, and a comic poem in which the unfortunate pupil is caned at the end of every line. These pieces and a number of marginal inscriptions elsewhere may reflect existence at Winchester College, closely associated with the cathedral at this period, and presided over by Wayneflete himself before his move to Eton.

Certainly the only other piece of evidence relating to the early history of Add. 60577 places it quite firmly in Winchester. This is its binding, of dark brown leather over wooden boards, decorated with a rather crowded and unequally spaced blind-stamped design (see Figure 1). Seven stamps are used, four of which occur on books bound by the 'Virgin and Child' binder, so named after the most distinctive of his tools.[10] Of the seven bindings known to be his work all bear stamps 1–3 (Figure 2), while two are also decorated with the fourth stamp, a small unframed rosette of five petals. The binding of Add. 60577 now presents an eighth example of this craftsman's work, moreover, an example which adds three further stamps (a branch, a lion and an eagle) to his known designs (Figure 3). This in

---

[8] Details from Sir B. Burke, *The General Armoury of England, Scotland, Ireland, and Wales . . . with a [Revised] Supplement* (London, 1884), p. 1085.

[9] See Chandler, *The Life of William Waynflete*, pp. 30–1.

[10] For details of this and what follows see N. R. Ker, 'The Virgin and Child Binder, LVL, and William Horman', *The Library*, 5th ser., vol. 17 (1962), pp. 77–85.

Figure 1. Add. 60577, front cover

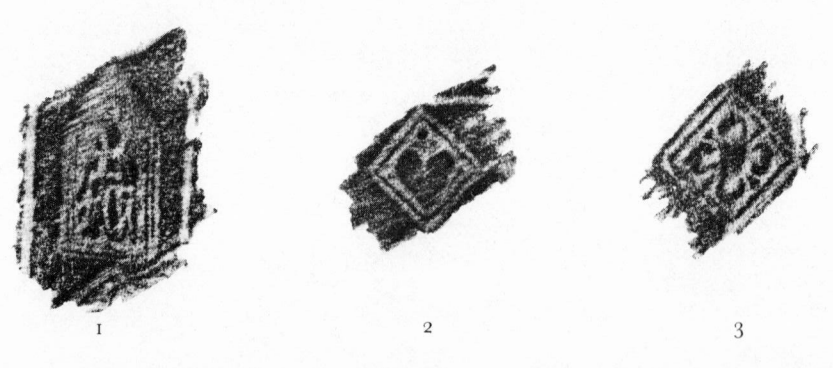

Figure 2. Tools of the 'Virgin and Child' binder from Cambridge, St John's College Library, MS G 7 (James 175), front cover

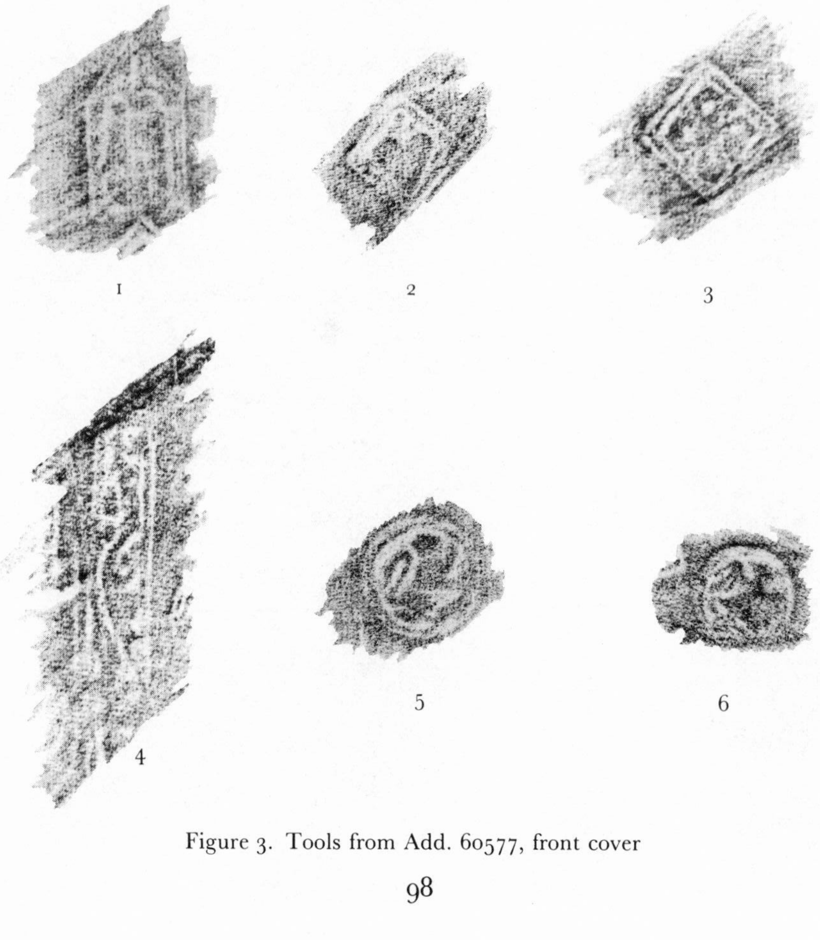

Figure 3. Tools from Add. 60577, front cover

turn suggests both the place and the approximate date when the work was carried out.[11] Four of the 'Virgin and Child' bindings were apparently done for William Horman, Headmaster of Winchester from 1495 to 1501 and later fellow of Eton; and a fifth occurs on a volume in the library at Winchester College. It seems likely that Horman's 'Virgin and Child' bindings were all executed before 1500, presumably by a local Winchester binder, and none of the 'Virgin and Child' bindings can be positively dated after 1497, the publication date of a copy of Philelfus's *Odae* owned by Horman. But while the presence of the 'Virgin and Child' binder's four tools on the covers of Add. 60577 indicates beyond reasonable doubt that it was bound in Winchester around if not before the turn of the fifteenth century, it is unlikely that the manuscript was owned by Horman himself. There are various signs showing that a given book was in Horman's ownership, including a title written on the tail, a table of contents copied on a flyleaf, a distinctive system of foliation, and an elaborate index. None of these are found in Add. 60577.

Once at Winchester, the manuscript seems to have remained there until at least 1549 and probably longer. Scribbled on the final pastedown is a series of payments to obedientiaries of the cathedral priory of St Swithun, and all but one of the functionaries whose positions are listed are also recorded in the document drawn up when Dr Hede, commissary of the Prior of Canterbury during the vacancy of the sees of both Canterbury and Winchester, made his visitation of the priory on 27 February 1500.[12] Furthermore, at the foot of the first folio is inscribed 'I. Buryton Monacus Sancti Swithuuni', and the same hand has written on the final pastedown 'Iohannes Buryton Monacus Sancti Swithuuni'. According to the published extracts from the obedientiary rolls of St Swithun's Priory,[13] John Buriton was sacrist there from at least Michaelmas 1536 until Michaelmas 1537; this is confirmed by the preamble to the surviving compotus roll (not written by Buriton himself) for that

[11] I am grateful to Howard Nixon, Librarian of Westminster Abbey Chapter Library, who confirms that, in his opinion, the decoration of the covers of Add. 60577 is undoubtedly the work of the 'Virgin and Child' binder.

[12] The list of names made at Hede's visitation is given in H. A. Doubleday *et al.*, *The Victoria History of the Counties of England. Hampshire and The Isle of Wight*, 5 vols. and index (London, 1900–14), II, p. 113.

[13] See G. W. Kitchin, *Compotus Rolls of the Obedientiaries of St Swithun's Priory, Winchester. From the Winchester Cathedral Archives* (Winchester, 1892), p. 201.

period.[14] Later, Buriton became one of the original pettycanons of the cathedral after the old Benedictine house of St Swithun was reconstituted as a secular cathedral in 1539–41.[15] A further note, almost certainly in Buriton's hand, occurs on the final pastedown and records that 'y bowthe hym [the book] of bry[n]stane coste me 3^{s}4$^{d'}$, and further comments, concerning 'Bry[n]stane', 'Erytike otherwyse callyd whythere postata. I pray God he may repent and recant.' (In both cases the final syllable of Buriton's surname is expressed by a rebus in the shape of a barrel (= tun).) The price which Buriton paid for the manuscript, a quarter of a mark, was a not inconsiderable amount, the same (incidentally) as that paid to an unnamed clerk for copying Buriton's own compotus roll for 1536–7.[16] 'Bry[n]stane' presumably refers to John Brynstone, another monk of St Swithun's, who was ordained deacon in 1520 and priest three years later.[17] A further inscription, on fol. 225v, refers to ownership of the volume by another of Buriton's contemporaries, William Wey. Written on that folio is the line 'Wylhelmus Wey Possessor Huius Libri', and both there and elsewhere (cf. fols. 224v and 225) there are prayers for the soul of William Wey. It is highly probable that this refers to the 'William Weye' listed as one of the 'xii laye men to singe and serve in the Quere daylly' in the cathedral's 'Boke of Portyons' dated 28 April 1541.[18] At Christmas 1541 Wey apparently received two payments, first as a lay singing-man (the list recording this payment is almost identical with that drawn up in April of the same year), and secondly an additional amount 'for repetinge in the quiere'.[19] After this nothing further is known of him.

Subsequently, Add. 60577 found its way into the hands of Thomas Dackomb (1496 – c. 1572), priest, canon of Winchester, and an active collector of medieval manuscripts.[20] The son of Thomas Dackomb of Stepleton in Dorset, one of a prosperous landed family, the younger Thomas is first recorded in the Winchester area in 1519 when he was inducted as rector of St Peter Colebrook, Winchester, at the

[14] G. W. Kitchin and F. T. Madge, *Documents Relating to the Foundation of the Chapter of Winchester, A.D. 1541–1547* (London, 1889), pp. 19ff.

[15] *Ibid.*, p. 18.   [16] *Ibid.*, p. 15.

[17] Kitchin, *Compotus Rolls*, pp. 479–80.

[18] Kitchin and Madge, *Documents Relating to the Foundation*, p. 55.   [19] *Ibid.*, p. 61.

[20] For the most complete account of his life and activities as a book collector, see A. G. Watson, 'A Sixteenth-Century Collector: Thomas Dackomb, 1496 – c. 1572', *The Library*, 5th ser., vol. 18 (1963), pp. 204–17.

presentation of the abbess and convent of St Mary's. By 1531 he had moved to the post of *vicarius ecclesiasticus* of Nutley, also in the diocese of Winchester. There he seems to have remained, at least until 1535; after that nothing is known of him until March 1541–2, when his name is registered as one of the newly appointed pettycanons of Winchester Cathedral, at a salary of fifty shillings a quarter.[21] The new foundation required twelve pettycanons – a large number, needed 'not merely that each canon might have a kind of curate or representative, but because there had to be provision made for the serving of the many Chantries in the Cathedral'.[22] More specifically, it can be inferred from Henry VIII's statutes dated 20 June 1544 that, from the beginning, the incumbents of these new posts were to be 'quantum fieri possit eruditi, famae bonae et conversationis honestae, denique cantando periti id quod constare volumus judicio eorum qui in eadem Ecclesia artem musicam callent'.[23] In the list of pettycanons given in the 'Boke of Portyons', Dackomb alone is described as a secular priest (the others presumably having been regulars), and it has been plausibly suggested that he was called to Winchester from Nutley precisely because of his musical accomplishments.[24] As will be seen, that suggestion gains additional support from the contents of Add. 60577. Not long after taking up his new post at the cathedral Dackomb was also reappointed to his old living at St Peter Colebrook. As far as is known he held this for the rest of his life, as he also did the living of Tarrant Gunville in Dorset, to which he was presented in 1549. He died, at Tarrant Gunville, in 1572.

Dackomb's ownership of Add. 60577 is beyond doubt. His hand is verifiable from inscriptions in printed books and manuscripts that he owned; the inscription on fol. 2 is quite clearly in his hand, and the same note, in the same hand, occurs partly erased at the foot of the first folio.[25] Furthermore, fols. 59–60 contain a long poem copied by

---

[21] *Ibid.*, p. 205. A 'Thomas Dackhinson' is recorded in the 'Boke of Portyons' as receiving a quarterly stipend on Lady Day 1541/2; this is presumably Dackomb. For the documents see Kitchin and Madge, *Documents Relating to the Foundation*, p. 55.

[22] Kitchin and Madge, *op. cit.*, p. 9.

[23] *Ibid.*, p. 130.

[24] Watson, 'A Sixteenth-Century Collector', p. 205. For the list see note 21, above.

[25] For a list of books and manuscripts that he owned, see Watson, *op. cit.*, pp. 211–17. A sample of his *ex libris* inscription taken from British Library, Harley MS 12, fol. 1, is shown in Watson's article on p. 210 as Fig. 1.

Dackomb and signed at the end 'Finis per me D[ominum] Thoma[m] dakcomb Anno Domini 1549'. It seems highly likely that Dackomb acquired Add. 60577 directly from Wey, since both men are recorded as singers at Winchester Cathedral during the same period, Wey as a singing-man and Dackomb as a pettycanon.[26] But Dackomb's motives for owning this manuscript, or indeed any of the other two dozen or so printed books and manuscripts which passed through his hands, are less easily ascertained. The four printed books which are known to have come from his collection are all theological, and may represent his genuine intellectual interests. On the other hand his acquisition of manuscripts seems to be yet a further example of monks and priests deliberately saving items from certain destruction, and it is noticeable that all Dackomb's manuscripts were collected after 1540 – that is, only after the dispersal of books and manuscripts from religious institutions had begun. After a group of acquisitions made early in the decade there seems to have been a gap, punctuated only by Add. 60577, until 1550 when, perhaps prompted by the Act against Superstitious Books and Images (3 & 4 Ed. VI, c. 10) which ordered the destruction of service books of all kinds,[27] Dackomb's interest seems to have been reawakened. And, as with his first acquisitions, his principal source seems to have been the old library of St Swithun's. Sir George Warner's judgement that Dackomb had 'reverence enough for the past to preserve [monastic manuscripts]' and 'was the means of saving most of the old Winchester MSS' seems justifiable, though recent identification of some seventy surviving items from the St Swithun's library necessitates modification of the latter claim.[28]

[26] Kitchin and Madge, *Documents Relating to the Foundation*, p. 55.

[27] J. R. Tanner, *Tudor Constitutional Documents, A.D. 1485–1603*, 2nd, rev. edn (Cambridge, 1930), p. 114.

[28] G. F. Warner and H. A. Wilson, *The Benedictional of Saint Æthelwold, Bishop of Winchester, 963–984. Reproduced in Facsimile from the MS. in the Library of the Duke of Devonshire at Chatsworth* (Oxford, 1910), pp. xxxii, n. 3, and xlii. In fact, although Dackomb acquired most of his manuscripts from the old library of St Swithun's, a large number of items from the library which did not pass through his hands have come to light since Warner's judgement. See N. R. Ker, *Medieval Libraries of Great Britain: A List of Surviving Books*, 2nd edn (London, 1964), listing over seventy books. There is a suggestion, though from a highly unreliable source, that the Old Hall Manuscript was used at Winchester and may have passed through Dackomb's hands. For a thorough discussion and evaluation of this idea see M. Bent, 'The Old Hall Manuscript: A Paleographical Study', Ph.D. diss., Cambridge University, 1968, pp. 21–6.

Unfortunately Dackomb's will has not been traced and no inventory of his property is known to survive; consequently, rather little is known of how he disposed of his books. A number were given away during his lifetime, and by the early years of the seventeenth century the more spectacular examples were finding their way into the libraries of bibliophiles such as Robert Cotton, Sir Simonds D'Ewes, and Baron Lumley.[29] The pattern is a familiar one: manuscripts dispersed at the Dissolution fell into the hands of a comparatively unknown collector, were released from his possession towards the end of the century, and by the first decades of the seventeenth century were being absorbed into the libraries of great collectors.[30] As a visually more modest item Add. 60577 probably remained in Dackomb's possession until his death (and there is some indication that, in contrast to the other manuscripts in his collection, it functioned in part as a commonplace book). Subsequently it disappeared into the obscurity from which it has only just emerged.[31]

The history of the manuscript, which seems to have been passed from hand to hand and to have served as a commonplace book for successive owners, is not untypical of such anthologies of the period. At some time towards the end of the fifteenth century a number of existing texts were gathered up and bound together with blank quires pricked and ruled for additions. Some pieces may have been added not long after the 'Virgin and Child' binder had finished his work, but a substantial body of material was also added about the middle of the sixteenth century. This includes some minor additions to the first, earlier section of the manuscript, including the poem copied by Dackomb and another English poem (fols. 57–58) concordant with *Tottel's Miscellany*, but most of the mid-century writing occurs in a single stretch at the end of the book. Among these additions, written in a number of hands, are some verse, a sermon, and music in both mensural notation and tablature, and it is noticeable that a number of the non-musical items have a distinctly

---

[29] Watson, 'A Sixteenth-Century Collector', pp. 209–10.

[30] F. Wormald and C. E. Wright, *The English Library before 1700* (London, 1958), p. 159.

[31] I have been unable to trace Henry Bavy, whose late-sixteenth-century signature occurs on fol. 86v. After this there are no further indications of provenance except for the illegible traces of a nineteenth-century *ex libris* pasted to the inside of the upper cover. The anonymous owner who sold the manuscript at Sotheby's in June 1979 had acquired it some twenty years earlier in Yorkshire.

recusant flavour. First, fols. 191–204 carry a substantial piece of prose headed 'sermon of the late bosshop of winton John whit made before quene Elizabeth' and with a note at the end: 'This sermon the busshop of winton made at the buriall of Queen Mary whose name was John whit And he was put in prison for his labor.' John White (*c.* 1510–1560) had his early education at Winchester College, where he was admitted as a scholar in 1521, and then went to New College, Oxford, where he held a fellowship during 1527–34.[32] Two years later he returned to Winchester as headmaster, and in 1542 became warden of the college, a post which he retained until 1554, the year in which he was promoted Bishop of Lincoln. By then his career had marked him out as a fierce opponent of Protestantism and he had, only a few years before, been excommunicated by his fellow-Wykehamist John Philpot, Archdeacon of Winchester, 'for preaching naughty doctrine'.[33] With Mary's accession White's fortunes changed. He now became a staunch supporter of the new regime and an important public figure, being one of the three commissioners for the trial of Bishops Ridley and Latimer in September 1555, and preaching at the opening of Mary's first parliament one month later. In the next year White's career advanced further with his appointment as Bishop of Winchester, but with Mary's death his fall from grace was rapid. At the Queen's funeral, on 13 December 1558, he preached a sermon on a text from Ecclesiasticus IV.2, which spoke warmly of Mary but was taken to be uncomplimentary to the new monarch. In particular, a passage in which, apparently referring to the preachers of the day, he remarked that 'melius est canis vivus leone mortuo' was thought to refer to Elizabeth.[34] As a result, White was commanded to 'keep his house', but then early in 1559 was called before the Council and 'after a good admonicion geven him, was sett at lyberty and discharged'. He voted against the Bill of Supremacy in the House of Lords in March, took part in the two abortive conferences between nine Romanists and nine Anglicans held in the choir of Westminster Abbey in March and April, and at

---

[32] For his biography see Emden, *Biographical Register*, pp. 621–2.

[33] R. Eden, *The Examinations and Writings of J. Philpot* (Cambridge, 1842), p. 82. For further details of Philpot himself see Emden, *Biographical Register*, pp. 449–50.

[34] Until now, the unique source for White's controversial sermon has been thought to be British Library, Sloane MS 1578. See S. Ayscough, *A Catalogue of the Manuscripts Preserved in the British Museum, Hitherto Undescribed*, 2 vols. (London, 1782), I, p. 8.

the close of the second of them was removed together with the Bishop of Lincoln to the Tower on account of the offence which his opposition had given. In June, after a fresh attempt to induce him to take the Oath of Supremacy had failed, he was deprived of his bishopric and sent back to the Tower. Here his health began to give way; in July he was released to live with relatives, and on 12 January 1560 he died.[35]

The special character of White's sermon, known from only one other copy, suggests that Add. 60577 was still in the Winchester area when this text was copied into it, most probably in the hands of Dackomb or one of his circle. Dackomb himself is known to have had Catholic loyalties,[36] and at least some of the pieces in the book would certainly have rendered it liable for destruction and its owner fit for prosecution had it come into the hands of the authorities. And it was during this final period of the manuscript's traceable history, while it was in the possession of Winchester recusants during the 1550s and 1560s, that the musical items were most likely copied into it. The connections between Dackomb and White are clear enough, but further links are provided by the music itself, and by a text on fol. 108 headed 'The copi of a letter written by Elis Heywood at Padua in Italie to John Heywood his father in London'. The Heywoods were a prominent recusant family. Together with his brother Jasper, one of the most important English Jesuits of his day, Ellis (1530–78) went to Italy in 1552, and was for some time at Florence where he enjoyed the patronage of Cardinal Pole. It seems unlikely that Ellis returned to England, and he seems to have spent the rest of his life in northern Europe, being received into the Jesuits at Dillengen in Bavaria in 1566 and living subsequently at the Jesuit Colleges in Antwerp and Louvain.[37] His father John (c. 1497–1580) was a well-known epigrammatist, musician and playwright whose best-known literary work, *The Spider and the Flie*, was written as a commentary on current social discontents and as a panegyric on the promise of the reign of Queen Mary, during which he enjoyed considerable favour.

[35] For further details see J. Strype, *Annals of the Reformation and Establishment of Religion, and Other Various Occurrences in the Church of England, during Queen Elizabeth's Happy Reign . . . with an Appendix of Original Papers*, 7 vols. (Oxford, 1824), I, p. 213, and the account in *Dictionary of National Biography*, ed. L. Stephen and S. Lee, 63 vols. (London, 1885–1900), XXI, pp. 52ff.

[36] Watson, 'A Sixteenth-Century Collector', p. 206.

[37] *Dictionary of National Biography*, XXVI, p. 329.

Traditionally, John is thought to have been introduced at court by Sir Thomas More. He was appointed first as a singing-man in June 1519, and by 1525 was being paid as a virginalist, a post which was confirmed with a life pension in 1528. Despite implication in a plot against Archbishop Cranmer in 1544, he managed to escape the severe penalties that could have resulted from his successful indictment for treason. Returning to court life, he continued to stage royal entertainments for both Mary and her successor, but on the appointment of the commission to enforce the Act of Uniformity he left England without licence, with his wife, and settled in Malines. Later, after his wife's death, quarters were found for him with the Jesuits by Ellis, first at Antwerp, and then at Louvain where he died.[38]

The original of Ellis's letter was presumably written before John left England in 1564, and this accords with what little is known of the dates of Ellis's time in Italy. The text itself is now mutilated in Add. 60577, but this copy was most probably made while the contents were still topical, and if not by Heywood himself at least by someone close to him. And, of course, the letter is interesting not only because it further strengthens the recusant character of the mid-century additions to Add. 60577, but also because Heywood's connection with the manuscript may help to explain the presence and character of the music in the book. Written by a number of scribes, these additions fall into three groups. The first (fols. 190–190v) consists of two dances in French lute tablature, one headed 'La Galantyne', neither attributed. The copy of Bishop White's sermon then intervenes (fols. 191–204), after which there is a long stretch of keyboard music written not on properly drawn or ruled staves but on the dry-point rulings made when the book was first put together and designed to carry additional literary items. The copying is clearly amateur, but the texts themselves are not without interest. This is particularly true of the first composition, a sequence of variations on the well-known bass pattern of 'Hugh Aston's Ground'. O. W. Neighbour has recently remarked, in his discussion of Byrd's set on this same ground, that Byrd may have taken the bass from one of Aston's pieces, most probably the set of twelve variations for three-

[38] The most recent general account of John Heywood is that in Emden, *Biographical Register*, pp. 288–9.

part consort called 'Hugh Aston's Maske'. That set survives complete except for the bass in Oxford, Christ Church Library, MSS 982 and 979, 'with a wretched additional part in 981 by William Whytbroke who adjusted Aston's parts here and there to make it fit'.[39] The original version occurs without attribution in Panmure MS 10 in the National Library of Scotland at Edinburgh, but without the last five variations. In Neighbour's opinion, it is unlikely that the final variations found in the Christ Church manuscripts were added entirely by Whytbroke since the inexpert part in Christ Church 981 gives the impression of an addition throughout the entire set.[40] In these circumstances, the presence of another text of 'Hugh Aston's Ground' (here also without attribution) is of considerable interest, though it hardly resolves the question of whether or not Aston's original keyboard version consisted of twelve variations, the usual number in a set at this time. Frustratingly, the version in Add. 60577 consists of ten statements of the ground, of which the last stops short of the cadence.

There follows a series of nine dances and other miscellaneous pieces, mostly in three parts, written by the same hand. One is headed (accurately) 'galliard', but the rest are undescribed and unascribed except for that beginning on folio 209v, which is signed at the end (in the same ink as the music) 'John Whit' after the bass stave and 'Whit' after the treble. Considering the context in which it is found, this undoubtedly refers to Bishop John White, otherwise unrecorded as a composer, and so considerably strengthens the links between the section of keyboard music in the manuscript and the Winchester Catholics. The style of the music suggests that it was composed around 1540; it is most likely to have been copied out shortly afterwards, while it was still fashionable.

After a further intervention of assorted miscellaneous entries and pen trials, there are some final music additions consisting of five canons (fols. 221–222). The first (fol. 221), in three parts, sets the text *Ave Maria*, though the significance of this should not be exaggerated. While a text of this kind would certainly have been contentious around the mid sixteenth century, Latin and even liturgical

---

[39] O. Neighbour, *The Consort and Keyboard Music of William Byrd* (London, 1978), p. 128.

[40] *Ibid*. I wish to thank Mr Fortune for his assistance.

texts are not uncommon in the early-seventeenth-century catch and round repertories, and Ravenscroft's *Pammelia* is full of them. The next canon (also fol. 221) is headed 'foure parts' and has the words 'As I me walkid in a May morning'; the piece is concordant with one in *Pammelia*, as is the fourth canon (fol. 221v), 'The old dog, the old dog as he lay in his den a buffa'.[41] Both these pieces also occur in the Lant Roll, a collection of fifty-seven rounds and canons copied by Thomas Lant and dated 1580.[42] That these pieces were also probably copied into Add. 60577 about the mid-century further underlines the highly retrospective character of *Pammelia*, as well as the intrinsic value of the manuscript itself as the only known source for some of them and the earliest for others. The third canon, 'Trol the bol [pass the bowl] and drink to me' (fol. 221v), may be the song begun by Old Merrithought in *The Knight of the Burning Pestle*, though given the traditionally accepted date of the play's composition that is more likely to be the different piece with the same opening words also published by Ravenscroft.[43] In the final piece, 'The mil gothe and let her go so merely' (fol. 222), the canonic voice generates three parts to be sung over an independent bass.

As a source of music, Add. 60577 is of considerable textual value, not only for the canons but also – since so few sources of any kind survive and since moreover it contains *unica* – for the keyboard music. The presence of music at all in the manuscript may be accounted for by its association with Wey, Dackomb, White or, most

[41] See *Pammelia. Musickes Miscellanie. Or, Mixed Varietie of Pleasant Roundelayes, and Delightful Catches, of* 3.4.5.6.7.8.9.10 *Parts in One . . .* (London, 1609), nos. 53 and 21 respectively. 'The old dogge' is a three-voice canon at the unison, and the version in *Pammelia* is close to though not identical with that in Add. 60577.

[42] Cambridge, King's College, Rowe Music Library MS 1. See J. Vlasto, 'An Elizabethan Anthology of Rounds', *Musical Quarterly*, 40 (1954), pp. 222–34. This source, consisting of a number of parchment strips glued together to form a roll sixteen feet long, contains forty-eight pieces which are also found in Ravenscroft's collections.

[43] Thus *The Knight of the Burning Pestle*:

To what end should any man be said in this world? Give me a man that when he goes to hanging cries

Troll the black bowl to me!

and a woman that will sing a catch in her travail.

(F. Bowers (ed.), *The Dramatic Works in the Beaumont and Fletcher Canon*, 1 (Cambridge, 1966), 11.430ff.) The play is thought to have been written in 1607–10, and the song from which Old Merrithought quotes is almost certainly *Pammelia*, no. 62, beginning 'Troll, troll. troll the bole to me and I will troll the same again to thee'.

intriguingly perhaps in view of his career as a court musician and impresario, John Heywood, or any combination of these. It is most likely though that the music was added after the manuscript had passed into Dackomb's hands – that is, at a time when a number of literary texts revealing continuing Winchester connections and strong Catholic sympathies were also copied into it. The prominent recusant tone of these later additions is not particularly surprising. Few counties had been more fundamentally Catholic in culture during the first half of the sixteenth century than Hampshire, a county which contains the ancient capital of England and where monastic institutions of all kinds abounded.[44] The roots of this culture lay deep in the past and were not easily destroyed when the doctrines of the Reformation spread through the country. As soon as attempts were made to enforce the services prescribed by the Act of Uniformity there was opposition in Winchester. The Act laid down that the new forms of service were to be introduced by 24 June 1559, but on 27 June the Spanish Ambassador was able to report encouragingly to Philip II that 'in the neighbourhood of Winchester they have refused to receive the church service book . . . and the clergy of the diocese had assembled to discuss what they should do. No Mass was being said, whereat the congregations were very disturbed.'[45] And Nicholas Sanders, an old Wykehamist and leader of the English Catholic exiles in Louvain, wrote afterwards that at the beginning of the reign 'not so many as one in a hundred are infected with the new religion',[46] though he was hardly unbiased in the matter. Bishop John White's refusal (together with all the Catholic bishops except possibly Kitchen of Llandaff) to take the Oath of Supremacy made him, in effect, the first Winchester recusant, and it is noticeable that his example seems to have been quite widely followed by the Hampshire clergy. This is yet further indication of how resilient Catholicism proved to be in the county since, throughout the country as a whole, no less than three-quarters of the

[44] The best general account of Hampshire recusancy during this period is J. E. Paul, 'The Hampshire Recusants in the Reign of Elizabeth I with Some Reference to the Problem of Church-Baptists', Ph.D. diss., University of Southampton, 1958.

[45] M. A. S. Hume, *Calendar of Letters and State Papers Relating to English Affairs (of the Reign of Elizabeth, 1558–1603), Preserved Principally in the Archives of Simancas*, 4 vols. (London, 1892–9), I, p. 78 no. 39.

[46] Sander's report to Cardinal Morone as cited in Paul, 'The Hampshire Recusants', p. 7.

priests forsook both the Mass and the Roman See with apparently no more misgivings than their Henrician predecessors had on abandoning the idea of Papal supremacy.[47] Arguably, it was the government's realisation of the strength of reaction in the Winchester diocese which caused it to allow it, together with that of Chichester, to escape the general visitation at the beginning of Elizabeth's reign and to delay consecration of White's successor, Robert Horne, until the early months of 1561. The surviving records of Horne's episcopate show him to have been energetic, regular and thorough in the visitations which he began shortly after his consecration; by exercising the power of excommunication and by insisting that the fine under the Act of Uniformity for abstention from church services be levied, he made a determined effort to eradicate Catholicism in his diocese. During the early years instances of recusancy or refusal to communicate are not recorded in great numbers, but it is clear that Horne was able to uncover a good deal of irregularity on the part of both clergy and laity. Horne himself seems to have been an ardent Puritan, grim and humourless, and an earnest and evidently efficient servant of the Crown, but despite the severity of his campaign, Catholicism seems to have lingered, supported by the educational and literary work of the Wykehamist exiles on the continent.[48]

Such a brief account can, of necessity, do no more than provide a preliminary examination of Add. 60577 as a document of literary, cultural and intellectual history. The process of identifying the musical and literary texts which it contains has not been exhaustive, and the factual and biographical information about successive scribes and owners is similarly far from complete. Yet apart from its obvious textual value, the manuscript is remarkably interesting as a document of taste and testimony to the growth of literacy (including musical literacy), and it is possible to draw some preliminary conclusions about these aspects of the volume. If the initial owner was William Wayneflete, the contents of the earliest layer fit well with what is known of his life and intellectual interests, and the circles in which he moved. His reason for compiling such a book, and the reason of others for preserving it, was almost certainly a desire to record works that appealed to the tastes of successive owners,

---

[47] P. Hughes, *The Reformation in England*, 3 vols. (London, 1950), III, p. 38.

[48] All details of Horne's episcopacy are based on the extensive discussion in Paul, 'The Hampshire Recusants', pp. 11ff.

improving and uplifting their spirits, educating them, delighting their ears with music, and healing their bodies with medical receipts. Although Add. 60577 probably remained within the precincts of Winchester Cathedral for at least half a century, the additions made by identifiable Winchester clerics during that period reflect the growing religious debate. Finally, as it passed out of the cathedral and into the hands of Thomas Dackomb, the book's contents began to mirror the religious sympathies and musical tastes of Winchester recusant circles. In their desire to preserve these texts, successive owners of the manuscript seem to underline an attitude typical of a society whose upper and middle reaches had, with growing enthusiasm, begun to accept the book as a natural and even vital part of its domestic life.

BRITISH LIBRARY, ADDITIONAL MS 60577 BRIEF DESCRIPTION AND SUMMARY INVENTORY

228 fols.; (i) + 226 + (i). Copied on vellum and paper, lacks at least one gathering after fol. 37, 2 leaves after fol. 66, 3 leaves after fol. 218, most of fol. 131* and half of fol. 108. There are single blanks after fols. 56, 116 and 189. The manuscript is now foliated in modern pencil (i) + 1–131, 131*–225 + (i). The gatherings are of 10 leaves except for i^8 [first pasted down], vii^6, xx^9 [but complete], last.[2] The gatherings are constructed with the outer- and innermost bifolia of vellum and the remaining leaves of paper; the only exception is the seventh gathering where the outer bifolium is of paper. The original contents, usually occupying 30 to 33 lines, are written by a single scribe in an English cursive bookhand. Some decorations, paragraph marks, headings etc. are executed in red ink. Many alterations and additions have been made by a number of sixteenth-century scribes. The binding is Winchester work by the 'Virgin and Child' binder using seven tools on tanned calf over wooden boards. The spine has been subsequently strengthened. One of the prose pieces in the original layer is dated 1487. Provenance: (1) The Cathedral Priory of St Swithun, Winchester, (2) John Brynstone, monk of St Swithun's, (3) John Buriton, monk of St Swithun's, (4) Thomas Dackomb, minor canon of Winchester Cathedral. A number of other names occur in a sixteenth-century hand, and there are traces of an illegible nineteenth-century bookplate, but nothing further is securely known of the book's history until it was bought in Yorkshire c. 1960 by the owner who subsequently sold it anonymously at Sotheby Parke Bernet and

Co. in London on 19 June 1979. It was subsequently acquired by the British Library who have now carried out extensive repairs using wheat-starch paste and handmade Bareham Green paper.

Pastedown	Various texts including notes on a great flood of 1442.
fols. 1–7v	A herbal, a lapidary, proverbs, rhyming prayers in Latin.
fols. 8–22	A dialogue headed 'Franciscus Petrarcha' followed by the invocation 'Assit principio Sancta maria meo'. It begins 'I am soore astoned when I remember me/ How I entred thys lyff & how I shal oute agayne'. This is an English translation of the Prologue and Book I of the dialogue between St Augustine and Petrarch from the latter's *Secretum*.[49]
fols. 22v–24	A poem, addressed to the Bishop of Winchester, opening '[R]yght noble & blessede fader to whom of excellence/ The flower ys proclamed thoroweought thys realme wyde'.
fols. 24v–37v	Verse headed '[T]his is the boke of the governaunce of kynges and princes', and opening '[G]od almyghti save & conferme our kynge/ In all vertue to hys encrees of glorye'. The text comprises the first 119 stanzas of Lydgate and Burgh, translation of the *Secretum secretorum*.[50]
fols. 38–44v	A prose treatise, lacking its opening, on virtues and morals.
fols. 44v–46	Tags and verses in Latin and English, including one very secular sixteenth-century addition (fol. 45v): 'Lyke as Women have facis/ to sat me[n]s harts on fyer/ So have they placis/ to quenche mens hot desyre'.
fol. 46v	Ruled, otherwise blank.
fols. 47–49	Verses on misfortune, opening 'Lyfte up the eeys of your wordly advertence/ Yee that be blynde with worldes vanytee'. On fol. 49 a sixteenth-century hand has written 'Dan

[49] W. H. Draper (trans.), *Petrarch's Secret, or the Soul's Conflict with Passion. Three Dialogues between Himself and S. Augustine* (London, 1911), introduction, p. xi, claims his to be the earliest English translation.

[50] See R. Steele, *Lydgate and Burgh's Secrets of Old Philosoffres. A Version of the 'Secreta Secretorum', edited from the Sloane MS. 2464* (London, 1894). Some other sources for the work are noted in D. W. Singer, *Catalogue of Latin and Vernacular Alchemical Manuscripts in Great Britain and Ireland Dating from Before the XVI Century*, 3 vols. (Brussels, 1928–31), I, pp. 27–31, and C. Brown and R. H. Robbins, *The Index of Middle English Verse*, p. 150, no. 935.

John lyddegate, monke of Bury'. The text presents fourteen verses from Lydgate's *A Thoroughfare of Woe*.[51]

fols. 49–50   Liturgical instructions, prayers.

fols. 50v–51   An account headed 'Oxenforde', and beginning 'Clerkys
of Oxenforde have determynid'. It deals with the appearance of comets.

fols. 51–51v   Short passages in English and Latin, including a cure for
headaches attributed to Abbot Stanley.

fols. 52–53   Poem on the imminence of death, each line partly in
English and partly in Latin, beginning 'When thous leste
wenythe. Veniet mors te superare/ Thus thy grave
grenethe. Ergo mortis memorare'.[52]

fols. 53–53v   A poem in English, beginning 'Lorde wherto ys this
worlde soo gaye/ Whos blysse so soone ys shake awaye'.

fols. 54–56   A sermon in English on the text 'Quis Ascendit in mon-
tem domini: aut quis in loco sancto eius?' It begins 'Lys-
tenythe a while: and thenke ye nott longe/ Turne to that
Lorde as the prophete can saye'.

fol. 56v   A verse alphabet headed 'C[r]ystys crosse be oure spede/
With grace mercye in all oure nede', and beginning 'A to
amerous to adventurous avyse or ye answere/ B to busye
to bolde bowdre not to broode'.[53]

fol. 57   Ruled, various pen trials.

fols. 57–58   A poem in English headed 'totus mundus in maligno est
positus', and beginning 'Complayne we maye wiche ys a
wise'. It is dated at the end 'yn the ere of o[r] lorde
Mcccccxlix'. The same piece is found anonymously in
Tottel's Miscellany.[54]

[51] See H. N. MacCracken, *The Minor Poems of John Lydgate*, 2 vols. (London, 1934), II,
pp. 822ff.

[52] See K. Brunner, 'Mittelenglische Todesgedichte', *Archiv für das Studium der neueren
Sprachen*, 167 (1935), p. 30, after London, British Library, Additional MS 37049.
A further source is noted in R. H. Robbins and J. L. Cutler, *Supplement to the Index
of Middle English Verse* (Lexington, Ky., 1965), p. 467.

[53] Rhyming alphabets are extremely common in prose and verse anthologies of the
period. See for example the one headed 'Cryste crosse me spede A.B.C./ The grace
of the graye distaffe' (otherwise quite different from the text in Add. 60577), in
T. F. Dibdin, *Typographical Antiquities; or, The History of Printing in England, Scotland
and Ireland*, 4 vols. (London, 1810–19), II, p. 368.

[54] This piece appears not in the first edition, but in all subsequent early ones. See
H. E. Rollins, *Tottel's Miscellany (1557–1587)*, 2 vols. (Cambridge, Mass., 1965), I,
pp. 232–4. According to M. Crum (ed.), *First-Line Index of English Poetry,
1500–1800, in Manuscripts of the Bodleian Library*, Oxford, 2 vols. (Oxford 1969), I,
p. 174, it is also found in MS Rawl. poet. 82, fol. 1 verso.

fols. 59–60v	A poem in English, beginning 'And yff thous wyst what thyng yt were'. It concludes 'per me dominum Thomam dakcomb A° d. 1549'.[55]
fols. 60v–61	Various short verses.
fols. 61v–62	Medical recipes.
fol. 62v	Ruled, pen trials.
fols. 63–64	Hymn in English and Latin, beginning '[O]mnipotentem semper adorant/ Operacious hevenly and erthely all'.
fols. 64v–65	Hymn in English verse, beginning 'Hyghe & almyghty, creator of alle/ Spyryte of lyff, & gyffer of gladnes'.
fols. 65v–66v	Poem against the rich, beginning '[O] lorde what ys thys worldes wele/ Rychesse revell or grate araye'.
fols. 67–77	A Latin–English *vulgaria* containing sentences to be used as translation exercises. A few are in verse.
fols. 77–78	Prayers in Latin beginning 'Omnes gentes plaudite', followed by indulgences and absolutions in English.
fols. 78v–80	Ruled, pen trials.
fols. 80v–81	French verse on the Siege of the Castle of Love, headed 'Dieu chastell damours vous demand' nomes le premier fundement', and beginning 'Apres nommer le maistre mure/ Qui plus le face fort et steure'.
fols. 81–85v	Bidding prayers in English, beginning 'In the honor reverence and wyrshype of oure lorde', and including prayers for the Pope, the Bishop of Winchester, the king and queen, etc.[56]
fols. 86–86v	Ruled, fol. 86v signed 'Henry Bavy' in a sixteenth-century hand.
fols. 87–89	Devotional prose in Latin.
fol. 89v	Latin verse, opening 'Si tibi pulcra domine'.
fols. 90–91v	The opinions of six masters on tribulation, beginning 'Here bygynnethe a lytyl shorte tret[is]'.[57]
fol. 91v	Poem on Fortune, beginning 'Ye that stonde in welthe & grete plesaunce', followed by four lines on the Name of Christ.[58]
fols. 92–92v	Seven-verse poem on the futility of human existence, beginning 'When lyff ys moost lovyde & dethe ys moost

[55] According to Crum (ed.), *First-Line Index*, 1, also in MS Gough Norfolk 43, fol. 52v.

[56] Cf. the traditions outlined in H. O. Coxe, *Forms of Bidding Prayer* (Oxford, 1940).

[57] See C. Horstman (ed.), *Yorkshire Writers. Richard Rolle of Hampole, An English Father of the Church and His Followers*, 2 vols. (London, 1895), II, p. 390, after British Library, MS Royal 17.A.xxv.

[58] Cf. Cambridge, Magdalene College, MS Pepys 2125, fol. 118a.

	hatyde/ Dethe drawythe a draught & makythe man full nakyde'.
fol. 93	A humorous verse (described in the text as 'bonus cantus') in Latin and English. It begins 'Amorning when I am callide to scola/ Da matre vel materia'.
fols. 93v–94v	Ruled, pen trials (on fol. 94v).
fols. 95–107v	A dialogue, often in straightforward terminology, between two lovers on the forms of love both courtly and physical. Headed 'Amor vincit omnia', it opens '[F]are sir, I aske you, whether ye hadde levyr rejoye without desyrynge', and ends 'Here endythe ye demaundes off love. M° CCCC° lxxx° vii°.
fol. 108	English verse beginning 'O splendid spectakyll'. Also 'The copi of a letter written by Elis Heywood at Padua in Italie to John Heywood his father in London'.
fols. 108v–110v	Ruled, pen trials and (fol. 110) a drawing labelled (somewhat unconvincingly) 'This is a fesant'.
fols. 111–114v	A version of the Nine Virtues, beginning: '[Y]t was an holy man'.[59]
fols. 114v–115	A version of the Short Charter of the *Carta Generis Humani*.[60]
fols. 116v–115v	(i.e. begun on one leaf and completed on the previous one). Poems in English, beginning 'Why dare I not compleyn to my lady?/ Whie woll I not aske grace in humble wyse?'. (See Postscript, p. 116 below.)
fol. 116	Ruled.
fols. 117–118v	Notes on astrology in Latin.
fols. 119–119v	Poem in English, beginning 'Maryegolde ys an herbe full gracyouse/ Who so knowethe all his vertuouse'.
fols. 120–181	English religious texts, prayers, Bible quotations etc., including the Seven Works of Bodily Mercy, the Five Bodily and Spiritual Senses, the Seven Gifts of the Holy Ghost, the Twelve Articles of Belief, etc.
fols. 181v–183v	Ruled.
fols. 184–189v	A treatise on the Twelve Degrees of Meekness preceeded by a dedicatory letter addressed to a '[R]elygiouse & goostyle belovyde Syster'.
fols. 190–190v	Two dances in French lute tablature, the first headed 'La galantyne'.

[59] See H. E. Allen, *Writings Ascribed to R. Rolle, Hermit of Hampole, and Materials for His Biography* (London, 1927), pp. 317–20.

[60] See M. C. Spalding, *The Middle English Charters of Christ* (Bryn Mawr, Pa., 1914), pp. 4–16.

fols. 191–204	A prose 'sermon of the late bosshop of winton John whit made before quene Elizabeth', in English, ending 'This sermon the busshop of winton made at the buriall of Queen Mary whose name was John whit And he was put in prison for his labor.'[61]
fols. 204v–208	Keyboard music.[62]
fols. 208v–209	Ruled, pen trials.
fols. 209v–214	Keyboard music. Fol. 212 also contains a four-line extract from Piers Ploughman beginning 'Whene you se the sonne a mysse . . .'
fols. 214v–215	Ruled.
fols. 215v–216	Medical remedies in English.
Fol. 216v	Ruled, pen trials.
fols. 217–219	Miscellaneous notes, pen trials, medical remedies etc.
fols. 219–220v	Ruled.
fols. 221–222	Five canons.[63]
fols. 222v–223	Ruled, various tags, pen trials.
fols. 223–224	Notes on digestion.
fol. 225	Ruled, various notes, pen trials.
fol. 226	(pasted down to back cover). Various notes of ownership, and a list of obedientiaries of Winchester Priory, *c.* 1500.

[61] The only known concordance is British Library, Sloan MS 1578: 'Queene Maries Funerall Sermon preached by Io White Bhp of Winchester at Westm[r] the viij[th] of December A.D. 1558', originally part of a larger (and now dispersed) manuscript.
[62] See above, pp. 106–7.   [63] See above, pp. 107–8.

POSTSCRIPT

A facsimile edition of Add. 60577 is to appear shortly with introductions by Edward Wilson and Iain Fenlon.

In 'Some New Texts of Early Tudor Songs', *Notes and Queries*, August 1980, Mr Wilson notes that the seven poems on fols. 116v–115v are in fact song texts. Two of these are concordant with the Fayrfax Manuscript (British Library, Additional MS 5465) and a third with the Ritson Manuscript (British Library, Additional MS 5665).

116

7

ON ITALIAN INSTRUMENTAL
ENSEMBLE MUSIC IN THE LATE
FIFTEENTH CENTURY

Louise Litterick

HISTORIES of Renaissance music tend, at least by implication, to locate the earliest substantial repertory of compositions for instrumental ensemble in mid-sixteenth-century Italy.[1] Such antecedents as are known seem to represent at best a sporadic activity; and the search for further candidates has suffered from a prevailing uncertainty as to just how they are to be recognised in the first place.[2] As I have reported elsewhere, however, an investigation into the performance practice of Franco-Netherlandish secular polyphony of the late fifteenth century has revealed an earlier instrumental repertory of surprising scope and depth. Briefly, it has become clear that virtually all Italian sources containing chansons and related genres – a sizeable body of manuscripts originating in Florence, Naples, and various north Italian centres, as well as Petrucci's first prints – were intended for use by instrumentalists and that virtually all of the music in them written by composers active in Italy was destined from the start for instrumental performance. Indeed, this large group of ensemble pieces, which drew on the talents of figures as significant as Martini, Josquin, Isaac, and others, represents the

---

[1] For example, the chapter 'Instrumental Music of the 16th Century' in Gustave Reese, *Music in the Renaissance*, rev. edn (New York, 1959) mentions no ensemble compositions by anyone earlier than Willaert; the comparable chapter in Howard Mayer Brown, *Music in the Renaissance* (Englewood Cliffs, N.J., 1976) expands this picture only to the extent of referring to Eustachio Romano's duos of 1521.

[2] Cf. *Petrucci: Harmonice musices Odhecaton A*, ed. Helen Hewitt and Isabel Pope, Mediaeval Academy of America Studies and Documents 5 (Cambridge, Mass., 1942), pp. 74–8; see also Dietrich Kämper, *Studien zur instrumentalen Ensemblemusik des 16. Jahrhunderts in Italien*, Analecta Musicologica 10 (Cologne and Vienna, 1970), pp. 39–43 (there is an Italian transl., *La musica strumentale nel rinascimento* (Rome, 1976); references in my notes are to the German edn).

chief focus of secular composition by Franco-Netherlanders in Italy.[3]

The very existence of such an extensive instrumental repertory so much earlier than formerly suspected naturally raises a number of questions. The compositions themselves, moreover, raise questions of their own; and it is with the music and the issues most immediately connected with it that the present discussion begins.

Although the repertory appears highly diverse, most of the compositions within it fall into three types. Not surprisingly, all three have vocal antecedents. One category of piece, usually for four parts, is based on a popular melody that is generally, although not invariably, treated in canon; examples of this genre include Josquin's well-known *Adieu mes amours* and *Basiez moy*.[4] Another type comprises compositions in which one or more voices of a *forme-fixe* chanson are set among two or three newly written parts often characterised by faster rhythmic motion and the repetition of short motives; pieces of this sort include the numerous settings of individual voices from Hayne van Ghizeghem's *De tous biens plaine* and Ockeghem's *D'ung aultre amer*.[5]

The third and most important type of composition, both quantitatively and artistically, is what might best be called the instrumental chanson[6] – a genre represented by such works as Josquin's *Cela sans plus*, Martini's *De la bonne chiere*, Isaac's *Helas que devera mon cuer*, or Ghiselin's *La Alfonsina*.[7] Like the preceding genre, the instrumental

---

[3] See Louise Litterick, 'Performing Franco-Netherlandish Secular Music of the Late 15th Century: Texted and Untexted Parts', *Early Music*, 8 (1980), pp. 474–85.

[4] See *Werken van Josquin des Prés*, ed. Albert Smijers, Myroslaw Antonowycz, and Willem Elders (Amsterdam, 1922–68), *Wereldlijke Werken*, nos. 35 and 20a.

[5] For lists of settings based on these compositions, see Howard Mayer Brown, *Music in the French Secular Theater, 1400–1550* (Cambridge, Mass., 1963), pp. 204–6 and 209–10.

[6] I have borrowed this term from Kämper, *Studien zur instrumentalen Ensemblemusik*, pp. 66–73, although I use it in a less restrictive sense than he does; as employed here, it covers not only the specific subgenre to which he applies it but also the type of piece that he labels 'Fantasia' (pp. 73–81), as well as a number of miscellaneous compositions discussed on pp. 57–64.

[7] *Cela sans plus* appears in *Werken van Josquin des Prés*, *Wereldlijke Werken*, no. 44; *De la bonne chiere* can be found in *Johannes Martini: Secular Pieces*, ed. Edward G. Evans, Jr, Recent Researches in the Music of the Middle Ages and Early Renaissance 1 (Madison, Wisc., 1975), pp. 7–9; *Helas que devera mon cuer* is published in *Heinrich Isaac: Weltliche Werke*, ed. Johannes Wolf, Denkmäler der Tonkunst in Österreich 27 (Vienna, 1907), p. 75; *La Alfonsina* appears in *Johannes Ghiselin-Verbonnet: Opera omnia*, ed. Clytus Gottwald, Corpus Mensurabilis Musicae ser. 23, vol. IV (n.p., 1968), no. 21.

chanson represents an offshoot of the *forme-fixe* chanson. But while it may occasionally draw thematic material from a specific model,[8] it never incorporates an entire pre-existent line; this formal autonomy makes it perhaps the first genre in the history of Western music whose structure unfolds without reference to any external scaffolding, be it a poem, a melody, or a series of dance steps. The debt of the instrumental chanson to its vocal antecedent is a more general one; what *forme-fixe* pieces, and more specifically the rondeau, provided was a precedent for how a small-scale composition might work in terms of continuity, architecture, and contrapuntal structure. Thus the instrumental chanson is typically built on the traditional foundation of superius and tenor with a supporting but non-essential contratenor; it divides into two main sections, often signalled by the presence of a *corona* or *signum congruentiae*; and its continuity is essentially a succession of clauses distinguished from one another by cadences and clearly profiled incises.

The instrumental chanson can, however, differ from analogous vocal pieces in several important ways. Freed from dependence on a text, it can have more than the four or five clauses typical of rondeau settings; the length of the individual clauses is less uniform,

---

[8] The frequency with which French catch-phrases appear at the start of these pieces could be taken as indicating some sort of borrowing from secular vocal compositions. For example, pieces such as Josquin's *La plus des plus* and Martini's *Des biens d'amour* (cf. *Werken van Josquin des Prés, Wereldlijke Werken*, no. 45, and *Martini: Secular Pieces*, pp. 11–12) – both clearly instrumental compositions according to criteria explored elsewhere (cf. note 3 above) and in the further course of this paper – could be based musically on settings, now lost, of extant rondeau poems with these incipits. Similarly, the title of Josquin's *Cela sans plus* (cf. the preceding note) might seem to suggest an association with the melody, apparently of popular origin, well known from the composition of the same title by Colinet de Lannoy (cf. *Ottaviano Petrucci: Canti B numero cinquanta, Venice, 1502*, ed. Helen Hewitt, Monuments of Renaissance Music 2 (Chicago and London, 1967), no. 16 and discussion, pp. 42–4). Nevertheless, caution seems in order. No setting of *La plus des plus* or *Des biens d'amour* has in fact been found; and there is no readily apparent connection between Josquin's *Cela sans plus* and its putative borrowed tune beyond two possible quotations of the head-motive – in inversion at the start of the composition and more or less literally in imitation at the close (cf. *Petrucci: Odhecaton*, pp. 76–7). Looking beyond these examples, moreover, one notes an extreme scarcity of fifteenth-century poems whose opening words correspond to the headings of instrumental pieces, let alone of settings of any of this poetry. The assumption, therefore, that the French words may in fact simply be titles, rather than incipits or references to musical models, would seem entirely plausible, although this conclusion does not lessen the mystery of why a given work would receive the title that it does.

moreover, and the differentiation between them is often less clear. The nature of the melodic writing also tends to differ from that of the rondeau, in which the superius generally begins each phrase with rather long, even note-values, and continues – after most of the syllables of the text phrase would have been sung – with shorter values frequently grouped in syncopated patterns (Example 1). In the instrumental offspring this rhythmic progression within a clause is commonly replaced by stasis and balance, with melodies built from compact motives similar to one another in their rhythmic makeup (Example 2). This uniformity of motion is often reinforced by the practice of linking superius and tenor in close imitation, usually at the octave or unison, over extensive stretches (Example 3). In some passages, the focus on smaller melodic units leads to a kaleidoscopic play of stereotypical figures treated in sequence, imitation, or both (Example 4); in a favourite manifestation of this procedure the outer voices, moving either in imitation or in parallel tenths, are pitted against a conjunct tenor moving in the manner of a cantus firmus in breves or even larger values (Example 5).

This catalogue of differences between the instrumental chanson and its vocal forebears exposes the first of the problems associated with the repertory under consideration. Of the various traits that I have described as characteristic of the instrumental pieces, only one – the sequential treatment of short motives – has traditionally been

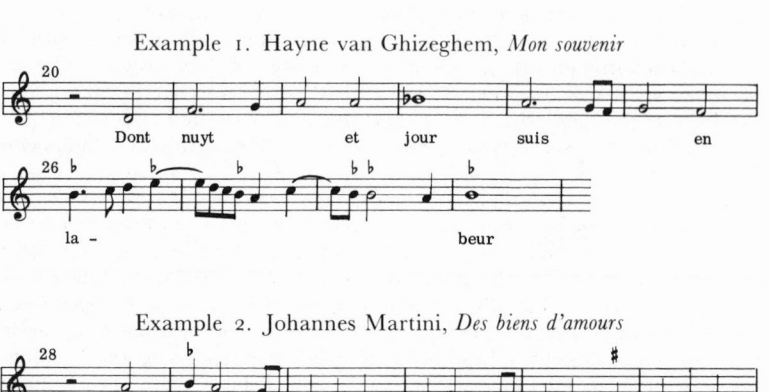

Example 1. Hayne van Ghizeghem, *Mon souvenir*

Example 2. Johannes Martini, *Des biens d'amours*

Example 3. Johannes Martini, *De la bonne chiere*

Example 4. Josquin, *La plus des plus*

isolated as particularly 'instrumental'.[9] Yet even writing of this sort is absent from a large percentage of instrumental chansons. Moreover, at the same time, it appears in a good number of pieces

[9] Cf. the discussion in *Petrucci: Odhecaton* cited in note 2 above, as well as Heinrich Besseler, 'Spielfiguren in der Instrumentalmusik', *Deutsches Jahrbuch der Musikwissenschaft für 1956* (Leipzig, 1957), pp. 12–38.

Example 5. Josquin, *La Bernardina*

undoubtedly written for voices. Example 6, for instance, offers a close parallel to Example 4, also by Josquin; and passages similar to those shown in Example 5 may be seen in another motet of Josquin (Example 7) or in numerous works by Obrecht, Isaac, and many others. All of this raises anew the old question of whether there exists any significant distinction between instrumental and vocal styles *per se* in the late fifteenth century, or whether differences such as we have found between vocal and instrumental pieces are rooted in the genre rather than in the medium.

On first glance, at least, the manner in which sequential patterning is used in vocal music would seem to support the latter answer. Rather than appearing equally in all sorts of works, this device is found primarily in large sacred compositions – motets and, especially, Masses.[10] In the chanson, sequences built around a slow-moving tenor never occur, and sequential writing of other sorts is extremely uncommon. When it is used, moreover, it never appears within the main body of a piece. Thus in Agricola's *A la mignonne de fortune* and Compère's *En attendant*, sequential passages close the

---

[10] In addition to the motets discussed earlier, see, to mention one particularly striking example, Obrecht's *Missa Je ne demande* (*Jacobus Obrecht: Opera omnia* 1, ed. Albert Smijers (Amsterdam, 1957), pp. 1–64), especially bars 74–80, 81–101, 126–34, and 139–65 of the Gloria.

Example 6. Josquin, *Vultum tuum deprecabuntur*

Example 7. Josquin, *Alma redemptoris mater / Ave regina celorum*

entire composition,[11] while Compère's *Chanter ne puis* – plainly a vocal work, despite the fact of its transmission solely in textless sources – shows sequential writing at the opening and close but nowhere in between.[12] Clearly, the small dimensions and, probably more important, the close relationship between music and verse typical of the chanson did not allow for any significant incorporation of an element so autonomous in its formation, while the more abstract relationship between text and music in the motet and Mass could more readily accommodate such a feature.

As this last observation suggests, however, generic constraints do not exist in a vacuum but rather reflect the specific conditions and assumptions that underlie each genre – and it would be shortsighted to imagine that the medium of a genre does not belong among these conditions. Thus if sequential patterning and similar repetitive designs cannot be associated with instruments alone, their use in the instrumental chanson is still hardly fortuitous. The absence of text not only encourages but virtually demands it as a means of generating and organising clauses.

It would be tempting to go beyond this conclusion and imagine that the frequent reliance on repetitive devices in the instrumental chanson springs not only from the demands of textless composition but also from an improvisatory instrumental practice in existence at the time the new genre was being shaped. Here too, however, caution is necessary. For one thing, sequences and other forms of patterned writing are not unknown in vocal music antedating the instrumental chanson by a considerable amount of time.[13] Moreover, what would appear to be the sole work from the period that can confidently be interpreted as an improvisation frozen in written form – the two-part *La Spagna* of M. Gulielmus found in the manuscripts Perugia, Biblioteca comunale Augusta, MS 431, and Bologna, Civico Museo Bibliografico-Musicale, MS Q 16 – shows no

---

[11] *A la mignonne de fortune* appears in *Alexandri Agricola Opera omnia*, ed. Edward R. Lerner, Corpus Mensurabilis Musicae ser. 22, vol. V (n.p., 1970), no. 2; *En attendant* in *Loyset Compère: Opera omnia*, ed. Ludwig Finscher, Corpus Mensurabilis Musicae ser. 15, vol. V (n.p., 1972), pp. 20–1.

[12] See *Compère: Opera omnia* V, p. 14; the arguments for considering *Chanter ne puis* a vocal composition can be inferred from the article cited in note 3, above.

[13] For some examples and commentary, see Edgar H. Sparks, *Cantus Firmus in Mass and Motet, 1420–1520* (Berkeley and Los Angeles, 1963), pp. 63 (in particular n. 24; the note itself appears on p. 438) and 229–35.

trace of patterned repetition.[14] Nevertheless, even if the origins of those aspects of the instrumental chanson that we may most wish to consider instrumental remain cloudy, there can be no doubt of the very real identification of the genre with its medium.

Many of the observations that I have made about the instrumental chanson apply equally well to pieces built around voices of *forme-fixe* chansons and even to many of the popular settings. In these genres, too, it is often easy to see stylistic traits growing out of the specific conditions set by the chosen medium.[15] That very choice of medium, however, presents something of a mystery. Traditionally, after all, the instrumental and vocal domains were sharply separated; composers were singers, and they belonged to organisations and fulfilled functions distinct from those of instrumentalists. It is not to be expected, therefore, that they would turn their attention in any great measure to the production of instrumental music.

Although it is impossible to say with certainty what accounts for this flourishing of instrumental ensemble music in the last decades of the century, an examination of the circumstances underlying that development may shed some light on the question. Despite considerable qualifications raised by new research, the fifty or so years surrounding the mid-century mark still show a relative dearth of musical activity in Italy, particularly in the realm of sophisticated

[14] On this composition, see Manfred F. Bukofzer, 'A Polyphonic Basse Dance of the Renaissance', *Studies in Medieval and Renaissance Music* (New York, 1950), pp. 190–216; a transcription of the piece appears on pp. 199–200. Pieces of the sort described earlier (p. 118) as settings of a voice from a polyphonic chanson are sometimes taken for improvised works or close reflections thereof. To cite just one recent instance, Walter H. Kemp, '"Votre trey dowce": A Duo for Dancing', *Music and Letters*, 60 (1979), pp. 37–44, seeks to relate an anonymous two-voice setting of a Binchois tenor to the tradition of dance music improvised above a cantus firmus borrowed from a *forme-fixe* chanson. Yet it seems characteristic of this tradition that the pitches of the tenor are stated in equal note-values, regardless of their original rhythmicisation (cf. Bukofzer, 'A Polyphonic Basse Dance', p. 194); Kemp's example retains the rhythm of Binchois's tenor literally. The very rigour of motivic patterning in the newly written voice, moreover, seems incompatible with improvisation: it would have taken remarkable skill indeed to create extemporaneously such a strict succession of sequences that at the same time formed perfectly acceptable counterpoint with a pre-existent voice of some melodic and rhythmic complexity.

[15] See, for example, the repetition of a single motive separated by rests in bars 3–8 in the superius of Josquin's *Adieu mes amours* (*Werken van Josquin des Prés, Wereldlijke Werken*, no. 35), or the discontinuous canonic lower parts at bars 5–9 of the same composer's *Una musque de Buscgaya* (*ibid.*, no. 37).

polyphony. Virtually no sources survive from this period, and what little archival evidence there is does not suggest the widespread maintenance of significant musical establishments.[16] All this changed dramatically, however, in the early 1470s with a notable upsurge of activity still visible today both in the archival records of *cappelle* being formed and expanded, and in the sudden proliferation of musical manuscripts.[17]

As already intimated, both the documents and the manuscripts themselves show that this new activity included a great interest in secular polyphony. This very partiality, however, seems to have created some difficulty. It is clear from the disappearance of texts after the earliest generation of Italian manuscripts transmitting French secular pieces that the *forme-fixe* chanson as a musico-poetic entity had no lasting appeal south of the Alps.[18] Presumably the charm of lengthy and repetitive pieces in a foreign language was limited, particularly when the text itself was obscured through

[16] For an overview of the situation, see Nino Pirrotta, 'Music and Cultural Tendencies in 15th-Century Italy', *Journal of the American Musicological Society*, 19 (1966), pp. 127–61. A specific instance from the archival realm may be seen in Ferrara, where documents indicate only sporadic maintenance of a *cappella* until 1472 (cf. Lewis Lockwood, 'Music at Ferrara in the Period of Ercole I d'Este', *Studi Musicali*, 1 (1972), pp. 101–31, esp. 104–6; *idem*, 'Pietrobono and the Instrumental Tradition at Ferrara', *Rivista Italiana di Musicologia*, 10 (1975), pp. 115–33, in particular 119–24; and *idem*, 'Dufay and Ferrara', in Allan W. Atlas (ed.), *Papers Read at the Dufay Quincentenary Conference, Brooklyn College, December 6–7, 1974* (Brooklyn, 1976), pp. 1–25, esp. 4–6 and 12). Between the 1430s – when Oxford, Bodleian Library, MS Canonici misc. 213 was completed (cf. Hans Schoop, *Entstehung und Verwendung der Handschrift Oxford Bodleian Library, Canonici misc. 213*, Publikationen der Schweizerischen Musikforschenden Gesellschaft II/24 (Bern, 1971), pp. 118–21) – and the period represented by the sources discussed in note 17 below, only the merest handful of Italian manuscripts survives; none of these, moreover (unless we consider such products of the German–Italian regions as the Trent Codices), can be securely dated after 1450.

[17] For some of the evidence of this activity, see the articles by Lockwood cited in note 16, above; Guglielmo Barblan, 'Vita musicale alle corte Sforzesca', *Storia di Milano*, IX (Milan, 1961), pp. 787–852, in particular 818–49; and Franz Xaver Haberl, 'Die römische "schola cantorum" und die päpstlichen Kapellsänger bis zur Mitte des 16. Jahrhunderts', *Vierteljahrsschrift für Musikwissenschaft*, 3 (1887), pp. 189–296, esp. 230–51. The upsurge in the production of manuscripts is best seen in the area of secular music; cf. the overview provided by Allan W. Atlas, *The Cappella Giulia Chansonnier (Rome, Biblioteca Apostolica Vaticana, C.G.XIII.27)*, 2 vols., Musicological Studies 27 (Brooklyn, 1975–6), 1, pp. 233–57 in particular.

[18] See the survey of texting practice in Italian sources of the late fifteenth century in Litterick, 'Performing Franco-Netherlandish Secular Music'.

increasingly melismatic phrases, rhythmic subtlety, and complex counterpoint. On the other hand, the continued textless transmission of chansons in Italian sources indicates that the pieces imported from the north retained their attractiveness when shorn of repetitions and performed on instruments. This attractiveness no doubt depended not merely on the music itself but also on the attainments of those who played it, for Italy boasted a wealth of native instrumental virtuosos.[19] In any event, it seems almost inevitable that the vogue for French vocal pieces in instrumental guise should have led to a demand for a music similar in nature yet more closely geared to the special capabilities of its performers. For composers, this development must have been a particularly happy one. The apparent distaste for *forme-fixe* chansons robbed Franco-Netherlanders at Italian courts of one of the principal outlets for their skills; and preference in settings of native poetry seems to have run to a simple, homophonic style that northerners clearly did not find sufficiently interesting to cultivate more than occasionally.[20] Writing for instruments, however, they could draw without reserve on their own sophisticated traditions; at the same time, the virtuosity of the musicians around them offered a stimulus for the exploration of new stylistic possibilities.

Despite its birth in what appears to have been such a favourable confluence of circumstances, the instrumental ensemble repertory did not outlive the vocal repertory that engendered it. Both appear to have died around 1500, presumably victims of a stylistic evolution that swept away many of the foundations on which they rested. The additive three-part contrapuntal framework gave way to so-called simultaneous conception of voices and a preference for four-voice texture, while new trends in melody and phrase structure, influenced

---

[19] Lockwood, 'Pietrobono', cites a number of contemporary references to the abilities of Italian instrumentalists; see in particular pp. 119 and 122–3.

[20] Even the earliest surviving settings of Italian poetry show this sort of simplicity; see, for example, *The Musical Manuscript Montecassino 871: A Neapolitan Repertory of Sacred and Secular Music of the Late Fifteenth Century*, ed. Isabel Pope and Masakata Kanazawa (Oxford, 1978), nos. 12, 13, 90, 128, and others. Northern composers' apparent lack of interest in this kind of music can be gauged by the measure of their contribution to both this repertory and its later successors in frottola production. For example, Petrucci's ten extant volumes of frottole include scarcely any pieces by northern composers, and of these only a small proportion corresponds to the 'normal' picture of the frottola as represented by composers such as Tromboncino, Cara, and their compatriots.

by popular elements, brought a tendency towards shorter phrases and increased symmetry.[21]

Yet while the chanson continued to evolve in the north, its instrumental counterpart in Italy found no replacement. The few Italian sources of secular polyphony other than the frottola to survive from the early 1500s either continue to transmit older pieces or place a strong emphasis on the most recent northern vocal music, which appears in fully texted form.[22] On reflection, this turn of events is not wholly surprising. The years surrounding the turn of the century were not favourable to the production of music in Italy, as repeated invasions by the French brought widespread hardship and instability. The powerful French presence, moreover, whatever its political implications, stirred up a fashion for things Gallic that surely included a new receptivity to the vocal chanson.[23] The newer chansons themselves – monostrophic, and with clear declamation and sprightly rhythms – were in any event more readily accessible musically than their predecessors.

The last question to be considered here concerns the relationship between the music that we have been investigating and the flourishing of instrumental composition in the mid sixteenth century. While both the considerable gap in time between the older and newer repertories and the apparent demise of the earlier tradition obviously warn against drawing connections too close and too direct, there is a strong temptation to see links nevertheless. The *canzon da sonar*, after all, appears to have evolved in more or less the same way

[21] Neither the *forme-fixe* chanson nor the instrumental chanson appears after the Petrucci editions except in manuscripts clearly copied from those publications, nor are such pieces written by composers of a later generation. For a discussion of some aspects of the transformation, see Howard M. Brown, 'Critical Years in European Musical History 1500–1530', *International Musicological Society, Report of the Tenth Congress, Ljubljana 1967*, ed. Dragotin Cvetko (Kassel, etc., 1970), pp., 78–94.

[22] This tendency is perhaps best exemplified in the Florentine partbooks Cortona, Biblioteca Comunale, MSS 95–6 / Paris, Bibliothèque Nationale, MS nouv. acq. fr. 1817, which would appear to date from no later than the middle of the second decade of the century and may in part precede this terminus by some years; on the question of dating, see in particular Atlas, *The Cappella Giulia Chansonnier*, I, pp. 469–73.

[23] An overview of the situation is presented by Heartz, '*Les Goûts Réunis*, or the Worlds of the Madrigal and the Chanson Conjoined', in James Haar (ed.), *Chanson and Madrigal 1480–1530. Studies in Comparison and Contrast* (Cambridge, Mass., 1964), pp. 88–99.

as did the fifteenth-century pieces; and while much about the history of the ensemble ricercar and the fantasia remains unclear, it is not impossible to find ties between these and the earlier compositions.[24] The case of the canzona in particular could suggest that the older and newer instrumental music were bound together by the thread of a continuing improvisatory instrumental practice focused on the adaptation of vocal polyphony. Seen from this perspective, the gaps in the written transmission would represent less periods of reduced activity than merely times when this activity did not find reflection in written form.

Attractive as this hypothesis may appear, however, it cannot be sustained. Written instrumental music clearly depends on the existence of a strong performance tradition, and it is equally clear that such a tradition can have considerable influence on written production. But it is unrealistic to regard the ensemble compositions that have come down to us as simply the notated tip of an oral-tradition iceberg. As we have seen, the men whose names grace the fifteenth-century pieces were not players but singer–composers, and even in the sixteenth century those most prominent in the creation of music for instrumental ensemble came from the vocal sphere or were organists – whose professional and musical status had been upgraded in the intervening decades to the point where they too could be seen as part of the singer–composer establishment.[25] However receptive they may have been to elements rooted in instrumentalists' practice, these figures still approached instrumental music essentially from the outside; the fundamental assumptions behind their pieces remained those with which they had long operated elsewhere. In the fifteenth century, moreover, it had clearly taken external factors to involve composers in instrumental music; and as the prevailing absence of instrumental compositions after 1500 shows, these factors did not themselves form part of a continuing tradition but were the momentary result of particular circumstances. Paradoxically, therefore, the fifteenth-century instrumental repertory does not truly alter our sense of the history of instrumental

---

[24] On the history of all three genres, see most recently Kämper, *Studien zur instrumentalen Ensemblemusik*, pp. 113–55 and 192–232.

[25] This change can perhaps best be seen in the example of the organists at St Mark's in Venice; both Jacques Buus and Andrea Gabrieli, for instance, published volumes of sacred and secular vocal pieces.

ensemble music. The music of the mid sixteenth century may have more antecedents than previously imagined, but it remains without true forebears. The fifteenth-century repertory left no heritage; instrumental ensemble music had to be re-invented.

8

INSTRUMENTAL VERSIONS, *C.* 1515–1554, OF A LATE-FIFTEENTH-CENTURY FLEMISH CHANSON, *O WAERDE MONT*[1]

H. COLIN SLIM

THIS paper examines six instrumental arrangements, made during the sixteenth century, of an apparently widely known song. Some, such as the lute tablature inscribed in a Flemish painting, are clearly instrumental; others, less obviously instrumental, will require comparison with the various vocal versions of the song.

A small panel painting around 1530 by an unidentified Flemish master close to Bernard van Orley, which is now in the private library of the Duke of Devonshire at Chatsworth, depicts a seated and presumably penitent Mary Magdalene reading from a rubricated prayer book (Figure 1).[2] During the 1520s and 1530s Flemish paintings of Mary Magdalene frequently include a lute and sometimes a clavichord.[3] While some of these paintings also include

---

[1] To those compositions which employ one or more voices of the song, cited in John Ward, 'The Lute Music of MS Royal Appendix 58', *Journal of the American Musicological Society*, 13 (1960), pp. 122–3, item 6, in Martin Picker, 'The Chanson Albums of Marguerite of Austria', *Annales Musicologiques*, 6 (1958–63), p. 215, in Daniel Heartz (ed.), *Preludes, Chansons and Dances for Lute published by Pierre Attaingnant, Paris (1529–1530)* (Neuilly-sur-Seine, 1964), p. lxvi, no. 5, and during the course of this paper, should be added Munich, Bayerische Staatsbibliothek, Mus. MS 34, fol 108v: (anon.), *Salve regina / O werde mont, a 4*, quoting the chanson's superius. Emil Weller, *Annalen der poetischen National-Literatur der Deutschen im XVI. und XVII. Jahrhundert* (Freiburg im Breisgau, 1862; repr. Hildesheim, 1964), I, p. 214, no. 66, cites *Ein ander lied, O werder mund* (Nuremberg, Kunegund Hergotin, n.d. [*c.* 1530]). This text is edited in anon., 'Alte Lieder', *Weimarisches Jahrbuch für Deutsche Sprache Literatur und Kunst*, 4 (1856), p. 230, no. 5.

[2] See H. Colin Slim, 'Mary Magdalene, Musician and Dancer', to appear in *Early Music*, 8 (1980), pp. 460–73.

[3] See, for example, Daniel Heartz, 'Mary Magdalen, Lutenist', *Journal of The Lute Society of America*, 5 (1972), pp. 52–67, plates A–E; Edwin M. Ripin, 'The Early Clavichord', *Musical Quarterly*, 53 (1967), pp. 518–38, plates 3 and 4.

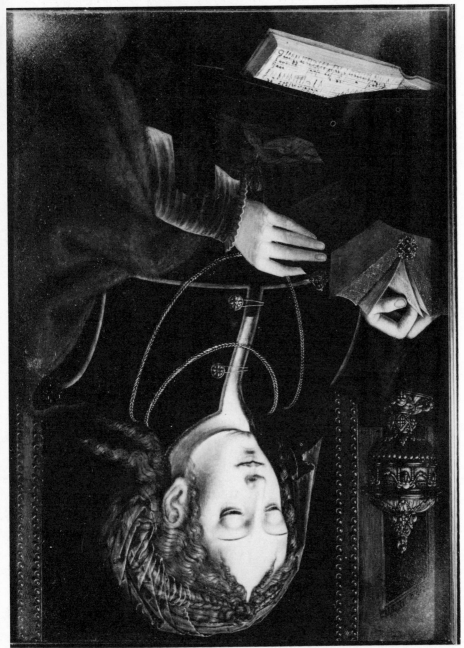

Figure 1. Anon., *Mary Magdalene*: Chatsworth, Derbyshire

Sixteenth-century instrumental music

stylised musical notation,[4] many present a genuine and readable version, either in tablature or in mensural notation,[5] and a few even include both.[6] Chatsworth's inscription is for six-course lute in French letter-tablature, identified on the left of its folio as *O waerde mont*. Before the lute case hides it, we encounter six and a half longae of the tenor and bass – that is, the song's first strain and the beginning of its second.[7] Apropos a similar selection for lute of just the tenor and bass in Royal Appendix 58, David Lumsden comments that its voices merely accompany the missing superius.[8] This is not the case here, for at least two reasons. First, the penitent Mary Magdalene who reads close-lipped clearly cannot be singing. Secondly, the lute itself is missing, or returned to its case – perhaps a reminder of her conversion. European literature often defines the worldliness of the Magdalene before she meets Christ by having her sing, or dance, or play a musical instrument. An example of the latter occurs in an early-sixteenth-century French farce wherein the wayward Magdalene, sought by her sister Martha, is finally located in the act of retuning one of the strings of her lute.[9]

The music of *O waerde mont* enjoyed a long life. And wherever this song appears its rhythm remains the same, as in (for example) its first appearance as a cantus firmus in a *Salve regina* setting *a 5* by Johannes Molunet, copied years later (around 1521) into Munich MS 34.[10] Its composer was presumably Jean Molinet, the great *rhétoriqueur*, poet, chronicler and sometime musician, who died in

---

[4] Ripin, *op. cit.*, plate 4.

[5] Heartz, 'Mary Magdalen, Lutenist', plates A, C, D, E.

[6] *Ibid.*, plate B; and see Slim, 'Mary Magdalene, *mondaine musicale*', to appear in the *Report of the Twelfth Congress of the International Musicological Society Berkeley 1977*.

[7] The transcription in Example 1 below is transposed to D tuning to correspond with the vocal versions.

[8] London, British Library, MS Royal Appendix 58: Lumsden, 'English Lute Music, 1540–1620 – An Introduction', *Proceedings of the Royal Musical Association*, 83 (1956–7), p. 9. See the transcription in Example 1 below, transposed to correspond with the vocal versions.

[9] Further details appear in the articles cited in notes 2 and 6 above.

[10] Munich, Bayerische Staatsbibliothek, Mus. MS 34, fol. 29v. See Julius Joseph Maier, *Die musikalischen Handschriften der K. Hof- und Staatsbibliothek in Muenchen* (Munich, 1879), p. 58, no. 88, item 7. On the date of the manuscript, see Herbert Kellman, 'Josquin and the Courts of the Netherlands and France: The Evidence of the Sources', in Edward E. Lowinsky and Bonnie J. Blackburn (eds.), *Josquin des Prez – Proceedings of the International Josquin Festival–Conference* (London, 1976), p. 215. Professor Kellman, in a letter to me of 10 October 1978, suggests 'closer to 1521 than to 1530'.

1507. Before his eyesight failed him, around 1497, Molinet apparently composed a considerable amount of music, most of which is now lost.[11] More than a century later *O waerde mont* makes a last bow when its tenor melody becomes the top voice in a four-voice Protestant chorale by Michael Praetorius in his *Musae Sioniae*, part 7, published in 1609.[12]

In between these years, we find the cantus and tenor in the tiny Brussels–Tournai partbooks, the tenor bearing the date 1511.[13] Brussels–Tournai contains mostly chansons with a few motets and Flemish songs. Except for a single Josquin chanson from shortly after 1508,[14] the dates of these works – mostly from the 1480s and 1490s – likewise suggest for *O waerde mont* an origin in the late fifteenth century.

Sometime between 1510 and 1519, Arndt von Aich published a four-voice version.[15] He provided a free German translation for the tenor part, though separately from the music. From this Valentin Triller made in 1555 a German Protestant contrafactum for three voices, deleting Arndt's altus and slightly recasting Arndt's bassus.[16]

---

[11] See Noël Dupire, *Jean Molinet, la vie – les oeuvres* (Paris, 1932), pp. 23–5, 135 and 140; and Slim, 'Mary Magdalene, Musician and Dancer', n. 39.

[12] Modern edition in Friedrich Blume (ed.), *Gesamtausgabe der musikalischen Werke von Michael Praetorius: Musae Sioniae 7 (1609)* (Wolfenbüttel, n.d.), pp. 231–2.

[13] Brussels, Bibliothèque Royale, MS IV. 90, fols. 12v–13, and Tournai, Bibliothèque de la Ville, MS 94, fols. 16–16v. See the *Census-Catalogue of Manuscript Sources of Polyphonic Music 1400–1550*, I (n.p., 1979), pp. 97–8. In the transcription in Example 1 below, the text underlay follows Tournai, Brussels having the first six words only.

[14] See Kellman, *op. cit.*, pp. 182–3 and 207–8.

[15] *In dissem Buechlyn fynd man LXXV. hubscher Lieder* (Cologne, n.d.), no. 16; see François Lesure (ed.), *Receuils imprimés 16ᵉ et 17ᵉ siècles*, in the Répertoire International des Sources Musicales (Munich and Duisburg, 1960): RISM [1519].⁵ Modern editions in Hans Joachim Moser and Eduard Bernoulli (eds.), *Das Liederbuch des Arnt von Aich* (Kassel, 1930), pp. 36–7, and Moser, *Paul Hofhaimer* (Stuttgart, 1929), pp. 162–3. See the transcription in Example 1. See the transcription in Example 1.
Yet another German version, *O wer dich mundt zu aller stundt so, a 4*, has gone unrecognised because of the loss of its tenor partbook in the collection of 56 Lieder without a title (Frankfurt, C. Egenolff, n.d.), no. 14, listed as [c. 1535]¹⁵ in RISM. Ernst-Ludwig Berz, *Die Notendrucker und ihre Verleger in Frankfurt am Main von den Anfängen bis etwa 1630* (Kassel, 1970), pp. 149–50, no. 10, dates it between 1537 and 1544. Incipits of the three surviving voices appear in Norbert Böker-Heil, Harald Heckmann, and Ilse Kindermann, *Das Tenorlied: Mehrstimmige Lieder in deutschen Quellen 1450–1580*, I: *Drucke* (Kassel, 1979), p. 60, no. 15.14.

[16] *Ein Schlesisch singebüchlein aus Göttlicher schrift* (Breslau, C. Scharffenberg, 1555), fol. m3; see Konrad Ameln *et al.*, *Das Deutsche Kirchenlied*, I, pt I (Kassel, 1975), p. 41. See the transcription in Example 1, below. Böker-Heil *et al.*, *op. cit.*, p. 18, no.

Whether the unknown composer's original setting was for three or for four voices remains uncertain. The repertory in the Brussels–Tournai partbooks preceding *O waerde mont* is for three voices in other sources; the repertory following it is for four voices, although in a few other sources these chansons and Flemish songs are three-voiced.[17] Possibly, then, *O waerde mont* in the late fifteenth century was for three voices and, like many such works from this period, quickly acquired an altus. Presumably at bar 10 the lost bassus part to Brussels–Tournai made the same octave leap across its tenor at the cadence as it does in Arndt.

None of the early texts, Flemish or German, fits the music very satisfactorily. Brussels and Tournai, for example, simply do not provide enough words. Even repeating whole lines and adding at bars 4–6 'mijns herten gront', an extra line which appears in the same poem in *Een schoon liedekens Boeck* of 1544,[18] fail to help much. Apparently the scribe of Brussels–Tournai gave up in despair (see Figure 2). Nor will any of the five Flemish sacred contrafacta for the superius found in 1539 in *Een devoot ende profitelyck boecxken* fit the music properly, even though each has a different number of lines.[19]

Arndt von Aich's German translation provides insufficient lines to accommodate his tenor's music. That Arndt's translation was specially commissioned seems likely from its simple-minded rhyme scheme. No other of the seventy-five poems in Arndt's collection ends every line the same: 'undt' in verse one, 'er' in verse two, 'ich' in verse three. This peculiarity suggests an unavailable translation and thus probably a hurried commission to meet a publishing deadline, which resulted in a clumsy translation. Perhaps Arndt's announcement on the title-page of the Lieder in his tenor partbook, wherein he mentions possibilities for instrumental performance, absolves him of properly connecting word and music: 'Auch etlich zu fleiten, schwegelen, und an deren musicalisch Instrumenten artlichen zu gebrauchen'. Arndt's mention of a tabor-flute (Schwegel) may be

---

5.16; p. 200, no. 41.49; p. 202, no. 42.49; p. 206, no. 43.49; p. 252, no. 54.42; and p. 277, no. 58.42, provide a useful list with incipits.

[17] See the composers cited in the *Census-Catalogue* (cited note 13, above).

[18] (Antwerp, Jan Roulans, 1544); modern editions by Hoffman von Fallersleben, *Antwerpener Liederbuch vom Jahre 1544*, Horae Belgicae XI (1855), pp. 196–7, no. CXXX, and K. Vellekoop *et al.*, *Het Antwerps Liedboek, 87 melodieën op texsten uit Een Schoon Liedekens-Boeck van 1544* (Amsterdam, 1972), I, pp. 140–1.

[19] (Antwerp, Symon Cock, 1539); modern edition by D. F. Scheurleer (The Hague, 1889), pp. 202–5, nos. CLXIX–CLXXIII; see also Vellekoop, *op. cit.*, II, p. 95.

Figure 2. *O waerde mont*; Tournai, Bibliothèque de la Ville, MS 94, fols. 16–16v.

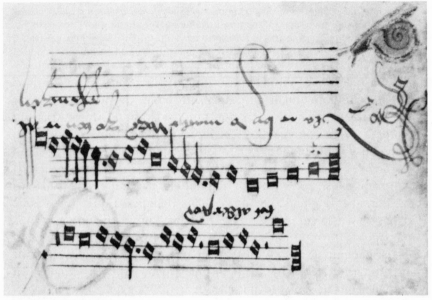

Sixteenth-century instrumental music

important, for *O waerde mont* also has a compelling association with dancing.[20] Not until 1549, when Caspar Othmayr's *Reutterische und Jegerische Liedlein* quotes the tenor of Arndt's *O werder mundt* as the top voice (mostly) in his own four-voice Lied,[21] does the German translation receive a plausible match with the music. Othmayr's text-setting for Arndt's tenor is more satisfactory than the version by Bernoulli or that by Moser in their editions of Arndt's Lied.[22] Finally, in his *Schlesisch singebüchlein* of 1555, Triller succeeded in taming the music with his three-voice Protestant contrafactum, 'O werder mundt, durch den mir kundt, wird des rechten glaubens grundt', but only by matching virtually every note with a syllable of text. Elevating Triller's tenor to the soprano, Praetorius also chose Triller's text-setting for his chorale.

Difficulties which arise when seeking to underlay the texts in sources from the first three decades of the century raise the question whether Flemish or German was the original language at all. Pierre Attaingnant provides a tantalising hint that it might have been French when he double-titled his lute arrangement in 1529 as *Alsov-verdonont / A toy me rendz*.[23] Attaingnant's subsequent quotation in 1532 of the bass of *O waerde mont* to the words 'A toy me rends' in the contratenor of a fricassée chanson[24] surely means that the French knew this song well as *A toy me rends* at least by the late 1520s. And the quotation of the opening of the tenor melody of *O waerde mont* in the superius of a Magdalene chanson which, though first published by Attaingnant in 1529, refers to events in 1518[25] may lend support for a

[20] See below, pp. 144–5.

[21] (Nuremberg, Berg and Neuber, 1549), no. 49; modern editions in F. Piersig (ed.), *Reutterische und Jegerische Liedlein, durch M. Caspar Othmayr mit vier stimmen componirt*, II (Berlin, 1933), pp. 145–7 (transposed up a fifth), and in Bernoulli, *Aus Lieder-büchern der Humanistenzeit* (Leipzig, 1910), pp. 102–3, after Basel, Öffentliche Bibliothek der Universität, MS F.X. 17–20, which lacks the text (see the *Census-Catalogue*, I, pp. 31–2). The transcription of Arndt's Lied in Example 1, below, adopts Othmayr's text-setting.   [22] See above, note 15.

[23] *Tres breve et familiere introduction pour entendre & apprendre par soy mesmes a jouer toutes chansons reduictes en la tabulature du Lutz.* See Heartz (ed.), *Preludes, Chansons and Dances for Lute*, Plate 1 and pp. 10–11. The transcription in Example 1 below, transposed a minor third lower, makes one correction to Heartz at bar 13, tenor, where the tablature gives 'e', i.e. (untransposed) db', not d♮' as in Heartz.

[24] See Heartz, *op. cit.*, p. lxvi, no. 5.

[25] *Tous nobles coeurs venez voir Magdalene* in *Trente et cinq chansons musicales*, listed in Heartz, *Pierre Attaingnant, Royal Printer of Music* (Berkeley and Los Angeles, 1969), pp. 215–16, no. 6, item 29. Further, see Slim, 'Mary Magdalene, Musician and Dancer', which includes a transcription.

French text to *O waerde mont* going back some considerable time. But until we recover more than just 'A toy me rends', a French origin for *O waerde mont* must remain in the realm of hypothesis.

Early in the century there is a flurry of cantus-firmus treatment for one or the other of two voices from *O waerde mont*. At first it is the superius, quoted by Johannes Heer in a song he copied at Paris in 1512.[26] Then in two works copied about 1516 it is the tenor's turn: once through in Franciscus Strus's motet *Sancta Maria*,[27] and six times complete and twice incomplete in the movements of a Mass preserved at Casale Monferrato and slightly later at Munich.[28]

The song's popularity in these early years brought forth a rash of instrumental arrangements. The simplest and, owing to its abrupt truncation, the shortest of these is in the Chatsworth painting, *c.* 1530, which intabulates only the tenor and the bass of the song. There is sufficient decoration of the tenor, such as splitting single notes into two (bar 1), coloration (bars 1 and 4), and cadential flourish (bar 5), to show that the painter either had readily available an instrumental version now otherwise unknown to us, or was handed such a one, possibly by his patron, for insertion into the painting. Decoration of this upper voice surely rules out any notion of the tablature being a mere accompaniment. The tenor *is* the melody here, a primacy already afforded it early in the century in works demonstrably composed before the painting, such as Attaingnant's Magdalene chanson of 1518, Strus's *Sancta Maria*, and the Casale Monferrato–Munich Mass, both around 1516. The primacy of the tenor after Chatsworth is confirmed in works such as Othmayr's Lied of 1549 and Praetorius's 1609 chorale wherein the tenor ascends to the top voice. Indeed, to judge from the selection of

[26] St Gall, Stiftsbibliothek, MS 462, fols. 54v–55; modern edition in Arnold Geering and Hans Trümpy (eds.), *Das Liederbuch des Johannes Heer von Glarus*, Schweizerische Musikdenkmäler 5 (Basel, 1967), pp. 109–10, no. 65.

[27] Strus's lied-motet, found in Basel, Öffentliche Bibliothek der Universität, MS F.X.1–4, and in London, British Library, Royal MS 8.G.VII, is edited (after Brussels, Bibliothèque Royale, MS 228) in Picker, *The Chanson Albums of Marguerite of Austria* (Berkeley and Los Angeles, 1965), pp. 270–4, no. 23. On Strus, see *ibid.*, p. 47.

[28] Casale Monferrato, Duomo, Archivio e Biblioteca Capitolare, MS L (B); see David Crawford, *Sixteenth-Century Choirbooks in the Archivio Capitolare at Casale Monferrato* (n.p., 1975), p. 115, item 2, and Munich, Bayerische Staatsbibliothek, Mus. MS F; see Maier, *op. cit.*, p. 2, no. 3, item 4. On the date of Munich MS F, see Kellman, *op. cit.*, p. 209; I am indebted to Professor Kellman for information on this manuscript. In his letter of 10 October 1978 he suggests *c.* 1519–23.

the tenor before all other voices of the song for cantus-firmus treatment early in the century and its triumphant emergence later on as an uppermost voice, we may well be dealing here with a fifteenth-century discant-tenor chanson.[29]

There are two less obvious instrumental arrangements of the kind, perhaps, which Arndt mentions on his title-page. One is in the British Library's so-called 'Henry VIII MS' of about 1515, Add. 31922, where it is called *Ough warder mount*.[30] The other, *O werder mŭndt*, is in Munich MS 718, a collection assembled by Jorg Weltzell between 1523 and 1524 for playing on discant, tenor, and bass viols da gamba.[31]

John Ward's discovery in Add. 31922 of a four-voice basse-dance setting[32] and Warwick Edwards's study on instrumental aspects of this manuscript[33] add a deal of precision and conviction to views on this source which I expressed in 1954 in an unpublished seminar paper at Harvard University. Edwards attacks the problem of those works which bear song titles and are thus readily identifiable as vocal and not instrumental in conception, but which, on certain criteria, may be suitable for instrumental performance. Some of Edwards's criteria are most helpful in examining *Ough warder mount*. For example, why did the copyist omit the song's text, while including texts for over fifty English songs? In other continental works, Edwards catches him joining together short repeated notes into longer ones: examples occur in *Ough warder mount* in bars 2–3 (tenor and bass) and 6–7 (tenor and superius). Such elisions effectively prevent texting. Edwards observes the scribe adding bar-lines and pauses to some chansons in the *formes fixes*, thereby making it impossible to fit the original text without violating its structural integrity.

---

[29] On this type, see Gustave Reese, *Music in the Renaissance*, rev. edn (New York, 1959), p. 54.

[30] London, British Library, Add. MS 31922. See John Stevens (ed.), *Music at the Court of Henry VIII*, Musica Britannica 18 (London, 1962), p. 34, no. 42, and the transcription in Example 1, below.

[31] Munich, Universitätsbibliothek, MS 718. See Clytus Gottwald, *Die Musikhandschriften der Universitätsbibliothek München* (Wiesbaden 1968), pp. 55–62, and Wolfgang Boetticher, *Handschriftlich überlieferte Lauten- und Gitarrentabulaturen des 15. bis 18. Jahrhunderts* (Munich, 1978), p. 226. I am indebted to Howard M. Brown for bringing my attention to this source.

[32] 'The maner of dauncying', *Early Music*, 4 (1976), pp. 131–6.

[33] 'The Instrumental Music of *Henry VIII's Manuscript*', *The Consort*, 34 (1978), pp. 274–82.

Bar lines and pauses also occur in *Ough warder mount*, but cause no problems because its text – whether German or Flemish – is not in a *forme fixe*. Nevertheless, adding these bar-lines to *Ough warder mount* must indicate the same scribal mentality that is distorting and reshaping other Continental vocal works in Add. 31922 to instrumental ends. Significantly, these bar-lines (shown as solid lines between the staves in the transcription below) also occur at three of the same places in Attaingnant's 1529 lute arrangement (bars 2, 6, and 15) and at two of the same places in the Chatsworth version (bars 2 and 6) and in Royal Appendix 58 (bars 2 and 15).[34] In bar 15 of Add. 31922 the absence of the breve rest from the superius, tenor and bassus probably also shows the arranger's hand. Surely the rest occurred in all voices in his source, as it does in all sources except Triller and Praetorius, the copyist merely forgetting to eliminate it from the altus in Add. 31922, where it still remains.

Perhaps owing to the heading in Add. 31922, Picker, Stevens, and Edwards all assume that *Ough warder mount* is modelled on Arndt von Aich.[35] Linguistically, their assumption seems dubious, for the heading could as easily be Flemish as German. While the scribe's joining and separating notes might be regarded as mere caprice and his differences from Arndt in signed accidentals might belong to the realm of musica ficta, some proof that the source of Add. 31922 is not Arndt is its lack at bar 10 of the old-fashioned octave bass leap over the tenor. Even if Add. 31922's copyist eliminated that archaism from his new instrumental version,[36] the presence at bar 16 of *signa congruentiae* lacking in Arndt, the different voice-leading of the superius in bar 8, and especially the conflicting ligature placement between manuscript and print must rule out Arndt.[37] Was there, then, a Flemish source for Add. 31922, such as Brussels–Tournai? While at bar 16 these two partbooks and Add. 31922 have the *signum*

---

[34] See the transcription in Example 1, below. I am grateful to Mr Arthur Searle of the British Library Department of Manuscripts for assistance in reading the heading in Royal Appendix 58 and for deciphering the word 'repete' at bar 19.

[35] See above, notes 1, 30 and 33. The index of Add. 31922 (fol. 2v) gives the title as *Ough warder mont*.

[36] It was perhaps not so archaic in 1515; it still appears in some madrigals by Verdelot, not earlier than the 1520s. See H. Colin Slim, *A Gift of Madrigals and Motets*, 2 vols. (Chicago and London, 1972), I, pp. 169–70.

[37] An examination of the transcription in Example 1, below, shows that the six ligatures in Add. 31922 enclose entirely different note-pairs from Arndt's five ligatures.

in common, and while the slightly decorated superius cadences at bars 10 and 14 of Add. 31922 might well be owing to instrumental concerns by its scribe, again, however, the different voice-leading in the superius in Brussels and differences in ligature assignment are probably sufficient to eliminate Brussels–Tournai as any direct source for Add. 31922.

Notwithstanding Jorg Weltzell's national origin and his manuscript's date, his source for *O werder mŭndt* in Munich 718 may not at first glance seem to be Arndt. It is true that at bar 10 Weltzell's bass viol crosses his tenor viol by octave leap as in Arndt, but where is Arndt's altus part? What about Weltzell's different rhythms in bars 1 and 5, discant and bass, and his joining Arndt's repeated notes across bars 2–3 and 6–7? What of Weltzell's low D at the close? Preliminary investigation of Weltzell's practice throughout Munich 718[38] with respect to his presumed vocal models shows him frequently omitting one or more voice parts. His final low D might be, as it is perhaps also in Add. 31922, for the sake of the sonority from an open string on the bass viol. And Weltzell's attitude towards rhythm seems fairly consistent throughout Munich 718. That is, he almost invariably combines repeated notes into one longer note, as in bar 11, discant and bass, and he almost always dissolves dotted notes into a long and a short, as in the latter half of bar 7, all three parts. Weltzell's practice of dividing longer sustained notes into two can be seen as early as bar 1, bass viol, but most tellingly at bar 8. In this second, unfinished version for discant viol,[39] he chose to split the breve c′, present in all vocal sources and even in his other discant part, into two semibreves. Weltzell hardly ever employs embellishment in Munich 718 and there is none in his *O werder mŭndt*. This timidity, along with several other features in the manuscript,[40] probably reveals him just learning to play his instruments and how to transcribe for them in German letter-tablature. Occasionally he adds quite sensible accidentals, such as the bass B♭ in bar 16, though he has forgotten it by bar 20. In this same measure his c♮′ c♯′

---

[38] I draw this information from a study and complete edition of Munich 718 by my student Hiro Minamino, to whom I express my thanks. See the transcription in Example 1, below.

[39] The last note of bar 12 and the two in bar 13 lack indications of rhythmic values in Munich 718.

[40] There are transposition tables for intabulating on discant, tenor, and bass viols (fols. 97–99v) and tables of note values, pauses, ligatures, etc. (fols. 101v–103v).

provides helpful evidence about early-sixteenth-century procedure when a leading note circles round a tonic.[41]

All the four-voice chansons which Pierre Attaingnant selected for intabulation in his *Tres breve . . . introduction* in 1529 lost their altus parts in the process.[42] Thus in Attaingnant's *Alsovverdonont / A toy me rendz*, bars 10, 12, and 15, the presence of a voice which corresponds to altus notes should probably be ascribed to Attaingnant's desire for a third in the chord and for full sonority at the ends of phrases, though the tenor f♯ in bar 21 is entirely his own. His restraint in decorating the song's tenor emphasises its primacy among his three voices. One difference may point to an unknown source. His tenor's second note in bar 7 repeats the a instead of proceeding to b, a passage found otherwise only in Add. 31922, in Strus's motet, and in Triller – none of which can be Attaingnant's source. However, the flat added to the tenor e' in bar 18 after the decorated e♮' is perhaps explainable only as an editorial error. Cadential procedures, such as raised sixth and seventh degrees and Picardy third, mark him as a pioneer in the new instrumental 'tonality'.

Twenty-five years after Attaingnant's lute print, Guillaume Morlaye published posthumously Albert de Rippe's intabulation, *O Verdémont*.[43] To what extent, if any, Morlaye modified de Rippe will never be determined unless we someday recover those de Rippe sources which Morlaye says he assembled over many years 'de divers endroitz'.[44] But even a de Rippe who, according to Morlaye,

---

[41] Note the different treatment by Attaingnant and de Rippe, similar to the more 'modern' accidentals applied by Joan Maria da Crema in his lute intabulation (1546) of a ricercar by Julio da Modena, edited in H. Colin Slim, *Musica Nova*, Monuments of Renaissance Music 1 (Chicago and London, 1964), p. 40, bars 5–6, and p. 42, bars 33–4. Warren Kirkendale, 'Ciceronians versus Aristotelians on the Ricercar as Exordium, from Bembo to Bach', *Journal of the American Musicological Society*, 32 (1979), p. 17, confuses this Joan Maria da Crema with an earlier Medici lutenist; see Slim, 'Gian and Gian Maria, Some Fifteenth- and Sixteenth-Century Namesakes', *Musical Quarterly*, 57 (1971), p. 571.

[42] Heartz, *Preludes, Chansons and Dances for Lute*, p. xix. See the transcription in Example 1, below.

[43] *Quatriesme livre de tabulature de leut* (Paris, Fezandat, 1554), fol. 20v. The transcription in Example 1, below, transposed a minor third lower, adopts the readings in Jean-Michel Vaccaro (ed.), *Oeuvres d'Albert de Rippe*, III, pt 2 (Paris, 1975), pp. 71–6, except for bar 13, last 'alto' and 'tenor' notes, and bar 19bis, last bass note, where it follows the tablature.

[44] Morlaye's dedication to Henri II in the *Premier Livre* (1552), quoted J.-G. Prod'homme, 'Guillaume Morlaye, éditeur d'Albert de Ripe, luthiste et bourgeois de Paris', *Revue de Musicologie*, 6 (1925), p. 164.

gave pleasure 'à ung Pape, à ung Empereur, à ung Roy d'Angleterre et à d'autres princes et infiniz Seigneurs'[45] had an upper limit to his finger velocity. De Rippe's shorter note-values in his coloration passages indicate a slowing-down of the tactus, a factor which contributes to masking the identity of the old song. So does de Rippe's apparent lack of concern for the song's metric structure when he drops beats at bars 2 and 10 (shown in Example 1 by arrows), unless this is just Morlaye's editorial carelessness.[46] As it stands, de Rippe's wealth of ornamentation moves in the direction of a free fantasy on *O waerde mont*. Certainly the primacy of its tenor is now gone; even its very first note disappears and thereafter it lacks several shorter notes (bars 7, 9, 11, 13, 18, 19).

Although de Rippe intabulated all four voices of the song, there is evidence that he knew Attaingnant's intabulation well. In bar 7 de Rippe adopts Attaingnant's tenor reading and in general follows Attaingnant's degree-inflections at cadences.[47] Two passages especially betray de Rippe's dependence on Attaingnant.[48] At bar 2 de Rippe's florid superius is identical to Attaingnant's, though twice as fast (Morlaye's error?). Beginning at the fourth beat of bar 6, de Rippe's second strain continues surprisingly close to Attaingnant throughout bar 7. However, certain other passages show de Rippe's originality. As de Rippe's intabulation proceeds, he prefers to animate Attaingnant's sustained chords with descending and ascending scales (bars 10, 12, 15, and 21). De Rippe's second major area of independence from Attaingnant is to observe the song's repeat of the last six longae from bar 16, as in Brussels–Tournai, Add. 31922, and Royal Appendix 58. From bar 16bis onwards, de Rippe gives us precious information about suitable melodic and harmonic procedures when varying a repeat.[49]

By means of letters or numbers, instrumental tablatures often specify accidentals not found in vocal versions, though some of these

[45] *Ibid.*

[46] Morlaye promised to 'faire les corrections de toutes fueilles' in his contract with Fezandat, 19 April 1552 (*ibid.*, p. 160).

[47] One notable exception occurs in the latter half of bar 8, where Attaingnant cadences on an A major chord, de Rippe on A minor.

[48] Heartz, *Preludes, Chansons and Dances for Lute*, p. xix, points also to Attaingnant's influence on Phalèse's lute books, beginning in 1545.

[49] Compare, for example, de Rippe's 'reharmonisation' of the first beat of bar 18 at bar 18bis; the minor mode of bar 21 and the major mode of bar 21bis; and the reworking of bars 16–17 on the repeat.

accidentals are presumably sung in performance by employing musica ficta. A case in point occurs in Weltzell, who at bar 9, last note, sounds b♮ and B♭ simultaneously in his discant and bass viols. While this clash and the great distances between parts in the manuscript may suggest that Weltzell's comprehension was more linear than intervallic, the partial signature in Add. 31922 confirms his reading. Characteristically, it is left ambiguous in Arndt's Lied, although presumably the bass singer would add a ficta B♭. Lute arrangements by Attaingnant and de Rippe avoid the clash by altering the superius – raising its seventh degree and eliminating its b♮. Triller's contrafactum merely hedges by changing the bass note to d. Clashes of this sort in Weltzell and in Add. 31922 probably should not be eliminated by adding musica ficta (as proposed by Stevens for Add. 31922)[50] or by editorial emendation, because they reveal the fascinating variety of instrumental performance practice early in the sixteenth century. Otto Gombosi spoke to this in his edition of Vincenzo Capirola's lute book (*c.* 1517) when he observed that in many instances Capirola's

controversial accidentals . . . [and] false cross-relations . . . while daringly nonconforming to theoretical standards as we understand them, are hardly the results of careless intabulation. They show a feeling for chord and harmony that is not commonly recognized as property of the early 16th century, although in this respect our notions may be in need of revision.[51]

An examination of chansons inscribed in several Flemish paintings of Mary Magdalene and the evidence found in other visual representations, in plays, and in poems pointing to her considerable Terpsichorean abilities have led me elsewhere to hypothesise that *O waerde mont* in the Chatsworth painting symbolises Mary Magdalene's secular dancing before her conversion.[52] In 1529 Antoine Arena cites *O waerde mont* as a basse dance, calling it, like de Rippe, *Verdemont*.[53] Heartz points to the twenty-one longae in *O*

[50] *Op. cit.*, p. 34, bar 10.

[51] *Compositione di Meser Vincenzo Capirola, Lute-Book (circa 1517)* (Neuilly-sur-Seine, 1955), pp. xxix-xxx.

[52] Slim, 'Mary Magdalene, Musician and Dancer'.

[53] *Ad suos compagnones studiantes . . . bassas dansas*, augmented edn (Lyons, 1529), no. 4; see Heartz, 'The Basse Dance. Its Evolution circa 1450 to 1550', *Annales Musicologiques*, 6 (1958–63), p. 335, and Robert Mullally, 'The Editions of Antonius Arena's *Ad suos compagnones studiantes*', *Gutenberg-Jahrbuch 1979* (Mainz, 1979), pp. 146–57.

waerde mont (without repeat) as suspiciously close to the nineteen longae that Arena requires for his dance.[54] Both Brussels and Tournai depict in their margins of this song a couple who are surely at some kind of dance (Figure 2).[55]

In light of these associations, I suggest that when Ward calls *warder mut* in Royal Appendix 58 a 'crude intabulation'[56] of the two lowest voices of the song and when Lumsden terms it 'no more than an accompaniment',[57] they possibly miss the point of this intabulation. The tenor's great popularity in the sixteenth century and the historic role of chanson tenors in dances might argue that its position as the top voice of Royal Appendix 58 and the rhythmic alterations in both tenor and bass indicate an English attempt at turning these two voices of *O waerde mont* into a dance. The first four notes of the intabulation could be considered an anacrusis to the next six breves (on e' in the tenor, the last one decorated). Supplementing the five beats of the vocal and other instrumental versions, the one-beat extension in Royal Appendix 58 thus forms a large 6/2 measure. Two more 6/2 measures follow up to bar 9, where the scribe drew his next bar-line across the tablature.[58] The remainder of the transcription proceeds mostly in similar triple rhythmic groupings (marked off by dotted barlines), except for bars 10 and 12, each of which lacks a crotchet (shown by arrows). However, even the scribe's crude execution of the lute pieces throughout Royal Appendix 58 and some rhythmically ambiguous passages, resulting from his apparent

[54] *Preludes, Chansons and Dances for Lute*, p. xxxii.
[55] Virtually the same miniature appears in the Brussels MS, fol. 13. Many scholars of these two partbooks point to the relationships between the texts of the music and the miniatures accompanying them, but only Louise Litterick (Rifkin), 'The MS Royal 20.A.XVI of the British Library', Ph.D. diss., New York University, 1976, p. 32, n. 34, has gone beyond such generalities. She identifies a miniature in an Ockeghem chanson, *Je n'ay dueil que je ne suis morte*, as a representation of melancholy.
[56] 'The Lute Music of MS Royal Appendix 58', p. 123.
[57] *Op. cit.*, p. 9.
[58] See the transcription in Example 1, below (transposed down a perfect fourth), which alters the length of several notes in Ward's otherwise exemplary version in 'The Lute Music of MS Royal Appendix 58', pp. 120–1, Ex. 6. At bar 19 I follow Ward's reading of a quaver rather than a crotchet (last note, lower stave). Alterations at bars 4 and 5 correct two other slight misreadings of rhythmic signs in the tablature. These and two editorial rests which Ward adds at bars 11 and 12 perhaps result from a desire to fit Royal Appendix 58's *warder mut* to the Procrustean bed of its vocal forebears (see Ward's general remarks, p. 118).

ignorance of the dot of augmentation, may not be sufficient, perhaps, to quell doubts in the reader's mind about the liberties taken in considering these two measures as part of large 6/2 and 9/2 groupings, respectively.

Royal Appendix 58 contains two compositions immediately preceding *warder mut* which might be dance music, i.e. *Heaven & earth* and an untitled setting of a variant on the *passamezzo antico*. However, the former is not assigned its 'Pavane' title (found in some other sources); and one cannot know whether either the composer or the copyist of the latter regarded it as dance music.[59] These factors and the considerable rhythmic problems in the notation of the manuscript should prompt caution at any attempt to view *warder mut* as a dance, despite the rhythmic suggestions offered in the transcription.

[59] See Ward, 'Music for *A Handefull of Pleasant Delites*', *Journal of the American Musicological Society*, 10 (1957), p. 179, n. 101. I am most grateful to Professor Ward for his letter of 11 December 1978 in which he expressed doubts about *warder mut* as dance music and offered me wise words of caution.

H. COLIN SLIM

O waerde mont,
ghi maect ghesont
mijns herten gront
tot alder stont;
als ic bi u mach wesen,
so ben ic al ghenesen.

Mer tscheyden quaet
von tfier gelaet
maekt mi dispereat,
ten baet gheenen raet;
wilt si mi nu begheven,
van vruechden moet ic sneven.

Haer schoon ghelu hayr,
haer oochskens claer
brenghen mi in vaer
nu hier nu daer,
dat icse soude verliessen,
oft si een ander soude kiesen.

Haer lippekens root,
haer borstkens bloot,
al sonder ghenoot,
maken mi vroecht groot;
als ic bi haer mach rusten,
boete ic mijns herten lusten.

Schoon lief, doet wel
ende kiest niemant el,
in narst en spel
doet mijn bevel
ende hout ghelofte in trouwen;
het en sal u niet berouwen.

Oh praiseworthy mouth,
thou healest
my heart's foundation
for always;
when I can be with you,
then I am already healed.

But the evil departure
of her spirited countenance
makes me desperate,
for which counsel is of no avail;
if she should forsake me now,
as a result I would perish.

Her fair blonde hair
her clear eyes
put me in fear
– now here, now there –
that I might lose her
or that she might choose someone else.

Her red lips,
her bare breasts,
all without enjoyment
make me greatly regret;
if I may rest with her
I shall give free reign to my heart's
  desire.

Fair love, do well
and choose nobody else;
in earnest or jest
do what I tell you
and keep faithful your vow;
you will not regret it.

Source: *Een schoon liedekens Boeck* (Antwerp, 1544). no. cxxx and in Fl. van Duyse,
  Het oude Nederlandsche Lied (1903), I, pp. 572–3, no. 152

Example 1

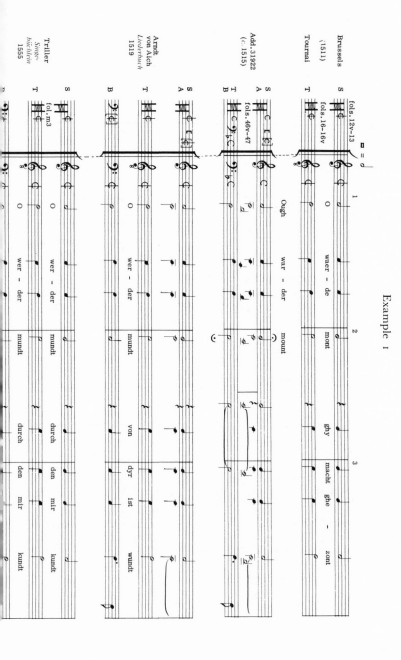

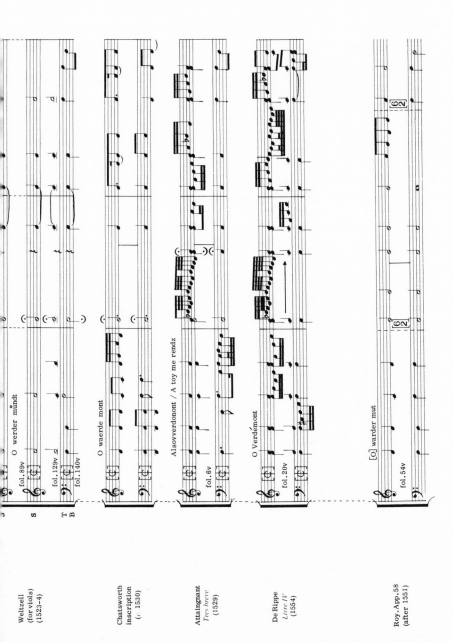

Weltzell
(for viols)
(1523–4)

O werder mündt
fol. 89v
fol. 129v
fol. 140v

Chatsworth
inscription
(c. 1530)

O waerde mont

Attaingnant
Tres breve
(1529)

Alsoverdonont / A toy me rendz
fol. 6v

De Rippe
Livre IV
(1554)

O Verdémont
fol. 20v

Roy. App. 58
(after 1551)

[O] warder mut
fol. 54v

149

Example 1 (cont.)

Weltzell

Chatsworth

Attaignant

De Rippe

Roy.App.
58

151

Example 1 (cont.)

Weltzell

Chatsworth

[no more in painting]

[2]

Attaignant

De Rippe

Roy. App.
58

[62]

Example 1 (cont.)

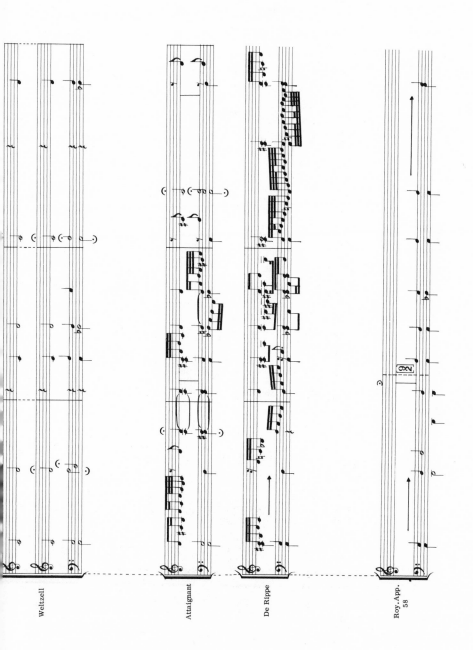

Weltzell

Attaignant

De Rippe

Roy. App.
58

155

Example 1 (cont.)

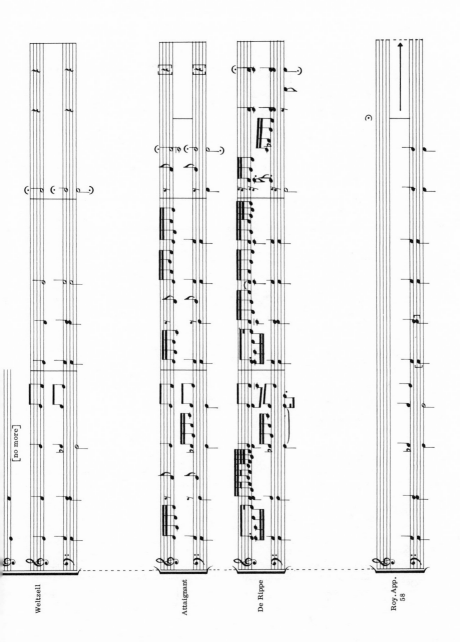

Weltzell

[no more]

Attaignant

De Rippe

Roy. App.
58

157

Example 1 (cont.)

Weltzell

Attaignant

De Rippe

repeat
of bars
16–21 in
De Rippe

Roy. App.
58

16bis

17bis

18bis

159

Example 1 (cont.)

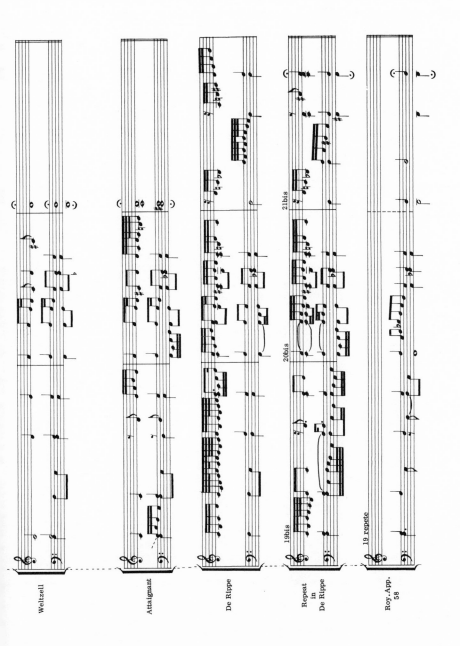

Weltzell

Attaignant

De Rippe

Repeat
in
De Rippe

Roy. App.
58

19bis

20bis

21bis

19 repete

161

PART III

MUSIC AND PATRONAGE IN ITALY 1450–1550

9

THE EARLY MADRIGAL: A RE-APPRAISAL OF ITS SOURCES AND ITS CHARACTER

James Haar

The genesis of the madrigal . . . is known: the transformation of the frottola from an accompanied song with a supporting bass and two inner voices serving as 'fillers' into a motet-like polyphonic construction with four parts of equal importance, can be followed as easily as the transformation of a chrysalis into a butterfly.[1]

Thus Alfred Einstein on the musical character of the early madrigal, giving in succinct and quotable form what probably remains the generally accepted view of the subject. Whether the madrigal of the 1520s and 1530s is best regarded as motet-like, as always having four equally important voices, or as emerging from the frottola are all of course debatable points, and that the transformation can be easily observed is a generously reassuring but not easily demonstrable statement.

The literary trend in secular music . . . grew in strength during the 1520s until classical verses of distinction and elegance became the norm. An already active and vigorous cult of Petrarca was to achieve such influence that in subsequent decades each of the master's lyrics was set to music not once but many times.

   This heightened artistry of text . . . was but one of the stylistic elements necessary to make up the balanced euphony of the madrigal.[2]

[1] Alfred Einstein, *The Italian Madrigal*, 3 vols. (Princeton, 1949), I, p. 121.
[2] Walter H. Rubsamen, *Literary Sources of Secular Music in Italy (ca. 1500)* (Berkeley and Los Angeles, 1943), p. 35.

In these words Walter Rubsamen summarised his view, also one quite generally accepted, of the literary background of the nascent madrigal. Again it seems debatable as to whether *petrarchismo*, even the more restrictive branch of it known as *bembismo*, can account for the poetic choices of composers – or, better, their patrons – in this period. An additional question is whether all or even very much sixteenth-century Petrarchistic verse aimed at the level of the genuine fourteenth-century article.

Scholars have been cautious about specifying time and place for the origins of the madrigal, but there is general agreement that Rome and Florence during the years 1515–30, with impetus given by the patronage of two Medici Popes, is about as close as one can come. In this view northern Italy is still preoccupied with the frottola, or is in the midst of Einstein's 'artistic pause', a larval stage of undetermined length and character.[3] What strikes me as questionable here is the rigidity of distinction in musical genre and in geographical–cultural boundaries; there is also some doubt in my mind as to the extent and importance of Medicean, at least Papal Medicean, patronage for the early madrigal.

Finally, everyone who has written on the rise of the madrigal has noted the paradox that this most Italian of genres appears on the musical side to be the creation of northern musicians, with only Costanzo Festa – for whom a French musical training has been postulated[4] – to represent native Italian talent. I would like to make a distinction here between visitors to Italy and thoroughly Italianised musicians, and incidentally to ignore the cultural stereotype of the polyphonic North versus the melodic South.

The traditional views of the madrigal thus far presented were formulated at the turn of this century, chiefly by Peter Wagner and Gaetano Cesari, the latter in a study that retains surprising vitality and freshness.[5] They were elaborated with inimitable grace and an abundance of detail, not all of it fully congruent with the major

[3] *Italian Madrigal*, pp. 139ff.
[4] See Edward E. Lowinsky (ed.), *The Medici Codex of 1518*, I: *Historical Introduction and Commentary*, Monuments of Renaissance Music 3 (Chicago, 1968), pp. 48–51.
[5] Peter Wagner, 'Das Madrigal und Palestrina', *Vierteljahrsschrift für Musikwissenschaft*, 8 (1892), pp. 423–98; Gaetano Cesari, *Die Entstehung des Madrigals im 16. Jahrhundert* (Cremona, 1908), issued in Italian as 'Le origini del madrigale cinquecentesco', *Rivista musicale italiana*, 19 (1912), pp. 1–34 and 380–428 (the Italian version will be cited here).

theses as I think he himself saw them, by Alfred Einstein, whose account of course remains of the greatest value despite errors of fact and what Iain Fenlon has called a point of view 'laced with Burckhardtian assumptions'.[6]

Before I venture on taking issue with aspects of these positions, attention should be called to more recent work that has already resulted in some modification of what one might call, without derogatory intent, the textbook view of the subject. Among contributions that may be singled out for their importance, and because exception will be taken with some of them as well, are Dean Mace's essay on the central position for madrigalists of Bembo's *Prose della volgar lingua*, Don Harrán's continuation of Cesari's work on verse types in the early madrigal, Ulrich Schulz-Buschhaus's informative if somewhat rigidly argued book on madrigal verse.[7] Verdelot as madrigalist emerges in sharpened focus as the result of Colin Slim's careful study of the Newberry manuscript, and Florentine patrons and native composers of the early decades of the sixteenth century assume new importance from the work of Frank D'Accone in a number of studies, particularly those devoted to Pisano and Layolle.[8] Valuable books by Nino Pirrotta and Wolfgang Osthoff on music in the Italian theatre in the Renaissance give much new detail on the public use of both frottola and madrigal.[9] Less has been done on questions of musical style in general, but hints for further work have been given by a number of scholars, particularly Walter

---

[6] Iain Fenlon, 'Context and Chronology of the Early Florentine Madrigal', to be published in the proceedings of the Convegno Internazionale di Studi held at Castelfranco Veneto in September 1978 to commemorate the fifth centenary of the birth of Giorgione.

[7] Dean T. Mace, 'Pietro Bembo and the Literary Origins of the Italian Madrigal', *The Musical Quarterly*, 55 (1969), pp. 65–86; Don Harrán, 'Verse Types in the Early Madrigal', *Journal of the American Musicological Society*, 22 (1969), pp. 27–53; Ulrich Schulz-Buschhaus, *Das Madrigal* (Bad Hamburg, 1969).

[8] H. Colin Slim, *A Gift of Madrigals and Motets*, 2 vols. (Chicago and London, 1972), and *idem*, *Ten Altus Parts at Oscott College Sutton Coldfield*, privately published (n.p., n.d. [1979]; Frank A. D'Accone, 'Bernardo Pisano: An Introduction to His Life and Works', *Musica Disciplina*, 17 (1963), pp. 117–35; *idem*, Introduction to *Francesco de Layolle: Collected Secular Works for 2, 3, 4 and 5 Voices*, Corpus Mensurabilis Musicae ser. 32 (n.p., 1969).

[9] Nino Pirrotta, *Li due Orfei. Da Poliziano a Monteverdi* (Turin, 1969; 2d edn, 1975), transl. as *Music and Theatre from Poliziano to Monteverdi* (Cambridge, 1981); Wolfgang Osthoff, *Theatergesang und darstellende Musik in der italienischen Renaissance* (Tutzing, 1969).

Rubsamen and Daniel Heartz.[10] Finally, the 'artistic pause' has been eliminated through the work of William Prizer on the continued life of the frottola into the 1520s, through Jeppesen's redating of some of the prints of the period, and through exploration of the manuscript sources for the early madrigal, begun by D'Accone, Slim, and Claudio Gallico and now continuing in the research of Iain Fenlon.[11] All of this work (and there is much more that could be cited were bibliographic completeness here the aim) has given grounds for a new interpretation of the early madrigal, even apart from the fact that a great deal of relevant music has been made available in modern editions.

In attempting a reconsideration of some of the basic problems in the early history of the madrigal I shall proceed from the sources to the texts to the music, with remarks on patronage and ambience scattered along the way. In order to be able to concentrate on some details I think of interest, I shall have to pass rather selectively over a good deal of important material; and this paper should be regarded more as a collection of notes aimed at the formulation of a new theory than as a finished product.

SOURCES

It may still seem convenient to place at the head of printed sources for the madrigal the first print to use the word in its title, the *Libro primo de la Serena* of 1530.[12] But one might just as easily take for a

---

[10] Walter H. Rubsamen, 'From Frottola to Madrigal: The Changing Pattern of Secular Italian Vocal Music', James Haar (ed.), *Chanson and Madrigal, 1480–1530* (Cambridge, Mass., 1964), pp. 51–87; Daniel Heartz, *'Les Goûts Réunis'*, or the Worlds of the Madrigal and the Chanson Confronted', *ibid.*, pp. 88–138.

[11] See William F. Prizer (ed.), *Libro Primo de la Croce (Rome: Pasoti and Dorico, 1526)*, Yale University Collegium Musicum 2d ser., vol. 8 (Madison, Wis., 1978), preface; on the later career of Marchetto Cara see Prizer, 'Marchetto Cara and the North Italian Frottola', Ph.D. diss., University of North Carolina, 1974, pp. 74–88. On revised dating for some of the prints of the 1520s and 1530s see Knud Jeppesen, *La Frottola. Bemerkungen zur Bibliographie der ältesten weltlichen Notendrucke in Italien* (Copenhagen, 1968).

A summary of recent scholarship dealing with manuscript sources for the madrigal is given in Iain Fenlon and James Haar, 'Fonti e cronologia dei madrigali di Costanzo Festa', *Rivista italiana di musicologia*, 13 (1978), pp. 212–42.

[12] The title *Madrigali novi de diversi excellentissimi autori. Libro primo de la Serena* is given to a reprint of 1533 (= RISM 1534[15] (n.s.)); it is assumed to be that of RISM 1530[2], of which only an untitled altus partbook survives. The title (lacking 'novi')

starting point volumes that advertise their contents as 'Canzoni', since much of what they contain is quite similar to the 1530 print. The Italian anthologies beginning with the Morgan Library print of 1520 and continuing through the decade (there are more of them than was once thought, and it is clear that some volumes have been lost) remain something of a puzzle, and their contents of Masses, motets, chansons, frottolas, villotas, and madrigals are in strong contrast to the unified series of Petrucci and even of Antico in the two preceding decades, and to the collected volumes of Verdelot and Arcadelt that came out in the 1530s.[13] Some manuscripts of the period also show mixed contents, but on the whole the manuscript sources are more orderly than the prints. Two reasons might be advanced for this. First, the prints containing secular music are frankly commercial in character, and are perhaps deliberately varied in the hope that they might appeal to a varied clientele. More importantly, the prints as opposed to the manuscripts do not represent a single repertory or even a limited provenance. These prints come mostly from Rome, at this time not a city prominent in the creation of the secular repertory – although connoisseurs of music among the princely ecclesiastics may of course have had private repertories of their own to which the printers did not have access. What the printers got hold of was music in wide circulation, much of it perhaps not very new; they supplemented it with bits of locally produced music such as the Petrarchan settings of Carpentras, a fair number of madrigals by Sebastiano Festa, and a few pieces by

is also found for the first edition in the purchase catalogues of Ferdinand Columbus; see Catherine Weeks Chapman, 'Printed Collections of Polyphonic Music Owned by Ferdinand Columbus', *Journal of the American Musicological Society*, 21 (1968), p. 72.

[13] Here follows an abbreviated-title list of these prints, dated according to the views of Jeppesen and others. All were printed in Rome unless otherwise indicated:

1520 *Motetti e canzone libro primo* (RISM [c. 1521]⁶)

c. 1520 fragments of a tenor partbook, printed in Fossombrone by Petrucci

1523 *Fior de motetti e canzoni* (RISM [c. 1526]⁵)

1524 *Canzoni strambote ode frotole soneti . . . libro 3° de la Croce* [lost; its existence, proved from Columbus's catalogue, indicates that earlier editions of Books I and II of this series must once have existed]

1526 *Canzone frottole e capitoli. libro primo de la Croce* (RISM 1526⁶)

1526 *Messa motetti canzonni . . . libro primo*

c. 1526 *Libro primo de la Fortuna* (RISM [c. 1530]¹)

1530 *Madrigali de diversi . . . libro primo de la Serena* (RISM 1530²)

1531 *Canzoni Frottole & capitoli . . . libro secondo de le Croce* (RISM 1531⁴)

Costanzo Festa.[14] Missing from these collections is a representative collection of the madrigals of Verdelot and other Florentines, found in abundance in manuscript sources of the period.

Two exceptional prints should be mentioned here. Both are from the press of Ottaviano Petrucci, at this time resident in his native Fossombrone. One is the *Musica di meser Bernardo pisano sopra le canzone del petrarcha*, dated 1520. The other is a fragment of one partbook of secular music, untitled and undated. The most recent hypothesis about its date, that of Stanley Boorman, places it shortly after the Pisano volume, perhaps in the same year.[15] If this is true the fact that the fragment contains a madrigal by Verdelot assumes special importance, and I shall return to it later. As for Pisano's collection, it is of course a landmark in the history of the madrigal, as Frank D'Accone has rightly stressed. It is rather an isolated monument, however, and although some of its contents are found in manuscript sources of Florentine provenance, I would think that much of the music was written in Rome and represents an approach to the setting of madrigalistic verse quite different from what the Florentines led by Verdelot were to do.[16] If one were to postulate a Roman school of madrigalists developing at this time, it is hard to see how Pisano and the two Festas fit together in it. The music of Sebastiano Festa is found in Florentine manuscripts, and so is much of the work of Costanzo Festa. The former composer is not known to have spent

[14] The pieces by Carpentras were printed by Antico in Rome, perhaps as early as the end of 1513; see Jeppesen, *La Frottola*, pp. 49ff and 128–29. Sebastiano Festa's first printed madrigal is in the *Motetti e canzone* of 1520; Costanzo Festa's earliest printed madrigal is in the *Libro primo de la Fortuna* of *c.* 1526. On a probable period of residence in Rome by Sebastiano Festa see Walter H. Rubsamen, 'Sebastian Festa and the Early Madrigal', *Bericht über den internationalen musikwissenschaftlichen Kongress Kassel 1962* (Kassel, 1963), p. 123.

[15] Professor Boorman's opinion on the Fossombrone fragment, a view concurred in by William Prizer, is as yet unpublished; it was kindly communicated to Iain Fenlon and to me. A description of the fragment may be found in Giuseppe Ceccarelli and Maurizio Spaccazocchi, *Tre carte musicali a stampa inedite di Ottaviano Petrucci* (Fossombrone, 1976).

[16] On the style of Pisano's Petrarchan settings see Einstein, *Italian Madrigal*, I, p. 172; D'Accone, 'Bernardo Pisano', p. 127. Pisano was in Rome a good deal of the time between 1513 and 1520; in D'Accone's opinion (*op. cit.*, pp. 121–2) his Petrarchan settings 'are to be associated directly with his early years of service at the Papal court'. Ottaviano Petrucci was himself in Rome on several occasions in the later years of Leo X's reign. See Augusto Vernarecci, *Ottaviano de' Petrucci da Fossombrone* (Fossombrone, 1881), pp. 132f and 142.

time in Florence and remains something of a musical enigma, but Costanzo Festa became, by whatever means, a thoroughgoing Florentine as a madrigalist. The extent of musical connections between Florence and Rome in the 1520s is for the most part unknown; there is one documented, and often-cited, visit of Verdelot to the court of Clement VII, a stray fact that makes one long for more information.[17] From the evidence of music printed in Rome during this period one could not guess that madrigals were being written in any number anywhere, but certainly not – apart from the modest number of works by the two Festas – in Rome itself.

Manuscripts containing early madrigals are far less dependent on printed sources than was once thought. Some of them are probably earlier than prints containing the same music, readings vary considerably, and there is a sizeable number of pieces surviving only in manuscript. A reconsideration of manuscripts devoted to this repertory is in progress, and some of the results have already been published.[18] Here only a few general remarks about these sources will have to suffice.

Although almost none of the manuscripts in question are explicitly dated, a number of them can be given approximate dates on the basis of musical and codicological evidence. They fall, roughly, into three groups: one from the early 1520s (Magl. XIX.164–7 and Basevi 2440 are examples), one from the middle years of the decade (the Newberry MS, Bologna Q 21), and one from the 1530s (Basevi 2495, Magl. XIX.122, and others).[19] With few exceptions all these manuscripts are of Florentine provenance; and indeed, except for the Marciana partbooks of c. 1520, which come from the Veneto or possibly from Venice itself, none of the known

---

[17] Slim, A Gift of Madrigals, I, pp. 52–3.

[18] See Fenlon and Haar, 'Fonti e cronologia', and the recent work on the subject cited there.

[19] The chief manuscripts in these three groups are the following: (1) early 1520s: Florence, Biblioteca Nazionale Centrale, Magl. XIX.164–7; Florence, Biblioteca del Conservatorio, Basevi 2440; Venice, Biblioteca Marciana, MS ital. Cl. IV.1795–8; (2) mid-1520s: Bologna, Civico Museo Bibliografico-Musicale, Mus. Q 21; New Haven, Yale University Music Library, MS 179; Modena, Biblioteca Estense, MS γ.L 11.8; Chicago, Newberry Library, Case MS VM.1578.M91; (3) 1530s: Florence, Biblioteca Nazionale Centrale, Magl. XIX.99–102; Florence, Biblioteca Nazionale Centrale, Magl. XIX.122–5; Florence, Biblioteca del Conservatorio, Basevi 2495; Brussels, Bibliothèque du Conservatoire Royal, MSS 27.731, FA VI.5 (2–4); Perugia, Biblioteca Augusta, MS I.M.1079.

manuscripts containing early madrigals can as yet be assigned to any place other than Florence.[20]

The repertory would appear to be mainly Florentine as well, with the exception of a group of villotas, the same ones that appear in the Roman prints of the 1520s. In the first group are pieces by Pisano and Layolle, the middle group is dominated by Verdelot but contains pieces by Corteccia and Layolle as well, and in the third group Arcadelt is the chief figure. Unrepresented are composers such as Willaert and Alfonso della Viola, early madrigalists working outside the Florentine orbit. The only non-Florentines included are, again, the two Festas.

Only the last of these groups seem close enough in date to printed collections to be related to them, and in some instances possibly dependent on them. Of all these manuscripts only the New-berry–Oscott partbooks can be thought to be a presentation copy;[21] the others, some of them closely interrelated in physical character, scribal concordances, and layers of repertory, appear to be collections made for private use. Bindings and other evidence suggest Florentine owners, among them members of the Strozzi and Capponi families.[22] One may speculate that men belonging to other Florentine families known for their patronage of the arts may also have had such collections copied for them.[23]

The apparent lack of manuscript sources for the madrigal outside

---

[20] Of the manuscripts listed in note 19 above, Modena *γ*.L 11.8 and Perugia 1079 may come from outside Florence. Two other manuscripts of the period, each containing a few early madrigals, are uncertain in provenance: Berkeley, University of California Music Library, MS 121 and Rome, Biblioteca Apostolica Vaticana, Mus. MS 571. For the latter see Alexander Silbiger, 'An Unknown Partbook of Early 16th-Century Polyphony', *Studi Musicali*, 6 (1977), pp. 43–67.

[21] On this see Slim, *A Gift of Madrigals*, chaps. 2, 5, *et passim*.

[22] For volumes of music with a Strozzi device on the bindings (including Basevi 2495 and the contemporary chanson manuscript Basevi 2442) see Frank D'Accone, 'Transitional Text Forms and Settings in an Early 16th-Century Florentine Manuscript', Laurence Berman (ed.), *Words and Music: The Scholar's View* (Cambridge, Mass., 1972), p. 35n; Howard Mayer Brown, 'Chansons for the Pleasure of a Florentine Patrician: Florence, Biblioteca del Conservatorio di Musica, MS Basevi 2442', Jan LaRue *et al.* (eds.), *Aspects of Medieval and Renaissance Music* (New York, 1966), pp. 56–66. For manuscripts that may have belonged to members of the Pucci and Capponi families see Fenlon and Haar, 'Fonti e cronologia', pp. 217–19.

[23] Some non-musical manuscripts of the period copied for members of the Rucellai and Ridolfi families are listed in Slim, *A Gift of Madrigals*, p. 40.

Florence does not necessarily give total priority for the genre to Florentine circles, but it is strongly suggestive that prior to 1530 the madrigal was cultivated with particular intensity in Florence, whether the Medici were present or absent from that city. More important than whether the Medici were in control or in exile was the ease of composition or at any rate of circulation of madrigalistic verse in Florentine society, and the presence of a nucleus of musicians who could match fashionable verse with fashionable musical settings.[24] No one poet dominated the Florentine literary scene, but it seems clear that Verdelot was the central musical figure, a *français italianisant* who supplied just what was wanted and needed and who, I suggest, dictated the formal and stylistic patterns of the music for the Florentine madrigal. Here seems the place to say that it does not matter very much that few of the early madrigalists were native Italians. To cultivate this genre one had to know the language well and to be thoroughly acclimatised; thus Verdelot and Willaert and Arcadelt may be thought of as naturalised Italians, in a way that Dufay, Isaac, perhaps even Josquin never were.

---

[24] Florentine aristocrats were, before the 1530s at any rate, perfectly capable of extending patronage to artists without dependence on the Medici; for long periods the Rucellai and Strozzi families were in fact rivals of the Medici in this regard. On the prominence of the Rucellai in this regard see Felix Gilbert, 'Bernardo Rucellai and the Orti Oricellari: A Study of the Origin of Modern Political Thought', *Journal of the Warburg and Courtauld Institutes*, 12 (1949), pp. 104ff. The munificence of Filippo Strozzi is described in glowing terms by Bernardo Segni, *Storie fiorentine* (Milan, 1805), [I], pp. 26–7. An example of this sort of patronage is the activity of the Compagnia della Cazzuola in presenting plays, with music, in the 1510s and 1520s; see Slim, *A Gift of Madrigals*, pp. 99–100. Also perhaps of relevance is the short-lived Accademia Sacra Medicea (1515–19), in which music played a part, and the activities of which interested Bembo though he was not a member. On this group (which may despite its name have had some anti-Medicean members) see Armand De Gaetano, 'The Florentine Academy and the Advancement of Learning Through the Vernacular: The Orti Oricellari and the Sacra Accademia', *Bibliothèque d'Humanisme et Renaissance*, 30 (1968), pp. 19–52.

Instances of Florentine patronage outside Florence itself are furnished by the dedications of Layolle's *Contrapunctus* of 1528 and of Naich's *Exercitium Seraficum*, a madrigal volume of *c.* 1540, both addressed to members of the Altoviti family (one in Lyons, one in Rome). One might also cite the patronage of Neri Capponi, a Florentine living in Venice in the 1540s, who according to Antonfrancesco Doni sponsored the musical circle in which *la Pecorina* performed and for which Willaert composed; see Doni's dedicatory letter to the tenor partbook of his *Dialogo della Musica* of 1544 (p. 5 in the edition of G. Francesco Malipiero (Vienna, 1965)).

TEXTS

One of Cesari's most interesting and least-noted contributions to the study of the early madrigal is a tabulation of types of poetry contained in the corpus as he knew it; what he found was a great preponderance of what he called poetic madrigals, with a fair number of ballatas and canzone stanzas but only a few sonnets and other verse types such as the sestina.[25] Even if one were to differentiate among the madrigal texts by use of Don Harrán's categories of hybrid forms mixing elements of ballata or canzone, the result would remain basically the same. Cesari's survey could be extended by inclusion of sources he was not acquainted with; I have not done this, but I did look through the sources, printed and manuscript, for the period *c.* 1510 – *c.* 40 in order to see how frequent the use of Petrarch actually was. Of the 366 poems in the *Canzoniere* seventy-four were set in full or in part (the number would be slightly higher if individual canzone stanzas were counted separately, but the number of Petrarchan verses would in this enumeration rise by a much greater factor).[26] Unlike Einstein I do not see that any particular part of the *Canzoniere* was stressed or neglected; both the *vita* and *morte* of Madonna Laura are represented. What is striking is that a good number, some thirty, of the texts used by the madrigalists had already been set by the frottolists of Petrucci's prints. Thus the Petrarchan verse favoured for musical setting early in the sixteenth century remained so through its fourth decade, with one rather telling exception: Petrarch's four madrigals were more popular with the madrigalists than they had been with the frottolists.[27] A change did come in the Petrarchan choices of Rore, the later Willaert, and members of their Venetian circle, but I would prefer to see this as a change of fashion rather than, as Einstein does, in itself a deepening and maturing of madrigalistic art, although his point remains of course a valid one.

[25] Cesari, 'Le origini', p. 14.

[26] Some poems were of course set by more than one composer. I counted a total of 131 settings in all (including those in the frottola prints).

[27] *Or vedi amor che giovanetta donna*, for example, has nine settings (Carpentras, *c.* 1513; Maio, 1519; Pisano [?] in Magl. 164–7; Arcadelt, 1539 and 1540; Alfonso della Viola, 1540; Matthias, 1541; anon. in Marciana 1795–8; anon. in Modena γ.L 11.8). Schulz-Buschhaus, *Das Madrigal*, p. 24n, points out that this madrigal is untypical of the fourteenth-century genre in its personal lyricism and lack of narrative tone; this is just what may have appealed to early-sixteenth-century tastes.

Why did the early madrigalists make such comparatively little use of Petrarch in this age of Petrarchism? I can suggest three reasons. One is the custom of reciting, or singing, with use of stock melodic formulas, of Petrarchan verse by *improvvisatori*, who played their own accompaniments. If the greatest recorded vogue for these poet–musicians was the turn of the century, we may be sure that the fashion did not end with the death of Serafino Aquilano in 1500. Castiglione attests to the continuing popularity of such figures in the first two decades of the sixteenth century, and Antonfrancesco Doni, among others, to their survival into the third and fourth decades.[28] These men sang poetry other than that of Petrarch, of course, but the tradition of performing Petrarchan verse in this way was nonetheless strong, and may in part account for the limited number of early madrigals using Petrarch.[29]

A second reason is that the *Canzoniere* is made up chiefly of sonnets; and the sonnet, it would seem, was no more popular or easy to handle for the first madrigalists than it had been for the frottolists. Petrarch's madrigals, individual canzone stanzas, and even sestina stanzas were composed more frequently than the sonnets, and very often when a sonnet was chosen only the octet was set. We shall look at an example by Verdelot in which it seems the composer did his best to disguise the form of the sonnet he chose. Of course the poets of the early sixteenth century wrote sonnets, most of them full of Petrarchan imagery and many of them crowded with direct citations

---

[28] Among musicians of this type mentioned in the *Cortegiano* are Bernardo Accolti (l'Unico Aretino), Terpandro, Cristoforo Romano, and Giacomo di San Secundo. Even Marchetto Cara is praised as a performer rather than as a composer. See James Haar, 'The Courtier as Musician: Castiglione's View of the Science and Art of Music', (to be published).

Doni's *Dialogo della Musica* ends with a performance of four sonnets improvised 'a la lira'; these are the only complete sonnets included in Doni's volume.

During this period *cantimbanchi* and *cantastorie* continued to travel about Italy reciting and singing poetry to their own accompaniment. For the career of a typical figure of this kind see Vittorio Rossi, 'Di un cantastorie ferrarese del secolo xvi', *Rassegna Emiliana di Storia, Letteratura ed Arte*, 2 (1889–90), pp. 435–6. Doni, in *I Marmi* (Venice, 1552; ed. Ezio Chiorboli, 2 vols. (Bari, 1928), I, p. 107), speaks of the custom of 'cantare all'improviso su la lira' in Florence in his time.

On the relation of this improvised music to that of the written madrigal see below, note 63.

[29] One reason for the existence of frottolistic settings of Petrarch is that they were meant as models to be used with other texts – were, in other words, 'modi di dir sonetti' or 'canzoni'. *Si è debile il filo a cui s'atiene*, a canzone stanza set by Tromboncino, is one such example; see Rubsamen, *Literary Sources*, p. 24.

from Petrarch, but even these seem not to have been regarded as *poesia per musica*. For example, Bembo's poetry enjoyed some popularity with the early madrigalists, but it was the ballate, canzoni and stanze of his youth, not the classically Petrarchan verse of his *Canzoniere*, that were chosen.

Finally, I would suggest that the madrigal, which throughout the sixteenth century was to some degree music written to order for single patrons or individual occasions, was particularly so in its early years. We know of patronage or event for only a few pieces;[30] but the suggestion is strong that the bulk of the repertory was written to order. To give this suggestion some tangible substance I might point out that although favoured texts were set repeatedly by composers working in the same or related milieux, the texts used by Alfonso della Viola writing in Ferrara, and those set by Hubert Naich writing in Rome, are different not only from each other but also from the madrigal literature of the Florentines, and the dedicatory letter to Naich's volume makes it clear that he composed music for the poetry of local friends and patrons.[31] Although one can imagine a request for a Petrarchan setting to be used on some occasion or other, it is much more likely that the poem would be a new one, containing an explicit or veiled reference to a specific person or place, or to another poem by a member of the local circle.

Is the poetry of the early madrigal, even if not very often that of

[30] Verdelot's music, commisioned for the madrigals serving as *intermedi* in Machiavelli's comedies, is one instance of music written to order; see Slim, *A Gift of Madrigals*, pp. 92–104, for these and other pieces by Verdelot on texts from poetic dramas. Corteccia's slightly later music for the comedies *Il Commodo* (1539) and *Il Furto* (1544) are other examples (on performances of *Il Furto* see De Gaetano, 'The Florentine Academy', p. 43). Many texts set by early madrigalists suggest festive occasions; see Pirrotta, *Li due Orfei*, 2nd edn, pp. 146 and 191–2 on a group of such texts by Arcadelt. Other kinds of texts likely to have had musical settings commissioned include those in praise of specific women such as the often-serenaded Tullia d'Aragona; poems addressed directly or indirectly to rulers or lesser dignitaries (Festa set a text, *Sacra pianta da quel arbor discese*, apparently in honour of Alessandro de'Medici; see Einstein, *Italian Madrigal*, I, pp. 157–8); and wedding poems. The texts set to order need not themselves have commemorated special occasions, of course; Arcadelt's settings of Michelangelo texts were apparently commissioned, some time after the poetry had been written, by the Florentine banker Luigi del Riccio: see Einstein, *op. cit.*, I, pp. 161–2.

[31] *Exercitium Seraficum. Madrigali di M. Hubert Naich* (Rome: Antonio Blado, n.d.). The dedication is in the altus partbook and was not noticed by Vogel. In it the composer refers to his madrigals as 'in maggior parte à richiesta di questo e di quello . . . composti'; one assumes that at least some among the 'questo e quello' had written the texts themselves.

Petrarch himself, nonetheless of 'high literary quality'? Throwing aside the caution an English-speaking musicologist properly feels on such subjects, I would say that on the whole it is not, that it is often frivolous in aim, tediously repetitious in theme, and mannered in execution. One is in fact tempted to set on end the traditional view of the subject by saying that frottolistic verse is fresher, more varied, and more interesting than run-of-the-mill 'Madonna' madrigals. What sets the two bodies of verse apart is less the quality of poetic thought than details of language and rhetorical plan (the madrigal being fuller of Petrarchistic turns of phrase and reserving its 'point' for the closing couplet), of form (the predictable repetition schemes of the barzelletta are no longer in use in the madrigal), and, above all, of metre (the regular trochaic octosyllables of the barzelletta, with their strong suggestion of dance rhythms, are replaced by the iambic metre of the madrigal with its freely alternating long and short lines punctuated by strongly marked caesuras).[32] Barzelletta and madrigal are sufficiently different as poetic types to call for distinctness of style when they are set to music. Not all of the poetic literature of the frottola is made up of barzellette, of course; but if one looks for similar verse types in order to compare the musical approaches of frottolists and madrigalists, I think the sonnet and the canzone stanza, which have been studied in this respect without much profit,[33] may be less important than the strambotto, the form of which lived on into the era of the madrigal as the eight-line stanza. What might repay study here is not general comparison of musical styles, which would only show how different the soloistic strambotto is from the chansonesque madrigal, but rather a study of declamation, treatment of poetic phrase and line segment, and rhetorical emphasis.

Another question about early madrigal texts, and their musical settings, is their relation to the theories of Pietro Bembo. The influence of Bembo's attitudes toward the *questione della lingua* was no doubt felt even before the publication of the *Prose della volgar lingua* in 1525. It is reasonable to suppose that poets in the Roman circles frequented by Bembo during the reign of Leo X (1513–21) were

[32] Observance of the poetic caesura by early madrigal composers is noted by Cesari, 'Le origini', pp. 26f and 32f.

[33] Both Rubsamen, *Literary Sources*, and Einstein, *Italian Madrigal*, emphasise these 'higher' forms; Einstein does of course give attention to other types of madrigal verse, but he is not very interested in declamatory rhetoric as a subject.

under his influence to some degree; but not every Petrarchising poet was necessarily a disciple of Bembo even in Rome. One may thus wonder if Luigi Cassola's madrigals, an important poetic source for early madrigal composers, are generally consonant with rather than reflecting in any specific way Bembo's doctrines about variety of metric form and of linguistic weight and colour.[34] It may be that Bembo even influenced, if only indirectly, musicians at Leo X's court; evidence of a tangible sort might be the fact that *Se 'l pensier che mi strugge* – the Petrarchan canzone Bembo thought to be the best example of Petrarch's mastery of *vaghezza, dolcezza*, and *piacevolezza* in the choice of words – was chosen for musical setting by both Carpentras and Sebastiano Festa.[35] Harder to claim as evidence but possibly important all the same is the musical style of Pisano's Petrarchan canzoni, elaborate and even somewhat pretentious, among the few genuine examples in the nascent madrigal of a deliberate attempt to make the music 'rise' to the level of the poetry.[36]

There is every reason to think that Bembo's influence was a real one on poets, critics, and composers in Venice and the Veneto during the 1520s and 1530s, especially near the end of this period. One might consider that, in choice of texts and in the increasingly sophisticated declamatory musical rhetoric with which they were set, Willaert and Rore exhibit a genuine musical *bembismo*. This music is, however, no longer the early madrigal; its pronounced novelty of style was felt and commented on as soon as it appeared.[37]

---

[34] Cassola, who visited Rome often but lived most of his life in his native Piacenza, published a volume of *Madrigali* in 1544. Settings of his verse appear as early as 1526 (*Se quanto in voi si vede*, in RISM [*c*. 1530]¹), and his poetry must have circulated widely in manuscript. Dale Hall is preparing a study of musical settings of Cassola's poetry.

[35] Carpentras's setting appears in Antico's *Frottole libro tertio*, first published *c*. 1513; cf. note 14, above. Festa's composition was printed in the *Libro primo de la Croce* (1526⁶); it is also found in a manuscript source of the 1520s, Bologna Q 21. Bembo cites this canzone (along with the next one in the *Canzoniere*, *Chiare fresche e dolci acque*) in the *Prose della volgar lingua*, ed. C. Dionissoti-Casolone (Turin, 1931), 11, xiii, p. 328.

[36] On the ambitiousness of Pisano's style see Einstein, *Italian Madrigal*, 1, p. 172; cf. Nino Pirrotta's comment in *Chanson & Madrigal*, p. 77.

[37] See, for example, the reaction of Antonfrancesco Doni to Venetian music of the early 1540s (*Dialogo della Musica*, ed. Malipiero, p. 5) as well as his references to the music of Arcadelt as 'troppo vecchio' and to music having recently surpassed all that Verdelot had done (*ibid.*, pp. 35 and 70).

It seems much less certain that Bembo was important to the circle of Florentine amateurs – some of them poets and probably nearly all of them, in their own minds, critics – in which the early madrigal was shaped. We know of no Florentine visit by Bembo to compare with those made by Giangiorgio Trissino in 1513–18; Trissino's ideas about vernacular literature were heard in the Orti Oricellari and were debated seriously by the Florentines, including one poet whose work was set by Verdelot and others, Lodovico Martelli.[38] It would appear that Trissino the 'Italianist' was taken more seriously in these years than Bembo the 'Tuscanist'; if Machiavelli's opinion was a typical one, Bembo as a Venetian was thought to be somewhat presumptuous in attempting to judge Florentine language.[39] Florentine poets, who in the opinion of Cosimo Bartoli were only mediocre at the turn of the century, improved their taste and technique in the next twenty-five years through study of Dante, Petrarch, and Boccaccio; Bembo is not mentioned as an intermediary.[40]

This argument against an early influence of Bembo's work in Florence suggests two things: first, that Florentine madrigalian literature and by extension the music that went with it was not only local in character but deliberately, even chauvinistically so; and second, that the blend of Petrarchism the Florentines espoused was a continuation of the fashionable, indeed dilettantish vogue of Petrarch already current during the frottolistic period rather than the more thoroughly reasoned academic approach of Bembo.[41]

It would be helpful to know how much of the poetry set by Verdelot, Pisano (in his Florentine years), Layolle, Corteccia, and

---

[38] Trissino's effect on the younger Florentines who heard him in the Orti Oricellari is described by Benedetto Varchi, *Lezzioni* (Florence, 1590), p. 647. On Martelli see Slim, *A Gift of Madrigals*, pp. 86–7, and the biographical sources cited there. Martelli's *risposta* in answer to Trissino is mentioned in Giuseppe Toffanin, *Il Cinquecento*, 7th edn (Milan, 1965), p. 116; I have not been able to find a copy of the work itself.

[39] See Niccolò Machiavelli, *Discorso o dialogo intorno alla nostra lingua*, ed. Bortolo Sozzi (Turin, 1976), introduction, p. lv. where this opinion, attributed to Machiavelli in Lenzoni's *In difesa della lingua fiorentina e di Dante* of 1556, is cited.

[40] Bartoli's opinion is given as an interlocutor in Giovan Battista Gelli's dialogue *Ragionamento sopra le difficoltà di mettere in regole la nostra lingua*, *Opere*, ed. Ireneo Sanesi (Turin, 1968), pp. 484–5.

[41] The passage in Gelli's *Ragionamento* cited above, note 40, implies that Florentine Petrarchism did mature and deepen between 1500 and 1530, with the discussions in the Orti Oricellari leading the way; but no theoretical work on the scale or level of Bembo's *Prose* arose out of these discussions.

Arcadelt was written by Florentine gentlemen. Frank D'Accone has shown that Lorenzo Strozzi's poetry was used; and from Colin Slim's research we learn that Machiavelli and Martelli wrote poetry that was set more or less on the spot.[42] For Machiavelli we even know the purpose of several madrigals being put to music, as *intermedi* for his comedies *Mandragola* and *Clizia*. In Martelli we have a critic, a poet, and a member of a family that included a real-life Petrarchist who literally died for love.[43] Of the other poets who frequented the Orti Oricellari before the group's dispersal in 1522 we know less with regard to music. Francesco Guidetti has one poem for which a musical setting survives, but Cosimo Rucellai and Luigi Alamanni are prominent members of this circle whose verse is not known to have been set to music in Florence.[44] The poetry of known author-ship that does appear in the Florentine musical corpus is not all of local origin, despite what I hinted above; the madrigalists knew the work of Roman-based poets such as Giovanni Brevio and Claudio Tolomei, the well-circulated madrigals of Luigi Cassola, and some poems by the Neapolitan Dragonetto Bonifazio.[45]

One problem with the poetry is that it, like the musical madrigal in its early days, seems to have circulated chiefly in manuscript. The printed collections of poetry in these years are few in number, and very mixed in character and quality – offering a striking analogy to the musical prints of 1515–30.[46] Poems circulated one by one, often

---

[42] On Strozzi and Florentine musicians see D'Accone, 'Transitional Text Forms', pp. 32ff; for Verdelot and the poetry of Machiavelli and Martelli see Slim, *A Gift of Madrigals*, pp. 85–6 and 92ff.

[43] Lodovico di Gianfrancesco Martelli, a first cousin of the Lodovico [di Lorenzo] in question here, is said by Varchi to have died in 1530 as the result of a duel fought over a married lady; see Benedetto Varchi, *Storia fiorentina* (edn of Cologne, 1721), pp. 349–52. According to Pompeo Litta, *Delle famiglie celebri italiane*, III, 1 (Milan, n.d.), *Martelli di Firenze*, Table 3, this duel was fought over political as well as amorous affairs; in the same table Litta says of Lodovico di Lorenzo that he died *c.* 1527 at Salerno 'con sospetto di veleno propinatogli per cagione di donna'.

[44] Guidetti's text *S'io pensasse Madonna che mia morte* (also ascribed to Molza) was set by Verdelot (RISM 1533², no. 2). On this poem, printed in *Rime di poeti italiani del secolo xvi*, Scelta di Curiosità Letterarie 133 (Bologna, 1873; repr. Bologna, 1968), p. 62, see Harrán, 'Verse Types', p. 33n. Alamanni's poetry enjoyed more favour with madrigalists later in the century than it did with the first generation, except for Francesco Layolle, a friend and fellow-exile, who set two of Alamanni's texts, *Lasso la bella fera* and *Infra bianche rugiadre et verdi fronde*.

[45] See Slim, *A Gift of Madrigals*, pp. 88–91.

[46] Cesari, 'Le origini', p. 387n. Cesari does not mention the poetry of Martelli, two volumes of which were printed in 1531 and 1533. One could also cite, as an

as part of epistolary exchanges,[47] and one suspects that musicians were given them one by one. Over this casual exchange a veil of anonymity has descended, and it seems unlikely that we will ever be able to track down the authorship of all or nearly all of the verse used by the early madrigalists.[48]

MUSIC

The poets of the early madrigal wrote verse that was freer in form than in content.[49] The conceit with which a poem ended might be – usually in fact was – new, since poets prided themselves on their ingenuity in this regard. But the opening and often the middle verses had strong resemblances one to another, including of course actual citation of phrases either from Petrarch or from a new poem in currency at the time. At an early stage composers learned to heighten the effect of such citation by including musical references from other settings of these phrases.[50] Certain individual poems appear to have been particularly appealing to composers; there are multiple settings of a number of poems, with examples by Bembo and by other contemporaries such as Cassola and Bonifazio in addition to those Petrarchan verses currently much in vogue. Here one is on the lookout for more frequent musical borrowings, perhaps even the use of parody technique within the genre itself. Examples do exist: a particularly interesting one is Cassola's *Altro non è il mio amor*, a poem

analogy to the villota's appearance in musical prints, the *opuscoli* issued by *cantastorie* throughout this period, little pamphlets containing popularised versions of well-known poetry.

[47] An example, one of many, is a sonnet, *Havea tentato il giovanetto Arciere*, by Machiavelli, included in a letter of 31 January 1514 [= 1515] to Francesco Vettori in Rome. See Niccolò Machiavelli, *Erotica*, ed. Gerolamo Lazzeri (Milan, n.d.), p. 207. On the exchange of poems among the 'eleganti del bel mondo', see Cesari, 'Le origini', p. 384.

[48] Madrigals flowed easily from sixteenth-century pens. Cf. the remark of A. F. Grazzini (Il Lasca): 'Non tengo conto già di un madrigale, ch'io ne fo cento il giorno', cited in Schulz-Buschhaus, *Das Madrigal*, p. 7n.

[49] This formal freedom of course had its limits; and the outlines of the canzone stanza, the ballata, and the old fourteenth-century madrigal tempted poets even though no necessity to observe them existed. On this see Harrán, 'Verse Types', *passim*.

[50] Examples of this kind of musical reference are cited often in Einstein, *Italian Madrigal*. See, for example, the sharing between Berchem (1544) and Animuccia (1547) of a common motive for the opening of a Petrarch sestina. Other examples from the early madrigal literature are cited by Cesari, 'Le origini', pp. 415–16.

existing in two textual parodies and a whole set of interrelated musical compositions.[51] Other, less striking examples are also found;[52] but the use of extensive musical parody within the madrigal now seems much less common than one would have supposed.

Beginning about 1540 the Venetian printers began to issue volumes of madrigals, usually for two and three voices but occasionally for four, books full of familiar titles. The composers, among whom are Gero, Lupacchino, Eliseo Ghibel, and the publisher Girolamo Scotto, may have been employed for the purpose of making settings of these well-known texts.[53] And yet the kind of parody-by-reduction that has been shown by Lawrence Bernstein to be a common practice in the French chanson would seem to be much less common in the madrigal.[54] If this is true (and not merely the result of my failure to spot musical resemblances) it is hard to resist the conclusion that, except for a relatively small number of musical favourites such as Arcadelt's *Il bianco e dolce cigno* or, a bit later, Rore's *Ancor che col partire*, it was the texts themselves that were popular and would sell the volumes of music. In other words, the new *poesia per musica* had a life of its own; madrigals were doubtless improvised as accompanied songs at the same time they were being set to more formal music, just as in the circles where the frottola had flourished.[55] In those circles composers like Marchetto Cara were still writing a few pieces, now to poetry of the newly fashionable cast. That such pieces are not madrigals in the sense that they do not sound just like Verdelot would not have bothered people very much; for once we may be more acutely aware of stylistic differences than most contemporaries of the early madrigalists would have cared to be.[56] The point to be made here is that our tendency to think of the music first – caused not only

[51] See James Haar, '*Altro non è il mio amor*', Berman (ed.), *Words and Music*, pp. 93–114.

[52] Slim, *A Gift of Madrigals*, pp. 208ff; Cesari, 'Le Origini', pp. 415–16.

[53] Gero's volume of two-voice madrigals and chansons is described in the dedication as having been written at Scotto's behest. See Lawrence Bernstein and James Haar (eds.), *Jhan Gero. Il Primo Libro de' Madrigali italiani et canzoni francese a due voci* (New York, 1980), pp. xxii–xxiv.

[54] See Lawrence Bernstein, 'Claude Gervaise as Chanson Composer', *Journal of the American Musicological Society*, 18 (1965), pp. 359–81; *idem*, 'The Cantus-Firmus Chansons of Tylman Susato', *ibid*., 22 (1969), pp. 197–240; Bernstein and Haar, *Gero*, pp. xxxviif.   [55] See note 28 above.

[56] This is not to say that sixteenth-century ears were not alert to novelties in musical style: cf. note 37 above. My point is that we attempt to define the madrigal by musical style; in the sixteenth century it was defined by the form and metre of the text.

by our professional bias but also by our continuing effort to define what is madrigalistic, and hence new and different, in the music – prevents our seeing the continuity of ambience and social practice that exists between frottola and madrigal.

An example may help to clarify this discussion. Dragonetto Bonifazio's madrigal *Amor mi fa morire* is a text known chiefly through its setting by Willaert, first printed in 1534.[57] Two other settings from the period are known to me: one is by Alfonso della Viola, the other by Girolamo Scotto.[58] Both of these might have been composed in emulation of Willaert; some musical evidence can be used to support this hypothesis (Example 1).

The musical resemblances are, admittedly, more marked between Scotto and Willaert. Even these are, however, superficial; in style the three pieces are quite different. Willaert's setting, more leisurely and more elaborate contrapuntally than the other two, is a working-out of a cantus–tenor framework.[59] Della Viola's piece is quite chordal, its top voice dominating, in the manner of Verdelot's more homophonic settings. Scotto's madrigal, also basically chordal, makes use of the fast patter and syncopated rhythms of the *note nere* style, here partly for visual novelty and partly to allow introduction of written-out *passaggi*.[60] These are all recognisable sub-types of the early madrigalian style. What they have in common is unity of rhetorical approach: precise declamation, emphasising the iambic rhythms of the text; some distinction in character between seven- and eleven-syllable lines (this is not uniformly observed);[61] emphasis

[57] Willaert's setting was printed in Verdelot's second book of four-voice madrigals (RISM 1534[16] and numerous reprints). Despite its position as the opening piece in the book it seems really to be by Willaert; it was included in the posthumous volume of Willaert's four-voice madrigals printed by Scotto in 1563. A modern edition of the piece may be found in Einstein, *Italian Madrigal*, III, no. 31.

[58] Viola's setting appeared in his *Primo libro* (Ferrara, 1539); Scotto's piece is in his four-voice *Primo libro* (Venice, 1542). No manuscript sources for these or for Willaert's setting are known to me.

[59] For a discussion of the form and style of this piece see Erich Hertzmann, *Adrian Willaert in der weltlichen Vokalmusik seiner Zeit* (Leipzig, 1931), pp. 39–41.

[60] Scotto's print seems aimed at capturing the widest possible market. Most of the texts are well known in the literature of the period; the title of the volume advertises its contents as having 'alcuni a la misura breve, et altri a voce pari'. It is a wonder he did not add the Italian equivalent of 'apt for voyces and viols'.

[61] Cesari, 'Le origini', pp. 32–3, discusses the tendency of early madrigalists to set seven-syllable lines syllabically and to reserve melismas for the tenth syllable of eleven-syllable lines. The observation is a valuable one but should not be taken as a rule, for exceptions abound.

Example 1. Dragonetto Bonifazio, *Amor mi fa morire*
A: Willaert; B: Scotto; C: Alfonso della Viola

Figure 1. Gentile Bellini, *Processione in San Marco* (1496), detail: Venice, Accademia di Belle Arti

was provided by the *cantadori nuovi*, with the participation of the instrumentalists. The musically accompanied observances on those days were usually limited to a Mass in the church or Scuola. The first Sunday of each month was celebrated with great ceremony at all of the Scuole. First, a Mass was held in the Scuola, followed by a procession to the church allied with each Scuola, where a second Mass was performed. The ceremonies concluded with a procession returning to the Scuola. Music for all four parts of the celebration was provided by the *cantadori nuovi* and instrumentalists, with the occasional participation of the *cantadori vecchi*. The same musicians were obliged to perform at major feasts, which were of two types, each observed in a particular manner. First, the feast-day of the patron saint of each Scuola was the occasion for a spectacular assemblage of musicians, as the host Scuola was joined in its celebrations by the other Scuole, with their musicians. The observances usually included Masses and processions, as on the first Sunday of the month, as well as Vespers. Second, the great civic feasts of St Mark, Corpus Christi, St Isidore, and St Vido also were events of great splendour. On those days a procession was held in the Piazza San Marco with all of the Scuole, accompanied by all of their singers and instrumentalists, the Doge and his retinue, including his private trumpets, the singers of St Mark's basilica, and the clergy of numerous churches and monasteries.

Music was of special concern to two of the Scuole, San Marco and San Rocco. At San Marco this took the form of increasing the number of musicians, both singers and instrumentalists, while San Rocco concentrated instead on obtaining fewer musicians, but of higher quality. The ensemble described at the beginning of this paper, that of the Scuola di San Marco in 1515, is an example of the increased number of musicians hired by this Scuola. The trumpets, shawms, recorders and cornets were all additions to its normal forces.

A practice unique to the Scuola di San Marco was that of hiring a third choir to supplement the *cantadori vecchi* and *cantadori nuovi*. These *cantadori solenni* were used only on the first Sunday of each month and other major celebrations. Their employment is first recorded in 1492, when the *maestro di cappella* of St Mark's, Piero de Fossis, and three of his senior singers were engaged.[12] These singers were clearly

---

[12] ASV, SSM, Registro 16bis, *Notatorio*, part 2, fol. 62. The other three men were pre Marco Bussati, pre Antonio Schatoler, and pre Nicolo Balanzer.

four of the best-known and best-trained in Venice, and they must have contributed greatly to the prestige of the Scuola and to the quality of its music-making. Singers of the basilica were employed as *cantadori solenni* until 1517 (or perhaps later), in which year all twelve adult singers of the *cappella* of St Mark's were employed.[13] During the 1520s and 1530s singers not connected with St Mark's were hired as *cantadori solenni*. The increased musical forces of the Scuola di San Marco are clearly set out in the payment records for Corpus Christi of 1494:

to the *cantadori da corpi* for their compensation for the day of Corpus Domini, one ducat, valued at 6 *lire*, 4 *soldi*
to the *cantadori de laude* for compensation for the said day, one ducat, valued at 6 *lire*, 4 *soldi*
to the singers of San Marco for the procession of Corpus Domini, 3 ducats, valued at 18 *lire*, 12 *soldi*
to the instrumentalists, that is maestro Zentil dal'Arpa and companions, for the said procession, 13 *lire*, valued at 13 *lire*, 0 *soldi*
(Doc. 6)

In contrast, the forces of the Scuola di San Giovanni Evangelista on the same feast in 1496, as depicted in Gentile Bellini's painting of the procession on that date, consisted only of three instrumentalists and five singers.[14]

From the very beginning of its existence, the Scuola di San Rocco paid attention to the quality of its musicians. The first singers hired in 1488 were lured from the other Scuole.[15] Clearly, San Rocco wished to employ singers of high quality, and selected men whose singing was well known to them. The concern of the officers of the Scuola for musical quality was expressed in an explanation of the dismissal of several singers in 1517:

It is now several months ago that our singers, viz. misser pre Sabastian and his companions, were dismissed for not being sufficient to our needs, and

---

[13] ASV, SSM, Registro 17, *Notatorio*, fol. 74. The singers hired were maestro Piero de Fossis, pre Antonio Schatoler, pre Nicolo di Leonardi, pre Sabastian di Leonardi, pre Zuan Zoto, fra Vizenzo Vituri, pre Franzescho Luchexe, pre Sabastian Corso, pre Franzescho Violante, pre Batista Paraviani, pre Marcho Antonio di Schavazoni, and Ser Nicholo de Felipo. It is almost certain that pre Marcho Antonio di Schavazoni is the organist Cavazzoni. The change in spelling is typically Venetian. This document is the earliest known reference to Cavazzoni's presence in Venice. The manuscript Venice, Biblioteca Nazionale Marciana, MS ital. IV.1795–8 contains a frottola by Franzescho Violante, *Forza d'amor da lo superno*.

[14] See p. 198 and Figure 1, above. [15] See note 7, above.

mostly for the salary they received, considering that at such a salary we could have the best singers in the world.   (Doc. 7)

In the other Scuole, dismissals were usually caused by failure to appear on required occasions or insolence to the officers, not by inadequate ability.

The clearest instance of the Scuola's insistence on musicians of high calibre was the selection, in 1524, of a new group of four *cantadori nuovi*.[16] Instead of hiring the first musicians who offered their services when a vacancy occurred, as seems to have been the normal procedure in other Scuole, an audition was held. Seven men participated, singing in three combinations, each of tenor, soprano, contralto, and bass. The specific procedure of the audition is not described in the document, but a vote was taken and the preferred group was hired. The quality of instrumentalists was also of concern to the Scuola di San Rocco, as evidenced by a decision, in 1531, to replace the players of harp, lute, and viol, 'who served very badly', with others who were more satisfactory.[17]

The reasons for replacing or dismissing musicians of the Scuole varied considerably. As has been discussed above, the quality of performance was a principal reason at the Scuola di San Rocco. Finances certainly also played a role, as at the Scuola di San Marco in 1527:

We find in our Scuola many expenses that are superfluous and of little value to the Scuola, such as the trumpets and shawms . . . [and] *cantadori solenni* . . . [They should be dismissed, and] in that way we will come to save . . . 20 ducats a year, which is certainly something worth doing, especially in these evil times that we now find ourselves in.   (Doc. 8)

The two most frequent causes of dismissal of singers were problems of discipline and failure to fulfil obligations, as shown in the following incidents at the Scuola di Santa Maria della Carità and the Scuola di Santa Maria della Misericordia, both of which had particular difficulty in maintaining complete choirs. At the Scuola della Carità in 1493 the *cantadori nuovi* were discharged with the following explanation:

For some time the aforesaid, or the greater part of them, have deliberately observed nothing of their promise, that is, they have totally broken that

16 ASV, SSR, Seconda Consegna, Registro 45, *Parti*, fol. 32.
17 ASV, SSR, Seconda Consegna, Registro 45, *Parti*, fol. 92.

order and promise made by them. [The result is] that when the tenors come the sopranos are missing, and when those two come the contras are missing, so that they are never in order and their songs are in great confusion . . .

(Doc. 9)

One *cantadore nuovo* of the Scuola della Misericordia went to great lengths to avoid serving in the procession of Corpus Christi of 1490. He had been receiving monthly alms instead of a salary in compensation for his services, but apparently wanted additional payment. On the day of Corpus Christi he declared that he was ill and could only be persuaded to come to sing by the payment of one ducat. The problems did not end with his arrival at the Scuola, however, as described in the *Notatorio*:

He then, immediately after arriving at the Scuola, went to the great altar of San Marco, and reaching there started bleeding from the nose. He got into a boat secretly and appeared [next] at the [Scuola's] arrival at the Palace [of the Doge], and then went for amusement to Mazzorbo, as he described to the Banca. This left the Scuola to go in shame and disgrace to the Piazza, [having no singers]. (Doc. 10)

Thus, he defrauded the Scuola of both one ducat and his services.

The Scuola della Misericordia continued to have problems with its *cantadori nuovi*, despite paying them salaries comparable to those of the other Scuole. In fact, in 1540 the entire choir had to be dismissed for reasons vividly explained in this excerpt from the Scuola's record book:

There is no money of our Scuola that is spent with less result and more shame and disgrace to the ministers than the payment made to the *cantadori nuovi*, because of their bad manner of singing, without any harmony and sweetness, singing in contempt of all rules, and with great dishonour in general to all; and more so in that they are unprincipled in conduct, behaving as they please and not as they should, [despite] having had courteous payment from us in the sum of about 40 ducats. (Doc. 11)

Certainly, in most cases the replacement of singers was necessitated not by lack of quality, money, or discipline, but by natural causes, that is death or illness. The situation of the *cantadori vecchi* of the Scuola della Carità in 1509, however, was exceptional:

The Guardian has found that our Scuola has need of *cantadori vecchi*, owing to the death of the late Ser Benetto di Struzzi, as well as to the infirmity of Ser Alvixe di Francesco Zotto who has become almost totally blind, and also because Ser Jachomo di Antonio Marangon, called Parza, has not filled the office of singer for a long time because he has been impeded by the *mal franzoxo*, which has caused him to lose his voice. (Doc. 12)

The music performed by the musicians of the Scuole at processions consisted chiefly of polyphonic *laude*, according to the documents, but nothing of the actual music performed is known beyond that general designation, and no information at all is provided on the music used at the Masses and Vespers. Not one extant musical source can be connected with the Scuole Grandi, and no specific pieces or composers are named in the documents. It is most likely that the music was quite simple, as in the *laude* published by Petrucci, some of which emanate from the Venetian monastery of San Salvador,[18] which was later to become the host of the sixth and last Scuola Grande, San Teodoro. All that is known of the training of the musicians of the Scuole is that on several occasions one singer was paid to teach some of his colleagues. It can be demonstrated, as has been illustrated above, that there was collaboration between the musicians of St Mark's church and those of the Scuole. However, as nothing is known of the music sung at St Mark's before the arrival of Willaert in 1527, it is impossible to determine anything about the music of the Scuole from that association.

The musical interrelationships among the various institutions of Renaissance Venice cannot be ascertained at present, but it is probable that the *cappella* of St Mark's basilica was the inspiration for many of the practices of the Scuole, as it was the best-trained and most renowned choir in Venice. In one area, however, I believe that the influence was reversed. It can be shown that until 1540, at least, no instruments other than organ were used at St Mark's, but it is well known that by the end of the sixteenth century the instrumentalists of the *cappella* were as famous as the singers. On the other hand, before 1500, singers and instrumentalists performed together at the Scuole Grandi, as demonstrated above. It is possible to conjecture that exposure to this practice may have played a large part in the decision to hire instrumentalists at St Mark's in the 1540s. In the selection of music, the Scuole Grandi were probably more conserva-

---

[18] *Laude Libro Primo, Innocentius Dammonis . . .* (Venice, 1508) and *Laude Libro secundo* (Venice, 1508) [R I S M 1508³]. Innocentius Dammonis was Prior of San Salvador in Venice in the first decade of the sixteenth century. For a study of these *laude* see Knud Jeppesen, *Die mehrstimmige italienische Lauda um 1500* (Leipzig and Copenhagen, 1935).

tive than the basilica, but the practice of using voices and instruments together was progressive.

It is conceivable that the Scuole Grandi contributed, in the long run, to the development of Venetian Renaissance music, but we cannot be sure. What is certain, however, is that each Scuola contributed greatly to the musical life of the district of Venice in which it was located. Public Masses with music were performed each Sunday at a local monastic church; and once a month, and at certain religious feasts, processions with music were held in the streets around the Scuola. These were undoubtedly the most important musical events to occur in the community. That they were greatly appreciated is made clear in the account of a public celebration of the Scuola di Santa Maria della Misericordia in December of 1530. The occasion was the annual granting of dowries to the daughters of deceased *poveri fradelli* of the Scuola. The ceremonies concluded with a solemn Mass as described in the records of the Scuola:

Afterwards was sung a solemn Mass in song, with deacon and subdeacon, players of trumpets, shawms, and cornets, and also [with] organ and singers, to the universal satisfaction of all. (Doc. 13).

APPENDIX: DOCUMENTS[19]

DOC. 1: (PRINCETON UNIVERSITY ART MUSEUM, 3(791), 'MARIEGOLA', FOL. 4V)

[undated; early sixteenth century]

Et così se obligano ditti preti a la nostra Schuola che ogni terza Domenega del mese per tutto l'anno . . . debano et sono tenuti de cantar una solenne messa in canto con tutte sollemnitade se rechiede al nostro altar con li cantadori et organi . . . Et el zorno dela nostra festa de Sancto Joseph: similiter ditti preti sono obligadi a far tutte sollemnitade sia conviene con procession, vespori, canti, et organo . . .

DOC. 2: (ASV, SSGE, REGISTRO 140, 'NOTATORIO', FOL. 157V)

1446 a dì 20 Luio

[in margin] Per elezer sie cantadori che serva la Scuola nelle sue solenità. . . . la ditta Scuola habbia de grandissima necesitade de cantadori, i quali

[19] For abbreviations, see note 1, above. In these transcriptions, the spellings have been left unchanged, but the punctuation, capitalisation, and accents have been normalised. The complete texts of these documents, and of many others on music at the Scuole Grandi, are provided in Glixon, *op. cit.*, vol. II.

acompagna quella cantar in procession di corpi et altre sue solenitade uzade . . . per puochi cantadori alla ditta Scuola come ancor per la vechieza de quelli che al presente sonno; alla qual cosa se el non se provede de cantadori che se rezeva sotto quelli, che son al presente, da i qualli imparà lo suo costume e modo uzado de cantar, de breve mancherà per muodo che la ditta Scuola non haveva cantadori . . .

MccccLx die xvii Martii

. . . quod cum cantores siu sint effecti ita senes, ut cum magna difficultate haberi possint ad corpora sepelienda, ad processiones, et ad devotiones per civitatem, quoniam infirmi sunt et non sit conveniens quod illi homines in illo habitu vadant per civitatem tacendo velut mortui sed vadant canendo laudes Deo, iuxta consuetum . . .

28 Junii [1452]

Ut ad laudem Dei et gloriose Crucis Domini Nostri Jesu Cristi, quando-cumque in processionibus et aliter portatur per civitatem cantetur amene et dulciter in cantu glorificetur Nomen Domini, et magnificetur exaltatio Santa Crucis . . .

Iesus 1493 a dì 8 Setembre

[in margin] Per nostri cantadori.

. . . fra le altre chose che son nezesarisime a questa nostra Schuolla sono i chantadori de laude, senza i quali mal se puol far l'onor dela Schuolla nostra . . .

Jesus 1494 a dì primo Zugno

Chasa de Schuolla de misser San Marcho . . .

. . . a chantadori da chorpi per suo regalia del dì del Chorpus Domini ducato uno, val   L.6 s.4

. . . a chantadori de laude per regalia del ditto zorno, ducato uno, val   L.6 s.4

. . . ai chantadori de San Marco per la prezision dela Chorpus Domini, ducati 3, val   L.18 s.12

JONATHAN GLIXON

. . . a sonadori, zoè a maestro Zentil dal'Arpa e compagni per dita prezision, L.13, val   L.13 s.o

DOC. 7: (ASV, SSR, SECONDA CONSEGNA, REGISTRO 45,
'PARTI . . .', FOL. 13)

1517 a di 22 Marzo
[in margin] L'ubligazion ano i chantadori in la nostra Schuola.
Esendo sta per noi za fu piui mexi chasado li nostri cantadori, vz., misser
pre Sabasttian ett compagni, per non esser a sufizienzia ett bixogno nostro,
ett maxime al salario i aveano, ett considerando che chon ttal salario se
potteremo aver di primi chanttadori dila ttera . . .

DOC. 8: (ASV, SSM, REGISTRO 18, 'NOTATORIO', FOL. 4)

Nel sopraditto giorno [A di x Fevrer M.D.xxvi] [1527]
[in margin] Che non si possa tener salariati, ne cantori sollenni, ne
sonadori.
Ritrovandosi nella Schuola nostra molte spese superflue e di poco frutto a
quella, come è gli trombi et pifferi . . . et . . . cantadori soleni . . . A questo
modo si vegnerà a sparagnar . . . ducati xx all'anno: cosa certo da far, et
massime ne gli tempi senestri, che hora si ritroviamo . . .

DOC. 9: (ASV, SSMC, REGISTRO 253, 'NOTATORIO', FOL. 18v)

A di xvi Zungno [McccLxxxxiii]
[in margin] De condar chanttadori nuovi.
. . . Da zertto ttempo in qual i ditti over la mazor partte de loro ano
deliberatto non observar alchuna chosa per loro promesa, anzi ttottalmente
ano interotto ttal ordene ett promision per loro fatta, in modo che quando
el vien i vien i tenori el mancha i sovrani, e quando ne son quelli duo el
mancha i conttra, per modo che mai sono in ordene ttal suo chantti,
grandissima confuxion . . .

DOC. 10: (ASV, SSMM, REGISTRO 166, 'NOTATORIO', FOL. 7)

A di dito [between July and November 1490]
[in margin] De retegnir duchato uno del mexe se da a Ser Domenego dale
Nape . . . .
. . . El qual subito abuto vene ala Schuola e seguito per in al'altar grando de
San Marco. Poi finise che lui fese sangue del naxo e monto in barcha,
ochultamente, la qual era apariada al'ariva de Palazo, et andosene asolazo

a Mazorbo, come lui a deto ala Bancha, e laso la Schuola andar con inchargo e vergogna per Piaza. . . .

DOC. 11: (ASV, SSMM, REGISTRO 166, 'NOTATORIO', FOL. 347)

[MDxl a dì 12 Settembrio, in zorno di Domenega]
[in margin] Cantadori

Non è danaro dela Schuola nostro che sia spexo con mancho fiato et con più vergogna et inchargo deli ministri quanto è 'l pagamento fato ali chantadori nuovi, quali per il suo mal modo di cantar, et senza alguna armonia et dolzeza de cantar, sono in contemptu et de suma desplizenzia in genere a tuti, et piui che nel sua servir se fano lizito che el sia al modo suo et non come sono obligati, havendo el pagamento da nui cortexemente che è ala suma de ducati 40 in zircha. . . .

DOC. 12: (ASV, SSMC, REGISTRO 253, 'NOTATORIO', FOL. 97[35])

Laus Deo a dì 2 Fievrer [Mccccviiii] [1509]
[in margin] Circha cantadori vechi.

La Schuola nostra che si attrova a Vardian Grando di bisognio di chantadori, si per la morte del condam Ser Benetto di Struzi, chome eziam per la infermità de Ser Alvixe di Francesco Zotto, el qual è diventado squasi ttottalmente horbo, e eziam per che Ser Jachomo di Antonio Marangon ditto Parza più ttenpo non exerzita più l'ofizio del chantar per eser impedimentta da mal franzoxo, per el qual ano perso la voxe. . . .

DOC. 13: (ASV, SSMM, REGISTRO 166, 'NOTATORIO', FOL. 225V)

A dì xiii ditto [Dezembre 1530]
Dovendose in questo zorno far la dispensa dele novize fiole de fradeli mortti dela Schuola . . . Da poi fu cantata una solene mesa in canto con diachono et subdiachono, sonadori de trombe e pifari et corneti et eziam organo et cantadori, con universal satisfazion de tutti. . . .

11

ANTONIO GARDANE'S EARLY CONNECTIONS WITH THE WILLAERT CIRCLE

Mary S. Lewis

TO the modern observer, Venetian musicians of the 1530s and 1540s appear to have had an enormous amount of music at their disposal. However, as the circulation and availability of that music is examined more closely, it is not always clear just who had easy access to various pieces and repertories. Composers undoubtedly wrote music for a variety of reasons – for use in the service of the Church, to provide entertainment for princely or intellectual gatherings, at the behest of a wealthy patron, to honour a potential or actual benefactor, or even for their own enjoyment. In at least some of these instances the original destination of a work may well have had some effect on its freedom of circulation. As long as a particular piece remained in manuscript, and so out of the public domain, control of its dissemination was at least possible, and, as we shall see, such control often seems to have been desired, either by a composer or by a patron.

Music available in manuscript probably circulated most frequently as single pieces, often enclosed in letters. Presenting a new work to a friend or patron was evidently considered a special favour; instances of such gifts are the motet included by Gombert in his famous letter to Ferrante Gonzaga[1] or the motet by Jachet Berchem enclosed by Doni in a letter of 1543 to Cosimo de Medici.[2] Some

---

[1] The letter is now in the Pierpont Morgan Library, New York; a facsimile appears in *Die Musik in Geschichte und Gegenwart*, v (Kassel, 1956), cols. 499–500.

[2] Antonfrancesco Doni, *Lettere* (Venice, 1544), fol. xxIIII, mentioned in James Haar, 'Notes on the "Dialogo della Musica" of Antonfrancesca Doni', *Music and Letters*, 47 (1966), p. 208. The passage reads in part: 'Io sono un prete, che familiarmente favello con V.S. Illustrissima; et mi chiamo il Doni. Sono presso à tre anni ch'io usci di Fiorenza: & son musico, scrittore, dotto in volgare, & di nove per greco. Son

individual collectors seem to have built up these single manuscripts into substantial holdings, such as that described in Doni's *Dialogo*.[3] One such anthology may be the group of manuscript leaves, written in various hands, now in the Bibliothèque Nationale in Paris (MS Cons. Rés. 1591).[4]

At times, manuscripts may even have been purchased from composers. Such a situation could be inferred from Doni's comment on Neri Capone:

Thanks to him I saw, heard, and felt all this divine music. This Messer Neri spends hundreds of ducats a year on such *virtù*, and keeps it all to himself; he wouldn't let a piece of music out of his hands, were it even to his own father. Now, since I can't send you that music, I send you this [the *Dialogo*].[5]

It is hard to say from Doni's description whether the money spent by Neri was merely for performances, or also for the music itself. If composers did sell their music in manuscript form, one can understand a certain reluctance on the part of both the patrons and the composers to let it out of their hands. Such a situation may also have lain behind the extraordinary negotiations and financial arrangements surrounding Alfonso d'Este's acquisition of the manuscript of Willaert's *Musica nova*.[6] Whether or not Polissena Peccorina actually purchased the manuscript from Willaert or, what is more likely, received it as a gift that reflected her long-standing friendship and association with the composer, the family clearly recognised that the value of the manuscript was financial as well as artistic.

It was within this atmosphere that publishers such as Gerolamo Scotto and Antonio Gardane gathered the repertory that they printed so prolifically in the second third of the century. How they obtained that music has, of course, been a central issue among

poeta; ch'io doveva dire inanzi. et perche mi conosciate, ch'io vi sono; oltra l'essere vassallo; affettionato; & vi vo bene, io mando à vostra eccellentia un mottetto di Giacchetto Berchem; degne certo di venire alle mani di tal signore et mando à vostri Cantori una mia Canzone mandovi due Sonetti composti dalla mia . . .'

[3] Haar, 'Notes on the "Dialogo"', p. 210.

[4] I would like to thank Professor Joshua Rifkin for first pointing out this manuscript to me, and for his suggestions as to its possible history and purpose.

[5] Doni, *Lettere*, fol. cxᵛ cited and translated in Haar, 'Notes on the "Dialogo"', p. 206.

[6] Anthony Newcomb, 'Editions of Willaert's *Musica Nova*: New Evidence, New Speculations', *Journal of the American Musicological Society*, 26 (1973), pp. 132–40.

editors and music bibliographers for some time. This paper will attempt to deal with one aspect of that issue – Gardane's acquisition not only of fresh repertory, but also of particularly accurate versions of older works by members of the most important group of musicians in the Veneto, those composers generally known as the Willaert circle.[7] While no clear-cut answers are as yet possible, there is enough circumstantial evidence to warrant at least a few speculations, and to point the way toward further research.

Gardane and his colleagues seem to have obtained the music they printed in three ways. One was the outright copying of music issued by other publishers. The most famous example of this is Gardane's admitted use of Moderne's *Motteti del Fiore* as a model for his *Fior de mottetti* series,[8] and at other times Gardane reproduced wholesale such works as Phinot's first book of five-voice motets, originally printed by the Beringen brothers of Lyons.[9] Furthermore, he seems to have borrowed individual works from miscellaneous editions by Attaingnant, Antico, Moderne, and others.[10] The exact nature of the numerous copyings that seem to have taken place between Gardane and Scotto – often in the form of editions with identical, or nearly identical, contents – is unclear;[11] but even in the case of such sibling editions, it appears that almost every pair represents a special case. Therefore, their problems, and the complexities of the relationship between the two great Venetian music printers, probably cannot be resolved until a great deal more preliminary work is done.

[7] The Willaert circle comprises those composers who studied with Adriano Willaert, or who were evidently associated with him in some way in Venice. They include Cipriano de Rore, Jacques Buus, Gioseffo Zarlino, Perissone Cambio, Baldissare Donato, Gerolamo Parabosco, and Domenico Ferabosco, and possibly Jachet Berchem and Jan Gero.

[8] Gardane acknowledges his debt to Moderne on the title-page itself: *Fior de mottetti tratti dalli Mottetti del fiore* (RISM 1539[12]).

[9] *Liber primus mutetarum quinque vocum, Dominico Phinot autore* (Lyons: Beringen, 1547; RISM P2015).

    Liber primus mutetarum quinque vocum Dominico Phinot autore (Venice: Gardane, 1552; RISM P2016).

[10] See Mary S. Lewis, 'Antonio Gardane and His Publications of Sacred Music, 1538–55', Ph.D. diss., Brandeis University, 1979, pp. 219–20.

[11] See for instance, *Musica quatuor vocum, que materna lingua moteta vocantur . . .* (Venice: Gardane, 1549; RISM 1549[9]) and *Musica quatuor vocum, que materna lingua moteta vocantur . . .* (Venice: Scotto, 1549; 1549[9 a]), or *Electiones diversorum motetorum distincte quatuor vocibus . . .* (Venice: Gardane, 1549; 1549[12]) and *Elletione de motetti non piu stampati a quatro voci . . .* (Venice: Scotto, 1549; 1549[15]). Cf. Norbert Böker-Heil, *Die Mottetten von Philippe Verdelot* (Wiesbaden, 1967), pp. 47f.

From time to time, publishers seem to have been approached by enterprising musicians intent on bringing their work before a larger public. Some were minor figures who provided financial backing for the printing of their music, either from their own pockets or, more frequently, through the generosity of a patron.[12] At other times, a composer of the first rank seems to have brought his music to a printer himself, perhaps to ensure, so far as possible, the accuracy of the publication.[13] In either case, the printer's role in obtaining the music was fundamentally a passive one.

Still, though there were some composers who were eager to see their works made widely available through the medium of print, publishers seem often to have had real difficulty in getting hold of good, new music in accurate copies, and competition for the best new repertory may have been keen. Many leading composers guarded their music jealously, as we learn from Rore, who was said to have asked a friend to keep his music from falling into the hands of those who would spread it about,[14] or Jachet Berchem, who complained in the preface to his first book of five-voice madrigals of 1546 about those who falsified the authorship of certain pieces, plagiarists whom he characterised as 'crows who dress themselves in the feathers of the swan'.[15] Thus, printers appear to have carefully cultivated sources from which they could obtain good new music – mutual friends of composers, musicians in leading establishments, patrons, collectors of manuscripts, and, ideally, the composers themselves. The process can be seen at work, for example, in a letter from Antonfrancesco Doni to Claudio Veggio asking for new madrigals by Veggio for

---

[12] See, for example, Gardane's editions of music by Castellino, Lucario, or Corvo.

[13] The well-known contract between Morales and Dorico is an excellent example of this. See Suzanne Cusick, 'Valerio Dorico: Music Printer in Sixteenth-Century Rome', Ph.D. diss., University of North Carolina, 1975, pp. 153f and 324f.

[14] '. . . per la gran familiarita, & amorevol servitu, che io longo tempo ho tenuta con l'eccellentiss. Musico M. Cipriano Rore benignamente per sua cortesia mi fece pertecipe d'alcuni suoi bellissimi Madrigali, a quattro, & a cinque voci, pregandomi li dovesse tenir appresso di me, accio le sue opere non cosi facilmente nelle mani di ciascheduno si divulgassero . . .' Giulio Bonagionta da S. Genesi, dedication to Anibale Del Forno in RISM R2514–1565[18], also partly quoted in Alfred Einstein, *The Italian Madrigal*, 3 vols. (Princeton, 1949), I, p. 385.

[15] '. . . acio che portandolo segnato in fronte possano con piu auttorita arditamente uscir in luce & si conoscano esser di Giachetto de Berchem suo amorevole domestico e non daltri che so hoggidi al mondo non manchar de i Corvi che si vestono ben spesso la piuma del Cygno . . .' Dedication by Berchem to Hieronimo Bragadino in RISM B1977–1546.

Scotto to print. The letter does not simply ask, but implores, beseeches, and pleads with the composer for some of the madrigals that Doni, a friend of Veggio's, knows that the composer possesses in abundant copies. One gains the distinct impression that Doni did not expect Veggio to part with his music freely.[16]

A particularly dramatic example of what may have been competition for a source for motets is the well-known quarrel between Gardane and the printer Johannes de Buglhat of Ferrara, reflected in a series of prefaces and title-page illustrations in 1539. Gardane's first motet book, the five-voice *Mottetti del Frutto*, appeared in September of 1538, its title-page decorated by a particularly elegant woodcut of fruit. Four months later[17] Buglhat issued a collection entitled *Moteti de la Simia*, the centre of whose title-page displays a rather grotesque monkey munching on some fruit. While the fruit-eating monkey was a common symbol of the time, its use here seems more than fortuitous, combining as it does the emblem of Gardane's first motet edition with a reference to that printer's address, the Calle de la Scimia.[18] That Gardane himself interpreted the symbolism not only personally, but as an insult and a threat, is amply demonstrated by his six-voice *Mottetti del Frutto* of 1539. The title-pages of the altus, quinta pars, and sexta pars of that edition bear a woodcut depicting a ferocious lion and bear attacking a monkey who lies supine, surrounded by the fruit he has presumably attempted to pilfer. In the preface, Gardane speaks indignantly of the malicious monkey who seeks to devour his fruit – fruit which, however, is vigilantly guarded by the lion and bear, the beasts, of course, that appear in Gardane's printer's mark.[19]

[16] 'A Messer Claudio Veggio Musico Eccellentiss. Messer Girolamo Scotto, amico honorato, ricerca dalla liberalita della vostra vertu un' libro di Madrigali nuovi; de i quali so che n'havete per il fertile intelletto vostro abondantissima copia . . . Cosi un prego, u'essorto, & u'astringo per il ben ch'io vi voglio, & per la gentillezza, ch'e in voi, a fargli parte delle vostre compositioni . . .' Doni, *Lettere*, fol. cxᵛ, cited in Haar, 'Notes on the "Dialogo"', p. 206.

[17] Lewis, 'Gardane', p. 9.

[18] Gardane's address is given on the tenor title-page of RISM 1538¹⁹.

[19] '. . . ho voluto questi presenti mottetti a quella dedicare, con questa letterina notificandoli, come una incauta piu, che malitiosa Simia, ad devorar piu presto, che a guardarse intenta, dico una certa Simia, non advertendo con quanto studio, et con quanta vigilantia dal feroce Leone et crudele Orso del continuo li mei frutti se custodiano, via piu avida de devorarseli, che canta de guardarse de la bona guardia da sopradetti fattali, non havendo pero mangiato, ne tra gollatoli in le loro ongie li capito . . .'

The exact nature of the dispute remains a mystery. It is conceivable that Gardane's ire may have been aroused over Buglhat's use of the single-impression process itself. Not only did both publishers print music in 1538 using the new method, but, in fact, both used the same music type-face. Perhaps Gardane had had that type-face cut for himself in order to be the first in the Veneto to print music in single impression. He may then have discovered that Buglhat had also obtained a fount of the same type, perhaps even being the first to employ it.[20]

It seems more likely, however, that repertory was at issue. There does not seem to have been any piracy, since Buglhat's *Simia* collection has almost no concordances with any of Gardane's editions. But its repertory is similar in many ways to that of the *Frutto* series. Many of the composers are the same, and the extent of its contents – twenty motets – also resembles Gardane's *Frutto* volumes, whose size ranged between seventeen and twenty-two motets each, significantly fewer than the forty motets of Buglhat's early motet edition, the *Liber cantus* of 1538. Gardane's *Mottetti del Frutto* contained a repertory that for the most part had not been previously published;[21] and it would appear that somewhere Gardane had found a source of new and potentially popular motets – a musician or patron, perhaps, who had influential contacts. It is entirely possible that Buglhat raided Gardane's source of supply; perhaps he even stole the contents of another intended motet volume. It is notable, indeed, that after the *Frutto* books Gardane's supply of new motets seems to have dried up for a few years, and he was forced to rely for the most part on previously published material. Could Buglhat even have interfered with Gardane's further access to new repertory? The extent of Gardane's rage is certainly evident in his willingness to spend what must have been a

[20] Buglhat's first known music book is dated March 1538, while the earliest surviving edition from Gardane's press is his *Venticinque canzoni* of April 1538. A mistake in the printer's name in the colophon of the Oxford (Bodleian Library) copy of the latter work would lend credence to the idea that Gardane was not well known at the time it was printed, even to his compositors, and that the *Venticinque canzoni* could well be his first publication. (See Iain Fenlon and James Haar, 'Fonti e cronologia dei madrigali di Costanzo Festa', *Rivista Italiana di Musicologia*, 13 (1978), p. 220.) On the other hand, the loss of all copies of Gardane's first edition of Arcadelt's four-voice madrigals, and consequently our ignorance of its exact date, make it impossible for us to decide the question of priority in favour of one printer over the other.

[21] Lewis, 'Gardane', pp. 192–6.

great deal of money on the symbolic woodcut, which was no doubt specially commissioned for his vehement protest.

Whatever his difficulties in securing repertory, during the first few years of his career in Venice Gardane published a great deal of new music, though very little of it stemmed from the musicians around St Mark's. From 1538 until 1541 the only work of Willaert's that Gardane printed was the four-voice *Pater noster*, a widely disseminated composition that he appears to have copied, as we have seen he did with other motets, from Moderne's *Motteti del Fiori*. Of composers active in Venice we find almost nothing in those years, with the possible exception of a large number of works by Jachet Berchem, whose music was part of Gardane's repertory from the beginning. The history of Berchem's tenure in Venice is extremely cloudy, though there is some evidence he may have been in Venice by the late 1530s.[22] He remains, in any event, the only composer with possible local connections published by Gardane until after 1540, a situation suggesting that most of the publisher's sources in his early years lay outside the Venetian Republic.

Scotto, meanwhile, was busily publishing the music of Willaert in great quantity. Not only did he put out two books of the master's motets in 1539, but he seems to have been the first to print, in 1540, ten of Willaert's secular works.[23] Whether or not Scotto obtained this music directly from the composer, he undoubtedly had a fertile source of supply for Willaert's works, whereas Gardane may even have been cut off for some reason from printing the music of most of the Venetians.[24]

In 1541, however, there began a slow but steady influx of music by local composers into Gardane's repertory. There is, first of all, a large amount of material by Jan Gero. While admittedly among the more shadowy figures of the period, Gero is one of a number of composers, all presumably from the Willaert circle, mentioned in a

---

[22] George Nugent, 'The Jacquet Motets and Their Authors', Ph.D. diss., Princeton University, 1973, p. 173.

[23] See RISM 1540[18] and 1540[20].

[24] Once the Willaert motets were published by Scotto, it is hard to see what prevented Gardane from re-issuing them as he evidently did with Gombert's works. The first book of Gombert's motets in Scotto's edition was even protected by a privilege, but that did not prevent Gardane from bringing out his own edition forthwith. Willaert's motets appear to have carried no such privilege, and yet Gardane waited until 1545 before re-issuing them in a thoroughly revised edition.

series of poems, probably by Gerolamo Fenaruolo, that were published anonymously in Padua in 1546.[25]

But above all, in 1541 Gardane printed two pieces by Willaert that appear never to have been published before, as well as eight others that had been printed by Scotto in 1540. Then, in 1542, Gardane published a volume of six-voice motets, fifteen of which were by Willaert. Of those, six were newly published. In another edition of the same year, 1542[17], Gardane printed what appears to be still another previously unpublished work of Willaert's along with a madrigal by Jacques Buus, organist of St Mark's. Moreover, in 1542 the works of Domenico Ferabosco, who seems to have been connected with the Willaert circle in some way, appear in Gardane's publications in substantial numbers; one edition is devoted exclusively to Ferabosco's madrigals.[26] Meanwhile, Scotto seems not to have published any new works by Willaert in 1541; and while in 1542 he did put out a few, there are problems of attribution in the most important of these, the hymn collection.[27]

In the next few years, Gardane enlarged his repertory of music by the Willaert circle. A 1543 book of chansons by Buus will be examined in detail below. Starting in 1544 Gardane published works by Perissone Cambio and Gerolamo Parabosco, not only in

[25] *Nuove rime di diversi eccellenti auttori le quali si leggono sparse hora raccolte e scelte* . . . (Padua, 1546). For an edition of these poems with commentary, see Remo Giazotto, *Harmonici concenti in aere veneto* (Rome, 1954). I would like to thank James Haar for calling Giazotto's study to my attention. Among other evidence for Gero's local connections is the fact that his duos, published in 1541 by Gardane, were, as the preface to the print tells us, commissioned by Scotto. Gero's music had not appeared at all prior to 1541, but why Gardane should then have printed it, rather than Scotto, who commissioned it, seems a mystery. Further, in the Bologna copy of Gardane's edition of 1545 of the Morales Magnificats, there is written in a margin, in a 16th-century hand, the name 'Jan Gero / Chioz', a rather cryptic inscription, possibly an owner's mark, that could possibly be interpreted as 'Jan Gero of Chioggia'. Unfortunately, the records of the *cappella* at the cathedral of Chioggia for those years are missing, and no other documentation has been found placing him in that city. See Iginio Tiozzo, 'Maestri e organisti della Cattedrale di Chioggia fino al XVII secolo', *Note d'Archivio*, 12 (1935), pp. 284–96.

[26] RISM F259. Einstein, *Italian Madrigal*, i, pp. 307–8.

[27] *Hymnorum musica secundum ordinem romanae ecclesiae excellentissimi Adriani Wilart et aliorum authorum* . . . (Venice: Scotto, 1542; RISM 1542[11]). While the title implies a number of composers, only Jachet of Mantua is cited in the body of the print, leaving some doubt as to just how many of the hymns are actually by Willaert.

collections but in individual editions as well.[28] Finally, by 1544 and 1545 Gardane had launched a full-scale project of publishing Rore's music.

Obviously, then, between 1541 and 1545 Gardane began to gain access to music by a group of local composers hitherto unavailable to him. How did this change in his fortunes come about? At least three possibilities present themselves.

One patron apparently connected in some way with the appearance of Willaert's music in Gardane's publications was Marco Trevisano, the dedicatee of the 1542 collection of Willaert's six-voice motets. Trevisano has generally been identified as the Marcantonio Trevisano who served as procurator of St Mark's starting in 1549, and as Doge of Venice for just under a year in 1553–4.[29] The presence of a possible connection between Marcantonio Trevisano and Jachet Berchem may be of importance as far as the relation between Trevisano and Gardane is concerned. The above-mentioned 1542 collection also contains three new motets by Berchem, one of which is unique to that edition. It would appear from Berchem's motet *Unica lux Venetum*[30] that Marcantonio Trevisano had been Berchem's patron since the late 1530s, and, as we have noted, Berchem's music figured importantly in Gardane's publications during that period, often appearing there for the first time. Thus it is certainly possible that Berchem formed some sort of link between Gardane and Trevisano.

As I have already noted, Gardane had begun his publishing

---

[28] A motet by Parabosco appeared in a 1544 collection featuring the works of Rore (RISM 1544[17]); moreover, it was Gardane who, in 1546, published the only print wholly devoted to Parabosco's works (RISM P885). Perissone Cambio's music first appeared in Gardane's publications in 1544, and Gardane put out a book of his canzone villanesche in 1545 (RISM C551). However, in that same year a book of his madrigals, for which he himself took out the privilege, was printed by an anonymous publisher who appears in fact to have been Scotto (C550). The privilege is found in Venice, Archivio di Stato, *Senato, Terra. Registro* 34: 'Die 11° Junii 1545 . . . et a Perison fiamengo per la musica per lui composta de madrigali sopra li sonetti del Petrarcha . . .' This privilege also provides us with the information that Cambio was Flemish. Concerning the printer of the madrigals, see Lewis, 'Gardane', pp. 314–29.

[29] Franceso Sansovino, *Venetia, citta nobilissima et singolare* (Venice, 1581), fols. 271v–272, and 'Cronico', fol. 36; Nugent, 'The Jacquet Motets', pp. 171f; Andrea da Mosto, *I dogi di Venezia nella vita pubblica e privata* (Milan, 1960), pp. 254–9.

[30] Published in RISM 1549[12] and 1549[15]. For a thorough discussion of this motet and Trevisano's patronage, see Nugent, 'The Jacquet Motets', pp. 171f.

career, so far as sacred music was concerned, with fresh material in the *Mottetti del Frutto*. But then, for some reason, he seems to have had difficulty in procuring new sacred works, and with a few exceptions he became reliant on material already in circulation. Therefore, it is no doubt significant that between the *Frutto* series and 1547 the only sacred editions from Gardane's press wholly independent of earlier publications of Scotto and Moderne are the Willaert six-voice motet book of 1542 and two Rore books of 1544 and 1545.[31]

Naturally, the question of the transmission of the Willaert pieces in the 1542 edition is thus paramount. Unlike Gardane's earlier publications devoted to the motets of Jachet and Gombert, the Willaert edition is in reality a collection. Of the twenty-three pieces it contains, fifteen are ascribed to Willaert, three to Jachet Berchem, one each to Pieton, Verdelot, Jachet of Mantua and Maistre Jan, and one is anonymous.

Early manuscript concordances confirm that many of the pieces in this book had been in circulation for some time. A surprisingly large number appear in one or both of the two earlier manuscripts Rome, Palazzo Massimo, Cod. VI.c.6.23–4, and Rome, Biblioteca Vallicelliana, MS s'35–40.[32] Moreover, three more were published in earlier collections by Attaingnant or Grapheus. But, even so, there is also a substantial amount of new material here. This collection is the earliest source for six of the works ascribed to Willaert and for four or five others, three of which are *unica*.[33] This book seems to be made up of a group of ten or eleven new works by Willaert, Jachet Berchem,

---

[31] The motets in the mixed collections for three voices also form a repertory separate from Scotto and Moderne, but they stand outside the main tradition and should be removed from consideration.

[32] On the Massimo partbooks, see Friedrich Lippmann, 'Musikhandschriften und -Drucke in der Bibliothek Massimo', *Studien zur Italienisch–Deutschen Musikgeschichte* XI, Analecta Musicologica 17 (Cologne, 1976), p. 267. I would also like to thank Professor Joshua Rifkin for communicating further information on the Massimo partbooks from the larger study promised in the above reference.

On the Vallicelliana manuscript (*olim* S. Borromeo E.II.55–60), see Edward E. Lowinsky, 'A Newly Discovered Manuscript at the Biblioteca Vallicelliana in Rome', *Journal of the American Musicological Society*, 3 (1950), pp. 173–232; Anne-Marie Bragard, *Etude bio-bibliographique sur Philippe Verdelot* (Brussels, 1964); Colin Slim, *A Gift of Madrigals and Motets*, 2 vols. (Chicago, 1972), I, pp. 55–60; Fenlon and Haar, 'Fonti e cronologia', pp. 216–17, n.12.

For a list, and dates, of sources concordant with the Willaert 1542 edition, see Lewis, 'Gardane', pp. 388–90 and 792–815.

[33] Lewis, 'Gardane', p. 219.

and Maistre Jan, supplemented by older pieces, primarily by Willaert. It would seem that Gardane had somehow obtained new motets by the three local musicians and then, in order to present a collection of proper magnitude, searched among sources at his disposal, perhaps including French and German editions, for suitable supplementary material. But where did he acquire such a large body of new works?

In the dedication to the 1542 edition, Gardane states that there has been considerable demand for the music in the collection, and in a show of exaggerated reticence, he protests that the publication of these motets by M. Adriano is more to meet this demand than to be of much practical benefit to himself.[34] He then goes on to describe his search for a suitable dedicatee, and his eventual choice of his friend and patron Trevisano. 'Therefore', Gardane tells Trevisano, 'I dedicate and give them to you, since their esteemed author allows me to do this.' He then asks Trevisano to have the motets performed at his 'most honoured salon', which has been chosen for that purpose, where the best music is played and sung by the finest performers, with the noblest personages in attendance. Gardane concludes, 'and thus you and the author will be, as usual, alone commended for it, and I, who am the servant of you both, will have paid my debt in regard to this affair'.[35]

A great deal has been made of this dedication, especially in citing it as evidence that Willaert organised the brilliant musical evenings at Trevisano's.[36] But much of Gardane's wording is at best obscure and ambiguous. Most directly stated are the facts that Willaert's music was in demand, that Gardane had received Willaert's permission to dedicate the collection to Trevisano, that Trevisano had particularly excellent musical performances in his home, and that Gardane commended the music of the collection to Trevisano for presentation there. But can we infer anything more from this dedication? If Gardane actually had to obtain Willaert's permission to dedicate the music to Trevisano, then we must assume he also had the composer's permission to print it in the first place. The slightly

[34] For the original text of the dedication, see the Appendix, below, p. 226.
[35] I would like to thank Richard Sherr, Allan Keiler, and Jeremy Noble for their help in the translation and interpretation of this preface.
[36] Einstein, *Italian Madrigal*, I, p. 320; Donna G. Cardamone, *Adrian Willaert and His Circle: Canzone Villanesche alla Napolitana and Villotte*, Recent Researches in the Music of the Renaissance 30, (Madison, Wisc., 1978), p. vii.

disgruntled tone of the opening and closing passages of the dedication could also imply that Gardane went to some trouble to obtain either the music or the permission, or both. Such a situation would be in accord with the theory that Willaert's music was not easily come by, a theory further reinforced by Gardane's assertion that many people had been demanding that he publish some of it, presumably to make it more readily available.

Though Gardane's detailed description would seem to imply that he himself had been at the gatherings at Trevisano's, no straightforward statement points to Willaert's presence. Still, Gardane's assertion that both Trevisano and Willaert, and only they, would be praised, 'as usual', for the performances, might be read as meaning that Willaert had been in attendance. Certainly the passage implies that Willaert's music had been performed before at Trevisano's, and while Willaert might have received his commendation *in absentia*, few composers in any age have been able to resist the opportunity to attend first-rate performances of their works.

Beyond this point, we swim out into the murky waters of speculation. If Gardane and Willaert were both at the musical evenings at Trevisano's, they presumably met, and Gardane's dedication to Trevisano may have been a way of thanking him for this opportunity. It is hard to decide just what 'the debt in this matter' that Gardane felt he had paid really was. Perhaps he felt obliged to publish Willaert's music, but for some reason had avoided doing so. Or perhaps he felt indebted to Willaert for allowing him to publish music, or to Trevisano for in some way making the publication possible. This debt was probably not monetary: considering Willaert's prestige, and the assumed commercial value of his music, it seems unlikely that Gardane would have sought financial aid from Trevisano for publication of this volume. In any case, the dedication was most likely simply an expression of gratitude.[37]

If Willaert himself did indeed (as the preface asserts) give some sort of approval to the project, we are probably safe in speculating that the 'new' repertory in the collection is closely related to the composer. If such is the case, this would strengthen our assumption that the 1542 collection could represent two separate transmissions –

[37] There is always the possibility that Gardane may have received aid from Trevisano in re-establishing his workshop after what appears to have been some sort of disaster in 1540. For details, see Lewis, 'Gardane', pp. 13–16.

the new pieces never before published, and the works already in circulation that may have been collected to fill out the volume.

The possible dual nature of the transmission would explain a serious defect, one that has cast a shadow over the reliability of the entire anthology – the attribution to Willaert in this edition of the motet *Salva nos Domine*.[38] Almost every other source for this work ascribes it to Mouton, and there seems little doubt that he was in fact the composer. The misattribution has been seen as placing Willaert at some distance from the actual publication of this edition.[39] But if, as suggested above, Gardane filled out the contents of the volume from earlier sources, he himself could have committed the error without in any way invalidating the authenticity of the readings of the pieces in the 'new' group.

There is another link between Gardane and the composers around St Mark's: his publication, in 1543, of a book of chansons by Jacques Buus. While all the extant copies of the work bear Gardane's distinctive printer's mark on the title-page, only some of them carry the usual designation 'Apud Antonium Gardanum'; the others have the imprint 'Apud ipsum authorem'. It would appear that Gardane and Buus were involved here in a joint publishing venture, an arrangement that seems to have been unique in Gardane's career; at least, no name besides his is known to appear on the title-page of any of his other editions. There is also evidence that Gardane and Buus were beneficiaries of the same patrons. In 1544, Gardane dedicated a collection of motets bearing Rore's name on its title-page to one Hieronimo Uttinger, whom he referred to as a 'very dear friend' of Rore;[40] the wording of the preface implies friendship between Uttinger and Gardane as well.[41] Then in 1547 and 1549 Buus dedicated his two books of ricercars to Uttinger as well.[42] And it was in 1549 that Buus published a book of motets which he dedicated to Francesco Palavicino, also the dedicatee of Gardane's first book of sacred music, the *Mottetti del Frutto* of 1538. Evidently Gardane and

[38] Lewis, 'Gardane', pp. 226f.

[39] Edward E. Lowinsky, *The Medici Codex of 1518*, I: *Historical Introduction and Commentary*, Monuments of Renaissance Music 3 (Chicago, 1968), pp. 177–80.

[40] '. . . l'Eccelentissimo musico Cipriano Rore vostro amico carissimo . . .'

[41] 'Considerando la nobilta del sangue, la grandezza de l'animo insieme la continua liberalita la quale se puo equiparar ad ogni gran principe & signore Per questo m'e parsso ufficio degno di vera amicitia dedicarvi, la presente opera . . .'

[42] B5195–1547 and B5196–1549.

Buus were both members of the same circle of musicians and patrons, one that included at least one other member of the Willaert circle, Cipriano de Rore.

Buus was elected organist at St Mark's in 1541.[43] While we do not know just when the association between Buus and Gardane began, Buus fiirst appears, as we have seen, in the latter's publications in 1542. It may not be coincidental that it was in 1541 and 1542 that Gardane began to gain access to the music of Willaert and his colleagues. As organist at St Mark's, Buus must have been able to lay hands on Willaert's music fairly easily. Still, if he did indeed pass some of Willaert's works on to Gardane, we have no way of knowing whether it was with the approval of the *maestro di cappella* of St Mark's.

Buus and Trevisano are not the only possible sources of Venetian music for Gardane. We must return here to Hieronimo Uttinger, member of a prominent German mercantile family resident in Venice, whose father, Georg, was the Venetian representative of the Augsburg trading company of the Rem family. Georg's importance in the German community of Venice is shown by the fact that he was elected a consul of the Fondaco dei Tedeschi on three separate occasions, in 1517, 1539, and 1540.[44] While Georg eventually left Venice for Graz, his children stayed on. A daughter, Catherina, married a member of the Medici family, while three sons, of whom Hieronimo appears to have been the eldest, resided in Venice at least as late as 1550.[45]

Unfortunately, although a number of documents on this family survive, none gives any further information on Hieronimo's friendship with Buus, Rore and Gardane. However, in his dedication to Uttinger, Buus mentions the fact that his patron has kept near him an abundant supply (*un gran copia*) of Buus's music for four, five, and

---

[43] Francesco Caffi, *Storia della musica sacra nella gia cappella ducale di San Marco in Venezia dal 1318 al 1797* (Venezia, 1854), pp. 107–9.

[44] Henry Simonsfeld, *Der Fondaco dei Tedeschi in Venedig und die deutsch-venezianischen Handelsbeziehungen.* (Stuttgart, 1887), II, p. 178, and Giovanni Bortalamio Milesio, 'Descrizione del Fontico dei Tedeschi in Venezia', 1715–24, fols. 47v–48, cited in *G. B. Milesio's Beschreibung des Deutschen Hauses in Venedig*, ed. G. M. Thomas (Munich, 1881).

[45] Information on the family is found in the following documents in the Archivio di Stato in Venice: *Atti Bianchi. Testamenti*, N. 383, fasc. 2, fols. 44v–45v; fasc. 3, fol. 12v; fasc. 4, fols. 36–37; *Notarile. Atti Bianchi*, N. 384, fasc. 1, fols. 24v–25; fasc. 2, fols. 1–2; N. 385, fasc. 1, fols. 43–43v.

six voices.[46] The implication here is that Uttinger, like Neri Capone and the protagonists of Doni's *Dialogo*, was a collector of music manuscripts. If this is true, then Gardane's choice of Uttinger as dedicatee of the Rore motet book of 1544 carries special significance. That book contains works not only by Rore, but by several other members of the Willaert circle – Cambio, Ferabosco, and Willaert himself. It is, in fact, among the earliest of Gardane's collections to contain works by a cluster of those composers known to be associated with the *maestro di cappella* of St Mark's. Moreover, the readings in the 1544 book stand very close to those found in at least one source believed to be related to Rore,[47] and it is likely that for the 1544 book someone close to Rore provided Gardane with copies of the motets of Rore and his circle that appear there. One could at least speculate that the source of those copies was Uttinger, the dedicatee of the volume, a professed dear friend of Rore's and a known collector of manuscripts, to whom the edition itself was dedicated.

Moreover, while Uttinger may have served as a connection, there is evidence that within a few years Gardane was in direct contact with Rore as well. In a separate study[48] I have shown that certain pieces by Rore in the 1544 collection reappear in a book of motets devoted entirely to his music and published by Gardane in 1545, and that those republished works show musical revisions pointing to the activity of the composer himself. Indeed, there is much to suggest that Rore supplied Gardane directly with the music of the 1545 volume and even took a hand in the supervision of its publication.

There seems to be little doubt that by the mid-1540s Gardane had become firmly established as a member of a circle of musicians and intellectuals that included the composers Willaert, Rore, Buus, Berchem, Gero, and the patrons Hieronimo Uttinger, Francesco Palavicino, and Marcantonio Trevisano, to name but a few. The evidence of the editions and their dedications is further strengthened

---

[46] 'Molto Magnifico M. Hieronimo poi che tanto vi son grati que frutti musicali che son prodotti da' l mio debole ingegno, che di essi cosi gran copia a quatro, e cinque, e sei appresso di voi teneti, e tanto vi mostrate apprezzarli, et haverli cari, ecco che io ora mando in luce il primo libro . . .'

[47] Lewis, 'Gardane', pp. 225–41.

[48] Lewis, 'Gardane', pp. 224–41.

by the series of poems mentioned earlier in connection with Gero.[49] Those poems place Gardane firmly in the midst of that circle; and indeed his shop may have served as a meeting place for the various members.[50] For instance, in verses praising Jan Gero, Gardane is invoked as 'il grand'Antonio'. Another poem is directed to Gardane himself, and links him to a number of prominent Venetian personages, among whom were the poetess Gaspara Stampa, and Francesco Sansovino, son of the architect Jacopo Sansovino and tireless chronicler of things Venetian. Gardane is depicted not only as being on friendly terms with this lively, influential, and literary group, but as the recipient of their praise. But this poem reveals even more, for it praises Gardane in these words: 'You unfold sweet rhymes and songs with Parabosco, Cambio, and Rore.' While this could, of course, mean merely that Gardane printed the music of these three composers, the general tone of the whole collection leads me rather to see it as evidence that they and Gardane actually performed music together.

There remains finally the question of Gardane's sources for his 1545 edition of Willaert's motets. Six of the forty-five motets in Gardane's edition are new. Most of the rest appeared in Scotto's earlier volumes, but ordered quite differently: the 1545 books are arranged by mode, with the first containing motets in modes with a major third, the second those with a minor third.[51] The difference in contents and ordering makes clear that Gardane did not simply copy the 1539 edition; indeed, even a perusal of Zenck's critical notes reveals numerous variants in accidentals, notation, etc.[52] Do we, then, have any indication as to the source of Gardane's variant readings?

A comparative study of the two editions and the manuscript

---

[49] Other verses in the group are addressed to Cipriano de Rore; Parabosco, Cambio, Rore, Willaert, and Menon as a group; Antonio Barges; Adrian Willaert; Tuttovale Menon; and Gaspara Stampa.

[50] Giazotto, *Harmonici*, p. 10.

[51] Cf. Hermann Zenck, Foreword to *Adriani Willaert Opera omnia*, Corpus Mensurabilis Musicae ser. 3, vol. 1 (n.p., 1950).

[52] Lewis Lockwood was the first to call explicit attention to these variants in a comparison of accidentals in the Gardane and Scotto versions of the *Pater noster* and found 'a number of discrepancies between the two editions'. See his 'A Sample Problem of Musica Ficta: Willaert's *Pater Noster*', Harold Powers (ed.), *Studies in Music History: Essays for Oliver Strunk* (Princeton, 1968), pp. 161–82.

RCM 2037 has indicated that the 1545 edition reflects the readings in the manuscript,[53] which was copied in Ferrara a few years after Willaert left that city, and which presumably represents readings close to Willaert himself.[54] A separate analysis of the readings in five of Willaert's motets has generally confirmed that the versions in the 1545 edition are not dependent on Scotto, and are similar to those in RCM 2037.[55]

The closeness of the readings in the 1545 print to those in the Ferrarese manuscript would seem to indicate that Gardane's edition is the more authoritative. Indeed, Gardane's apparent membership by 1545 in the Willaert–Rore circle might have gained him access to revised and corrected versions of these motets, as well as to new pieces. Still, while we have evidence to support Gardane's closeness to Willaert's circle, we have no documentation of Willaert's directly supervising either the Scotto or Gardane editions.

In sum, then, it emerges that after his first years of publishing in the highly competitive world of Venetian music printing, Gardane finally began to find a place in the leading musical circles of that city. Through friendship with some of those who were close to some of the most important composers, as well as with the composers them-selves, he seems to have had the opportunity to obtain their music in accurate copies. While each edition must still be considered as a special case, there is at least some support for the theory that Gardane's editions of the music of the Willaert circle may carry a special authority.

[53] Carla Pollack, 'Willaert's Four-Part Motets: The Ferrarese Tradition and the Venetian Prints', unpublished seminar paper, Brandeis University, 1972.

[54] London, Royal College of Music, MS 2037. See Lowinsky, *Medici Codex*, I, pp. 116–17, and Joshua Rifkin, 'New Light on Music Manuscripts at the Court of Ferrara in the Reign of Alfonso I and Hercules II', unpublished paper presented to the New England Renaissance Conference, Durham, N.H., 26 October 1974.

[55] Personal communication from Professor Rifkin. See also his notes for *Adrian Willaert: Motets for Four Voices* (New York: Nonesuch Records, 1977). The readings were studied in connection with a new edition prepared for the recording. The motets in question are *Benedicta es, celorum regina; Magnum hereditatis misterium; Quem terra, ponthus, ethera; Saluto te, sancta virgo Maria*; and the *Pater noster*.

APPENDIX: DEDICATION FROM *ADRIANI WILLAERT . . . MUSICORUM SEX VOCUM . . . LIBER PRIMUS* (VENICE: GARDANE, 1542)

AL MAGNIFICO M. MARCO TRIVISANO

Antonio Gardane

HAVENDO io, Nobilis. signor mio, piu à sodisfatione di molti: quali commandare mi possano, che per l'utile, che per cio mi dè sequire, à donare al mondo per lo mezzo delle mie impressioni quello, che, l'eccelentissimo M. Adriano: maestro meritissimo de la capella del sacro santo Domo di MARCO Euangelista, non guari compose. Dico gli non mai basteuolmente lodati suoi motetti à Sei voci, che hora vsciranno in luce. Per bon spatio restai sospeso, à cui delli miei amici & padroni, cosi grata cosi dolce, & honorata compositione dedicare douessi, a fine, che à tale io ne la indricciassi, che egli à lei, & essa à lui piu che ad altri si conuenisse: & hauendo tra me medèsimo pensato & ripensato, ludicai à voi signor mio piu che ad alcuno altro couuenirse donare. Perche io à V. S. affetuasamente li sacro & dono, poscia che il pregiato suo Autore questo mi concede poter fare: & ben si deue, da che voi siete parimente & nobile & virtuoso, & che della Musica non pure sopramodo vi dilletate: ma di lei ne siete buonissimo professore, ne solamente nella pratica, ma nella Theorica altresi. E si nel Canto, come nel Suono: Impercio che non è stromento Musicale, che con merauigliosa harmonia, & con dolcissima attentione di cui vi ode, non sia da voi ottimamēte suonato. Pero io nō mi affatichero altrimente, della musica alcuna cosa à dirui, come de l'origine sua, de l'antichita sua, de la nobilta, de la eccellenzza, de la autorita & del dolce diporto suo ne di tante altre sue & infinite, lode, (come si suole) perche voi molto meglio di me tutte le sapete, senza, che tale carico à me non appartiene, ma io solamente debbo, quanto piu vi posso pregarui: che con quel bon animo debbiatte, questa cosi cosi[sic] rarra coppia di motetti accetare: con il quale à voi, & li dedico, & li sacro & li dono. & etiādio fare che essi siano vditi dal Mondo, nel vostro honoratissimo Ridutto a cio eletto: Doue ogni sorte di stromenti Musicali in buona quantita tenete, & oue le piu eccelente cose, che altri cātano, sono continoamente da i piu perfetti Musici cantate, & suonate, & quindi v̀ li piu nobili personaggi, che di canto, di suono si dilettano, molto volentieri si riducono, & cosi voi & l'Autore ne sarete al solito, solamente commendati & io, che di ambi doi son seruidore, il mio debito in questa parte harò pagato & à V. S. mi raccomando.

12

STRATEGIES OF MUSIC PATRONAGE IN THE FIFTEENTH CENTURY: THE *CAPPELLA* OF ERCOLE I D'ESTE

Lewis Lockwood

IN the well-known preface to his *Proportionale* Tinctoris divides all of music history into three broad phases. The first is Antiquity; the second, the Christian middle ages from the time of Jesus Christ ('the greatest of musicians') to Jean de Muris; the last is Tinctoris's own time. Writing about 1476 and addressing himself to his royal Neapolitan patron, King Ferrante d'Aragona, Tinctoris first comments on his own period not in terms of its regional and personal musical styles and qualities, but as one in which a new flowering of patronage has made possible a vast increase in the cultivation of music. He writes: 'the most Christian princes . . . desiring to augment the divine service, founded chapels after the manner of David, in which at extraordinary expense they appointed singers to sing . . . praise to our God with diverse (but not adverse) voices'. He then continues, not without a touch of irony: 'And since, if their masters are endowed with the liberality which makes men illustrious, the singers of princes are rewarded with honour, glory, and wealth, many are kindled with a most fervent zeal for this study.'[1] Although a closer look at the status of singers may arouse scepticism as to how much wealth, honour, and glory they typically received, still this shrewd appraisal of the current musical scene by one of its leading thinkers and practitioners gives us a key with which to interpret the development of musical patronage in the complex Italian domain of the last quarter of the fifteenth century. It reinforces plentiful documentary evidence that *cappelle* of court musicians were indeed being founded or strengthened in certain Italian centres in the 1470s

[1] C. E. H. Coussemaker, *Scriptorum de medii aevi nova series* (Paris, 1864–76), IV, p. 154; English transl. in O. Strunk, *Source Readings in Music History* (New York, 1950), pp. 194f.

and it also hints that this development was closely bound up with the reciprocal interests of both patrons and musicians. In this paper my purpose is to look at certain strategies of patronage (and I am aware that the term may evoke images of diplomatic and even military planning, which would not be historically inappropriate) under three headings. The first concerns the particular court *cappella* with which I am best acquainted, that of Ferrara, and the means by which it was established and controlled by Duke Ercole d'Este between 1471 and 1505;[2] the second aims to deal with the founding of the Ferrarese *cappella* in close conjunction with its most important early rival, the *cappella* of Galeazzo Maria Sforza of Milan; the last is a brief attempt to suggest some lines of interrelationship between the patronage developments in Milan and Ferrara in the early 1470s and the apparent tendencies of these two centres to foster specific and locally defined musical styles and usages.

In the crowded and suspicious world of the Italian courts, the year 1471 was marked by two events of importance for politics and music. In June, Pope Paul II died at Rome under mysterious circumstances and was succeeded by Sixtus IV, Francesco della Rovere of Savona. The Papacy of Sixtus became as famous for its artistic and architectural contributions to the renewal of Rome as for its extraordinary nepotism and political ambition. As Machiavelli put it, 'Sixtus was the first who began to show how far a Pope might go, and how much that which was previously considered sinful lost its iniquity when committed by a Pope.'[3] By 1473 Sixtus had begun the construction of what would be called the Sistine Chapel, and he was establishing a new *cappella* of singers for St Peter's; in that year he also issued the first of four bulls conferring new provisions for benefices on the Papal singers and confirming the extension of their privileges.[4] The second event in politics in 1471 was the death of Borso d'Este at Ferrara, in August, and the immediate seizure of power by his half-brother Ercole, who beat back a threat by Niccolò d'Este, the son of Borso's predecessor Leonello.[5] The advent of Ercole and Sixtus brought to

[2] For a brief account of Ercole's patronage in local cultural context see my 'Music at Ferrara in the Period of Ercole I d'Este', *Studi Musicali*, I/1 (1972), pp. 101–32.

[3] *History of Florence*, transl. of *Istorie fiorentine* (New York, 1960), p. 338.

[4] See F. X. Haberl, *Die Römische 'Schola Cantorum' und die Päpstlichen Kapellsänger bis zur Mitte des 16. Jahrhunderts* (Leipzig, 1888), pp. 42–5.

[5] On the campaign of Niccolò di Leonello to seize power, which ended with his death in 1476, see W. Gundersheimer, *Ferrara: The Style of a Renaissance Despotism* (Princeton, N.J., 1973), pp. 180–2.

power two of the major figures in the newly developing patronage of *cappella* singers. If we look across the Italian landscape at the beginning of 1471, we find not more than four court centres that maintained companies of singers capable of mounting performances of sacred polyphony of the more complex varieties: Savoy, Florence, the Papal court, and Naples.[6] More numerous were those principalities that did not then have this capability, among them Milan, Ferrara, Mantua, Urbino, Monferrato, and many other smaller states. But by the end of the year 1471 important new initiatives toward the founding of court *cappelle* had been not only announced but begun by Ercole and Galeazzo, and a new phase of competition for talent had begun.

When Ercole took power at Ferrara in August of 1471, he was the first of his venerable line to enter the succession with the title of Duke of Ferrara, an investiture conferred on Borso only a few months before his death. Just as the Burgundian court had established a level of opulence that could rival that of the Kings of France themselves, one of Ercole's earliest major steps in transforming the character of the court, as a seat of power and propaganda, was to build and staff a new court chapel. From Borso he had inherited a group of secular court musicians of considerable talent, dominated by the famous lutenist–singer Pietrobono and by other instrumentalists and improvisational singers; but a company of singers of sacred music had not been in existence at Ferrara since the death of

---

[6] Recent studies based on substantial research on these centres include the following for Savoy: M.-Th. Bouquet, 'La Cappella Musicale dei Duchi di Savoia dal 1450 al 1500', *Rivista Italiana di Musicologia*, 3 (1968), pp. 233–85, and 5 (1970), pp. 3–36. On Florence the many important studies by Frank D'Accone are the essential basis for all future work: see his 'The Singers of San Giovanni in Florence during the Fifteenth Century', *Journal of the American Musicological Society*, 14 (1961), pp. 307–58. On the Papacy, the earlier work by Haberl is now being superseded by the research of several scholars, including Jeremy Noble, Richard Sherr, and Christopher Reynolds. See in particular R. J. Sherr, 'The Papal Chapel ca. 1492–1513 and Its Polyphonic Sources', Ph.D. diss., Princeton University, 1975; J. Noble, 'New Light on Josquin's Benefices', in E. E. Lowinsky and B. J. Blackburn (eds.), *Josquin des Prez – Proceedings of the International Josquin Festival– Conference* (London, 1976), pp. 76–102. Christopher Reynolds has a Ph.D. dissertation now (1980) in progress at Princeton University, entitled 'The Basilica San Pietro and the Cappella Sistina: Musicians and Polyphonic Masses, c. 1460–1500'. For Naples, we now have the valuable research of Allan Atlas, e.g. his 'Alexander Agricola and Ferrante I of Naples,' *Journal of the American Musicological Society*, 30 (1977), pp. 313–19.

Leonello in 1450.[7] With Ercole's advent the emphasis shifted strongly. While maintaining secular music as entertainment and recreation (in short, as *sollazo*), he also wanted a prominent *cappella* that would serve both personal religious purposes and musical ambition. Unlike Borso, Ercole was a serious religious devotee, concerned not only with observance but with public religious displays that would fortify the bonds of religion by which he could rule effectively. From a contemporary description we know that the chapel of Santa Maria di Corte (which survives now as a cinema) was the locus of court religious life. Thaumaturgic miracles were attributed to Ercole's prayers of intercession in this chapel.[8] Normally there, sometimes in other churches of the city, he heard Mass every morning and Vespers every evening, sung in polyphony on more important days by his singers, with organ alternation or accompaniment. As another eyewitness tells us, it was in the chapel that he habitually gathered with his singers or knelt in prayer as they sang; and in the late 1490s, when he had published a special volume of devotional prayers for the Virgin, it was there that he sang or intoned its texts. Beginning in 1475, he heard what a chronicler called the 'Messa del Duca', evidently a special Mass for his personal use, of which he was particularly proud.[9] It is entirely likely that it was for this specific tradition that Josquin composed the *Missa Hercules Dux Ferrarie*, which I attribute to the period 1480–1 when Josquin was probably residing in Ferrara with his patron Ascanio Sforza. Among other features, the division of the final six-voice Agnus dei of the *Hercules* Mass into contrasting upper and lower three-voice groups, noted

[7] On Borso as music patron, see Lockwood, 'Pietrobono and the Instrumental Tradition at Ferrara in the Fifteenth Century', *Rivista Italiana di Musicologia*, 10 (1975), pp. 115–33.

[8] On Ercole's construction and use of the *cappella di corte* see the principal Ferrarese chronicles of the period, especially the *Diario ferrarese dall'anno 1476 sino al 1504* (= Diary of Bernardino Zambotti), in *Rerum Italicarum Scriptores*, rev. edn, vol. XXIV, pt 7, pp. 5, 24, 28, 46, 83, 88, 184, and 220; Ugo Caleffini, 'Croniche . . . 1471–1494', Rome, Biblioteca Vaticana, MS Chigiano I.I.4, fols. 43v, 53v, etc.). Also G. Sabadino degli Arienti, *De triumphis religionis*, as published by W. Gundersheimer under the title *Art and Life at the Court of Ercole I d'Este* (Geneva, 1972), p. 89.

[9] Caleffini, fol. 37 (for 28 July 1475): '. . . sonata le 14 hore se comenciò la messa in canto del Duca nel suo palatio nostra dona che durò una bona hora . . .' In 1481 Ercole proudly wrote to his wife, Eleonora d' Aragona, from Mantua (24 February 1481): 'Hogi se ne andassimo a Messa in Domo dove facessimo cantare la nostra Messa secundo usanza . . .'

also by Osthoff, would exactly fit the double-chorus structure of the Ferrarese *cappella* as it was organised through the 1470s and up to 1482, but not beyond.[10]

Through the first years of his reign Ercole built his staff of singers by every means of recruitment then available to him. Four months after becoming duke he wrote to the Bishop of Constance and asked for a musician named 'dominus Martinus de Alemania' of whom he had heard good reports, since, as he said, he had determined to create a 'most celebrated *cappella*' and wanted 'excellent musicians, whom we are looking for everywhere'.[11] Despite some scepticism among earlier scholars, I see no reason to doubt that this 'don Martinus' could be Johannes Martini, since by little more than a year later a 'Govanni d'Alemagna' was installed in the *cappella* and this can hardly refer to anyone else. Except for a portion of the year 1474, Martini's entire later career was centred at Ferrara, where he remained for twenty-five years until his death in 1498. In the 1470s the number of musicians is impressively high for a smaller Italian court: by 1472 there were fifteen singers, by 1473 at least thirteen adult singers and eleven imported German choirboys. By 1476 the choir had grown to twenty-seven singers, and though it fluctuated at a somewhat lower figure (around twenty) through these years, by

[10] In his study 'Josquin des Prez and Ascanio Sforza', *Congresso internazionale sul Duomo di Milano, Atti*, ed. M. L. Gatti Perer, II (Milan, 1969), p. 19, Edward Lowinsky expressed the view that the probable date of the *Hercules* Mass was 1487, when Ercole paid a visit to Rome and was received cordially by Ascanio Sforza. In the absence of any documentation the point is moot. Yet at present I lean to 1480–1 for the reasons expressed above. Professor Lowinsky has agreed with the view that in all probability Josquin came to Ferrara with Ascanio in 1480–1: see E. E. Lowinsky, 'Ascano Sforza's Life: A Key to Josquin's Biography and an Aid to the Chronology of His Works', in Lowinsky and Blackburn (eds), *Josquin des Prez – Proceedings*, pp. 31–75. On the division of the *cappella* into a double chorus up to 1482, see Sabadino degli Arienti, *Art and Life . . .*, p. 89, and my review in *Renaissance Quarterly*, 26 (1973), pp. 494–7.

[11] The text of this important letter is now extant only in a corrected ducal minute: Archivio di Stato di Modena (hereafter AS M), Fasc. Borsii et Herculis I, Epist. reg. 1471–75, p. 87. Its text was first published by L. Valdrighi in 'Cappelle, concerti e musiche di case d'Este (dal sec. XV al XVIII)', *Atti e Memorie delle RR. Dep. di Storia Patria per le Prov. Modenesi*, 3rd ser., vol. 2 (1884), p. 443, but without the original corrections to the text. It was recently discussed by Manfred Schuler in 'Beziehungen zwischen der Konstanzer Domkantorei und der Hofkapelle des Herzogs Ercole I. von Ferrara', *Analecta Musicologica*, 15 (1975), pp. 15–20, but unfortunately again without showing the original corrections. A full discussion and text will be given in my forthcoming book on music in fifteenth-century Ferrara.

1481 and the end of Ercole's first decade it again had twenty-seven mature singers, plus choirboys.[12]

In writing to the Bishop of Constance in 1471, Ercole had sought musical talent in a city in which he maintained no diplomatic agents and had no known political business.[13] Probably he had heard of singers at Constance through other musicians. But in his other recruiting in this period he made extensive use of the expanding network of diplomatic contacts created by his resident orators at the courts of France, Rome, Milan and Florence, and by special agents, chiefly musicians, sent on particular missions.

It now seems clear that Ercole's entire effort to launch his *cappella* was not a wholly independent venture but was aimed at competing directly with Galeazzo Maria Sforza at Milan. Galeazzo was an apt rival for Ercole in recruitment of musicians and similar matters; as a man he was a sharply contrasting personality. Ercole in 1471 was a middle-aged man for his time – forty years old when he became duke – and he soon gained a reputation for political prudence in guiding his small and continually threatened state through the political dangers around him. He gained a considerable reputation for the sizeable expansion of the city and its new architectural achievements; and he also spurred its cultural growth by sponsoring the first revival of Classical theatre in the Italian Renaissance. At the same time he managed to project the image of a pious and elderly leader, more distant and abstracted from the people than the popular Borso, but evidently supported by the local nobility and gentry.[14] Galeazzo on the other hand was a mere twenty-six in 1471, and after only five years as duke had lost the confidence of almost every Milanese political faction. To call him impetuous, extravagant, autocratic and vain would be bland understatement. His conspicuous love of display, as on his famous journey to Florence in February 1471, overshadowed even his most ambitious contemporaries. As ruler of a state much more powerful than that of Ercole, he handled foreign

---

[12] For a preliminary survey of the numbers of singers in cathedral *cappelle*, and in some court *cappelle*, in this period see F. D'Accone, 'The Performance of Sacred Music in Italy during Josquin's Time, *c.* 1475–1525', in Lowinsky and Blackburn (eds.), *Josquin des Pres – Proceedings*, p. 665.

[13] The few surviving diplomatic papers that document Ferrarese missions to German cities and courts in this time are preserved in ASM, Ambasciatori, Germania, B.I. No letters to or from Constance are included in this collection.

[14] On Ercole's rule see L. Chiappini, *Gli Estensi* (Varese, 1967); and Gundersheimer, *Ferrara*, pp. 173–228.

affairs with some ability. As local ruler he was wholly unable to reconcile his thrust towards despotism with the expectations of civic influence that were rooted in the nobles. The result was his notorious assassination in 1476 by a group of conspirators who thought of themselves as Milanese patriots, liberating the city from a vicious tyrant. They stabbed him to death in the church of Santo Stefano in full view of a throng of citizens and courtiers and of his assembled singers.[15]

In the years between 1471 and 1476, Galeazzo and Ercole had used essentially the same tactics as music patrons, and probably acted with close awareness of one another's moves. Beginning in October 1471 (two months before Ercole's first recruiting letter) Galeazzo sent his singer Raynerio to England for singers, armed with a letter to King Edward IV, and he sent subsequent recruiters, including Gaspar Weerbecke, on similar missions to the courts of France and Burgundy and to Flanders. He sent for singers of the court of Savoy and then tried to keep them for himself, arousing angry reactions from the Duchess Yolanda of Savoy; but this in no way dissuaded him from sending other agents to Naples and Rome to try to lure their singers away.[16] By 1474 Galeazzo had formed an establishment of forty singers (twenty-two *da cappella*, eighteen *da camera*), by far the largest of its time, and although it was reduced to thirty-two and then to twenty-six members by the end of the year 1475, it was a sizeable special group even within his well-populated court. Wages for singers were not high, even for the leading figures, but clothing and housing were supplied and benefices were sought for them. By 1476 Galeazzo was spending some 5,000 ducats annually for the *cappella*, and it is therefore hardly surprising that after his abrupt demise in 1476 the *cappella* was cut to half this size by his successors, who kept the best of the singers but let the others go.[17]

---

[15] On Galeazzo see the excellent recent summation by Caterina Santoro, *Gli Sforza* (Varese, 1968), pp. 111–73. On the plot leading to his death, see B. Belotti, *Il dramma di Gerolamo Olgiati* (Milan, 1929). Discussion of his music patronage began with E. Motta, 'Musici alla corte degli Sforza', *Archivio storico lombardo*, 2nd ser., vol. 4 (1887), and has been continued by C. Sartori, art. 'Sforza', *Die Musik in Geschichte und Gegenwart*, 12 (1965), cols. 604–7; G. Barblan in *Storia di Milano*, IX, pp. 818–37; and Lowinsky, 'Ascanio Sforza's Life'.

[16] Motta, *op. cit.*, pp. 301ff and especially 302–3, for the Savoy episode.

[17] Motta, *op. cit.*, p. 319. Lowinsky, 'Ascanio Sforza's Life', pp. 40f, presents a newly found document of 1477 showing travel passes for a group of singers, including Compère.

Yet, although this figure has been cited as a very high one, for a chapel of forty singers it averaged a little more than 120 ducats per singer per year, and in contrast to some of Galeazzo's other extravagances this may not have seemed truly excessive. Allowing for slight variations in the local value of currencies, 120 ducats was exactly the figure that Ercole offered to three Milanese singers when he tried to recruit them in 1479, and it was also, we remember, the figure at which Isaac was said to be willing to come to Ferrara in 1502.

In sending recruiters on far-flung missions and in their steady raiding of one another's *cappelle*, these Italian princes were obviously competing for talents that were not in plentiful supply in their own populations. In the matter of raiding, there were calculable political risks. Galeazzo had managed to exchange instrumentalists cordially with Borso in the late 1460s, but Borso had not been a collector of singers. Among Ferrarese agents, the notorious Gian, early in 1502, was actually imprisoned in Savoy for tampering with singers, and a messenger had to be sent to free him.[18] Ercole was more courteous in 1479 when recruiting in Milan; first he told his ambassador to keep it all as quiet as possible, and then solemnly advised the singer Victor Tarquinio de Bruges that 'before you leave you should ask permission from Her Ladyship . . . since if you don't have it we don't see how we can honourably accept you'.[19] That Galeazzo and Ercole understood each other perfectly in the busy years between 1471 and 1476 is clear from the cool and courteous tone of Galeazzo's letter to Ercole of 24 July 1476:

We are certain that your Lordship would neither wish nor permit that any of your singers should steal away any of ours, just as we would shun such behaviour, since we are brothers and comrades . . . but we must advise you that a certain Michele Feyt, a singer of ours, has left our service [along with a] Daniele, another of our singers . . .[20]

Recruiting abroad, although more uncertain, was relatively freer of political complications, especially if the source of singers was not a

[18] See my 'Josquin at Ferrara . . .', in Lowinsky and Blackburn (eds.), *Josquin des Prez – Proceedings*, pp. 125f, Docs. 7–9.

[19] These letters from Ercole are important as evidence of his recruiting methods and for the specific inducements he offered singers to join his service. Their texts are given in full in the Appendix to this article, pp. 245–8 below.

[20] See my 'Music at Ferrara in the Period of Ercole I d'Este', *Studi Musicali*, I (1972), p. 118, n. 49, for the original text.

rival court but the towns and churches of France and the Low Countries, with their streams of talent flowing from the *maîtrises*. As with Constance in 1471, Ercole had no other diplomatic relations with the Low Countries, and as a vassal of the French court he kept away from its singers, seeking only music from them. Nor, so long as the Burgundian *cappella* lasted (until 1477), is there any evidence of his attempting to subvert its members. But in 1487 he sent his singer Cornelio to Bruges with letters addressed to the canons of the collegiate church of Saint-Donatien, asking them to give Obrecht a six-month leave of absence to come to Ferrara.[21] Cornelio was a faithful agent to Ercole but had also once served in Milan, and he was accompanied on this journey by the prominent Milanese singer Jean Cordier, who explained to the canons that Ercole was an exceptionally avid patron of music. Sometimes the search was aimed at just the singers needed to balance voice-ranges in the *cappella*. In 1503 Ercole allowed his contralto Bartolomeo di Fiandra to go back to his native territory, and when Bartolomeo sent in a report on certain gifted singers he had heard in Antwerp, Therouanne, and Bruges, Ercole gave the list to Alfonso a year later and urged him to bring as many as he could hire, 'but we do not want singers who are not really perfect'.[22]

Far from being merely passive or captive participants in the patronage process, the singers whose training and experience qualified them for positions in *cappelle* emphasising devotional and liturgical polyphony began to develop their own tactics for self-advertisement and advancement, rapidly developing the celebrated mobility that historians have come to see as a typical hallmark of Renaissance musicians. Tinctoris in 1476 hints that the number of musicians was increasing to meet the new opportunities, which in Italy seems certain to have been true. For some foreigners who had musical training the Italian princely *cappelle* provided convenient temporary means of support while they pursued other goals. The young Rudolph Agricola, from Groningen, later a famous humanist and an influential writer, spent three years as organist in Ercole's

[21] See Bain Murray, 'New Light on Jacob Obrecht's Development – A Bibliographical Study', *Musical Quarterly*, 42 (1957), pp. 510–15; two additional documents on Obrecht's benefices are presented in Lockwood, 'Music at Ferrara in the Period of Ercole I d'Este', pp. 127–9.

[22] See my 'Messer Gossino and Josquin Desprez', in *Studies . . . in Honor of Arthur Mendel* (Kassel and Hackensack, N.S., 1974), p. 22.

cappella while he was enrolled as a student in the University of Ferrara.[23] And a full-time singer from Constance, Uldrich Pelczer, left Ercole's *cappella* in 1487 after fifteen years as a member, and took a degree in medicine at the university, thereafter abandoning music.[24]

Some singers improved their status by offering their services as recruiting agents. Thus in October of 1472 the singer Thomaso Leporis is recommended to Galeazzo by one of his counsellors in the following terms: he is a Frenchman, he is newly arrived from Rome where he had obtained certain benefices, he had been since childhood a singer in the Burgundian *cappella* and later in the Papal *cappella*; he is an excellent singer, trained in both practical and theoretical matters; he is a very tractable and accessible man (this carries echoes of the famous Josquin–Isaac comparison of 1502); and finally, says the writer, 'he is known by all the good singers of France and the court of Rome; and he similarly knows all of them, so that for managing and governing a *cappella* he would be as suitable as anyone else'.[25] Accordingly, Thomaso was hired at once by Galeazzo and was sent immediately to France to round up new singers. Similarly, in 1474 Agricola informed Galeazzo from Florence that while passing through Ferrara he had heard a gifted young organist named Bernardo Todesco, who had promised to make Milan his first choice of a new position and had given Agricola several compositions as evidence of his ability.[26] For Ercole this role seems to have been played in earlier years mainly by the lay singer Cornelio di Lorenzo of Antwerp, whom Ercole trusted despite his tendency to rove to

[23] On Rudolph Agricola as organist at Ferrara see his letter of Easter 1475 or 1476, as published by K. Hartfelder, 'Unedierte Briefe von Rudolf Agricola', *Festschrift der Bodischen Gymnasium gewidmet der Universität Heidelberg . . .* (Karlsruhe, 1886), p. 17.

[24] Documentation of the degree awarded to Ulderichus Pelczer was published by G. Pardi, *Titoli dottorali conferiti dallo Studio di Ferrara nei secoli XV e XVI* (Lucca, 1900), p. 81. The degree was granted on 10 April 1488 to 'Ulricus Pilcer de Constantia cantor ducis Ferrariae'; two of the three witnesses were ducal singers. Close relationships that might be inferred between the northern European students and ducal singers from the same territories are confirmed by frequent references to singers who served as witnesses for the conferral of degrees. This sheds some light on the tendency of the northern singers to retain their status as members of a foreign minority in the small urban environment of an Italian city such as Ferrara, which lacked commercial bases for foreigners.

[25] Motta, 'Musici alla corte degli Sforza', pp. 304f.

[26] C. Sartori, 'Organs, Organ-Builders and Organists in Milan, 1450–1476; New and Unpublished Documents', *Musical Quarterly*, 43 (1957), p. 64.

other courts, and whom he three times rehired. Cornelio was in Milanese service from 1474 to 1477, in Florence in 1482–4 (during the Ferrarese–Venetian war), and again in Florence in 1488–90. But during both of his Florentine stays Cornelio continued to act as agent by sending music (e.g. in 1484 the 'new *L'homme armé* Mass of Philippon'), and it is indicative of his good relations with Ercole that in this same post-war year, 1484, Cornelio was encouraging Ercole to reconstitute his *cappella* and was telling him of a singer at Florence whom he'd 'risk his soul' to bring back to Ferrara.[27] In later years, as Ercole's seven children rose to maturity, the relationships of local patrons and musicians become dense with intrigue and court politics. Accordingly the agents also multiply in numbers, as we know from the famous conflict over Josquin and Isaac in 1502. The two protagonists are both court agents, spies, and informers; one of them, Gian, tells Ercole that Isaac composes quickly, is easy to get along with, will come for a lower salary, and is thinking it over. The opposing agent, Girolamo da Sestola, 'il Coglia', tells Ercole that if he brings Josquin to the *cappella* 'neither Pope nor king will have a better chapel than Your Lordship'. Vanity, the dream of outdoing kings and Popes, wins out even over avarice, and Josquin is hired. Incidentally, Coglia, who acted as agent for virtually every member of the family at one time or another, survived to tell his tales for many years thereafter. Gian, on the other hand, made a vital miscalculation when he sided with two lesser sons of Ercole in an attempted *coup d'état* in 1506, and was publicly tortured and executed.[28]

That the principal singers of polyphonic music at this period were northern Europeans, not Italians, is by now the most obvious of historical commonplaces, but I believe that a close look at the rosters of the *cappelle*, even in the 1470s, will serve to modify it substantially. It is true that the leading figure in each of the principal new or strengthened *cappelle* was a Northerner: Tinctoris at Naples, Martini at Ferrara, Weerbecke at Milan. At the Papal chapel in these years we find no quite comparable figure, as it now appears, but among its members in these years was Guillaume Garnier, who is said by Gaffurius to have been a composer. The same position of

[27] D'Accone, 'The Singers of San Giovanni', p. 343, n. 170.

[28] See R. Bacchelli, *La Congiura di don Giulio d'Este* (Milan, 1929; 2nd edn, 1958), pp. 511f. For Ariosto's views of Gian, see my 'Musicisti a Ferrara all'Epoca di Ariosto', to appear in a *Quaderno* of the *Rivista Italiana di Musicologia*, 1980.

leadership by a northern musician doubtless governs the installation of Isaac in Florence in the 1480s; and when Johannes Martini died early in 1498, Ercole at first sought to obtain Weerbecke from Milan, then turned to Josquin and to Obrecht to fill the post of *maestro di cappella*. At the same time, the number of native Italian singers in the *cappelle* of the 1470s is by no means negligible, so far as we can tell, with the inevitable exception of the Papal *cappella* and even the choir of St Peter's. At Milan under Galeazzo Maria, there were some seven Italian singers in the *cappella* in 1474. And at Ferrara during the 1470s the proportion of Italians rose from almost one-fourth of the *cappella* in 1472 to two-fifths in 1477 and one-third in 1481 (nine out of twenty-seven).[29] Despite the late and slow development of Italian cathedral schools in which mensural polyphony could be taught, it appears that native singers were becoming available in some numbers as early as the 1470s, just thirty years after the reforms of Eugenius IV. Possibly Tinctoris's programmatic series of treatises of the 1470s, which cover the field of mensural polyphony and its notation, should be seen in this context – that is, as being intended to teach correct principles of composition and above all notation to a newly established and visibly inexperienced generation of singers, of whom only a very small minority are also known as composers.

Without doubt one of the most important and enduring of Ercole's strategies for music patronage was his pursuit of a Papal Indult that would give him the right to confer benefices on his singers within his own dominions. This too would have been a means of surpassing Galeazzo, who had tried without success to obtain the same privilege. Since the surviving documentation on Ercole's singers and their benefices is immense, both individually and in relation to his Indult, only the barest outline of the matter can be given here.[30] The business of conferring benefices in Ferrarese lands was complicated, as elsewhere, by the inexact correlation between the political bound-

[29] Of these nine, seven were called 'don', indicating at least minor clerical status; several were *cappellani*, and may have been products of the scuola attached to the Cathedral of Ferrara, in which singing had been taught since the 1440s when the great theorist Ugolino di Orvieto was archpriest of the cathedral chapter and an important member of the local hierarchy.

[30] The correspondence between Ercole and his ambassadors at Rome on the Indult is very extensive; it forms one of the principal topics in the entire Ferrara–Rome diplomatic material of this period from about 1484 to 1505. It is preserved in ASM, Cancelleria, Ambasciatori, Roma, B.1–17.

aries of the state and the boundaries of the ecclesiastical jurisdictions that governed its parishes, churches, and other religious institutions.[31] Ferrara itself was then the seat of a bishop, but so were Modena and Reggio, its main subordinate cities, and in many instances a particular parish or church in a border area could be subject to the conflicting claims of two ecclesiastical authorities. Like his predecessors Ercole regarded it as within his power not merely to influence but to control appointments to benefices in his lands, and in 1476 he issued a local proclamation declaring that right and threatening fines for infringement.[32] But this was a long way from actually being able to confer a benefice, since most of these were actually controlled on a grand scale by the enormous Papal bureaucracy, set up to manage the process and to reap profits from it. During the entire Papacy of Sixtus (down to 1484) Ercole was able to secure only a handful of small-scale local benefices for several singers. But when Sixtus was succeeded by Innocent VIII in 1484, Ercole embarked on a long campaign to persuade the new Pope to give him an Indult that would allow him to distribute his own benefices to his singers. At first the Pope refused and offered Ercole nothing but vague promises to respect his requests for appointments whenever benefices might fall vacant in his lands. Only after three years of negotiations, after Ercole had invoked the powerful help of his old friend Ascanio Sforza, then Papal Vice-Chancellor, and had himself gone to Rome to see the Pope about it, was the Indult granted, on 2 June 1487.[33] Although it provided Ercole with the right to confer benefices in his duchy up to a total of twenty singers, all of whom are named in the document, it was nevertheless hedged about by a large number of conditions and limitations that prevented Ercole from interfering with the prerogatives of various groups in regard to really major benefices. The granting of even this sort of Indult to an Italian prince was most exceptional, and in Rome it was observed that only the King of Naples had received one (in 1479, for forty singers).[34]

---

[31] See A. Prosperi, 'Le istituzioni ecclesiastiche e le idee religiose', in *Il Rinascimento nelle Corti Padane, Società e Cultura*', (Bari, 1977), pp. 125–64. This study deals primarily with ecclesiastical institutions in Ferrara in Ercole's time.

[32] Caleffini, 'Croniche', fol. 86; Zambotti, *Diario ferrarese*, p. 26.

[33] The original Indult is preserved in ASM, Principi Esteri, Roma, Papi, B.9.

[34] Ercole was told by his ambassador at Rome in November–December 1484 that a similar concession had been granted by the Papacy only to 'His Majesty'; in the

In 1492 another change of Popes required the Indult to be reconfirmed, and Alexander VI eventually did so a year later, after suitable delays. And in 1503 the brief Papacy of Pius III and the rapid advent of Julius II once more complicated the matter, together with the unexpected and bitterly ironic competition for a similar Indult on the part of Ercole's son, Cardinal Ippolito I. For almost a year after Pope Julius's election, the Pope found one reason after another for postponing a decision on Ercole's Indult for his singers, among them the necessity of providing suitably for Ippolito, who by now, at the age of twenty-two, was not only a Cardinal but Archbishop of Eztergom and of Milan, and also Bishop of Ferrara. On 26 November 1503, the very day of Julius's consecration, he confirmed Ippolito's Indult to confer benefices on his familiars and singers in the territory of Milan and in part in his other jurisdictions, while Ercole had to suffer not only the embarrassment of further delay but of seeing his son as a successful rival for the same privileges to which he had been devoting twenty years of struggle, and even challenging his jurisdiction in his own territories.[35] The antagonism between Ercole and Ippolito was made worse when Ippolito refused even to be formally courteous; in April 1504 the Pope demanded that Ippolito furnish in writing his approval of any Indult given to Ercole that would apply to benefices in Ippolito's diocese of Ferrara. When Ippolito declined to put such assurances in writing, Ercole exploded in a letter to his ambassador in Rome:

Seeing the obstinacy and tenacity that our son the Cardinal uses with us about the Indult, and since we are extremely unhappy over this inconvenience, we have had him notified that he should take himself out of our dominions, and go to Rome or Milan, or wherever he likes, as long as he doesn't stay in our lands . . .; because it doesn't seem to us proper that we should have with us a son who is so obstinate in dealing with our wishes, and so disobedient . . .[36]

Two months later Julius gave Ercole his own Indult again, and the matter was temporarily settled, but within another half-year Ercole was dead. The story of the court *cappella* and its Indult then con-

Italian context, this can only mean the King of Naples. In fact an Indult of this type was issued by Sixtus IV to Ferrante of Naples in 1479, as I am informed by Jeremy Noble, to whom my thanks for the information.
[35] Julius's confirmation of Ippolito's Indult is dated 26 November 1503; the Papal breve is in ASM, Principi Esteri, Roma, Papi, B.11.
[36] ASM, Ambasciatori, Roma, B.20, Ercole to Gian Luca Pozzi, 8 April 1504.

tinued one more step when Alfonso, in November of 1506, secured a Papal letter confirming earlier provisions for his court singers, and sent a new set of twenty names. Thereafter the collapse of good relations between Alfonso and Pope Julius cancelled any further steps in this direction, and there were no similar efforts during the Papacy of Leo X or for the rest of Alfonso's rule down to 1534.

Finally, I wish to consider briefly the interplay between the patronage of Galeazzo and Ercole in the early 1470s and the directions of style-development that seem to emerge in Milan and Ferrara in these years. First, it appears that we can distinguish in these two patrons not only sharply contrasting aspects of personality and governance but to some degree also attitudes towards the role of music and of their court *cappelle*. Both had considerable musical backgrounds and evident practical ability. Galeazzo's early education had conspicuously included music, principally French secular music of the 1450s; and in later years he knew enough of international musical culture to collect music as well as musicians, mainly secular music so far as we know.[37] Ercole had been exposed to music and probably to musical training during his early years of long residence at Naples in the 1440s and 1450s; during his thirty-four years as duke he kept up the musical forces needed for a wide variety of secular and sacred purposes, ranging from recreational instrumental and vocal music to music for *sacre rappresentazioni* for the public, and to the repertories of Santa Maria di Corte. I interpret Galeazzo and Ercole as patrons holding very different points of view. Galeazzo's ambitious efforts to develop his company of singers were grandiose, and among his explicit aims was to build a *cappella* not only superior in quality to any Italian rival but of greater size and even greater volume. In a letter to the Duke of Mantua reported by Canal and Motta, written in 1473, he says that he would like to have a *cappella* not only better than others but also such that when he wants to hear a really big noise (*un gran rumore*) he would 'call the singers together and have them shout all at once so that their voices would resound up to heaven'.[38] Although Ercole also sought a

---

[37] On Galeazzo's early exposure to music see *Storia di Milano*, IX, p. 818, especially the letter of 1452 reporting that the young Galeazzo was 'learning to sing diligently, has already learned eight French songs, and is learning others every day'.

[38] Motta, *op. cit.*, p. 309.

cappella of large size, he sought more differentiated and subtle means of management, achieving a special mode of organisation in its formation as a double chorus. His strong and consistent attention to civic and courtly religious observance gave his entire regime a flavour quite different from that of the extravagant Galeazzo. Balancing the important Ferrarese traditions of secular music, which emphasised both vocal and instrumental genres, by the end of the first decade of Ercole's *cappella* (1471–81) a large body of polyphonic works had also been assembled for the use of his singers.[39] These fall precisely into those categories of sacred music that Ercole especially favoured, as the chroniclers tell us: first, Masses; secondly, music for Lent and Holy Week, especially Vespers, psalms and hymns. By 1481 his scribes had completed at least two large volumes of Masses and a special pair of manuscripts for Vespers in Lent containing double-chorus settings of psalms, hymns, Magnificats and two Passion settings.[40] The Masses as preserved in one of these manuscripts – Biblioteca Estense, α.M 1.13 – comprised an international repertory headed by Martini and probably collected by him. The manuscript has eighteen Masses as presently preserved, of which thirteen are attributed; six of these are assigned to Martini (by far the leading figure), two to Faugues (including his *L'homme armé*), and one each to Dufay, Caron, Weerbecke, Vincinet, and Domarto. Ercole's interest in the current Italian vogue of *L'homme armé* settings is equally reflected three years later when he sends for the new *L'homme armé* Mass by Philippon. The manuscript as a whole shows the increasing variety of secular melodies used for settings of four-voice tenor Masses in the closing years of the Dufay era; these Masses are broadly representative of the types cultivated in the decade marked by the death of Dufay and the early maturity of Josquin and Obrecht. The Masses of Martini are not yet published in full, but those that are available display a

[39] I have made a preliminary survey of the Ferrarese music manuscripts of the 1470s and the extant documentation for them in an unpublished paper, 'Musical Sources from Renaissance Ferrara: The Reconstruction of a Manuscript Tradition', given before the New York Chapter of the American Musicological Society on 15 May 1976.

[40] The Mass manuscripts are: (1) Modena, Biblioteca Estense, MS α.M. 1.13 (Lat. 456); (2) ASM, Manoscritti, Frammenti Musicali (three leaves of a large MS of Masses of the same type and format as the preceding); (3) the paired choirbooks Modena, Biblioteca Estense, α.M. 1.11–12 (Lat. 454–5).

tendency to envelop a tenor cantus firmus with highly imitative trios having substantial motivic and rhythmic animation in all voices. In the double-chorus settings of psalms and hymns, on the other hand, both Martini and Brebis write one setting after another in which simplicity of style is of the essence: many settings are explicitly in fauxbourdon. The two choirs alternate between odd and even verses, many of which are set in simple fauxbourdon patterns for two voices, some for three. As Kanazawa suggests, Martini surpasses Brebis in discovering ways of enlivening the textures with brief imitations, but taken as a whole the style of these settings is rigidly severe: as Kanazawa puts it, a minimal compositional effort.[41] Since Martini is manifestly capable of music of much greater complexity, I am inclined to believe that the simplicity of style in these settings may have been specifically designed to reflect and enhance the clarity of text declamation, perhaps in accordance with the patron's views on the efficacy of religious observance and ritual. These works in short may represent an instance of the so-called 'intelligible style' ninety years *avant la lettre*. That this could be the case may be inferred from indirect but relevant evidence. In the mid-1490s Ercole was on good terms with Savonarola, who was in fact a native Ferrarese, and he even tried to institute some of Savonarola's reforms in Ferrara during the 1490s. From Savonarola in his prime we have a typically violent attack on the princely *cappelle* of this time, not only as immoral concessions to secular frivolity but also because their polyphonic music obscured the intelligibility of sacred texts:

These princes have their *cappelle* of singers which are a great confusion, because there stands one singer with a big voice who sounds like a calf, and the others howl around him like dogs, and no one understands what they are saying [*E non s'intende cosa che dichino*]. So let these *canti figurati* go and sing instead the *canti fermi* ordered by the church . . . [42]

To put it briefly, then, I take the deliberate simplicity of the double-chorus music of the Modena choirbooks to represent a style that is in part consistent with traditions for office compositions of this category since Dufay, but also as reflecting specific and demonstrable

[41] See M. Kanazawa, 'Martini and Brebis at the Estense Chapel', in S. Bertelli and G. Ramakus (eds.), *Essays presented to Myron P. Gilmore* (Florence, 1978), II, p. 431.

[42] See Nino Pirrotta, art. 'Italien, 14.–16. Jahrhundert', *Die Musik in Geschichte und Gegenwart*, VI (Kassel, 1957), col. 1492.

qualities of expression imposed by, or at least well suited to, a patron of unusually strong religious proclivities.

In Milan, on the other hand, a quite different mixture of developments is visible. Owing to his brief presence in Milan in 1474 Martini has often been included in a putative Milanese group of this period; but actually he is by far the most representative figure in the Ferrarese development, and his output as a whole seems to me to mirror precisely the musical preferences of his patron and the musical talents available to him.[43] Subtracting Martini, we can regard as his principal Milanese counterpart Gaspar Weerbecke, vice-abbot of the *cappella* under Galeazzo, along with his collaborators, Compère and Josquin. This group was certainly active in the *cappella* between about 1472 and 1477. Recently the emergence of specific style-tendencies at Milan at this time has been effectively suggested by Joshua Rifkin, extending some earlier comments by Wolfgang Stephan and linking these to the recent dating of Josquin's *Ave Maria* in 1476 by Thomas Noblitt through watermark evidence.[44] What seems to emerge from comparison of relevant motet settings by Weerbecke, Compère and Josquin is a four-voice style entailing much use of voice-pairing and chordal textures, abandonment of cantus firmus in favour of the balanced functions of all voices, and a tendency towards symmetry of phrase-organisation. One may speak here of simplicity but certainly not in the degree entailed by the Martini and Brebis psalms in fauxbourdon. Nor is the double-chorus principle anywhere visible in the Milanese circle. The repertories tend to emphasise the motet rather than psalms or hymns – above all, motets as substitutes for portions of the Mass in the Ambrosian liturgy, the well-known *motetti missales*.[45] The larger spectrum of composition in Milan in these years, paradoxically, gives the

[43] Thomas Noblitt, accepting the apparent evidence that Martini was in Milan for an extended period, ascribed to him two unattributed cycles of *motetti missales*: 'The Ambrosian Motetti Missales Repertory', *Musica Disciplina*, 22 (1968), p. 84. Despite the presence of similar pieces in Munich, Bayerische Staatsbibliothek, MS Mus. 3154, where music by Martini also appears, I doubt that his residence in Milan was long enough to warrant attaching him to a specifically Milanese group.

[44] J. Rifkin, 'Josquin in Context: Towards a Chronology of the Motets of Josquin', Paper delivered at the 44th Annual Meeting of the American Musicological Society, 1978 (*Abstracts*, pp. 36f); Wolfgang Stephan, *Die Burgundisch–Niederländische Motette zur Zeit Ockeghems* (Kassel, 1937), especially p. 68.

[45] On the *motetti missales* see Noblitt, *op. cit.*, pp. 77–104.

impression of great flexibility in the relationship of liturgy and polyphony, especially choice of texts, despite the well-known and self-conscious tendency of the Ambrosian clergy to faithfully preserve indigenous liturgical features. In Ferrara, on the other hand, which had no special liturgy, a strict and rigid observance of usage, certainly under the rule of Ercole, seems to have been current. Admittedly we have no basis for attributing to Galeazzo any special influence over particulars of style, and if we read his attitudes correctly, he was probably an entirely lenient patron concerned with what was pleasing, or loud, not with strictness of observance and religious fervour. Unlike Ercole, we cannot imagine Galeazzo kneeling with his singers in daily worship or obsessed with the salvation of his soul. That the two patrons shared methods of management, then, should not obscure their differences in purpose. If these distinctions of style are indeed genuine, and are borne out through further explorations of works and repertories, they may show that strategies of patronage not only were effective in relation to the societal status of musicians but had some reflection as well in the development of local styles.

APPENDIX: TWO LETTERS FROM DUKE ERCOLE I D'ESTE TO MILAN (1479 & 1480) ON THE RECRUITMENT OF SINGERS

I

Letter from Ercole d'Este to Cesare Valentino, Ferrarese ambassador in Milan, dated Ferrara, 22 November 1479. Source: ASM, Cancelleria, Ambasciatori, Milan, B.2.

Ad eundem [follows another ducal minute of the same date on the same page]:

Messer Cesare: Voi fareti chiamare quello messer Gasparo gyletto Cantore & gli fareti intendere como havemo riceuuto la sua per laquale havemo inteso la dimanda ni fano lui & zohane et ottinetto. Et che per parte nostra vui gli haveti arispondere come siamo contenti didarli li x. ducate ogni mese arasone de paga XII. lano segondo che ni richedono. [Item] ducati 50. lano de beneficij senza cura per cadauno quando accaderano vacare nel dominio nostro che geli potiamo dare et per questo non gli mancharemo dela provisione. Et che quando caso venisse che perdessino la voce che li sia licito lassareli permutare epsi beneficij ben cum nostra volunta segondo che loro domandono et che do li dui ducati che dimandano il mese quando gli accaderà astare fuora de Ferrara per le spexe. Il non mi pare de dargeli senon quando gli accadesse venire cum nui fuora del dominio et terre nostre. Et che siamo contenti di darli ducati x per cadauno de loro per potersi comprare uno cavallo. Ma che in Milano non ni pare defargeli dare perche si veniria adiscoprire la cosa laoltra. Et giunti qui incontinente geli faremo dare. Et che ali Cavalli soi non li volemo far le spexe ne ala stalla nostra ne altrove. Et cussi li faremo dare et li vestimenti segondo il nostro costume. Ma la casa che ni dimandano per habitatione se la haverano a trovare loro a sue spexe. Et questa e la risposta che facemo a tute le parte dele sue lettere liquali gli fareti intendere in nostro nome.

Et haveriti etiam arispondere a Torquin da p[er]si [Victor Tarquinio de Bruges] che nui siamo contenti dedarli il Cavallo per venire qua & cussi li dinari per le spexe et per la via segondo il ni richede per la sua scripta. Et se li compagni non voleno venire al presente, ma expectare anadale [i.e., a Natale] per intendere come passarano quella cosa de la sia col nome de Dio. Et acio che epso Torquin possi venire auraiti de comprarli un Cavallo da x in xii ducati et dargelo & dargeli dui ducati daspendere per la via perche li bastarano dinanzo per il venire fin qui. Et advisaritimi de quello che haveriti conclusi cum loro.   Ferrariae xxij Novembre 1479

Messer Cesare: You will call in that messer Gasparo Gyletto, the singer, and you will explain to him that we have received the request made by him and by Zohanne and Ottinetto. And you will tell him on our behalf that we are glad to give him the ten ducats every month on the basis of twelve months a year, as they request, [and also] fifty ducats a year in benefices *senza cura* for each one, when they fall vacant in our dominions and when we are able to bestow them. Thus we will not be lacking in providing for them, and if it should happen that they lose their voices then it will be understood that they will exchange these benefices, but with our approval, as they may request. As for the two extra ducats a month that they request for expenses, when they have to travel outside Ferrara, I will not agree to give them these unless they are asked to accompany me outside my dominions and lands. Also we are glad to give them ten ducats each to enable them to purchase a horse. But do not give them this in Milan because people up there would find out about the whole affair; so when they arrive here we will gladly give it to them. As for their horses, we are not going to pay for their stables either here or elsewhere. We will give them clothing as we are accustomed to do. But the housing that they ask for they will have to find at their own expense. And this is the reply that we make to all the sections of their letter, which you will communicate to them in our name.

246

And also you will reply to Torquin da p[er]si that we are content to give him the horse to come here, that is, the money for his expenses along the way as he requests in his letter. And if his companions don't want to come here at present, but wait until Christmas to see how that matter will go up there, then let it be so in God's name. And so that Torquin may come you will have to buy him a horse for ten or twelve ducats and give it to him, and give him two ducats to spend for travel expenses, since that will be enough for his trip here. And you will inform me of what you have concluded with them.   Ferrara, 22 November 1479

2

Letter of Ercole d'Este to the singer Victor Tarquinio de Bruges, dated Ferrara, 12 January 1480. Source: ASM, Archivio per Materie, Musica e Musicisti, B.2.

Venerabilis nobis dilectissime. Respondendo ala vostra lettera dicemo che siamo contenti di farui dare al nostro Ambassatore lie ducati dieci da comprarvi uno cavallo da potere venire qua. Et altri ducati dieci per levarvi cum le vostre cosse et per farvi le spexe per via. Et questi vinte vi donaremo de bona voglia: et cussi a scripto e dicto nostro Ambassatore. Et restaremo etiam contenti che la vostra provisione cominci a Kalende de zenaro presente, et che habiati ogni mese ducati dieci de provisione. Et ogni anno una veste come hanno li nostri cantori: Et cussi che vi sia pagato la pisone de una casa per vostra habitatione: Et anchora vi provederemo da beneficij per cento ducati, et al presente gli sera modo da darvene parte, forsi per la mitade o circa, et comperassi fin ala dicta summa, quando lo accadera che vachino de li benefitij sul nostro dominio. Ma non volemo obligarsi de haverveli dati de qui ala festa de Sancto Zoanne baptista, perche el potria essere che fra questo tempo non vi vaccaria da potervene dare, o a li haverete quanto piu presto si potria. Et per piu vostra chiareza havemo sotto scripto questa lettera de nostra propria mano . . . habiate a mente Inanti che vi partiati de havere bon licentia da quella Illustrassima Madona perche non havendo non vedemo come vi potessemo acceptare cum nostro honore. Bene valeat.   Ferrarie xij Januarij 1480.

Venerabilis nobis dilectissime. Replying to your letter, we tell you that we are glad to have our Ambassador give you the ten ducats that you need to buy a horse to be able to come here, and another ten ducats for your expenses en route. And this twenty we give you out of our good will, as we have written to our Ambassador. And we will be glad to have your payment begin on the calends of this month, and that you will receive ten ducats a month as payment, and each year a suit of clothes such as our singers have.

And also we will provide for you the rental of a house you can live in, and further we will provide you with benefices up to a hundred ducats; at present we can provide you with a part of that, perhaps about half of it, and it will be increased to the full amount when a benefice falls vacant in our territory. But we cannot promise to give them to you before the festival of St John the Baptist, because it might happen that between now and then no benefice would fall vacant that we could give you; but you will have one as soon as possible. And to clarify the matter for you all the more we have signed this letter with our own hand . . . Have in mind that before you leave you should ask permission from Her Ladyship there, since if you don't have it we don't see how we can honourably accept you. Bene valeat.

Ferrara, 12 January 1480

PART IV

STEMMATICS AND MUSIC SOURCES

13

CONFLICTING ATTRIBUTIONS IN ITALIAN SOURCES OF THE FRANCO-NETHERLANDISH CHANSON, C. 1465– C. 1505: A PROGRESS REPORT ON A NEW HYPOTHESIS[1]

ALLAN W. ATLAS

PERHAPS by now one may hope that would-be editors of fifteenth-century *opera omnia* have come to realise that their obligations do not end with the transcription of a piece from one source or another and the compilation of an uncritical catalogue of variant readings that so often passes for a 'Critical Report'. Rather, whether they try to construct precise stemmata or simply group the sources into families or traditions, they must come to terms with the problems involved in evaluating the sources and determining the interrelationships among them.[2] Yet even before the editor of a 'Complete Works' reaches this stage in the editorial process, he must often face an even more fundamental question, that of authenticity: which pieces are by the

[1] I worked on this project while I was a Fellow at the Villa I Tatti, Florence, 1978–9. Aid was also received in the form of a Fellowship from the American Council of Learned Societies. On a more personal note, I am indebted to Howard Mayer Brown for having sent me his inventory of the manuscript Florence 229, his edition of which will appear in the series Monuments of Renaissance Music.

For fuller references to all the sources discussed in this paper, see the lists on pp. 285–8 and 289–90, below.
[2] For the two different approaches, see, among others, Martin Staehelin (ed.), *Heinrich Isaac: Messen*, I–II, Musikalische Denkmäler 7 (Mainz, n.d.) p. 97, and 8 (Mainz, 1973), pp. 150 and 160; Allan Atlas (ed.), *Robert Morton: The Collected Works* (to be published, New York, 1980).

composer and which are not. The problem, of course, comes about chiefly because of conflicting attributions, wherein the same composition is ascribed to two or even three or four different composers in the various, roughly contemporary sources in which it appears.[3] What I should like to do here is to present a new approach to the problem of conflicting attributions as it affects the Franco-Netherlandish chanson repertory of the late fifteenth and early sixteenth centuries.[4] I do so, however, with an important caveat, and that is that the presentation be considered a preliminary or progress report, based on research that has yet to be completed. Indeed, further work on the subject may cause some of my tentative conclusions to be altered or at least to be stated in even more qualified terms than they are at present. Finally, since my views on conflicting attributions have much to do with variant readings, scribal practices, and rather basic problems of the transmission of music, this discussion demonstrates how the results of the systematic collating of readings may be put to practical use in problems other than those concerned purely with editing.

In the past, unless the conflicting attributions involved a composition to which a *si placet* altus or other voice had been added – in which case one of the composers has generally been credited with the added voice part only – the conflicts have been treated in a rather black-and-white fashion: one attribution has been assumed to be correct, the other incorrect. And traditionally, four methods have been used

[3] The problem of authenticity can of course arise even when there are no conflicting attributions, as when an editor rejects an unchallenged ascription on stylistic or other grounds; see, for example, Heinrich Besseler (ed.), *Guglielmi Dufay: Opera omnia*, Corpus Mensurabilis Musicae ser. I, vol. VI (n.p., 1964), p. xiv, where, among others, a setting of *Le Serviteur* that is ascribed to Dufay in Montecassino 871 and not challenged elsewhere is considered to be the work of a composer belonging to a younger generation. I have not considered this type of authenticity problem in the present report.

[4] Other repertories in which conflicting attributions are especially vexing are the sixteenth-century motet and the instrumental music of the eighteenth century. On the latter, see, among others, Jan LaRue, 'Major and Minor Mysteries of Identification in the 18th-Century Symphony', *Journal of the American Musicological Society*, 13 (1960), pp. 181–96; Eugene K. Wolf, 'Authenticity and Stylistic Evidence in the Early Symphony: A Conflict in Attribution between Richter and Stamitz', E. H. Clinkscale and C. Brook (eds.), *A Musical Offering: Essays in Honor of Martin Bernstein* (New York, 1977), pp. 275ff, and the bibliography cited in nn. 5 and 10. There is no specialised study on the conflicts in the motet repertory. However, I suspect that the conflicting attributions in motets could be subjected to much the same methods that I have used here for the chansons of the late fifteenth century.

to determine which was which. The oldest and still most commonly employed is style analysis, which can seemingly be applied convincingly in instances in which the composers involved belonged either to different generations (and such conflicts occur but rarely) or to different national or regional 'schools' (something that is of slight import in the chanson repertory), or otherwise displayed some truly marked, personal stylistic traits that readily identify their work. The trouble with this approach, though, is obvious; it is difficult to reach firm conclusions when the composers involved wrote in fairly similar, impersonal styles or, as sometimes happens, when one or both of them has left us so little music that there is no reliable base against which we can measure the style of the disputed piece.[5]

Recently, another method has gained currency, in part as a result of increased knowledge regarding the precise provenance of many fifteenth-century manuscripts. Here one tries to determine which of the sources containing an ascription stands closest to the composers concerned and is therefore most likely to be telling the truth.[6] Although this method is somewhat more objective than the first, it too has its limits, as when the sources with the attributions are equally close to or equally far removed from the composers that they name, or when filiation shows that a source that is seemingly distant from the composers on chronological–geographical grounds is closely related to or even ultimately derived from an earlier source that is quite central, in which case its ascription counts heavily.[7]

[5] Among composers in this category are Barle, Basin, Boris, Bourdon, Congiet, and Malcort, to name but a few.

[6] See, for example, the discussion of the conflicting attributions involving Morton in Atlas, *Robert Morton: The Collected Works*, where I briefly allude to the idea developed in the present paper.

[7] An example of such may possibly be found in certain sections of Copenhagen 1848, which, though apparently compiled at Lyons, possibly in the third decade of the sixteenth century, demonstrates in part some striking relationships with two Florentine manuscripts of the 1490s, Florence 229 and Rome XIII.27. Thus, its attribution of *La saison en est* to Agricola, an ascription that is challenged by attributions to Compère in four seemingly more central sources of the late fifteenth century (see no. 12 in the Table p. 279 below), cannot be summarily dismissed solely because of the peripheral origins of the manuscript. Indeed, Agricola's presence at Florence in the early 1490s (see note 12, below) may, given the connection between Copenhagen 1848 and Florence, imbue the Copenhagen 1848 attribution with no less authority than we grant to the Compère ascriptions that appear in Paris 2245 and the final section of Washington L 25, both of which can be associated with the royal court of France during the period in which Compère is presumed to have been active there. On the provenance of

About a third method, which simply tallies up the number of sources in which each composer is named and then awards the piece to the winner,[8] there is little to say; its wrong-headedness is evident in that it forgets that all the ascriptions to one composer may be dependent upon a common parent or, once we reach the era of printed music, even on one another. Finally, the fourth approach seeks to find corroboration of one of the attributions in the works of a contemporary theorist,[9] once again forgetting that the theorists sometimes derived their ascriptions from the same sources that we use today.

As I have noted, all four methods start with the assumption that one of the conflicting attributions must be wrong. And to judge from statements frequently encountered, to the effect that the ascriptions in a given source are unreliable either as a whole or for an individual composer,[10] there seems to be the further assumption that the root of the problem lies in scribal–editorial carelessness, confusion, invention, or even partiality,[11] either on the part of the scribes and editors

Copenhagen 1848, see Henrik Glahn, 'Et fransk musikhåndskrift fra begyndelsen af det 16. århundrede', *Fund og forskning i det kongelige Biblioteks samlinger*, 5–6 (1958–9), pp. 90ff. A brief hint at the Copenhagen 1848–Florence relationship is given in Atlas, *The Cappella Giulia Chansonnier (Rome, Biblioteca Apostolica Vaticana, C.G.XIII.27)*, 2 vols., Musicological Studies 27 (Brooklyn, 1975–6), I, pp. 221–3 and 228, where, however, the lack of significant agreement between the Copenhagen 1848 and Florentine readings is perhaps unduly emphasised at the expense of the significant concordances among the sources. On the provenance of Florence 229 and Rome XIII.27, see *ibid.*, I, pp. 23ff and 248, and the forthcoming edition by Howard Mayer Brown. On the French ties of Paris 2245 and the final section of Washington L 25, see Louise Litterick (Rifkin), 'The Manuscript Royal 20.A.XVI of the British Library', Ph.D. diss., New York University, 1976, pp. 40 and 66–7).

[8] For an example of this method, see the discussion of the Ockeghem–Martini–Malcort *Malheure me bat* in Edgar H. Sparks, *Cantus Firmus in Mass and Motet: 1420–1530* (Berkeley and Los Angeles, 1963), p. 470, n. 24.

[9] *Ibid.*

[10] See, for example, Ludwig Finscher, *Loyset Compère (c. 1450–1518): Life and Works*, Musicological Studies and Documents 12 (n.p., 1964), p. 47, n. 4, and p. 54, nn. 9 and 11, where the ascriptions in Segovia to Compère in particular and to other composers in general are questioned: and Besseler, *Guglielmi Dufay: Opera omnia*, VI, p. xviii, who, in discussing Montecassino 871, writes: 'The names of composers are often wrong' (in fact, they are not) and then goes on to reject two ascriptions to Dufay that are challenged in other sources and one other that is not (see note 3, above).

[11] Thus Theodore Karp, 'The Secular Music of Johannes Martini', Jan LaRue *et al.* (eds.), *Aspects of Medieval and Renaissance Music: A Birthday Offering to Gustave Reese* (New York, 1966), p. 457, n. 12, on *Malheure me bat*: 'If one seeks to confirm Ockeghem's claim to the piece, one may . . . disclaim the evidence of [Florence] Banco Rari 229 on the ground that the compiler was simply displaying favoritism toward Martini.'

of the extant sources themselves or perhaps on the part of those who compiled the examplars from which the former group worked. Yet perhaps these assumptions are wrong, for if the scribes and editors worked carelessly or were confused or sometimes took the matter of attributions into their own hands – that is, deciding between composers or supplying names when there were none before them – the overall picture of conflicting attributions would probably be quite different in three significant ways. First, there would probably be an even greater number of such ascriptions, which, numerous as they may seem, still comprise a relatively small percentage of the total number of attributions. Secondly, there would probably be a greater number of attributions in general and fewer anonymous compositions. And thirdly, and most important, the conflicts would – unless the scribes possessed an acute stylistic–historical awareness – probably form a rather haphazard pattern, with composers conflicting with one another in a rather random fashion. Yet a review of a substantial number of conflicting attributions – seventy-six so far – shows that the pattern of conflicts is not entirely haphazard. Rather, many of them seem to form a rational pattern in which certain composers tend to conflict frequently with a select group of certain other composers. Indeed, it was this tendency that first led me to question the traditional assumptions about conflicting attributions and to investigate the problem at greater length.

Before considering a few examples, however, an important ground rule must be explained. I have limited my study to those conflicting attributions in which at least one of the composers involved is named in a source of Italian provenance that was compiled between the mid-1460s and the opening years of the sixteenth century. I have concentrated on what I call the twenty-three 'base sources' (see the Appendix, pp. 285–8 below) because they are – though with some exceptions – fairly homogeneous in character, show definite signs of interrelatedness, and do not contain a large number of concordances with sources that are either much earlier or later in date. This makes the task of tracking down the conflicting attributions somewhat easier, yet still provides enough such ascriptions on which to test an hypothesis.

Returning to the conflicts, one may look at the pattern that has begun to emerge as it is illustrated by three composers who are represented in the base sources by the major part of their secular output: Agricola, Caron, and Martini. Of the thirteen different composers with whom Agricola disputes authorship, there are five with whom he conflicts two or more times. Leaving aside both Obrecht, who admittedly does not help my hypothesis, and for the moment the somewhat problematical Hayne van Ghizeghem, whose biography may actually be expanded by it and to whom we shall, therefore, return presently, we are left with Compère, with whom Agricola conflicts four times, and Fresneau and Isaac, each of whom conflicts with Agricola twice. What these three composers have in common is that each of them was at one time or another a colleague of Agricola's – Compère at Milan and then at the French royal court, Fresneau at the French court and possibly also at Milan, and Isaac at Florence.[12] Thus Agricola had close personal contacts with at least three, and perhaps four, of the composers with whom he conflicts most frequently. A similar pattern emerges with respect to Caron: each of the three composers with whom he conflicts, Busnois three times and Morton and Dusart once each, had Burgundian or Cambrai connections of his own, with the first two having been members of long standing of the Burgundian court *cappella*.[13] Finally,

[12] I use the term 'colleague' with a little elasticity in that I do not insist that the composers had to have been at the same place on precisely the same day. Thus, while Agricola–Compère were at Milan together, and while Agricola–Isaac were at Florence at the same time, the paucity of documents from the French royal court permits us only to presume that Agricola–Compère–Fresneau were personally in touch with one another at some time during their respective periods of service at that court. In any event, even if the trio Agricola–Compère–Fresneau were never in attendance at the French court at precisely the same time, they were certainly there – and at Milan as well (this with respect to Fresneau) – in short succession and would certainly have known about and had access to one another's music. The chronological–geographical relationships among the three composers may be pieced together from: Atlas, 'Alexander Agricola and Ferrante I of Naples', *Journal of the American Musicological Society*, 30 (1977), pp. 316 and 319; Frank A. D'Accone, 'The Singers of San Giovanni in Florence during the 15th Century', *ibid.*, 14 (1961), p. 344; Finscher, *Loyset Compère*, pp. 17–18; Edward E. Lowinsky, 'Ascanio Sforza's Life: A Key to Josquin's Biography and an Aid to the Chronology of his Works', Lowinsky and Bonnie J. Blackburn (eds.), *Josquin des Prez: Proceedings of the International Josquin Festival–Conference* (London, 1976), pp. 40–1; Emilio Motta, 'Musici alla corte degli Sforza', *Archivio storico lombardo*, 2nd ser., vol. 4 (1887), pp. 322ff and 532; Martin Picker, 'A Letter of Charles VIII of France Concerning Alexander Agricola', *Aspects of Medieval and Renaissance Music*, p. 669; Craig Wright, 'Dufay at Cambrai: Discoveries and Revisions', *Journal of the American Musicological Society*, 28 (1975), pp. 206–7.

[13] There is, of course, some uncertainty about Caron's identity. He may be either Jean Caron, a *petit vicaire* at the Cathedral of Cambrai in 1455–8, 'Carron', a

there is the situation of Martini, who, in addition to conflicting once each with Busnois, Malcort, and Ockeghem, disputes the authorship of three compositions with Isaac. And though there is no proof of any personal contact between the two composers (see below, however, p. 276, note 39), that their relationship must have been a special one seems evident from the opening section of Florence 229, where the scribe or editor of that manuscript throws them into a competition of sorts by presenting a long series of their pieces in strict alternation.[14] In all, there is a rational pattern in these and other conflicts; and it seems that the composers who most often conflict with one another enjoyed some special bond, often in their having been colleagues at the same court or cathedral.

A definite pattern also emerges with respect to the conflicts among the sources. As one would expect, a base source will generally conflict most often with sources that belong to a tradition or family other than its own. Thus the northern Italian *Odhecaton* contains a total of nine conflicting attributions with Neapolitan and Florentine manuscripts, but only one with a fellow northern Italian source.[15] And while not all the base sources demonstrate so dramatic an adherence to the pattern, fourteen of the eighteen sources that have conflicting attributions with other base sources do conform to it. Also noteworthy is the tendency of the conflicting attributions in

singer in the retinue of Charles the Bold in 1475, Philippe Caron, a choirboy at Cambrai about 1471, 'le Caron 1441', cited in Cambrai, Bibliothèque Municipale, MS 24, or Firminus Caron, mentioned by Tinctoris and apparently to be identified with a musician at Amiens in 1422. Though Philippe has recently been judged to have been too young to be the composer just as Tinctoris's Firminus is considered too old, it should be remembered that the chanson *Rosa plaisant*, which is attributed to 'Caron' in Florence 229 and to Dusart in Rome 2856, is ascribed to 'Philipon' in *Canti C*. Does this last ascription refer to Philippe Caron or to still a third composer? At any rate, since the trio of composers with whom Caron conflicts had connections with both Cambrai and the Burgundian court, their proximity and probable contact with any of the Carons cited above (except the unlikely Firminus) is probable. On the problem of Caron's identity, see Leeman L. Perkins and Howard Garey, *The Mellon Chansonnier*, I (New Haven, 1979), p. 9; Geneviève Thibault, art. 'Caron', *Die Musik in Geschichte und Gegenwart*, II (Kassel, 1952), cols. 859–60; James Thomson, *An Introduction to Philippe (?) Caron*, Musicological Studies 9 (Brooklyn, 1964), pp. 4–5; Wright, 'Dufay at Cambrai', p. 205, and 'Musiciens à la cathédrale de Cambrai, 1475–1550', *Revue de Musicologie*, 62 (1976), pp. 215–17.

[14] For an explanation of this unusual series of pieces, see the forthcoming edition of Florence 229 by Howard Mayer Brown.

[15] On the sources of the three traditions, see Atlas, *The Cappella Giulia Chansonnier*, I, pp. 234ff.

some sources to cluster about a particular composer. For example, both disputed attributions in Montecassino 871 concern Dufay,[16] while three of the six conflicts in Perugia 431 involve Morton.[17] Similarly, five of the seven conflicting attributions that I have so far found in Paris 15123 occur in connection with Busnois, who is especially troublesome in Bologna Q 17, all four of whose ascriptions to him are challenged elsewhere, three times by Japart. Thus, unless we are content to charge the scribes and editors of these manuscripts either with whimsically ascribing works to favourite composers or with falling prey to whole batches of faulty exemplars involving individual composers, we must conclude that the conflicting attributions result from some quite unaccidental process that took place during the course of the transmission of the chansons, one that formed the patterns just described.

Is there an explanation for these patterns? I believe that there is and should like to suggest that it may lie in the variant readings with which so many of the chansons were disseminated. Let me state the hypothesis immediately and then turn to the evidence both for and against it and to the problems that arise in trying to sustain it. To put the hypothesis in the form of a question: Could the combination of conflicting attributions and variant readings mean that the conflicts are not a matter of one being right and the other wrong, but rather an indication that one composer should be credited with the original composition, while the other was responsible for the revised or variant version?

Although this interpretation of the conflicts raises new problems, the main question obviously concerns the variant readings themselves, and not so much their number or even whether there are variants for every piece, but rather their nature or character. Are the variants such that they constitute true 'compositional' variants by the generally well-known, professional composers who are named in the ascriptions, or could they just as well be the work of non-composer scribes (see below, note 22)? A number of examples may double as evidence and matter for discussion.

---

[16] See Isabel Pope and Masakata Kanazawa, *The Musical Manuscript Montecassino 871: A Neapolitan Repertory of Sacred and Secular Music of the Late Fifteenth Century* (Oxford, 1978), pp. 555ff.

[17] See Atlas, 'On the Neapolitan Provenance of the Manuscript Perugia, Biblioteca Comunale Augusta, 431 (G 20)', *Musica disciplina*, 31 (1977), pp. 78ff.

A variant that will support the hypothesis appears in the *Des biens* attributed both to Martini and to Isaac (no. 3 in the Table on p. 278 below). Here, in addition to the added altus in Bologna Q 18, three manuscripts – one of which, Florence 27, ascribes the piece to Isaac – transmit a reading that substantially alters the entire polyphonic fabric (Example 1).[18] At bar 17, the version attributed to Isaac expands a passage of two semibreves into one of three, while beginning at bar 23, it contracts nine semibreves of music into five. Such changes are not likely to have been made by a scribe, and it seems reasonable to conclude that one of the composers revised the other's music.

Admittedly, such large-scale revision as occurs in Example 1B is rare: in the pieces that I have already collated, the only other examples appear in the *Malheure me bat* attributed to Ockeghem, Martini, and the otherwise unknown Malcort (Example 2; Table, no. 14), and the setting of *La Martinella* ascribed to Martini and Isaac (Example 3; Table, no. 11).

Example 1. Martini/Isaac, *Des biens* (without added altus of Bol Q 18)
a = all sources except those in *b* (Fl 178 and Fl 229 attr. Martini)
b = Cape 3.b.12, Fl 27, Ber 40021

A: bars 16ff

---

[18] Unless otherwise noted, the variant readings given in the music examples are derived from my own collations.

B: bars 22ff

Less extensive is the alteration that affects all three voices of the Obrecht–Virgilius *Nec michi, nec tibi* (Example 4; Table, no. 15). Here, the entire polyphonic texture as it is notated in Rome XIII.27 expands first by one minim and then, fifteen bars later, by another,

Example 2. Malcort/Martini/Ockeghem, *Malheure me bat*
a = Rome XIII.27 (attr. Martini)
b = all other sources (attr. all three composers)

A: bars 7ff

B: bars 42ff

1. 𝅗𝅥 - in *Odh* and SG 461, the sources that name Ockeghem
2. 𝅗𝅥. 𝅘𝅥 e–c in Bol Q 18

c: bars 50ff

so that by the end the piece has gained an entire semibreve. In addition, the piece appears *a 2* in some sources, *a 3* in others; while the Latin title itself alludes to the probable division of labour on the part of the two composers.[19]

Far more common than variants or revisions that affect the entire polyphonic texture, however, are those that occur in a single voice part, usually the contratenor. In rare cases, a piece may be transmitted with two entirely different contra parts, as in the Busnois–Caron *Cent mille escus* (Example 5; Table, no. 1), the Busnois–Ockeghem *D'ung aultre amer* (in which Seville/Paris transmits both the original voice part and a 'bassus ab alio' which may be performed in its place), and the previously cited Martini–Isaac *La martinella*. In general, though, the variants affect but a few bars of the contratenor. Four examples, among others, may illustrate the type: the Busnois–Hayne *J'ay bien choisie* (Example 6; Table, no. 6),[20] the Busnois–Isaac *Sans avoir* (Example 7; Table, no. 24), the Josquin–Japart *J'ay bien rise*

[19] Atlas, *The Cappella Giulia Chansonnier*, I, p. 132.
[20] Variants after Barton Hudson (ed.), *Hayne van Ghizeghem: Opera omnia*, Corpus Mensurabilis Musicae ser. 74 (n.p., 1975), pp. 42–3.

tant (Example 8; Table, no. 7), and the Agricola–Compère *La saison en est* (Example 9; Table, no. 12).[21] Finally, there is the type of variant that takes the form of a short 'codetta' to the original. Such extensions appear in both the Congiet–Japart *Je cuide* (Example 10; Table, no. 8) and the *Mais que ce fust secretement* attributed to Compère and Pietrequin (Example 11; Table, no. 13).

Example 3. Martini/Isaac, *La Martinella*

A: bars 81ff (Bol Q 16 ends at bar 79)

a = Fl 229, Formschneyder 1538, Tr 89 (Fl 229 and Tr 89 attr. Martini)
b = Par 15123, Rome XIII.27, SevPar, Ver 757 (SevPar attr. Martini)
c = Ber 40098, Rome 2856, Tr 91 (Rome 2856 attr. Martini)

The sources that attribute the piece to Isaac are Seg, which has a different contra and which is not included above, and the tablature Bas F.IX.22.

a

b

c

as in version *b* until bar 87

[21] After Edward R. Lerner (ed.), *Alexandri Agricola: Opera omnia*, Corpus Mensurabilis Musicae ser. 22, vol. v (n.p., 1970), pp. lxxxviii and 19.

Example 3A (cont.)

B: bars 29ff – contratenor

a = all sources except those in *b*
b = Fl 229, Formschneyder1538, Tr 89

Example 4. Obrecht/Virgilius, *Nec michi, nec tibi*
a = Rome XIII.27 (attr. Virgilius)
b = Fl 229, Per 431 (*a 2*), Seg (attr. Obrecht), Speciálník, Tur I.27 (*a 2*)

A: bars 72ff

B: bars 87ff

Example 5. Busnois/Caron, *Cent mille escus*, bars 1ff – contratenor
a = Par 15123 (attr. Busnois)
b = Per 431
c = all other sources (incl. Fl 229 attr. Busnois, Rome 2856 attr. Caron)

Example 6. Busnois/Hayne, *J'ay bien choisie*, bars 32ff
a = Rome 2856 (attr. Hayne)
b = Par 15123 (attr. Busnois)
c = Fl 229

In all, each of the eleven examples so far cited contains variants that go beyond the type of alteration to which I believe a non-composer scribe – whose main task I assume to have been a fairly faithful copy of his exemplar – would probably have limited himself.[22] Rather, the variants represent what I would call 'composi-

[22] There were, of course, instances in which composers doubled as scribes. Yet in these cases it is still a composer who would be making the revisions, and it is just as reasonable to suppose the composer–scribe to be one of the composers to whom the work is attributed as it is to introduce a third party. As for the possibility that the revisions were wrought by performers, again we may speculate that the

Example 7. Busnois/Isaac, *Sans avoir* (= *Malagrota*), bars 43ff
a = Per 431 (attr. Busnois)
b = Par 676 (attr. Isaac)

Example 8. Japart/Josquin, *J'ay bien rise tant* (*J'ay bien nourri*), bars 47ff
a = Fl 229 (attr. Japart), Seg (attr. 'Johannes Joye')
b = Fl 178 (attr. Josquin), Rome XIII.27

tional' variants and serve as evidence that the conflicting attributions may signal instances in which one of the composers to whom
the composition is ascribed revised the work of the other. And among
the seventy-six chansons with conflicting attributions that I have so

inventive performer was also one of the composers named. Finally, I think it
unlikely that less illustrious performers would have made such extensive revisions
or that those alterations that they might have contributed would have had great
authority. It is one thing for a Wagner or a Mahler to tamper with earlier music; it
is another for a second bassoonist to do so. In all, I see no reason, when faced with
two musical versions and the names of two composers, to seek to complicate the
matter still further by attempting to credit one of the versions to a third or fourth
party.

Example 9. Agricola/Compère, *La saison en est*, bars 15ff
a = all sources except that in *b* (attr. Compère in Fl 178, Par 2245, Rome 2856,
    Wash L 25; attr. Agricola in Cop 1848)
b = Lon 31922

Example 10. Congiet/Japart, *Je cuide*, bars 54ff
a = all sources except that in *b* (attr. Japart in Rome 2856, attr. Congiet in Fl 229)
b = Par 676

far tracked down and the fifty-three that I have collated either myself
or with the aid of the critical notes of various editions, I would place
twenty-eight in a group that contains either compositional variants
or added voice parts and thus supports the hypothesis.

At the other end of the spectrum are those pieces with conflicting attributions in which the variants are so slight as certainly to
be the work of the scribe. Thus the only two redactions of the

Example 11. Compère/Pietrequin, *Mais que ce fust secretement*, bars 31ff
a = Bol Q 17 (attr. Pietrequin), Fl 178 (attr. Pietrequin), Fl 229, *Odh* (attr.
   Compère), Lon 35087
b = Rome 2856, Cop 1848
c = Rome xiii.27 (attr. Pietrequin)

Agricola–Fresneau *Notres assouemen* (Table, no. 51) are virtually
identical,[23] as are the readings for such pieces as the Josquin–
Compère–Ninot Le Petit *Lourdault, Lourdault* (Table, no. 50),[24] or
the Agricola–Brumel *Du tout plongiet* (Table, no. 47).[25] That the eight

[23] Lerner, *Alexandri Agricola: Opera omnia*, v, pp. xci and 122.
[24] Helen Hewitt (ed.), *Ottaviano Petrucci: Canti B numero cinquanta, Venice, 1502,*
   Monuments of Renaissance Music 2 (Chicago, 1967), pp. 108–10.
[25] Lerner, *Alexandri Agricola: Opera omnia*, v, pp. xciii–xciv and 124–5.

chansons so far placed in this category argue against my hypothesis cannot be denied; yet that they may not be altogether damaging will be seen when we return to the problem presently.

Ultimately, whether the hypothesis is convincing or not may depend upon those pieces in which the character of the variants is somewhere between the two extremes, a category in which I have so far placed the variants of seventeen compositions. Do the variants in this group stand closer to the compositional variants of the first group or to the minor, scribal alterations of the second? Two pieces involving Walter Frye may serve to introduce the problem. In *So ys emprentid*, the authorship of which is disputed by Bedingham (Table, no. 44), Washington L 25 presents a variant reading at bars 17–18 (Example 12).[26] Unobtrusive as it might seem, the variant skilfully decorates the reading found in all the other sources and at the same time increases the rhythmic drive in the approach to the coming cadence. I am inclined to think that it could be by one of the composers to whom the work is ascribed and that it therefore supports the hypothesis. Example 13 shows fourteen variants in the Frye–Binchois *Tout a par moy* (Table, no. 5).[27] Here, we can probably dismiss most of the differences in the sources as the work of scribes; however, one or both of the variants at (*i*) (bars 28–9 in the contra) might belong to the compositional category. The next two examples

Example 12. Bedingham/Frye, *So ys emprentid* (= *Pour une suis*), bars 17ff
a = all sources except that in *b* (attr. Bedingham in Fl 176; attr. Frye in NH 91)
b = Wash L 25

[26] After Sylvia Kenney (ed.), *Walter Frye: Collected Works*, Corpus Mensurabilis Musicae ser. 19 (n.p., 1960), pp. viii–xi and 5–6.
[27] *Ibid.*, pp. vi–vii and 1.

call for more difficult decisions. However, I believe that the variants in the contra of *Madame faites moy* (Example 14; Table, no. 43), which is attributed to Basin and to a composer whose name is now only partially visible because of the trimmed margin in Paris 15123, supports the hypothesis.[28] Finally, we may consider the two variants in the Barbingnant–Fedé *L'homme banni* (Example 15; Table, no. 41).[29] Could either of these represent a revision by one of the composers named? Perhaps the answer is Yes for the variant at bar 13 (Example 15B), which alters the harmony as well as the melodic

Example 13. Binchois/Frye, *Tout a par moy*

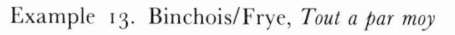

[28] From the fragment of the attribution that remains, we can be sure that it did not name Basin.

[29] After Bernhard Meier (ed.), *Jacobi Barbireau: Opera omnia*, Corpus Mensurabilis Musicae ser. 7, vol. II (n.p., 1957), pp. iv–v and 13–14.

Example 13 (cont.)

Variants:

a. Par 2973, Wash L 25, Wolf 287:

b. Par 2973, SevPar, Wash L 25, Wolf 287:

c. SevPar:

d. Ber 78,C.28, Fl 2356:

e. SevPar:

f. Ber 78.C.28, Fl 2356, Niv,
Par 2973, Wolf 287, Wash L 25:

g. Wash L 25:

h. Niv:

i. Wash L 25:   Ber 78.C.28, Fl 2356, Niv,
Par 2973, SevPar, Wolf 287:

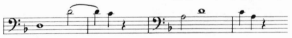

j. Par 2973:

k. Wash L 25:

l. Ber 78.C.28, Fl 2356, Niv,
Par 2973, SevPar, Wash L 25:

m. Ber 78.C.28, Fl 2356, Niv, Par 2973,
SevPar, Wash L 25, Wolf 287:

270

n. Ber 78.c.28, Fl 2356, Niv, Par 2973,
   SevPar, Wash L 25, Wolf 287:

Example 14. Basin/[illegible], *Madame faites moy* (= *Mad*

a = Fl 229, Bol Q 16, SevPar, Par 15123 (attr. [illegible]
b = Rome 2856 (attr. Basin)

contour of the contra; it is probably No for that at
15A).

Before concluding, I should like to gather to
ends both by returning to a number of problems t
unresolved or skipped over entirely and by addit
speculation in connection with the possible applic
ideas presented here. To turn to the problems: Fi
reconcile the hypothesis with those pieces for wh
flicting attributions but no compositional variant
argued elsewhere against appealing to hypothet
lost, about which nothing can really be known,[30] I
contradictory position of perhaps having to fall ba
lity of lost versions and variant readings. Yet th
rare though they might be, when one can make at
guess about the existence and character of a read
already noted, the only two sources for the Agricola
assouemen, the early 1490s Florentine manuscripts

[30] Atlas, 'La provenienza del manoscritto Berlin 78.c.28: Firer
   Italiana di Musicologia, 13 (1978), p. 26, n. 51.

Example 15 Barbingnant/Fedé, *L'homme banni de sa plaisance*
a = all sources except that in b
b = Par 2973

A: bars 4f

B: bars 13f

1. e–d in Fl 176; g–f in Par 15123   2.   g–f in Pav 362

ome XIII.27, present virtually identical readings (see note 7,
bove). Now, assuming that the chanson originated within the
usical circle at the French royal court, where both Agricola and
resneau are known to have been active (on this assumption, see
elow), and given the frequency with which the readings in the
anuscripts from that court tend to disagree with those of concor-
ant pieces in the Florentine manuscripts, perhaps we may hazard
at another version of the piece – one with compositional variants –
rculated in the French musical circle. Yet attractive as such a
olution might seem, its application is purely hypothetical and

perhaps rather limited even at that. For in still another conflicting attribution in which Fresneau figures, that for *De vous servir*, which is also ascribed to Hayne, the readings in the Florentine manuscripts Bologna Q 17 and Rome XIII.27 fail to differ in any significant way from the redaction in the royal French manuscript Florence 2794.[31] Thus, unless one is adamant – as I am not – about having recourse to lost sources and versions as a general principle, the problem remains unresolved, though possibly pushed slightly into the background at least for the moment on the ground that of the fifty-three pieces so far collated, those in which there are definitely no compositional variants comprise a small minority of eight.

A second problem concerns the frequent lack of coincidence between the sources in which the conflicting attributions appear and those in which the compositional variants are contained. Two examples may suffice to illustrate the problem. First, though it is only Paris 15123 and in part Perugia 431 that transmit *Cent mille escus* with a contratenor that differs from that in the other sources (see Example 5), Paris 15123 is joined by Florence 229 in attributing the work to Busnois. Thus there is a contradiction in Florence 229, which has the 'normal' contra part, between the attribution on the one hand and the reading on the other. At the same time, the contra in Perugia 431, which contains elements of both contratenor parts, shows that the original and revised versions could quickly become conflated. The second example concerns *Malheure me bat*. Although both Florence 229 and Rome XIII.27 name Martini as the composer, only Rome XIII.27 transmits the extensive compositional variants (see Example 2); Florence 229 has basically the same reading as do Rome 2856 and the *Odhecaton*, which name Malcort and Ockeghem respectively. Again, I must risk a contradiction and draw on an explanation that I was not willing to accept for the problem of conflicting attributions as a whole, and that is confusion on the part of the scribes or editors of the sources. There is, however, an important difference, for now the names are not being 'made up', so to speak. Rather, each of the composers who disputes the authorship of a chanson has, according to the hypothesis, a legitimate place in the transmission of the work. What has become confused is now simply a matter of which version should be credited to which composer.

---

[31] On the provenance of the source, see Litterick, 'The Manuscript Royal 20.A.XVI of the British Library', pp. 66–7 and 71.

Finally, there is the question of who revised whose music and why. The first part of the question might perhaps be answered if either of two sets of conditions prevails: first, that there is a clear chronological gap both between the careers of the composers involved and between the sources that both name them and transmit the compositional variants; or, secondly, that one variant is recognisably superior in a conflict between composers of obviously disparate abilities, there being once again a coincidence of composer and variant in the sources. Using the first set of conditions, one might reasonably conclude with respect to the Busnois–Isaac *Sans avoir* that it was Isaac, named in connection with the variant in the early-sixteenth-century Paris 676, who revised the chanson by Busnois, who is credited with the work in Perugia 431, which dates from the 1480s.[32] Using the second set, perhaps it may be agreed that it was Isaac who revised Martini's *Des biens* (see Example 1) – and this is also suggested by the first set of conditions – and that it was Josquin who made the revisions in the contra of Japart's *J'ay bien rise tant* (see Example 8). In most cases, however, the problem is not easily resolved. As to the question of why one composer would revise the work of another, the answer would seem to vary according to the nature of the revision. Certainly, one can understand a composer's adding a fourth voice to a chanson in order to increase the sonority and at the same time bring it up to date once a four-part texture had become the norm; and in some instances, the addition of the fourth part no doubt led to other revisions. Nor can we doubt that the fashioning of an entirely new contratenor constituted a legitimate compositional act by the standards of the period. Indeed, both of the creative processes just described had long histories. What is more difficult to understand is why a composer would trouble himself to revise just a few bars of the polyphonic texture or sometimes just a bar or two of only the contratenor. Perhaps such revisions simply represent in miniature the kind of compositional competitiveness that on a far grander scale led Brumel and Josquin to vie with one another in the composition of their *De beata virgine* Masses.[33]

[32] On the dates of the two manuscripts, see Nanie Bridgman, 'Un Manuscrit italien du début du XVIe siècle à la Bibliothèque Nationale (Département de la musique, Rés. Vm⁷ 676)', *Annales musicologiques*, 1 (1953), p. 180; Atlas, 'On the Neapolitan Provenance of the Manuscript Perugia 431', p. 58.

[33] See the remarks of Glareanus, in Clement A. Miller (ed. and trans.), *Heinrich Glarean: Dodecachordon*, Musicological Studies and Documents 6 (n.p., 1965), I,

Turning now to the final round of speculation, I should like to suggest that one of the ideas presented here may, in addition to its application in the problem of conflicting attributions, be relevant in an entirely different area – that is, in helping to fill the gaps in the biographies of certain composers. I have already noted a tendency – admittedly stronger in some instances than in others – for repeated conflicting attributions between two composers to involve persons who were colleagues (and again I allow for some chronological elasticity in the use of the term) at one time or another in their careers. Should this tendency or pattern prove compelling enough, could it be used to fill in the biographies of certain composers about whom little is known or whose biographies are problematical, but who frequently dispute authorship with composers whose lives are better documented? A promising figure in this respect is Hayne van Ghizeghem. Hayne's two conflicts with Busnois are no doubt explained by their joint ties with the court of Burgundy, from which Hayne seems to have vanished after July 1472.[34] Though the lack of subsequent references to him has led to the assumption that he died at that time,[35] Louise Litterick has recently suggested that Hayne may have moved on to the French court, this on the ground that he is mainly represented not in the manuscripts normally associated with the court of Burgundy, but rather in somewhat later sources (or sections thereof) that demonstrate ties with the royal court of France.[36] And this is precisely the same conclusion that one would draw from the remainder of Hayne's conflicting attributions (two with Agricola and one each with Ockeghem and Fresneau) – that is, with composers who had their own ties with the French court. Another composer about whom it is interesting to speculate in this regard is Johannes Japart, whom we know only through his activities at the court of Milan in 1476–7 and that of Ferrara about 1479–80.[37] Could even the single Japart–Josquin conflict point to an association between the two composers? Surely such an hypothesis gains sup-

p. 186. For the interpretation adopted here, see Gustave Reese, *Music in the Renaissance*, rev. edn (New York, 1959), pp. 243–4.

[34] Jeanne Marix, 'Hayne van Ghizeghem: Musician at the Court of the 15th-Century Dukes of Burgundy', *Musical Quarterly*, 28 (1942), p. 279.

[35] *Ibid.*, p. 279; Reese, *Music in the Renaissance*, p. 99.

[36] Litterick, 'The Manuscript Royal 20.A.XVI of the British Library', p. 69, n. 82.

[37] Lowinsky, 'Ascanio Sforza's Life', pp. 40–1; Lewis Lockwood, 'Music at Ferrara in the Period of Ercole I d'Este', *Studi musicali*, 1 (1972), p. 119.

port from the supposed reference to Japart in a now-lost chanson by Josquin.[38] And given the three conflicting attributions between Japart and Busnois – all in a single manuscript, Bologna Q 17 – and the three conflicts between Martini and Isaac, I should not be surprised if we should someday find some convincing documentary evidence that links each of those pairs of composers.[39]

Finally, perhaps this speculative method of biography could be taken one step further and used as an aid in determining the approximate chronology of some of the chansons. In other words, is it possible to hypothesise that the four pieces attributed both to Agricola and to Compère are most likely to have been written and revised while the two composers were in the same employ? Or if we accept the hypothetical possibility of Hayne's having gone from the court of Burgundy to that of France at some time after 1472, can those chansons that are attributed both to him and to either Agricola, Fresneau, or Ockeghem be dated from no earlier than Hayne's arrival at the French court? Since our knowledge of the chronology of this repertory is so vague, any dating tool – however hypothetical it may seem at first – deserves close consideration.

[38] The chanson is *Revenu d'oultremonts, Japart*; the chanson was last seen by Fétis, *Biographie universelle des musiciens*, 2nd edn, IV (Paris, 1862), p. 429. Although its existence is questioned by Helmuth Osthoff, *Josquin Desprez*, II (Tutzing, 1965), p. 154, it is accepted as a possibility by Lowinsky, 'Ascanio Sforza's Life', p. 41, n. 30.

[39] As Lewis Lockwood kindly pointed out to me after the present paper was read, Martini made journeys to Rome in February 1487 and November 1488. Perhaps he passed through Florence and came into personal contact there with Isaac. Significantly, the Florentine manuscripts of the early 1480s contain almost nothing by Martini (the sole exception seems to be the appearance of the disputed *La martinella*, which appears in Paris 15123; see Edward G. Evans, Jr (ed.), *Johannes Martini: Secular Pieces*, Recent Researches in the Music of the Middle Ages and Early Renaissance 1 (Madison, Wisc., 1975), p. x), while Florence 229, written *c.* 1490–1 – that is, just a few years after Martini's sojourns to Rome and presumed stopovers at Florence – is, with its twenty-four chansons by the composer, including those in the Martini–Isaac series, the second most important source of Martini's secular compositions. Nor can the lack of pieces in the Florentine manuscripts of the early 1480s be a consequence simply of chronology, since Rome 2856, the most extensive Martini source, also dates from that period: see Lewis Lockwood, 'Pietrobono and the Instrumental Tradition at Ferrara in the Fifteenth Century', *Rivista Italiana di Musicologia*, 10 (1975), p. 133. Thus, the sudden flourish of Martini compositions in Florence 229, together with the Martini–Isaac 'contest', speaks strongly both for Martini's having stopped at Florence and for an association with Isaac.

To deal with problems concerning the transmission of music in the fifteenth century is to deal to a large extent with possibilities or perhaps at best with what is merely probable. That the traditional assumptions about conflicting attributions may be correct is of course possible, and presumably some of the conflicts could arise from scribal errors.[40] Yet to the presumed accidents that such assumptions hold to have occurred in the transmission of the chansons must now be added such further 'accidents' as the patterns of conflicts that have begun to emerge, as well as the large proportion of pieces with conflicting attributions that were transmitted with widely varying readings. At some point, the notion of what is possible sheerly as a result of coincidence becomes strained. And I think, therefore, that it is not only possible but actually quite probable that many – perhaps most – of the conflicting attributions in the Franco-Netherlandish chanson repertory arose not from scribal confusion or carelessness, but from one composer's having revised the work of another.

[40] I am certainly willing to attribute the conflicting ascriptions to Pietrequin and Pierre de la Rue for the chanson *Adieu florens* (Table 2, no. 54, a piece for which my collations are still incomplete) to scribal confusion caused by the similarity of the composers' names.

Table of conflicting attributions in Italian sources of the Franco-Netherlandish chanson, c. 1465 – c. 1505

Conflicts are listed only if at least one of the composers involved is named in one of the 'base sources'. Sources that transmit the piece without an attribution are not listed. *Sigla* are explained below, pp. 285–8 and 289–90. The table is indexed according to composers on pp. 291–3.

I. PIECES IN WHICH VARIANTS OR ADDED VOICE PARTS SUPPORT THE REVISION HYPOTHESIS

1	*Cent mille escus*	Busnois (Fl 229, Par 15123); Caron (Rome 2856, Rome XIII.27)	Par 15123 and Per 431 contain a contra that differs from that in all other sources; see Ex. 5
2	*De tous biens plaine*	Agricola (Seg); Bourdon (*Odh*)	variant in contra, bars 24–6; attribution in *Odh* in index only
3	*Des biens*	Isaac (Fl 27); Martini (Fl 178, Fl 229)	see Ex. 1; ascription to Isaac in Rome XIII.27 was rubbed out
4	*D'ung aultre amer*	Busnois (Par 15123); Ockeghem (Bol Q 17, Dij 517, Fl 2794, Niv, Par 2245, Rome 2856)	three sets of variants; SevPar has a 'Bassus ab alio'
5	*Fortuna desperata*	Agricola (Augs 142A); Busnois (Seg); Felice (Rome XIII.27)	versions given to Agricola and Felice have three and two added voices respectively
6	*J'ay bien choisie*	Busnois (Par 15123); Hayne (Rome 2856)	see Ex. 6
7	*J'ay bien rise tant*	Japart (Fl 229); Josquin (Fl 178); Johannes Joye (Seg)	see Ex. 8; Joye=Japart?
8	*Je cuide*	Congiet (Fl 229); Japart (Rome 2856)	see Ex. 10
9	*Je ne fay plus*	Busnois (Bol Q 17, Fl 229); Compère (Seg); Mureau (Fl 176, Par 2245, Rome XIII.27)	*Odh* has added altus
10	*Je suis venu*	Busnois (Par 15123); Hayne (Rome 2856)	variants in contra
11	*La martinella*	Isaac (Bas F.IX.22, Seg); Martini (Fl 229, Rome 2856, Rome XIII.27, Tr 89)	see Ex. 3

12	*La saison en est*	Agricola (Cop 1848); Compère (Fl 178, Par 2245, Rome 2856, Wash L 25)	see Ex. 9
13	*Mais que ce fust secretement*	Compère (*Odh*); Pietrequin (Bol Q 17, Fl 178, Rome XIII.27)	see Ex. 11
14	*Malheure me bat*	Malcort (Rome 2856); Martini (Fl 229, Rome XIII.27); Ockeghem (*Odh*, SG 461, *AronTrattato*)	see Ex. 2
15	*Nec michi, nec tibi*	Obrecht (Seg); Virgilius (Rome XIII.27)	see Ex. 4; added voice in some sources
16	*Nunca fue pena major*	Enrique (Rome XIII.27); Urrede (Mad 1335, Per 431, Sev 7-1-28)	variants in bassus; added voice in some sources
17	*O vos omnes*	Compère (Bol Q 17, Rhau1542); Obrecht (SG 463)	variant at opening of contra in Rhau1542
18	*Pour tant se mon valoir*	Busnois (*AronTrattato*); Caron (Fl 229, Rome 2856)	variants in contra; could Aron be citing another composition on the same text?
19	*Pues serviçio*	Enrique (Mad 1335); Morton (Per 431)	variants and added altus in Mad 1335
20	*Quant ce viendra*	Busnois (Dij 517, Wash L 25); Ockeghem (Esc IV.a.24)	added altus in NH 91 and Tr 91
21	*Que vous madame – In pace*	Agricola (*Canti C*, Rhau1542, War 2016); Isaac (Bas F.IX.22); Josquin (Bol Q 17, Fl 178, Fl 229, Lon 20.A.XVI, Rome 2856, Rome XIII.27, Seg)	added altus in *Canti C* and Rhau1542
22	*Rosa plaisant*	Caron (*Canti C*, Fl 229); Dusart (Rome 2856)	variants (see n.13)
23	*Royne du ciel – Regina caeli*	Boris (Bol Q 17); Compère (*Odh*)	variants
24	*Sans avoir*	Busnois (Per 431); Isaac (Par 676)	see Ex.7

TABLE OF CONFLICTING ATTRIBUTIONS (*cont.*)

25	*Se brief je puis voir madame*	Busnois (Par 15123); Caron (Fl 229)	variants
26	*Se je vous eslongue*	Agricola (Fl 178); Hayne (Fl 2794)	Fl 2794, Lon 20.A.XVI, and Par 1597 expand a single bar into three bars
27	*Si dedero*	Agricola (Bol Q 17, Fl 27, Fl 178, Fl 229, *Odh*, Par 676, Rome 2856, Rome XIII.27, Seg, SG 530, Aron*Trattato*); Isaac (Bas F.IX.22); Obrecht (Newsidler1536); Verbonet (SG 463)	Barc 454 and Par 676 transmit different added altus parts
28	*Vien avante morte dolente*	Basin (Rome 2856); Morton (Per 431)	variants

II. PIECES IN WHICH VARIANTS MAY POSSIBLY SUPPORT THE REVISION HYPOTHESIS

29	*Ave ancilla trinitatis*	Brumel (*Canti B*, Seg); Mouton (Petreius1541)	*Canti B* transmits unique variants
30	*Ce n'est pas jeu*	Hayne (Fl 2794, Par 2245, Seg); Ockeghem (Rome 2856)	Seg and Lon 20.A.XVI have variants in bassus
31	*Cela sans plus*	Colinet de Lannoy (Bol Q 17, *Canti B*, Fl 229, Rome 2856, Rome XIII.27); Josquin (Fl 178)	variants in Rome 2856, which also contains an added bassus by Martini, that part alone being attributed to him
32	*C'est temps perdu*	Caron (Rome 2856); Morton (Per 431)	variants
33	*Departes vous male bouche*	Dufay (MC 871); Ockeghem (Par 15123)	differences could be the result of errors rather than conscious revision
34	*Durer ne puis*	Bedingham (Porto 714); Dunstable (Esc IV.a.24)	variants in superius

35	*Fors seulement*	La Rue (*Canti B*); Pipelare (Bas F.X.1–4, Bol Q 19, Reg c 120, Seg, SG 461)	variants in *Canti B*
36	*Fortuna desperata*	Isaac (Seg); Martini (Rome 2856)	one set of variants corrects the voice-leading of the other
37	*Helas madame*	Agricola (Seg); 'P . . .' (SevPar)	variants in contra; ascription in SevPar no longer legible
38	*Il n'est vivant*	Agricola (Cop 1848, Fl 178, Fl 229, Rome 2856); Compère (Rome XIII.27)	Rome XIII.27 differs slightly from all MSS that name Agricola
39	*J'ay pris amours*	Busnois (*Odh*); Martini (Seg)	variants
40	*Je ne vis onques*	Binchois (Niv); Dufay (MC 871)	variant in superius
41	*L'homme banni*	Barbingnant (NH 91, Tinctoris *Imp*); Fedé (Fl 176)	see Ex. 15
42	*Les grans regretz*	Agricola (Bruss 11239); Hayne (Bol Q 17, Par 2245, Wash L 25)	variant in tenor
43	*Madame faites moy*	Basin (Rome 2856); [illegible] (Par 15123)	see Ex. 14
44	*So ys emprentid*	Bedingham (Fl 176); Frye (NH 91)	see Ex. 12
45	*Tout a par moy*	Binchois (Niv); Frye (NH 91, Wash L 25)	see Ex. 13

III. PIECES IN WHICH THERE ARE NO VARIANTS TO SUPPORT THE REVISION HYPOTHESIS

46	*De vous servir*	Fresneau (Fl 2794); Hayne (Bol Q 17, Rome XIII.27)	
47	*Du tout plongiet / Fors seulement*	Agricola (*Canti C*); Brunel (Fl 2439, Reg c 120, SG 461)	*Canti C* and Mun 1516 are notated a fifth higher than the other sources
48	*Fille vous have mal garde*	Isaac (Bol Q 17, Fl 178, Fl 2442, Rome XIII.27, Vienna 18810); Puchner (Ber 40026)	Puchner might be responsible for the instrumental arrangement

TABLE OF CONFLICTING ATTRIBUTIONS *(cont.)*

49	*Ha traite amours*	Compère (Par 504); Rubinet (Bol Q 18); Stockem (Bol Q 17, Fl 178, Fl 229, *Odh*, Rome XIII.27)	the attribution to Compère in Par 504 appears in the place normally reserved for the text incipit
50	*Lourdault, Lourdault*	Compère (*Canti B*, Reg c 120); Josquin (Bas F.X.1–4); Ninot Le Petit (Bol Q 17)	
51	*Notres assouemen*	Agricola (Fl 229); Fresneau (Rome XIII.27)	
52	*Tous les regretz*	Josquin (Reg c 120); La Rue (Bas F.X.1–4, Bruss 11239, *Canti B*, Fl 2442, Rome 11953, Vienna 18810)	
53	*Veci la danse barbari*	Compère (Seg); Vaqueras (*Canti B*)	

IV. PIECES FOR WHICH COLLATIONS ARE NOT COMPLETE

54	*Adieu florens*	Pietrequin (Fl 178, Fl 229); La Rue (Vienna 18810)	here the scribe may have confused the name Pietrequin with that of Pierre de la Rue
55	*Adieu mes amours*	Josquin (Bol Q 17, Fl 178, Fl 229, *Odh*, Rome 2856, Rome XIII.27, Fl 107bis, Fl 2794, Reg c 120, SG 463, SG 530, Newsidler 536); Isaac (Bas F.IX.22)	
56	*Amours amours*	Busnois (Bol Q 17); Japart (*Odh*)	collation of Fl 229 and *Odh* shows no variants; Bol Q 17 remains to be collated
57	*Amours fait molt tant / Il est . . . / Tant que*	Busnois (Bol Q 17); Japart (Fl 229, Rome 2856); Pirson (Bas F.X.1–4)	Pirson=La Rue
58	*Dat ic een byden aldus helen moet*	Jannes Agricola (Fl 229) Petrus Elive (Seg)	
59	*Et qui la dira*	Busnois (Bol Q 17); Japart (Fl 107bis)	

283

60	*Ha qu'il m'ennuye*	Agricola (Fl 178); Fresneau (Par 2245)	
61	*Helas le bon temps*	Compère (Seg); Tinctoris (Fl 27, *Odh*)	
62	*Het es al ghedaen*	Barle (Fl 229); Isaac (Seg)	
63	*He logerons*	Agricola (SG 530); Isaac (Bol Q 17, Fl 178, Fl 229, Rome XIII.27)	
64	*J'ay beau heur*	Agricola (Fl 178, *Odh*, Ver 757, Zwick 12); Compère (Seg); Robert (Par 504)	
65	*Je ne puis plus*	Agricola (Fl 178); Compère (Seg)	
66	*La stangetta*	Isaac (Seg); Obrecht (Zwick 12); Weerbecke (*Odh*)	the ascription to Weerbecke appeared only in the 1501 edition of *Odh*; it was withdrawn in subsequent editions
67	*Madame helas*	'Dux Carlus' (Bol Q 16); Josquin (*Odh*)	the attribution in Bol Q 16 appears in the place normally reserved for the text incipit; the ascription in *Odh* was withdrawn after the 1501 edition
68	*Mijn hert altijt heeft verlanghen*	La Rue (*Canti C*, Fl 2439); Obrecht (SG 463)	
69	*Mon seul plaisir*	Bedingham (Porto 714); Dufay (Fl 176)	
70	*O gloriosa regina mundi*	'Cecus' (Per 431); Touront (Rome 2856)	perhaps 'Cecus'=Touront, in which case there is no conflict
71	*O venus bant*	Josquin (*Odh*, SG 463, AronTrattato); Weerbecke (SevPar)	collations made so far—*Odh*, SG 463, and SevPar – reveal no variants; Mun 1516 remains to be collated
72	*Pour mieulx valoir*	Isaac (Seg); Rubinet (Fl 229)	
73	*Si sumpsero*	Agricola (SG 530); Obrecht (Ber 40026 Canti B, Heil x.2, Newsidler1536)	Formschneyder1538, in which an ascription to Obrecht was added in a later hand, notates the piece a fourth lower than the other sources

TABLE OF CONFLICTING ATTRIBUTIONS (cont.)

74	So lang so meer	Braxatoris (Esc IV.a.24); Pullois (Tr 90)
75	T'meiskin was jonck	Isaac (Schlick1512, Odh); Japart (Fl 178); Obrecht (Seg)	the attribution in Odh was withdrawn after the edition of 1501
76	Vray dieu, quel paine m'esse	Compère (Canti C); Pipelare (SG 530); Weerbecke (Fl 2442)	in SG 530, the piece is used as the secunda pars of a motet

V. ALTERNATIVE TEXT INCIPITS FOR PIECES IN THE TABLE ABOVE

Au joly moys de may = 9
Ave amator castir = 3
Ave Maria = 29
Ave rex regnum ditissime = 22
Ave sanctissima Maria = 48
Benedic anima mea Domino = 65
Carmen = 54
Ce n'est pas = 66
Comment hier = 72
De tusche in busche = 75
Donzella non me culpeys = 13
Elaes Abraham = 60
Exortum est in tenebris = 35
Fortuna esperée = 5
Gaude mater misericordiae = 20
Helas = 15
In pace = 21
J'ay bien nourri = 7
Je ne puis haver = 65

Laus virginis Mariae = 69
Les biens = 3
Madame m'amie = 43
Malagrota = 23
O devotz cueurs = 17
O stella maris = 10
Omnis habet finem labor = 3
Ortus de celo flos est = 66
Pensées vivant = 38
Poi che t'hebi nel core = 5
Pour une suis = 43
Primum querite regnum dei = 8
Quadraginta annis = 76
Quanto magnus es humila te = 43
Regina caeli = 23
Sancta Maria succurre = 44
Si mieulx ne vient = 30
Tant ay d'ennuy = 17

284

ALLAN W. ATLAS

LIST OF 'BASE SOURCES' WITH THEIR
SIGLA AND BIBLIOGRAPHY

NAPLES:

Ber 78.c.28 Berlin, Staatsbibliothek der Stiftung Preussischer Kulturbesitz, Kupferstichkabinett, MS 78.c.28 (no attributions)

Peter Reidemeister, *Die Chanson-Handschrift 78C28 des Berliner Kupfer-
stichkabinetts: Studien zur Form der Chanson im 15. Jahrhundert*, Berliner
Musikwissenschaftliche Arbeiten 4 (Munich, 1973) (general discussion, inventory, partial modern and facsimile editions); Atlas, 'La
provenienza del manoscritto Berlin 78.c.28: Firenze o Napoli?', *Rivista
Italiana di Musicologia*, 13 (1978), pp. 10–29.

Esc IV.a.24 El Escorial, Biblioteca del Monasterio, MS IV.a.24

Eileen Southern, 'El Escorial, Monastery Library, MS IV.a.24',
Musica Disciplina, 23 (1969), pp. 41–79 (inventory); Martha K. Hanen,
'The Chansonnier El Escorial, Ms. IV.a.24', Ph.D. diss., University of
Chicago, 1973 (edition and general discussion).

NH 91 New Haven, Yale University, Beinecke Library, MS 91

Leeman L. Perkins and Howard Garey, *The Mellon Chansonnier*, 2 vols.
(New Haven, 1979) (modern and facsimile editions, inventory, general discussion).

SevPar Seville, Biblioteca Colombina, MS 5-1-43 / Paris, Bibliothèque
Nationale, nouv. acq. fr. MS 4379

Dragan Plamenac, 'A Reconstruction of the French Chansonnier in
the Biblioteca Colombina, Seville', *The Musical Quarterly*, 37 (1951),
pp. 501–42, and 38 (1952), pp. 85–117 and 245–77 (inventory, general
discussion); *idem, Facsimile Reproduction of the Manuscripts Sevilla 5–I–43
and Paris, N.A.Fr. 4379 (Part I)*, Publications of Mediaeval Musical
Manuscripts 8 (Brooklyn, 1962); Atlas, *The Cappella Giulia Chansonnier
(Rome, Biblioteca Apostolica Vaticana, C.G.XIII.27)*, 2 vols., Musicological Studies 27 (Brooklyn, 1975–6), I, p. 257 (provenance).

MC 871 Montecassino, Archivio della Badia, MS N 871

Isabel Pope and Masakata Kanazawa, *The Musical Manuscript Montecassino 871: A Neapolitan Repertory of Sacred and Secular Music of the Fifteenth
Century* (Oxford, 1979) (modern edition, inventory, general discussion).

Per 431 Perugia, Biblioteca Comunale Augusta, MS 431 (G 20)

Atlas, 'On the Neapolitan Provenance of the Manuscript Perugia,

Biblioteca Comunale Augusta, 431 (G 20)', *Musica Disciplina*, 31 (1977), pp. 45–105 (inventory, general discussion).

Bol Q 16   Bologna, Civico Museo Bibliografico-Musicale, MS Q 16

Edward Pease, 'A Report on Codex Q 16 of the Civico Museo Bibliografico Musicale (Formerly of the Conservatorio Statale di Musica 'G. B. Martini'), Bologna', *Musica Disciplina*, 20 (1966), pp. 57–94 (list of contents with musical incipits; general discussion); Sarah Fuller, 'Additional Notes on the 15th-Century Chansonnier Bologna Q 16', *Musica Disciplina*, 23 (1969), pp. 81–103 (partial inventory, provenance, general discussion); Atlas, *The Cappella Giulia Chansonnier*, I, pp. 235–6 (provenance).

FLORENCE

Fl 176   Florence, Biblioteca Nazionale Centrale, Magl. MS XIX.176

Bianca Becherini, 'Autori minori nel codice fiorentino Magl. XIX.176', *Revue Belge de Musicologie*, 4 (1950), pp. 19–31 (defective list of works, general discussion); Atlas, *The Cappella Giulia Chansonnier*, I, pp. 246–7 (provenance); Knud Jeppesen, *La frottola*, II. *Zur Bibliographie der handschriftlichen musikalischen Überlieferung der weltlichen italienischen Lieds um 1500*, Acta Jutlandica 41/1 (Aarhus, 1969), p. 10 (corrections to Becherini); Joshua Rifkin, 'Scribal Concordances for Some Renaissance Manuscripts in Florentine Libraries', *Journal of the American Musicological Society*, 26 (1973), p. 318 (scribal concordances).

Fl 2356   Florence, Biblioteca Riccardiana, MS 2356 (no conflicts)

Dragan Plamenac, 'The "Second" Chansonnier of the Biblioteca Riccardiana (Codex 2356)', *Annales Musicologiques*, 2 (1954), pp. 105–87, and 'Postscript', *ibid.*, 4 (1956), pp. 261–5 (general discussion, inventory); Atlas, *The Cappella Giulia Chansonnier*, I, p. 256 (provenance); Rifkin, 'Scribal Concordances', p. 318 (scribal concordances).

Par 15123   Paris, Bibliothèque Nationale, f. fr. MS 15123

Edward Pease, *Music from the Pixérécourt Manuscript* (Ann Arbor, Michigan, 1960) (list of works); Atlas, *The Cappella Giulia Chansonnier*, I, pp. 254–5 (provenance).

Fl 229   Florence, Biblioteca Nazionale Centrale, Banco rari MS 229

Howard Mayer Brown, forthcoming edition and study in the series Monuments of Renaissance Music.

Rome XIII.27   Rome, Biblioteca Apostolica Vaticana, Cappella Giulia, XIII.27

Atlas, *The Cappella Giulia Chansonnier*, i–ii (partial edition, inventory, general discussion).

Fl 178   Florence, Biblioteca Nazionale Centrale, Magl. MS xix.178

Bianca Becherini, *Catalogo dei manoscritti musicali della Biblioteca Nazionale Centrale di Firenze* (Kassel, 1959), pp. 75–7 (defective list of works); Atlas, *The Cappella Giulia Chansonnier*, i, p. 247 (provenance).

Bol Q 17   Bologna, Civico Museo Bibliografico-Musicale, MS Q 17

Richard Wexler, 'Newly Identified Works by Bartolomeo degli Organi in the MS Bologna Q 17', *Journal of the American Musicological Society*, 23 (1970), pp. 107–18 (partial inventory); Atlas, *The Cappella Giulia Chansonnier*, i, pp. 236–7 (provenance); Craig Wright, 'Antoine Brumel and Patronage at Paris', in this volume, pp. 51–2 (provenance).

NORTHERN ITALY

Rome 2856   Rome, Biblioteca Casanatense, MS 2856

José M. Llorens, 'El Códice Casanatense 2.856 identificado como el Cancionero de Isabella d'Este (Ferrara), esposa de Francesco Gonzaga (Mantua)', *Anuario Musical*, 20 (1965), pp. 161–78 (general discussion, defective list of works); Arthur S. Wolff, 'The Chansonnier Biblioteca Casanatense 2856: Its History, Purpose, and Music', Ph.D. diss., North Texas State University, 1970 (general discussion, edition, inventory); Lewis Lockwood, 'Musical Sources from Renaissance Ferrara: The Reconstruction of a Manuscript Tradition', paper read at a meeting of the Greater New York Chapter of the American Musicological Society, 15 May 1976 (provenance).

Wash M 6   Washington, Library of Congress, MS M 2.1 M 6 Case (attribution in later hand)

Rifkin, 'A "New" Renaissance Manuscript', *Abstracts of Papers Read at the Thirty-Seventh Meeting of the American Musicological Society* (Chapel Hill, 1971), p. 2 (provenance).

Odh   Ottaviano Petrucci, *Harmonice musices Odhecaton A* (Venice, 1501)

Helen Hewitt and Isabel Pope, *Ottaviano Petrucci: Harmonice musices Odhecaton A*, Mediaeval Academy of America Studies and Documents 5 (Cambridge, Mass., 1942) (edition, inventory, general discussion); *Monuments of Music and Music Literature*, ser. 1, vol. 10 (New York, 1973) (facsimile edition); Stanley Boorman, 'The "First" Edition of the *Odhecaton A*', *Journal of the American Musicological Society*, 30 (1978), pp. 183–207 (bibliographical analysis, stemmatics).

Stemmatics and music sources

Canti B Ottaviano Petrucci, *Canti B numero cinquanta* (Venice, 1502)

Helen Hewitt, *Ottaviano Petrucci: Canti B numero cinquanta, Venice, 1502*, Monuments of Renaissance Music 2 (Chicago, 1967) (general discussion, edition, inventory); *Monuments of Music and Music Literature*, ser. 1, vol. 23 (New York, 1975) (facsimile edition).

Par 676 Paris, Bibliothèque Nationale, Rés. MS Vm⁷ 676

Nanie Bridgman, 'Un Manuscrit italien du début du XVIe siècle à la Bibliothèque Nationale (Département de la Musique, Rés., Vm⁷ 676)', *Annales Musicologiques*, 1 (1953), pp. 177–267 (inventory, general discussion, provenance).

Canti C Ottaviano Petrucci: *Canti C numero cento cinquanta* (Venice, 1504)

Claudio Sartori, *Bibliografia delle opere musicali stampate da Ottaviano Petrucci*, Biblioteca di Bibliografia Italiana 18 (Florence, 1948), pp. 69–74 (list of works); *Monuments of Music and Music Literature*, ser. 1, vol. 25 (New York, 1978) (facsimile edition).

Cape 3.b.12 Cape Town, South African Public Library, Grey Collection, MS 3.b.12 (no attributions)

Giulio Cattin, 'Nuova fonte italiana della polifonia intorno al 1500 (MS. Cape Town, Grey 3.b.12)', *Acta Musicologica*, 45 (1973), pp. 165–227 (general discussion, inventory); Atlas, *The Cappella Giulia Chansonnier*, I, p. 238 (provenance); Cattin, *Italian Laude and Latin Unica in MS Capetown, Grey 3.b.12*, Corpus Mensurabilis Musicae ser. 76 (n.p., 1977).

Bol Q 18 Bologna, Civico Museo Bibliografico-Musicale, MS Q 18

Jeppesen, *La frottola*, II, p. 10 (general description); Atlas, *The Cappella Giulia Chansonnier*, I, p. 237.

Fl 27 Florence, Biblioteca Nazionale Centrale, Panciatichi MS 27

Becherini, *Catalogo dei manoscritti musicali*, pp. 118–22 (list of works); Atlas, *The Cappella Giulia Chansonnier*, I, p. 252 (provenance).

Ver 757 Verona, Biblioteca Capitolare, MS 757 (attributions in later hand)

Giuseppe Turrini, *Il patrimonio musicale della Biblioteca Capitolare di Verona* (Verona, 1952); Atlas, *The Cappella Giulia Chansonnier*, I, p. 257 (provenance).

LIST OF SOURCES CITED WITH THEIR *SIGLA*
(OTHER THAN 'BASE SOURCES')

Aron*Trattato*	Pietro Aron, *Trattato della natura e cognizione di tutti gli tuoni di canto figurato* (Venice, 1525)
Augs 142A	Augsburg, Staats- und Stadtbibliothek, MS 142A
Barc 454	Barcelona, Biblioteca Central, MS 454
Bas F.IX.22	Basel, Universitätsbibliothek, MS F.IX.22
Bas F.X.1–4	Basel, Universitätsbibliothek, MS F.X.1–4
Ber 40021	Berlin, Staatsbibliothek der Stiftung Preussischer Kulturbesitz, MS 40021
Ber 40026	Berlin, Staatsbibliothek der Stiftung Preussischer Kulturbesitz, MS 40026
Ber 40098	Berlin, Staatsbibliothek der Stiftung Preussischer Kulturbesitz, MS 40098
Bol Q 19	Bologna, Civico Museo Bibliografico-Musicale, MS Q 19
Bruss 11239	Brussels, Bibliothèque Royale, MS 11239
Cop 1848	Copenhagen, Kongelige Bibliotek, Ny Kgl. Samling, MS 1848$^{2\circ}$
Dij 517	Dijon, Bibliothèque Publique, MS 517
Fl 107bis	Florence, Biblioteca Nazionale Centrale, Magl. MS XIX.107bis
Fl 2439	Florence, Biblioteca del Conservatorio 'L. Cherubini', MS Basevi 2439
Fl 2442	Florence, Biblioteca del Conservatorio 'L. Cherubini', MS Basevi 2442
Fl 2794	Florence, Biblioteca Riccardiana, MS 2794
Formschneyder1538	Hieronymus Formschneyder, *Trium vocum carmina* (Nuremberg, 1538)
Heil X.2	Heilbronn, Stadtarchiv, MS X.2
Lon 20.A.XVI	London, British Library, Royal MS 20.A.XVI
Lon 31922	London, British Library, Additional MS 31922
Lon 35087	London, British Library, Additional MS 35087
Mad 1335	Madrid, Biblioteca de Palacio Real, MS 1335 (*olim* 2-1-5)
Mun 1516	Munich, Bayerische Staatsbibliothek, MS 1516
Newsidler1536	Hans Newsidler, *Ein newgeordnet kunstlich Lautenbuch* (Nuremberg, 1536)

Niv	Paris, Bibliothèque G. Thibault, Chansonnier Nivelle de la Chaussée
Par 504	Paris, Bibliothèque Nationale, Rés. MS Vm^7 504 (Christian Egenolff, *c.* 1535)
Par 2245	Paris, Bibliothèque Nationale, f. fr. MS 2245
Par 2973	Paris, Bibliothèque Nationale, Collection Rothschild, MS 2973
Pav 362	Pavia, Biblioteca Universitaria, Aldini MS 362
Petreius1541	J. Petreius, *Trium vocum cantiones* Nuremberg, 1541)
Porto 714	Porto, Biblioteca Comunal, MS 714
Reg c 120	Regensburg, Proske Bibliothek, MS c 120
Rhau1542	Georg Rhau, *Tricinia* (Wittenberg, 1542)
Rome 11953	Rome, Biblioteca Apostolica Vaticana, MS Vat. Lat. 11953
Schlick1512	Arnolt Schlick, *Tabulaturen etlicher lobgesang und lidlein* (Mainz, 1512)
Seg	Segovia, Catedral, MS without number
Sev 7-1-28	Seville, Biblioteca Colombina, MS 7-1-28
SG 461	St Gall, Stiftsbibliothek, MS 461
SG 463	St Gall, Stiftsbibliothek, MS 463
SG 530	St Gall, Stiftsbibliothek, MS 530
Speciálník	Hradec Králové, Krajske Muzeum, Knihovna, MS II A 7 (Speciálník Codex)
Tinctoris*Imp*	Johannes Tinctoris, *De imperfectionis notarum musicalium*
Tr 89	Trent, Castello del Buonconsiglio, MS 89
Tr 90	Trent, Castello del Buonconsiglio, MS 90
Tr 91	Trent, Castello del Buonconsiglio, MS 91
Tur 1.27	Turin, Biblioteca Nazionale, Riserva musicale, MS 1.27
Vienna 18810	Vienna, Österreichische Nationalbibliothek, MS 18810
War 2016	Warsaw, Uniwersitiet, Muziekolowskiego Institut, MS mf. 2016
Wash l 25	Washington, Library of Congress, MS M 2.1 L25 Case
Wolf 287	Wolfenbüttel, Herzog August Bibliothek, MS Guelf. extravag. 287
Zwick 12	Zwickau, Ratsschulbibliothek, MS 12

INDEX OF CONFLICTING ATTRIBUTIONS
ARRANGED ACCORDING TO COMPOSERS

The numbers following each composer's name in the right-hand column refer to the serial numbers in the Table, pp. 278–84 above.

Alexander Agricola	Bourdon 2; Brumel 47; Busnois 5; Compère 12, 38, 64, 65; Felice 5; Fresneau 51, 60; Hayne 26, 42; Isaac 21, 27, 63; Josquin 21; Obrecht 27, 73; 'P . . .' 37; Robert 64; Verbonet 27
Jannes Agricola	Elive 58
Barbingnant	Fedé 41
Barle	Isaac 62
Basin	[illegible] 43; Morton 28
Bedingham	Dufay 69; Dunstable 33; Frye 44
Binchois	Dufay 40; Frye 45
Boris	Compère 23
Bourdon	Agricola 2
Braxatoris	Pullois 74
Brumel	Agricola 47; Mouton 29
Busnois	Agricola 5; Caron 1, 18, 25; Compère 9; Felice 5; Hayne 6, 10; Isaac 24; Japart 56, 57, 59; La Rue 57 Martini 39; Mureau 9; Ockeghem 4, 20;
Caron	Busnois 1, 18, 25; Dusart 22; Morton 32
'Cecus'	Touront 70 ('Cecus'=Touront?)
Colinet de Lannoy	Josquin 31
Compère	Agricola 12, 38, 64, 65; Boris 23; Busnois 9; Josquin 50; Mureau 9; Ninot Le Petit 50; Obrecht 17; Pietrequin 13; Pipelare 76; Robert 63; Rubinet 49; Stockem 49; Tinctoris 61; Vaqueras 53; Weerbecke 76
Congiet	Japart 8
Dufay	Bedingham 69; Binchois 40; Ockeghem 33
Dunstable	Bedingham 34
Dusart	Caron 22
Petrus Elive	Jannes Agricola 58
Enrique	Morton 19; Urrede 16
Fedé	Barbingnant 41
Felice	Agricola 5; Busnois 5
Fresneau	Agricola 51, 60; Hayne 46

Frye	Bedingham 44; Binchois 45
Ghiselin-Verbonet	Agricola 27; Isaac 27; Obrecht 27
Hayne	Agricola 26, 42; Busnois 6, 10; Fresneau 46; Ockeghem 30
[illegible]	Basin 43
Isaac	Agricola 21, 27, 63; Barle 62; Busnois 24; Japart 75; Josquin 21, 55; Martini 3, 11, 36; Obrecht 27, 66, 75; Puchner 48; Rubinet 72; Verbonet 27; Weerbecke 65
Japart	Busnois 56, 57, 59; Congiet 8; Isaac 75; Josquin 7; 'Johannes Joye' 7 (probably a corruption of Japart, not a conflict?); La Rue 57; Obrecht 75
Josquin	Agricola 21; Colinet de Lannoy 31; Compère 50; Isaac 21, 55; Japart 7; Johannes Joye 7; La Rue 52; Ninot Le Petit 50; Weerbecke 71
Johannes Joye	probably a corruption of Johannes Japart: Japart 7 (not a conflict); Josquin 7
La Rue	Busnois 57; Japart 57; Josquin 52; Obrecht 68; Pietrequin 54; Pipelare 35
Malcort	Martini 14; Ockeghem 14
Martini	Busnois 39; Isaac 3, 11, 36; Malcort 14; Ockeghem 14
Morton	Basin 28; Caron 32; Enrique 19
Mouton	Brumel 29
Mureau	Busnois 9; Compère 9
Ninot Le Petit	Compère 50; Josquin 50
Obrecht	Agricola 27, 73; Compère 17; Isaac 27, 66, 75; Japart 75; La Rue 67; Verbonet 27; Virgilius 15; Weerbecke 66
Ockeghem	Busnois 4, 20; Dufay 33; Hayne 30; Malcort 14; Martini 14
'P ...'	Agricola 37
Pietrequin	Compère 13; La Rue 54
Pipelare	Compère 76; La Rue 35; Weerbecke 76
Puchner	Isaac 48
Pullois	Braxatoris 74
Robert	Agricola 64; Compère 64
Rubinet	Compère 49; Isaac 72; Stockem 49
Stockem	Compère 49; Rubinet 49
Tinctoris	Compère 61
Touront	'Cecus' 70 (Touront='Cecus'?)
Urrede	Enrique 16
Vaqueras	Compère 53

Verbonet	see Ghiselin-Verbonet
Virgilius	Obrecht 15
Weerbecke	Compère 76; Isaac 66; Josquin 70; Obrecht 66; Pipelare 76

14

SOME CRITERIA FOR ESTABLISHING RELATIONSHIPS BETWEEN SOURCES OF LATE-MEDIEVAL POLYPHONY

Margaret Bent

THE principles governing the establishment and definition of relationships between sources have long been accepted in other fields of scholarship. Perhaps best known to musical scholars is the exposition by Paul Maas of the guidelines for editing Classical Greek and Latin texts. It is not my intention here to give a full account of the important refinements made to it by other Classical scholars, but it will be convenient at this stage to summarise the concepts and terminology.[1]

The purpose of textual criticism is to produce a text as close as possible to the lost original. Although not in practice carried out in self-contained stages, the procedures are as follows. *Recensio* is the reconstruction from the surviving copy or copies of the earliest recoverable version of what is transmitted. It is achieved largely by accumulating and sifting the evidence provided by variant readings and errors. If there is a single witness, it must be deciphered. If there are several, their relationship to each other must be established. If the tradition is 'closed' (i.e. with no source being copied from more than one exemplar), a *stemma* may be drawn up. In an 'open' tradition, *contaminatio* has taken place through promiscuous copying. (Martin West's acceptance of contamination as a normal state of affairs rather than as a deviation which impedes normal critical procedures leads him to offer some sensible guidance on this

---

[1] Martin L. West, *Textual Criticism and Editorial Technique* (Stuttgart, 1973) goes further than Paul Maas, *Textual Criticism*, trans. Barbara Flower (Oxford, 1958) in allowing for some of the eventualities which arise in music. I wish to thank Professor Michael Connolly of Boston College for a stimulating exchange of ideas which benefited the final form of this paper.

subject.) Any sources that are totally dependent on others should be eliminated from consideration (*eliminatio*). Then the lost version from which the survivors ultimately descend should be reconstructed as far as the evidence permits. The text thus achieved, whether deriving from one source or several, is examined for correctness and plausibility (*examinatio*), and subjected where necessary to *emendatio* by conjecture. In some cases the emendations may have the corroboration of the scribe–editors who are our witnesses to the tradition, and in other cases they may depend solely on the modern editor's judgement.

These procedures can, with some refinements, be applied to most written verbal texts, including music theory, though the susceptibility of theoretical writings to modernisation, amplification or summary treatment sets them apart from the products of scribes who were trying to transmit an ancient or sacrosanct text intact. Although both Classical scholars and music historians share the problem of lost originals, the differences in nature between their raw materials impose substantial refashioning of the editor's tools. Music affords text-critical opportunities that are both more and less precise than those afforded by words. It is the purpose of this paper to set out some of the conditions pertinent to musical transmission. I shall first outline some general ways in which the differences demand modification of the text scholar's approach, and then proceed to the suggestion of some criteria for evaluating variants – the main business of recension.

The Classical text *is* more nearly the literary work than the musical notation is the music. Musical notation is only an approximate and incomplete record of sound, and while we can recover most of the essential features (pitches and rhythms), we are never likely to be able to piece together a full understanding of the performance conventions with which the early performer was armed, and which are arguably more fundamental to the essence of music than are uncertainties about pronunciation and dialect that may underlie a literary text. There is a stronger possibility for music than for literature that we may misunderstand, neglect or overvalue such evidence for these conventions as finds its way into the surviving manuscripts on the initiative of scribes and performers. Our task is rather different from that of the text critic who, when isolating glosses and annotations that have been incorporated into his text, is not faced with such a strong likelihood that these additions in fact represented a realisation of the author's intentions. The musician is trying not only to retrieve the text as the composer wrote it, but also to take account of such accretions, some of which the composer may have supplied, some of which he may have presumed, while yet others may have counted as acceptable options or indeed as rejects. Even though these features may be in practice inseparable from the composed 'essentials', a hierarchy of judgement between them is important. The process of recension may eliminate some sources because of their textual dependence on others. These sources, however, may still carry valuable evidence about performance licences and constraints which the editor, in making the music accessible to modern users, must take account of.

(a) In terms of the editorial policies of the major critical editions of composers from Bach onwards, even the existence of autograph material does not exonerate the editor from serious consideration of the evidence about authentic alternative versions and performance solutions which is to be gleaned from non-autograph copies and parts. How much less should the reconstruction of a less complete tradition depend on a relatively arbitrarily chosen witness.

(b) In one of the very few identified cases of medieval autographs or near-autographs, some of the later additions to the Old Hall Manuscript, the modern editor is, in the few available cases of concordances copied from them, grateful for the clarification by a musically skilled professional scribe of features such as text underlay, despite the stemmatic demand for elimination of the musical text of such a copy. Knowledge of textual dependence makes it possible to isolate scribal initiatives with some certainty.

(c) In the case of the Trent MS 90, much of which is largely a literal copy of Trent 93,[2] the copy is textually worthless for the pieces so reproduced, though it presents us with a large body of fascinating material in the form of later revisions. While a few of these revisions may have some stemmatic value in deriving from an independent source,[3] being separable from the

---

[2] I argued for this connection between these two sources, and not the opposite as previously assumed, in 'The English Countenance behind a Continental Mask', a paper read at the annual meeting of the American Musicological Society at Los Angeles in 1975. Some supporting material is given in my edition of *Fifteenth-Century Liturgical Music*, ii: *Four Anonymous Masses*, Early English Church Music 22 (London, 1979).

For the *sigla* used in this paper, see note 21 on pp. 316–17 below.

[3] Notably in the Sanctus of the *Quem malignus spiritus* Mass; see Early English Church Music 22, p. 174.

tradition presented by M S 93, the majority must be seen as stemming from the initiatives of the scribes or performers who used the manuscript, and thus as conveying information about their mensural and rhythmic preferences.

Whereas sources of Classical texts may be spread over many centuries, allowing an approximate preliminary chronology to be set up before detailed work begins, this is rarely the case with musical sources, which usually survive from a time-span too short to permit safe datings on paleographical grounds alone. Maas asserts that knowledge of manuscript datings is a prerequisite for establishing a stemma; it has proved possible, however, under the special conditions of musical transmission, to establish certain directional and even direct relationships between musical sources and thus to ascertain their chronology, rather than vice versa. Classical texts survived long-term chronological transplanting in a way that late-medieval polyphony never did. This point bears out the greater dependence of musical material on knowledge of how it was performed, and on changing fashion. Moreover, because they are contemporary or nearly so with the compositions themselves, musical sources transmit more evidence of the underlying assumptions of their repertory than do copies of Classical texts widely separated in time from their originals. The music historian is protected from the effects of fashion changes on his material to a greater degree than is the student of material whose actual substance was less quickly superseded than that of polyphony. Conversely, the smaller time-lag between musical composition and copy, and the nature of the tradition that binds them, make it more difficult for the modern scholar to separate accretions from original matter, to distinguish a composer's revision from a scribal reworking.

Another factor distinguishing most pre-1600 polyphony from Classical verbal texts is that in music smaller units of original material are transmitted. Because almost every polyphonic source is a uniquely compiled anthology, the concern of the musical text critic must be with each individual piece. Any discussion of the relationship between entire manuscripts is premature until it can rest on the sum of individual case histories of its individual component pieces. Each case has to be built brick by brick. Individual judgements about individual variants may lead to judgements about various copies of the single pieces; judgements about single pieces may lead to judgements about the sources in which they appear. The process should not be applied in reverse. Stemmatic work of this kind bears radically on larger-scale repertorial work, but general notions insecurely founded should not condition judgements at the fundamental level. As Martin West has put it: 'Since the collective judgment is derived from individual judgments, it cannot be a ground for modifying any of them, but only a ground for making a judgment where none could be made before.'[4]

The construction of stemmata for individual pieces, or at least the identification of broad transmission patterns or groups for each piece, is thus the only secure way of establishing tributary groups of pieces within a homogeneously copied source. This principle should override the frequently made assumption that the reliability of a reading or an attribution for one piece in a source can be assumed by contagion for other pieces in the same manuscript. It is safer to proceed from the expectation that all pieces in a source had different exemplars until evidence to the contrary emerges. 'Shared repertory' is a premature starting-point for considering two sources to be related, though it is an obvious place to start looking.[5]

In certain exceptional cases (such as Trent 93–90 and the Machaut MSS Vg and B) which share a very substantial repertory, in the same order, and with variants and identities which establish not only the direction but the directness of the copy, the 'unique anthology' principle is clearly overruled. But it is only by examining the text of each piece in each manuscript, note by note, that the nature of the relationship can be securely established.

The retention of a certain grouping of pieces from one manuscript

---

[4] Martin West, *op. cit.*, p. 50.

[5] Allan Atlas, *The Cappella Giulia Chansonnier (Rome, Biblioteca Apostolica Vaticana, C.G.XIII.27)*, 2 vols., Musicological Studies 27 (Brooklyn, 1975–6) has made a valuable contribution to establishing stemmatic tools for the musicologist. Insofar as the present discussion raises some quibbles with his statements of principle, it should be borne in mind that different repertories have different problems which may demand different solutions. Atlas (vol. I, chap. IV) gives shared repertory as one of two conditions for considering sources to be related. Since he finds no direct copies amongst the surviving manuscripts, we must presume that more sources must once have existed for the pieces copied from them which now survive in only a few manuscripts. Although the statement that a piece enjoyed wide or limited dissemination, on the basis of its surviving copies, may be broadly true, it cannot take full account of lost sources and random survival.

to another may carry significant information about their common origin. Lack of such groupings, however, does not disprove connections, since for many practical reasons (such as the common expedient of working on more than one part of a manuscript concurrently while ink dries), and on the initiatives of different compilers, pieces may be copied in an order different from that in which they appeared in the exemplar. If pieces in the copy appear in the same order, the sequence in which they were actually written down is quite likely to have been a different one, even though its intention (and effect) was to preserve the original order. If pieces in the copy appear in a different order, however, this by no means excludes their having been copied consecutively from the same exemplar.

In order to explain why 'compositions preserved in two or more manuscripts often agree so closely in all details of notation and even layout that they cannot be far removed from a common source', while 'If one of the manuscripts had been copied from the other, or from a copy of the other, . . . there should be some vestige of common structure and many of the common pieces should be in the same order', Charles Hamm put forward an attractive and widely accepted hypothesis that music circulated primarily in small fascicles destined for independent existence rather than for incorporation in larger manuscripts such as those which preserve most of the repertory.[6] Copying from such 'fascicle manuscripts', however, accounts no more readily for the order of the surviving collections than would copying from larger compilations in just the manner indicated above. We can no more presume that details of piece-ordering in surviving manuscripts would preserve the order of pieces copied from small autonomous fascicles than that the order of a larger collection would be retained. Hamm posits that fascicles not destined for inclusion in a particular compilation were the normal means of transmitting music. While much music was undoubtedly circulated in, sung from and copied from fascicles, I wonder whether the practice of compiling autonomous fascicles was as widespread as he implies. He distinguishes two main types of manuscript compilation: first, the relatively disorderly result of copying music as it came to hand, but with the retention of the internal groupings of the individual fascicles themselves, so that these groupings are assumed

[6] 'Manuscript Structure in the Dufay Era', *Acta Musicologica*, 34 (1962), pp. 166–84.

to be recoverable by us; and secondly, the more common procedure whereby a scribe copied pieces according to an overall plan, thus submerging the structure of his exemplars. The latter point is incontrovertible, but it is quite possible that such manuscripts could have been selected, rearranged and copied from other larger compilations as often as they were copied from small, separate fascicles. But in the case of the former point – manuscripts with a less detectable plan – Hamm not only discerns groupings of pieces implying their adjacence in a self-contained exemplar, but finds that these manuscripts themselves were in some cases 'planned originally as a collection of independent fascicles, not as a single large manuscript'. This should at least be modified to allow that even if the final order and exact contents were not fixed at the outset, such fascicles were planned in such a way that it would be physically possible to bind them together. The considerable differences in paper size and in the area ruled for writing among the manuscripts from which he makes his case weaken the concept of easy interchangeability of fascicles. The written area may vary within a manuscript, but not so much as to prevent uniform trimming.

The Machaut manuscripts are in some ways a special case, but they do illustrate some of the dangers that Hamm's approach may hold for the unwary. To start with, Machaut's own testimony that his works were copied from *pièces* into manuscripts for his patrons[7] has not resulted in the kinds of rearrangement that might be expected. Elizabeth Keitel's useful examination of the underlying structure of the Machaut manuscripts comes up with relationships based on groupings and manuscript order, rather than demonstrating on the basis of readings that such groupings survived transmission.[8] I established recently not only that the MS B was copied from Vg to the extent of preserving its gathering structure and line ends – an example of retained order – but that about half the music in MS E was copied directly from B.[9] The two main factors that have led to scholarly discounting of MS E are its 'disorderly' presentation and its poor readings. These two elements should in fact be disentangled. Now that many of E's

---

[7] See Sarah Jane Williams, 'An Author's Role in Fourteenth Century Book Production: Guillaume de Machaut's "livre ou je met toutes mes choses"', *Romania*, 90 (1969), pp. 433–54.

[8] 'A Chronology of the Compositions of Guillaume de Machaut based on a Study of Fascicle-Manuscript Structure in the Larger Manuscripts', Ph.D. diss., Cornell University, 1976.

[9] In a paper entitled 'Another Bite at Machaut, or, Too Many Sources Spoil the Stemma', read at the national meeting of the American Musicological Society, Minneapolis, 1978, and now in preparation for publication.

poor readings can be blamed on those of B (whose scribe made a far worse job of copying Vg than did E's in copying B), we should be prepared to trust the scribe of E a little more when he was copying from another, unknown exemplar. In addition, E presents a selection of the contents of B, not a complete copy. The pieces appear in a different order, intermingled with pieces *not* copied from B, though present in it, for which the scribe preferred to use other exemplars. MS A purports to present the order of pieces approved by Machaut. Only MS E departs radically from that order. There are many possible reasons for this, including even that Machaut changed his mind, but this non-conformity cannot affect judgements about the readings themselves. If indeed any of E's readings were 'contaminated' by combination with others, they are no longer detectably 'copied from B'.

Not only differences of page size but differences of format and local or national practice sharply diminish the chances that fascicles representing anything close to the original would often have been suitable for incorporation into manuscripts elsewhere, or indeed that even their general layout would have been reproduced.

I have pointed out elsewhere that continental scribes copying English music in the first half of the fifteenth century often made substantial editorial changes.[10] Apart from mensural changes, these included changing the order of the parts on the page, changing the vocal scoring and texting, 'translating' the notation from black to void and, most significantly for the present argument, redistributing Mass movements that appear in the earlier English sources on a single opening of large format to occupy two openings of smaller format. In addition, we now know, the English Kyries were often suppressed. Thus an English Mass, occupying its own fascicle-

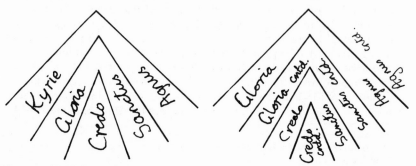

Figure 1. English Mass-fascicle: large format, parchment (hypothetical)

Figure 2. Continental copy of the same Mass: small format, paper

[10] See note 2, above.

manuscript according to Hamm's hypothesis, would have been arranged as in Figure 1, whereas its continental copy would have been like Figure 2. Despite the very large amount of English music in Trent and Aosta there is no single piece copied in an English hand in these manuscripts, although it is very likely that Aosta's exemplars were English or at least retained many English features.

Whatever arguments may be advanced for the fascicle-manuscript status of an individual case – and Hamm's own examples of 'fascicle-manuscripts preserved by the accident of being incorporated' into larger manuscripts are open to question[11] – we no longer need to posit their autonomous and plentiful existence in order to explain how manuscripts were compiled. Once the issues of anthology order and of variant readings are separated, the need of which Hamm's theory was born becomes much less pressing. A more refined method of dealing with variants offers the possibility of

---

[11] Of the surviving original fascicle-manuscripts instanced by Hamm the following may be said (references in brackets are to his points 1–5 on p. 168): (a) The last 23 folios of Aosta (1, 4) are inaccurately described by de Van; although he saw the manuscript before restoration, the watermarks preclude the structure he proposes and disqualify the separate existence of the alleged fascicles. (b) The fact that the Aosta examples are all copied by the same scribe weakens the claim of independent copying (1, 4). The scribe's 'reluctance' to recopy the English pieces is undermined by his evident willingness to copy other pieces. The order of copying of the Brassart duplicates appears to be more complex than Hamm's statement implies. (c) The English pieces in Aosta (4) are further disqualified. Not only are they in the Germanic hand of the scribe of this section of the manuscript, and cannot therefore be claimed to originate from the circle of the composer, but they have clearly undergone editing of the type discussed elsewhere in this paper. (d) A binder does not normally require 'one small fascicle to complete his binding'. Considering the format of San Pietro B.80, it is likely that the Josquin fascicle was copied in such a way that it could be added to the earlier corpus (2). (e) The fifteenth fascicle of Trent 87 indeed contains the Pylois Mass (3), but the next three gatherings – blank, except for an interpolation – have the same paper type. Although the scribe of this gathering is indeed 'found nowhere else in the manuscript', he is no stranger to the Trent collection, being almost certainly identifiable as Johannes Wiser. (f) Some of Hamm's assumptions about the compilation of Trent 87 seem to be uncertainly founded. Rather than having their 'own foliation', fascicles II–XIII have original gathering signatures which indicate that they were destined to be bound together. Fascicles I and II have a piece bridging the join, and they seem to have been added as a unit to III–XIII. The original order of these gatherings, judging from the signatures, was intended to be: V, XI, XIII, VI, VII, XII, X, III, IX, VIII, IV. At some stage after the signatures were supplied, some compositions were copied across gathering joins in a manner which imposed some of the present deviations from the order originally intended.

establishing at least some transmission patterns independently of how pieces are grouped in surviving manuscripts.

In some ways, musical notation is less subject than verbal text to serendipitous, correct scribal emendation; music does not 'make sense' horizontally in quite the same way as do words. Polyphony offers the opportunity for setting up objective criteria for musical sense; vertical corroboration of sense or correctness is not available to the scribe at the time of copying each individual part (unless by memory: see below). Thus, whereas the text scribe is in a position to understand and control what he is copying, perhaps making spontaneous emendations as he proceeds, the music scribe, unless he knows the piece, will know that certain kinds of initiative, applied to individual parts, would have consequences for the whole texture, and is less likely to make them, not being at that moment in control of the other parts.

Thus, when we encounter certain kinds of plausible variants which do affect the whole texture, we have to infer that they were made by someone who did have such control. They may result from a different version circulated by the original author, but this is very hard to detect because of the relative proximity in culture and chronology of composers, performers and scribes of a given repertory. Alternatively, such a variant may result from the conjectural emendation of an error detected when the parts were put together in performance, or indeed from a change made from choice rather than necessity.

Some modern writers express incredulity that a manuscript with errors could have been used for performance and remain uncorrected. This reflects our higher dependence on visible signs and our lower memory capacity. I find no difficulty in accepting that many errors were solved in performance after the initial learning had been done from the faulty parts. The role of memory may have considerable importance in our assessment of variants. Without very complete recall of the sound of what he is 'copying', a scribe's freedom to introduce spontaneous variation is very confined, and his copy is more likely to be faithful to an exemplar. How far, then, do we have to make allowance for such recall?

I believe that memory is relatively unimportant at the copying stage, and that much of the identity and variation we find between sources can be explained (sometimes wholly explained) mechanically, i.e. by 'blind' copying of individual parts. There are enough demonstrable instances of pieces copied, in this sense, to encourage the conviction that it was at least a normal means of transmission, if not the only possibility. But if more of our 'copies' were the result of memory or dictation, we should expect to find more instances of pieces notated in different manuscripts at varying pitch levels and in different note-values. The few types of such change that regularly occur are explicable by fairly obvious practical considerations (such as the transposition by a fifth of some of the very low-lying songs in Brussels MS 228,[12] the bringing up-to-date with notational change of a number of trecento pieces,[13] or the editing of mensural practices to conform to different local conventions, as applied to English music exported to the continent). Examples falling outside definable and specific repertories such as these are very rare.

I do believe that memory played an important role in the learning and preparation of a piece. Many of the surviving copies appear to have been made prior to that stage.

While the written transmission of most pieces is relatively consistent in just those features we might expect to fluctuate more widely, were we dealing with a large ingredient of memory, we cannot discount the possibility that dictation played a role in the initial stage of transmission. Composers must have been musically literate, if only because many of their creations depend on thorough notational understanding (extreme examples being the mensuration canon or proportional essay) and were constantly conditioned by the available notational possibilities. However, the blind Landini presumably dictated his compositions, and Machaut leaves us some very suggestive hints in the *Voir Dit* that he may also have depended on a musical as well as a literary secretary.[14]

The physical layout of a text manuscript may provide occasional clues related to its exemplar, notably anomalies associated with line, column, page and gathering ends. Musical notation, with its high

---

[12] Brussels, Bibliothèque Royale, MS 228: see Martin Picker, *The Chanson Albums of Marguerite of Austria* (Berkeley and Los Angeles, 1975).

[13] See Kurt von Fischer, 'Zur Entwicklung der italienischen Trecento-Notation', *Acta Musicologica*, 16 (1959), pp. 87–99.

[14] See the article by Sarah Jane Williams cited in note 7, above.

dependence on accurate spatial presentation both of tangible symbols and of less tangible spaces and spacings, offers immeasurably greater opportunities for such clues: for the reproduction or creation of error, significant identity, variation and ambiguity. Even short pieces of music may carry rich evidence of their copying procedures because of the many opportunities for mechanical error and change. Because normal copying circumstances do not foster exact reproduction of the exemplar, no music scribe can avoid revealing his strengths, weaknesses and personal habits as well as conveying information about his exemplar. The music scribe has to take initiatives which require at least rudimentary notational understanding, and he may take initiatives which demonstrate advanced musicianship. The copying process is one of constant interpretation, even in a 'faithful' copy. While the intentions may or may not be clear, the exact representation of text underlay is virtually impossible to transmit, whether from scribe to scribe or from scribe to modern editor, and is especially resistant to commentary formulation. Lack of musical skill is probably more detectable in music copying than is minimal literacy in a text scribe.

Maas's understatement of the nature of evidence for vertical relationships or for direct copying has prompted some musicologists also to underplay these possibilities. In fact, the evidence in musical sources is very rich, and the criteria involved are very much commonsense. They have been spelled out to some extent by West and have long been taken for granted in other musical areas, e.g. Bach scholarship. Failure to apply them to music manuscripts of earlier periods, however, has led to some ill-founded claims, and it is probably worth recapitulating the criteria as they apply to music.

A directional or filial relationship may exist if all omissions and errors of the exemplar are transmitted to the copy and no more than about half of its ambiguities correctly resolved. The extent to which allowance should be made for scribal initiative will depend on the picture of that scribe's habits yielded by his other work. Allowing for this factor, there should be nothing correct in the copy that is wrong in the exemplar. Any further errors or omissions in the copy should not be such as could derive from another extant source.

In order to demonstrate that such a relationship is not merely directional but also direct, further evidence must be present, such as the reproduction of calligraphic idiosyncrasies, details (not necessarily errors) relating to the physical layout and notably associated with line ends, clef changes and accidental placing. (To copy a passage in a different clef is not to miscopy it, but the chances of pitch error by a third in the affected portion will be greatly increased.) Examples of both directional and direct transmission exist, often with intermediate ambiguity, among the Machaut manuscripts Vg, B and E. It has often been said that manuscripts – and variants – should be weighed and not counted. Statistical counts of readings tell us nothing unless it is clear that the versions are stemmatically independent. However, although the strongest evidence for relating sources comes from variants that are not only shared but 'significant' (that is, variants not likely to be arrived at independently by two scribes), a compelling number of mechanical agreements or variants may give valuable evidence of relationship, including directional or direct transmission. A clear perspective should also be maintained on the distinction between agreements, variants, errors and ambiguities. Ambiguities may be immediately apparent as such; readings which differ or agree between sources can be established by comparison. But the distinction between plausible variants and errors is crucial to directional relationships, and errors must be carefully evaluated before source dependency can be claimed.

I now come to a review of what a scribe may do when he copies a piece; this will partly duplicate and partly complement some of the points already made. These possibilities will underlie our diagnosis and treatment of each stage of a scribe's work.

(1) The copy may be a faithful interpretation of the exemplar. Because of the high potential of musical notation for mechanical and graphic change, a high degree of identity of such features may point to a relationship.

(2) If the scribe combines faithful copying with fidelity to the music and with some intelligence and musical skill, he may improve upon his exemplar by correctly resolving certain kinds of ambiguities and self-evident errors, even without memory-knowledge of the piece.

(3) The scribe may be copying a piece which he knows from performance to be corrupt. He may seek to emend it by memory of a performance which was correct or in which a conjectural emendation was devised by the performers. Such emendations may affect

more than one part of the texture and thus appear to give a fundamental difference of versions. If such emendations are successful,
they may be impossible to distinguish from 'authentic' different
versions, and I am personally convinced that they are a more common cause of variation. A scribe may copy an emended exemplar,
embodying the emendation so that it is not visible in his copy but
detectable only by divination.

(*a*) An example of this may be the opening of Dunstaple's *Alma redemptoris
mater* (no. 40 in the *Complete Works*, Musica Britannica 8), of which the Trent
copy presents a rewritten opening duet which eliminates the probably more
authentic chant paraphrase of the other versions. I am disinclined to regard
the Trent version as an equally authentic one originating from the composer; this leaves the alternative that other musicians supplied the new
opening from choice, or from some such necessity as having a damaged
exemplar for the piece.

(*b*) The opening of Machaut's Ballade 26 survives in two very different
versions in two branches of the Machaut manuscript tradition. It is hard to
judge which is the more correct, but it is very probable in this case that one
of them resulted from a conjectural emendation of a corrupt version of the
other. The same may be true for Rondeau 18, of which E's reading differs
considerably from that of the other manuscripts and is in some ways more
satisfactory. The difference may otherwise be due to compositional
revision.

(4) The scribe or editor of a manuscript may introduce deliberate
and unnecessary editorial change of a more or less radical nature.
Examples include the addition or substitution of a part; the substitution, embellishment or simplification of a part; the rescoring or
restructuring of a composition.

Examples of rewriting are numerous and include the different versions
(ornamented and plain) of *Merce merce* in BU and Paris n.a.fr.4917, and of
the Zacharias Credo in Modena 568 and Bologna Q 15; the partial rewriting
of Dunstaple's Magnificat to a different alternatim and mensural scheme
by the scribe of the MS San Pietro B.80, and the version in the same
manuscript of the Kyrie of Dufay's *Ave Regina celorum* Mass with composed links obliterating the sectional joins of the Brussels version; the *a
cappella* arrangements of Dufay's Savoy Masses made for the Sistine
Chapel.[15]

[15] For details of the latter see Alejandro Enrique Planchart, 'Guillaume Dufay's
Masses: A View of the Manuscript Traditions', in *Papers Read at the Dufay
Quincentenary Conference, Brooklyn College, December 6–7, 1976*, ed. Allan W. Atlas
(New York, 1976), pp. 26–60.

justification, and in the absence of other techniques for explaining their existence we have traditionally regarded them in one of two lights: either as random changes on the part of the scribe, or as evidence for the existence of the same variant in the (lost) exemplar for the surviving source.

This has had two results, neither satisfactory, in the pursuit of stemmata and of Urtexts. The first is that many published stemmata have as many unknown (lost) sources as surviving ones – examples abound in musical studies. The second is that more and more scholars have turned to what is benignly called the 'best-text' method of editing. In this, the editor may or may not have attempted a stemmatic analysis, but he eventually falls back on using one source as the prime, with or without considerable emendation from other sources.[9] However, there is no reason to believe that a text accepted as the most attractive by a modern editor need bear any relation at all to that preferred by the author or composer. Fortunately, musicologists have begun to turn away from the concept of the original composer's version as being a valid or useful object of pursuit, and have started to accept that we will probably not get much closer than an understanding of the form of the original – number of voices, relative levels of dissonance and so on. Such a point has long been understood by other scholars, who have written, for example, of being able to reconstruct only small parts of an earlier version, or of the impossibility of providing a complete reading for even a lost exemplar, much less an original version.[10]

Types of Trecento Music', *L'ars Nova Italiana del Trecento*, iv, ed. A. Ziino (Certaldo, 1978), pp. 211–23.

[9] This was first formally proposed as a procedure by Dom Bédier (Bibliography 2 and 3) and has been adopted by many editors of early French texts since then. It has recently received indirect support from Thorpe (Bibliography 36). It is normally criticised on the ground that no single text can be completely reliable, and that the adoption of the method does to some extent allow the editor to evade his responsibility of considering amendment in other situations than those of obvious error.

A common position is that of using a stemmatic analysis to determine not the original form of readings (though here see below), but rather which is the best recension and its best manuscript – this then being used for the edition, without regard to the other results of the analysis. This position is described in Marie-Joseph Lagrange, *Introduction à l'étude du Nouveau Testament*, ii, pt 2: 'La critique rationelle' (Paris, 1935), p. 25, and to some extent justified by A. E. Housman, as quoted in Bibliography 40, p. 50.

[10] Colwell, 'Method in Grouping New Testament Sources', pp. 15–18, argues that we should abandon the attempt at reconstructing the original form and readings

MARGARET BENT

Such changes may be linked to regional, institutional or personal policy.

(5) The scribe may carelessly introduce ambiguities of pitch register, text underlay or lateral grouping.

(6) The scribe may unintentionally miscopy his exemplar. 'Miscopying is far from being the only cause of textual variation, and misreading is far from being the only cause of miscopying.[16] West goes on to give examples of textual variation in which a word may be miswritten without having been misread, especially by partial assimilation of the ending to that of a nearby word. This can happen easily with similar and proximate musical phrases; the psychological miscopyings he cites have clear parallels in music, but the opportunities occur much more frequently because of the mechanical and space-dependent elements in musical notation. Miscopying may be easily diagnosed and emended (as in the case of dittography, or of a clef-change-related error), or it may not be detectable as such (as in some cases of the substitution of a dot for a rest or vice versa). It may or may not have been encouraged by an anomaly or ambiguity in the exemplar.

(7) The scribe may introduce melodic or rhythmic variation to the individual part in such a way as to define for us the normal range and type of legitimate variation in performance. These changes may be spontaneous or memory-fuelled. They mostly concern cadential figures, anticipations, dotted patterns versus even pairs, passing notes and other slight rhythmic and melodic changes that can be made without fear of polyphonic consequences. Changes in text underlay and in ficta indications may fall into the same category, which presumes considerable musical ability and probably the innate musicianship of a practised performer.

(8) Much other change results from the capacity of mensural notation for expressing similar or identical results in more than one way. Some cases of mensural or colorational synonymy may be the result of editorial decisions reflecting local or personal preferences, as in the continental transcriptions of English music, where black notation with red and void coloration was changed to void notation with only black coloration, proportions translated from colours to numerals, rests or tacet indications substituted for different or non-existent indications of reduced scoring. Changes of ligaturing and

[16] West, *op. cit.*, p. 15.

309

certain alternative notations for coloration groups may bear upon performance practice, in ways yet to be explored. Most such changes, however, can probably be regarded as the exercise of free variation on the part of the scribe, notably reversals of dotted and coloured patterns, and all graphic peculiarities, including the forms of ligatures and accidentals. Clef changes may similarly reflect personal preferences, but they not infrequently arose from the simplest expedient for correcting the most common pitch-copying error of a third.

In order to assess as closely as possible which of the above each of our scribes may be responsible for, we need to build up as complete a picture as possible of the detectable habits of each scribe we are dealing with – his tastes, tendencies, types of common errors and initiatives, musicianship, priorities, intelligence. By the time the possibilities of change for each note have been multiplied by an unknown number of copying processes underlying each surviving source, we have to admit that the consistency of what is transmitted is more remarkable than the changes. The text-critical principle of *praestat difficilior lectio* must be used with great caution in music. Apart from avoiding the obvious trap of equating 'more difficult' with 'less plausible', it should also not necessarily be equated with 'more elaborated'. In some circumstances it may apply to composer attributions: an attribution to Forest of a piece ascribed elsewhere to Dunstaple should be seriously considered. Composer attributions moreover should be evaluated separately from other kinds of scribal reliability, in that they are more easily separable from the transmission of the music.

Musical manuscripts, as multi-exemplar anthologies, give us a unique basis for appraising scribal habits. If a consistent pattern emerges in a scribe's handling of pieces known from other sources, we may in turn begin to use that knowledge in our *examinatio* of his *unica*, and allow it to guide our emendations. Even without concordances for comparison, certain personal idiosyncrasies may be apparent as such, and we may therefore be able to reconstruct some features of his exemplar by eliminating them.

Examples include, in the Machaut MS B, poor pitch register, retention of exemplar line ends, leaving us uncertain about the scribe's ability to take even the simplest musical initiatives; unconcern for mutual placement of text and music; some misunderstanding of the significance of stem direction; mimicry of some graphic peculiarities of his exemplar. This manuscript is an excellent example of an attempt to copy literally by a musically weak scribe, from whom therefore certain kinds of errors but no initiatives can be expected. The scribe of M S E tends to place accidentals at the same horizontal location as in the exemplar but at the pitch of the adjacent rather than the applicable note. The scribe of LoF likes to write long compound ligatures including successions of semibreve pairs. The scribe of Old Hall enjoys elongated oblique ligature forms (often to fill space), is fastidious in text placement (evidenced by erasures), and editorially changes final longs of sections to breves. The scribe of Bologna Q 15 writes compatible double clefs. The scribe of MuEm frequently transgresses the *similis ante similem* rule. B U's scribe tends to give two-voice versions of pieces surviving elsewhere *a 3*. The scribe of Trent 90 copied literally and mindlessly, even to the point of copying correction signs rather than incorporating the correction, but later made some corrections and reworkings; his pitch register is poor. Strahov's scribe shows a great fondness for replacing dotted-minim–semiminim pairs by *minor color* groups. These are random samples. We need data like this, in much more detail, including procedural information about how scribes ruled up pages and the order in which they wrote text and music under various circumstances, before we can properly evaluate their work for text-critical purposes.

Peculiarities noted in a single piece or group of pieces probably reflect those of the exemplar, and may be a valuable guide to transmission grouping. A scribe's known preference for adding or removing accidentals or adding or simplifying cadential ornament may likewise assist editorial decisions. Carefully built knowledge of a scribe's reliability may enable us to conjecture in what precise respects his exemplar was good or bad.

Two fundamentally different positions have been taken by most recent editors of late-medieval polyphony. One of these is that the editor should select a 'main' source from those available and present the readings of that source, resorting to others only when 'necessary' (a loophole of indeterminate scope). He will thus produce what somebody, somewhere, at some time performed from, rather than a conflated hybrid version corresponding to no single surviving source. Such an approach seems to have gained currency only for a period which is virtually devoid of extant musical autographs, and has been stated thus:

When a composition has been preserved in two or more manuscripts, I have followed the practice of Heinrich Besseler by selecting what seems to be the best source and deviating from it only in the case of flagrant errors ... I prefer this method to that of piecing together variants from various sources and offering a transcription that does not agree with any of the manuscripts. After having selected the best source, I have made as few alterations as possible in this version ...[17]

If we should beware of 'the absurdity of following whatever is regarded as the best manuscript as long as its readings are not impossible',[18] even where there is a reasonably authoritative main source, how much more careful should we be when there is not?

To select one source for an edition, where others exist, is certainly justified to the degree that that source has a claim to authority, use or supervision by the composer or his circle. One such source is the M S Brussels 5557 for the late Masses of Dufay. It is far from being true, however, that we have equally good sources for all of Dufay's music. Hence it will not do to apply a uniform editorial approach to the variously disseminated works that may be assembled for a collected edition. Despite our evidence from his own testimony that Machaut supervised compilations of his own manuscripts (possibly including some of the surviving sources), no one of them is free from error to a degree that permits us to assume careful proofreading by and therefore authority from the composer. However impressive the pedigree of a chosen source, the editor is not relieved of the duty to examine and emend the text it yields. If there is no authoritative source (and, as just stated, even the obvious cases turn out to be fallible), there is little sense in investing the best of a bad bunch with an authority it would immediately lose were a better one to turn up. This is not to deny that in practice it is often necessary to use as a 'copy text'[19] an admittedly inferior source which may be the only complete one, or to select such a copy for details which are resistant to qualitative or stemmatic evaluation.

The one-source approach may have its justification if we are to recognise more than one authentic version of a work of art, and to be prepared to produce as many editions as the number and distinct-

---

[17] C. Hamm (ed.), *Leonel Power: Complete Works*, Corpus Mensurabilis Musicae ser. 50 (n.p., 1969), vol. I. p. xix.

[18] West, *op. cit.*, p. 50.

[19] The term is used by W. W. Greg, 'The Rationale of Copy-Text', *Studies in Bibliography*, 3 (1950), pp. 19–36.

ness of versions warrants. Practical and economic considerations are in general against the proliferation of editions of only slightly differing versions. We should in any case assure ourselves that 'independent' versions really deserve that status and do not merely represent editorial credulity, indecision, laziness, or failure to apply rudimentary notions of transmission. To pass such indecision on to the bewildered consumer in the form of multiple editions of the same undigested material would be sheer irresponsibility.

The second approach recognises the fallibility of scribes and maintains that the editor's duty goes beyond respect for manuscripts. Even more respect, surely, is owed to the original intentions of the composer. The fact that these intentions include unnotated performance conventions as well as notated essentials must be taken account of in adapting text-critical principles for use in music. Thorough knowledge of his materials may permit an editor to establish a text better than any that has survived the hazards of repeated copying and physical jeopardy – indeed, better than what some medieval performers had to make do with, which, however, they were arguably better equipped to do than we are.

An editor who draws on all available witnesses to an imperfectly preserved tradition is not necessarily conflating their readings indiscriminately, but rather attempting to establish the best reading for every note, on the assumption that any source may have transmitted some things correctly and some incorrectly. The magistrate will listen to all witnesses, and may place different weight on different parts of the testimony of each. Each witness will be treated with as much respect and as much scepticism as its testimony commands, and the coherence of its version will be tested as though it were the sole witness before being compared with others.

Because the evaluation of what has been transmitted to us must take account of lost as well as surviving sources, a *unicum* is just as likely to contain error and require emendation as is a piece surviving in several sources, some of which appear more 'correct' than others. The following therefore takes account of both one-source and multiple-source situations.

If there is only one source, the readings of its individual parts may be perceived as being clear or ambiguous, and the resulting pitches and rhythms may be adjudged plausible or implausible. Next, when fitting the individual parts together, it may be possible to resolve ambiguities, and in addition to identify anomalies that range from obviously erroneous to merely stylistically dubious. If the piece is tested, as it must have been by contemporaries, by performance rather than by putting it into written score, the anomalies will emerge aurally. What may be ambiguous in an individual part may be resolved by aural considerations without creating any uncertainty for the performer. If there is more than one source, the above operations should ideally be carried out on each before they are compared. The failure of many critical commentaries to make clear when they are recording errors and when they are recording plausible alternatives often results from a one-source approach in which not all witnesses have been fairly heard.

The nature of music copying, with its mechanical aspects and with the separation of polyphonic parts, makes contamination, in the literary sense of copying from more than one exemplar at a time, rather unlikely for music. The relatively short time-span within which each repertory was circulated also reduces the likelihood. Music, unlike text, is not normally subject to the kind of learned emendation and criticism by contemporaries that was normal for ancient texts. Because of the different nature and status of the material, it lent itself far more readily to other kinds of change by editors and scribes, as discussed above. It is in this way that musical sources are 'contaminated' – or, rather, enriched. If a source has been changed after copying (Trent 90 is a clear case, and we have its exemplar, Trent 93), the layers of activity will be visible. But if we had a copy of Trent 90 in which the changes were presented integrally, it might be very much harder to identify them as such, or to establish the derivation from Trent 93. A single source may embody more than one version, and may itself represent just the sort of conflation that the one-source editors abhor. It may even contain incompatible alternatives, whether or not the copy is scribally homogeneous. Conversely, different sources may present complementary indications, and to recognise them as such need not yield an undiscriminating conflation of readings. The editor should be alert, therefore, to the possibilities that a single source may tell more than one story, and that many sources in combination may paint a single coherent picture.

A modern edition of mensural notation is a transliteration of a different notational system. The conceptual basis is inevitably changed; therefore to preserve orthographic features of the original (clefs, note-values etc.) is relatively pedantic. (Most deceptive in this respect are diplomatic transcriptions that appear to preserve the original notation while, for example, rewriting altered semibreves as breves and breaking up ligatures to facilitate score presentation.) It should, however, be possible for a user who knows the original language to translate it back in all essential details. If the copy on which we are dependent is itself a translation or adaptation, we may similarly be able to restore many essentials (if not all details) of its original form. The use of features such as mensural usage to establish the chronology of sources or of a composer's works[20] should be undertaken with as much caution as is necessary in the case of paleographical datings, because they are subject to the same hazards of time-lag and individual scribal habit. As the continental interpretations of the English repertory show, it was the mensural aspect that was least proof against scribal editing.

In practice, the modern editor may be able to 'de-edit' a source. Changes may have been made to the structure, scoring, text underlay and mensurations in such a way that the original written form can be reconstructed with confidence, by analogy with similar compositions and with knowledge of the regional differences that prompted the changes. The editor may then be able to apply text-critical principles to the recovery of pitches and rhythms, establishing dependencies, evaluating alternatives, making emendations. Finally, he will be faced with a variety of evidence at the level of scribal and performing freedom, concerning ligaturing, ornament, ficta, underlay. It is only at this level, I suggest, that a copy text may be useful and that a relatively arbitrary decision to follow one source for the majority of such details is justified. Here, in particular, the editor must draw on his knowledge of the habits of his individual scribes in selecting such a source and evaluating the scribal contribution to the version in question. Even the use of such a copy text should not reduce the editor's freedom of judgement in complementing the last category, especially in details of underlay and ficta, whether his decisions are supported by other sources or not. The consequences of responsible text-critical procedures are that, at any of the above three levels, the editor may present material which is in

[20] Notably the pioneering and valuable study by Charles Hamm, *A Chronology of the Works of Guillaume Dufay Based on a Study of Mensural Practice* (Princeton, 1964).

any of his sources, and material for which none of them gives him a direct mandate.

Time and space do not permit a fuller formulation of detailed procedures, but I hope I have indicated the direction and kind of approach I believe to be fruitful in questions of source relationship, even though it may only rarely be possible to produce directional or stemmatic evidence rather than grouping patterns. The plea for more thoughtfully based editorial procedures springs from the desire to present to the performer and analyst (or indeed to ourselves in those capacities) a worthy basis for their best efforts. Analysis provides the criteria that should raise the process of *examinatio* to a higher degree of refinement than the hit-or-miss methods often employed. This in turn is only possible if the analysis is based on decent texts, and if its procedures are sufficiently subtle to take into account the variable elements (successively added or optional voices, text placement, ficta alternatives, ornamentation or mensural variants, as well as alternative readings). All we can hope for at present is to produce musical texts which reflect as faithfully as possible what the composer might have written, with some overlay of contemporary performance evidence and editorial common sense. The experience and instincts of the editor will have to serve for the finer points of critical examination and emendation until analysis of these repertories is further advanced, and can furnish more objective bases for making attributions for anonymous or disputed works as well as criteria for emending our texts. Finally, we should remind ourselves that the modern editor is just as fallible as the medieval scribe, a condition from which he can no more escape by taking the 'safe' course of literal copying than by exercising his mind and judgement.[21]

---

[21] The following *sigla* are used in this paper:

Machaut sources: A = Paris, Bibliothèque Nationale, fonds fr. 1584
B = Paris, Bibliothèque Nationale, fonds fr. 1585
E = Paris, Bibliothèque Nationale, fonds fr. 9221
Vg = New York, Wildenstein Collection, MS Vogüé
Inventories, bibliography, etc. in RISM B/IV/2

Aosta = Aosta, Biblioteca del Seminario, MS A¹D 19. Inventory by G. de Van, *Musica Disciplina*, 2 (1948), pp. 5–74. See also M. Cobin, 'The Aosta Manuscript: A Central Source of Early-Fifteenth-Century Polyphony', Ph.D. diss., New York University, 1978

Bologna Q 15 = Bologna, Civico Museo Bibliografico-Musicale, MS Q 15. Inventory by G. de Van, *Musica Disciplina*, 2 (1948), pp. 231–57

Brussels 5557 = Brussels, Bibliothèque Royale, MS 5557. See Sylvia Kenney, *Walter Frye and the Contenance Angloise* (New Haven and London, 1964)

BU = Bologna, Biblioteca Universitaria, MS 2216. See H. Besseler, *Musica Disciplina*, 6 (1952), pp. 39–65, and A. Gallo, *Monumenta Lyrica Medii Aevi Italica*, III: *Mensurabilia*, vol. 3, parts 1–2 (Bologna, 1968–70)

LoF = London, British Library, Add. MS 40011B (the 'Fountains Fragment')

Modena 568 = Modena, Biblioteca Estense, MS α.M5.24 (*olim* lat. 568). Inventory, bibliography etc. in RISM B/IV/4

MuEm = Munich, Bayerische Staatsbibliothek, MS mus. 3232a. Inventory by K. Dèzes, *Zeitschrift für Musikwissenschaft*, 10 (1927–8), pp. 65–105

Old Hall = London, British Library, Add. MS 57950

Paris n.a.fr.4917 = Paris, Bibliothèque Nationale, nouv. acq. fr. 4917

San Pietro B.80 = Vatican City, Biblioteca Apostolica Vaticana, Archivio di San Pietro, MS B.80. Inventory by C. Hamm, *Revue Belge de Musicologie*, 14 (1960), pp. 40–55

Strahov = Prague, Strahov Monastery, MS D.G.IV.47. See R. J. Snow, 'The Manuscript Strahov D.G.IV.47', Ph.D. diss., University of Illinois, 1968

Trent 87–92 = Trent, Museo Provinciale d'Arte, MSS 87–92. Trent 93 = Trent, Biblioteca Capitolare, MS 93. See *Die Trienter Codices*, Denkmäler der Tonkunst in Österreich 7, 21, 40 (Vienna 1900, 1924, 1933)

15

LIMITATIONS AND EXTENSIONS OF
FILIATION TECHNIQUE

Stanley Boorman

THE practice of stemmatics as a method of evaluating source readings is now almost a century old, if its beginnings are traced to the fundamental statement of Karl Lachmann.[1] Since that time there has been a stream, bordering on a flood, of articles and books, both employing the method adumbrated by Lachmann and also criticising, expanding and modifying his techniques: these techniques have been employed in numerous fields, though principally those of Classical and patristic studies, of research into the sources and texts of

---

[1] K. Lachmann, 'Rechenschaft über seine Ausgabe des Neuen Testaments', *Theologische Studien und Kritiken*, 63 (1890), pp. 817–45. Of course, as Timpanaro shows in Bibliography 38, this was not the start of textual criticism or of the use of variants to provide relationships between sources, both of which lie at the heart of, for example, the fifteenth-century study of Classical texts. A summary discussion of earlier methods can be found in Bibliography 27, pp. 149–55; more detailed comment is in, among others, A. Casacci, 'Per la critica del testo nella prima metà del Quattrocento', *Memorie dell'Istituto Lombardo, Accademia di Scienze e Lettere*, 59 (1926); K. Hulley, 'Principles of Textual Criticism known to St Jerome', *Harvard Studies in Classical Philology*, 54 (1944), pp. 87–109; S. Prete, *Observations on the History of Textual Criticism in the Medieval and Renaissance Periods* (Collegeville, Minn., 1969); S. Rizzo, *Il lessico filologico degli umanisti*, Sussidi Eruditi 26 (Rome, 1973); or R. Sabbadini, *Storia e critica di testi latini*, Medioevo e Umanesimo 11, 2nd edn (Padua, 1971).

Details of some of the more important studies in the field are given in the Bibliography at the end of this paper. This merely provides a guide to the principal approaches and the main critical arguments: it does not include the myriad books and articles employing stemmatic procedures when they do not raise methodological questions of value to musicologists. Nor does it include many important studies of detailed theoretical points, such as the work of Havet or Hruby, or that of Turyn on local divergent traditions. Some of these are cited below: others are referred to in studies listed. I am indebted to Geoffrey Chew, Edward Roesner and John Stevens for drawing my attention to omissions in this bibliography after the paper was read.

When an item in the Bibliography is referred to in the notes, it is cited in the form 'Bibliography 76'.

scripture, and study of the sources of medieval and later writers in Latin, Italian and French, as well as of English literature, both manuscript and printed.

By contrast, the use of filiation techniques in musicology is of a very recent birth: Atlas, in his dissertation on the Cappella Giulia chansonnier,[2] was able to cite only a few other works discussing the method as applied to musicological research, and the list cannot, even now, be extended very much further. None the less, as the present collection of papers bears witness, the subject has acquired a certain vogue interest among musical scholars. While some have claimed that there are major differences between the transmission of musical sources and that of almost any other range of material, I believe that there is no characteristic of musical manuscripts and transmission patterns which cannot also be found elsewhere.[3] The combination of problems faced by the musicologist is admittedly unusual, and it does demand some modifications of technique, but these are already available to us, tried and tested elsewhere in the literature on the method.

There are three critical problems that arise in attempting a stemmatic study of early musical sources, and one other which plagues such study in most fields: the three seem to me to be (1) the small size of most individual pieces (even in the case of whole Masses), resulting in relatively little evidence;[4] (2) the fact that most surviving sources were probably copied from more than one exemplar;[5] (3) the

[2] Bibliography 44.

[3] Reference to some instances is made in notes 4–6, below: others might include different spellings and notations (in, for example, Latin manuscripts, Bibliography 42) or the possibilities of open recensions and authorial revision (Bibliography 5; 28 vol. II, pp. 29–40; 30, pp. 395–469; 38; and see note 12, below). Blackburn (Bibliography 46, p. 35) says: 'we must understand that sixteenth-century scribes of music had an entirely different attitude toward the text of a piece of music than did the copyists of classical authors. The basic assumption of the filiation method is that a scribe copied a text from a particular manuscript with the intent to transmit it as faithfully as possible. Such an assumption is not necessarily valid in music . . .' With the second sentence I have no quarrel, except for the tense of the verb – it has indeed been the basic assumption of filiation. However, as greater numbers of scholars outside musicology have been realising, such an assumption is also not necessarily (indeed, not very frequently) valid in other fields, either.

[4] Musical sources have this in common with poetical anthologies and with collections of letters. Examples of and studies on both abound from both the Classical and later periods (Bibliography 6, part 2).

[5] This situation also exists in the classes of literature mentioned in note 4, as well as

possible confusion between editorial and accidental changes to both substantive and non-substantive elements of the text.[6] Each of these may seem to be a limitation of the possible applications of stemmatics to music, though, in returning to them later in this paper, I hope to show that they work to our advantage. The additional problem that I have mentioned is the most crucial of all, and requires that we move outside the field of stemmatics before we can solve it.

This general, and very real, problem concerns the question of how and why variants appear in sources.[7] The number of variants in a given source for which we can advance a satisfactory (or even plausible) explanation is always slight – perhaps an incidence of haplography or dittography, or a demonstrable textual modification.[8] For the great majority of variants, however, we have no such

in play texts and collections of treatises (Bibliography 4 is a valuable case-study). It is the situation that has led to attempts at relating sources on the basis of contents rather than readings (Bibliography 53, 59 and, in particular, 51; see also *Paléographie musicale*, xiii (Tournay, 1925), pp. 42–53, for a further simple example in chant sources).

[6] This is a standing problem in all cases where the stemma is at all obscure: it merely appears worse for musical sources as a result of the apparent freedom which the scribe felt (at both the conscious and unconscious levels) to ornament and vary readings. However, it has been discussed in other fields (Bibliography 11, 15, 25, 29, and 42).

[7] Many writings on textual criticism have attacked the problem of scribal error and its detection. Among them, often the most attractive blend of erudition and literary style, are those of A. E. Housman: see Bibliography 22 and many of the articles collected in *The Classical Papers of A. E. Housman*.

[8] The classic field for the deliberate textual change, establishing new lines of tradition, is that of scripture, where there were good doctrinal reasons for change – even though these reasons seem, in their morality, to be opposed to the very intent of scripture. A standard discussion of the theory of local texts remains Bibliography 35. Colwell (Bibliography 11, p. 83) says that 'the theory of so-called local texts is a snare and a delusion', even though he elsewhere states: 'Certain scholars, interested in history, have argued convincingly that the variant readings in any particular manuscript have something to tell us about the history of the Church' ('Method in Grouping New Testament Sources', Bibliography 9, p. 9).
There is little reason to doubt that local traditions of style as well as of notation were important in the transmission of several repertoires of music (perhaps most obviously chant): these will clearly affect our view of a stemma. Indeed, one of the weaknesses in the premises behind Charles Hamm's *A Chronology of the Works of Guillaume Dufay Based on a Study of Mensural Practice* (Princeton, 1964) is just this, that scribes *did* make deliberate changes. While this has not yet been seriously investigated for the early fifteenth century (though see the remarks of M. Bent in the preface to *Fifteenth-Century Liturgical Music*, ii: *Four Anonymous Masses*, Early English Church Music 22 (London, 1979)), it is certainly true for the end of the century, and has been hinted at, albeit indirectly, by E. Fellin in 'The Notation-

For as long as variants have to be described either as random-and-non-significant or as significant-and-related-to-the-exemplar, we will continue to get little further, either in attempts at reconstructing readings or in essays at constructing stemmata. The situation will continue in which sources are merely grouped into families without further distinction,[11] or else many hypothetical sources and cross-fertilisations will be produced to account for the variants and patterns. Neither of these yields any guidance as to readings, particularly in those frequent cases where a stemma or grouping of sources suggests the presence of only two families of readings.[12]

However, a number of studies, both in and outside stemmatics, have indicated an approach to the crux of the problem – why the variants appear. The key lies in an analysis of the working habits and characteristics of the scribe.[13] Students of the scribal process and of scribal habit have examined all the aspects that musicologists need for the study of stemmatics – the copying process itself,[14] accidents, errors and faults of copying,[15] the manner in which different scribes

of the text, and Silva Lake, *Family π and the Codex Alexandrinus: The Text According to Mark*, Studies and Documents 5 (London, 1937), p. 5, says of surviving sources that 'each of them has been so considerably modified by successive copying, or even revision, that this archetype can be only approximately reconstructed, with due allowance for alternative possibilities in almost every reading'. See also Bibliography 4, pp. 142–7.

[11] Bibliography 44, p. 47. See also Bibliography 20, 31, and 55.

[12] One of the traditional methods for selecting between readings involves the presence of one (the acceptable) in more than one family of sources. With a two-branched stemma, this evidence is valueless. Many of the variants will have been used to construct the stemma, having no further sources to weight the evidence; in such a stemma, it is no more than theoretically possible to distinguish between those variants which should represent the stemma and those which should be the result of conflation or contamination. See Bibliography 37 in particular, and also 3 and 16, and P. Canivet and P. Malvaux, 'La tradition manuscrit du *Περὶ τῆς θείας ἀγάπης*, (Recherche d'une méthode mathématique de classement des manuscrits et critique textuelle)', *Byzantion*, 34 (1964), pp. 385–413. It is at this point that the comments by Thorpe, Bibliography 36, on the aesthetics of editing are valuable.

[13] I use the word 'scribe' here to include the type-setter of printed music. The differences in copying procedure do not materially affect the analytical processes described in the present study, although they do influence details of technique.

[14] See, in particular, Bibliography 12. Although this may be one of the few places where some modification of the applications to textual study of music may be necessary in the light of the special nature of music copying, it seems unlikely that the basic processes of copying were drastically altered.

[15] See Bibliography 42, and 40, pp. 15–29.

copy and the impact of that on the resulting readings,[16] ranges of deliberate scribal change,[17] and the changes that a scribe will make, largely unconsciously, as a result of training and background.[18] I have written elsewhere[19] on the use of scribal habit in analysing readings, but some of the points are relevant here also. The first and most important is that so-called 'accidentals' or 'non-substantives' in the readings are just as important as changes to the text; indeed, the former may lie at the root of the analysis.[20] It might seem, at first sight, that the study of 'accidentals' is of little value, in particular to the musicologist, who regularly argues that early music has a higher proportion of irrelevant accidental variation than does other material – citing as examples added accidentals, ligatures, coloration, decorated cadences, etc. Thus, Cook claims that 'since the work itself does not change, variants of this type have no bearing on its transmission'.[21] At the same point, however, he cites the verdict of Willis, who points out that the only variants in Latin texts that have no bearing on the transmission are those that are purely orthographical.[22] Colwell[23] uses such variants, among others, to evaluate

---

[16] These are discussed in some detail in Bibliography 7 and brilliantly illustrated in Bibliography 11.

[17] See Bibliography 25, 35, 39, 42, and 24, pp. 115–73, which also discusses the unconscious changes made by scribes.

[18] See Bibliography 39, and 29, part III. Already in 1940, Bibliography 28, II, p. 2, recognised the need for study of 'the habits of scribes and the transmission of texts', and used this as justification for recording 'the readings of *codices eliminandi* and *codices deteriores* as faithfully as those of the most important MSS' in the last four of eight volumes. The authors go on (p. 21) to point out that many variants occur 'not by the common possession of a MS tradition, but as a result of similarities in the habits and ideas of scribes, due to similarities in training and experience'.

[19] See Bibliography 47; and Boorman, 'The "First" Edition of the *Odhecaton A*', *Journal of the American Musicological Society*, 30 (1977), pp. 198–207.

[20] Kane, Bibliography 24, makes the point that 'dramatic' changes in the text are of much less value in studying the tradition than are the casual ones made routinely as either lapses or editorial emendation.

[21] Bibliography 48, pp. 12–13. See also Bibliography 46, p. 35. I should add that I am far from convinced that these elements have no bearing on the transmission or, for that matter, that they have no bearing on the music itself. Apart from the second point (which deserves fuller treatment elsewhere), the abandonment of 'accidentals' leads directly to ignoring subtle details both of transmission and of changes in notation and interpretation. It is also often associated with the pursuit of the mythical Urtext, a pursuit in which any 'fortunate' congruence of these 'accidentals' is cited as evidence and any disagreement can safely be ignored.

[22] Bibliography 42, p. 36.   [23] Bibliography 11.

the readings of his text; and study of the spelling habits of type-setters has become crucial in establishing the quality of the texts of Shakespeare plays.[24] Indeed, in music, it is because so many of the variants (often dismissed as insignificant) lie in the shadowy ground between the light of clear error and editorial change and the dark night of simple spelling variants that they are so useful in our evaluations of scribal behaviour.[25]

The term 'scribal habit' covers several things: there is the range of practices of spelling, notation or underlay, for example, that are peculiar to the individual; there is the range proper to his locality and time – what one might call dialect; and there is the range of required changes peculiar to his place of employment. All these are bound up, almost inextricably, with one another and are further confused by the occasional errors and lapses from consistency that are the failings of all scribes. However, there will normally be a consistent enough picture for the student to be able to deduce a great deal about the scribe's habits, conscious or unconscious or, more often, only partly conscious.[26]

The value of such a detailed study (and it is certainly laborious) lies in the light it casts on the exemplar. We can say with some confidence that a scribe who unexpectedly, or occasionally, breaks his normal habit is likely to be reflecting a feature of his exemplar. The analysis of his habit will have revealed characteristics that are to be found regularly across all layers of his work. When they are present, they tell us nothing of his exemplar, for we cannot know whether the scribe followed copy or adapted it to his own taste. When, however, they are absent, we may reasonably infer that this reflects something in the source – it is unlikely that the scribe would

[24] Almost any study of the transmission and texts of the quartos, for example, touches on spelling habits or related matters of little textual significance (according to the traditional view); among the most recent is T. Berger, 'The Printing of *Henry V*, Q1', *The Library*, 6th ser., vol. 1 (1979), pp. 114–25. A classic study of the subject is Bibliography 21.

[25] See Bibliography 28, 11, pp. 22–3.

[26] A valuable example, involving an important though often disregarded aspect of source transmission, is Howard Brown's 'Words and Music in Early 16th Century Chansons: Text Underlay in Florence, Biblioteca del Conservatorio, Ms Basevi 2442', to be published in the proceedings of the Kolloquium über Formen und Probleme der Überlieferung mehrstimmiger Musik im Zeitalter Josquins Desprez, Wolfenbüttel, 1976. I am grateful to Professor Brown for giving me a full text of this paper in advance of publication.

abandon what was his normal habit without some clear reason for doing so.

As an example, the pattern of copying underlay in the chansonnier now split between Seville and Paris (hereafter *Sev*) may be cited (Table).[27] The habits of the three scribes are markedly different. Scribe III copies only Italian texts: this says nothing about the presence or absence of French texts in his exemplars, for he may have chosen to omit such as were present. Scribe II (and IIa) texts everything he can: the assumption would seem valid that he had no text available for those few pieces in which he copied the top voice without text.[28] The demonstration may seem simplistic, but the method is identical to that adopted for more complex situations, and its implications have been overlooked. For Scribe I, incidentally, the evidence is not conclusive as it stands. I suspect, for other reasons, that he also copied text when he had it.

It will be noted that I have discussed scribal habit as if one (the last) of my three problems peculiar to musical sources did not exist – that is, as if there were no difference between substantive and non-substantive elements of the text nor between editorial and accidental change. For the first part, I am sure that there is no difference. The same patterns of behaviour while copying will have affected the scribe, no matter whether he were thinking about readings or about notation, about underlay or about accidentals or ligatures. Indeed, study of sources of the chanson repertoire shows clearly that some scribes had specific approaches to each of these elements.[29] For the second part (the congruency between patterns of editorial and accidental change), I believe that the same holds. For one thing, we can seldom distinguish the two, itself an indication that they had similar

---

[27] MS Seville, Biblioteca Colombina, 5-1-43 and Paris, Bibliothèque Nationale, nouv. acq. fr. 4379 (part 1). The principal description of the source (including an inventory) is Dragan Plamenac, 'A Reconstruction of the French Chansonnier in the Biblioteca Colombina, Seville', *Musical Quarterly*, 37 (1951), pp. 501–42, and 38 (1952), pp. 85–117 and 245–77. Plamenac has also edited a facsimile of the whole source, as vol. 8 of *Publications of Mediaeval Music Manuscripts* (New York, c. 1962), with amendments to the earlier study: and an edition has appeared in Alice Moerk, 'The Seville Chansonnier: An Edition of Sevilla 5-1-43 and Paris N.A.Fr. 4379 (pt 1)', Ph.D. diss., West Virginia University, 1971.

[28] Of the seven pieces that Scribe II copied without text, five lack text in all sources and perhaps never had it.

[29] See note 26, above, and Bibliography 47. The distinctive approach can also be shown in several other sources of the period.

STANLEY BOORMAN

The manuscript Sev *(Seville, Biblioteca Colombina, MS 5-1-43, and Paris, Bibliothèque Nationale, n.a.fr., MS 4379 (pt 1))*

Collation: a–d^{10} ($-a$10, b6–10), e–o^{12} ($-f$3, g2), p–q^{10}, r^{78}

Folios	Hand	Contents	Texting [I = Italian text]
a1r–2r	I	part of an index	
a2v–5v	I	theoretical writings	
a6r–9v		blank	
(a10)			
b1r–5v	I	music: 1–5 (1 and 5 incomplete)	3
(b6r–10v)			
c1r–e1r	I	6–25 (6 incomplete)	7, 8, 24[I], 25
e1v–f2v	II	26–37 (37 incomplete)	all (34 only in part)
(f3)			
f4r–12v	II	38–46 (38 and 46 incomplete)	all
g1r		blank	
g1v	III	47 (incomplete)	
(g2)			
g3r–4r	III	48 (incomplete) and 49	
g4v–12r	I	50–57	50, 51[I], 54
g12v		blank	
h1r–12v	II	58–70 (58 incomplete)	59–70
j1r–12v	I	70 (T & C) – 82 (S)	74, 75, 82
k1r–m2r	IIa	82 (T & C) – 105	all except 95, 97, 98
m2v–n11r	IIIa	106–126	111[I]
n11v–12r	III	127	
(n11v, foot	I	additional voice for 127)	
n12v	I	128 (S)	128
o1r–p1r	II	128 (T & C) – 136	130, 131, 132, 133, 134
p1v–3r	III	137	137
p3v–q2v	I	138–151 (151 unfinished)	141–148 [all I]
q3r		blank	
q3v–5r	III	152–153	
q5v–7r	I	154	
q7v–r5r	III	155–163	156, 158, 159, 162, 163 [all I]
r5v–6r	II	164	
r6v–8v	III	165–167 (167 incomplete)	

Amount of texting by scribes:

Scribe I: 22 (out of a possible 59), of which 11 are in Italian

II: 37 (out of a possible 41)

IIa: 20 (out of a possible 23)

III: 6 (out of a possible 18), all of which are in Italian

IIIa: 1 (out of a possible 21), an Italian text.

327

origins (I except here those clearly editorial changes that almost amount to re-composition): a conscious decision to change details in the text will be reflected just as surely (and also as surely with occasional exceptions) as will the unconscious decision based on habit. It seems to me, therefore, that an analysis of scribal behaviour will yield considerable (though admittedly limited) information about the exemplar – information usually of a negative kind.[30]

It may well be asked: how can one tell that the detected patterns of change are those of the scribe of the source studied and not those of his exemplar? After all, the copy that survives is a fusion of the scribe's patterns and those of the copyist of the exemplar (as well as, to decreasing extents, those of each of the precursor sources). Each will reflect its place of origin and the local habit and dialect of the scribe, and each will itself be reflected in the later sources to the extent that the next scribe did not wish (or omitted) to amend certain features.

If one had to study merely a single piece – one chanson, for example – I am sure one could not tell the difference.[31] There would not be enough information, as I suggested at the start of this paper when listing three apparent limitations to the technique of stemmatics. However, the analysis I have outlined here is concerned, at this stage, not with filiation, but with the present source: the habits of the whole source are the object of investigation. Therefore, we normally have enough material from each scribe at each stage of his work to give us some idea of his habits; and the second apparent limitation – that of the multiple exemplars for the majority of sources – is itself the key to the answer to this question.

Any habit that is peculiar to the scribe of the surviving source should appear throughout his work, in all pieces copied at one stage and perhaps, unless it is a feature that changes with the passage of time, across all layers of his work. By contrast, any patterns that survive only in certain parts of the source, perhaps in one or two

[30] This information must normally be 'negative'. It will never tell us certainly what was in the exemplar, although it can sometimes give us a strong clue (see Bibliography 47). It is much more likely to show, by explaining the taste of the scribe, what cannot have been in the exemplar.

[31] In this respect, the analysis of scribal behaviour differs from the subsequent stemmatic analysis: the former must be concerned with all the work of one scribe, the latter can only succeed when concentrated on separate units, in this case individual chansons.

fascicles or in selected pieces, is more likely to be that of the exemplar (or even of a more distant source). In other words, the pattern of distribution of categories of change throughout the source tells us something about whether they belong to the scribe or not, and thence tells us even more about the nature of the exemplars. The layered nature of a manuscript is in fact an advantage in the study of the readings preserved, and thence of the filiation.

(Stemmatics, as a study, is not really concerned to examine the situation in which a source is copied from another surviving source: that is more related to paleographical questions, and only thence to matters of content. Most studies on such situations have been more concerned to prove the connection, either for the whole source or for some layers: however, study of such related sources would tell us much about the patterns of *change* that particular scribes adopted and thence also about the stemmatic process in general, where these changes can only be postulated.)

In *Sev*, I believe one can identify the basic habits of each of the scribes. Scribe III, for example, always presents a simple version of the music, with very little decoration: every example of an ornamental figure in his work that I have collated so far also survives in other sources. The patterns suggest that he may well have simplified versions on occasion. Scribe II is an editor, within limits: he tends not to fill in leaps of a third or fourth and prefers the first notation of Example 1 to the others. This seems to be a characteristic across the

Example 1

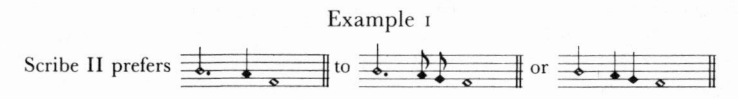

whole of his work. However, he does show some habits that are probably not his, but belong to the exemplar. There is a curious notational change that occurs almost excusively in gathering *h* (Example 2). Since this does not appear to be a habit of Scribe II, I believe it to have been in the source from which he was working.[32]

Scribe I is perhaps the most interesting: he has certain characteristics which recur throughout his copying. First, he regularly

---

[32] This was first pointed out to me by Barbara Strauss, a member of a graduate seminar on the *Odhecaton A* at the University of Wisconsin in 1978. I am grateful to her and to other members of the class (Diantha Clark, Merryn Ledbetter and Richard Manner) for other comments on this repertoire.

Example 2

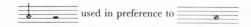

presents simple, lightly decorated cadence figuration. However, in a number of pieces he provides additional more complex decoration, for the final cadence only.[33] Secondly, he occasionally fills in leaps of a fourth or fifth. This does not seem to me to be a consistent habit, and probably reflects the exemplars. Thirdly, he tends to preserve fusae: these have begun to disappear from the figuration in two of the closely related sources, *Pix* and *F229*.[34] Fourthly, he regularly takes an independent line over long notes and repeated pitches, breaking up the former and tying together the latter, apparently as whim or notational appearance take him.[35]

An attractive example of the manner in which this works is Joye's chanson *Ce qu'on fait* (Example 3), on fols. *j*12v–*k*1. The tenor and contratenor stand at the beginning of a fascicle of over two gatherings copied by Scribe II. The superius, at the end of the previous gathering, is the work of Scribe I, a later copyist.[36] The music

---

[33] This does not happen very frequently, perhaps because the scribe was not working from score: however, its appearance is frequent enough, and spread widely enough through his work, to suggest that it is one of his characteristics and not one from his exemplars.

[34] Paris, Bibliothèque Nationale, f.fr. 15123 (Pixérécourt) and Florence, Biblioteca Nazionale Centrale, Banco rari 229. An incomplete edition and an inventory (with few concordances) of the former is in Edward Pease, 'An Edition of the Pixérécourt Manuscript: Paris, Bibliothèque Nationale, *fonds fr. 15123*', Ph.D. diss., University of Indiana, 1960, while Howard Brown, in 'The Transformation of the Chanson at the End of the Fifteenth Century', *International Musicological Society, Report of the Tenth Congress, Ljubljana 1967*, ed. Dragotin Cvetko (Kassel, etc., 1970), was the first to demonstrate convincingly that the manuscript was written in Florence. In his forthcoming study and edition of the second manuscript, Professor Brown shows that the two were probably copied in the same workshop. A list of contents of the Florence manuscript appears in Bianca Becherini, *Catalogo dei manoscritti musicali della Biblioteca Nazionale di Firenze* (Kassel, 1959), pp. 22–9, and in Anne-Marie Bragard, 'Un manuscrit florentin du quattrocento: le Magl. XIV, 59 (B.R.229)', *Revue de Musicologie*, 52 (1966), pp. 56–72.

[35] This is perhaps the most common trait, for there are many examples throughout his work.

[36] This is not the place to discuss the paleographical evidence that demonstrates that the work of Scribe I is the latest layer in the source; however, some of the reasons for this conclusion will be immediately apparent on examining the Table.

Example 3

A. Version in *Sev* on the topmost staff, variants in other sources underneath

A = a notational change, with no effect on pitch or rhythm
B = a change in the rhythmic treatment of long or repeated notes
C = a change in decorative figuration
D = an 'error' or minor variant
E = a major variant – shown in score in Ex. 3B (p. 334)

Example 3A (cont.)

Example 3A (cont.)

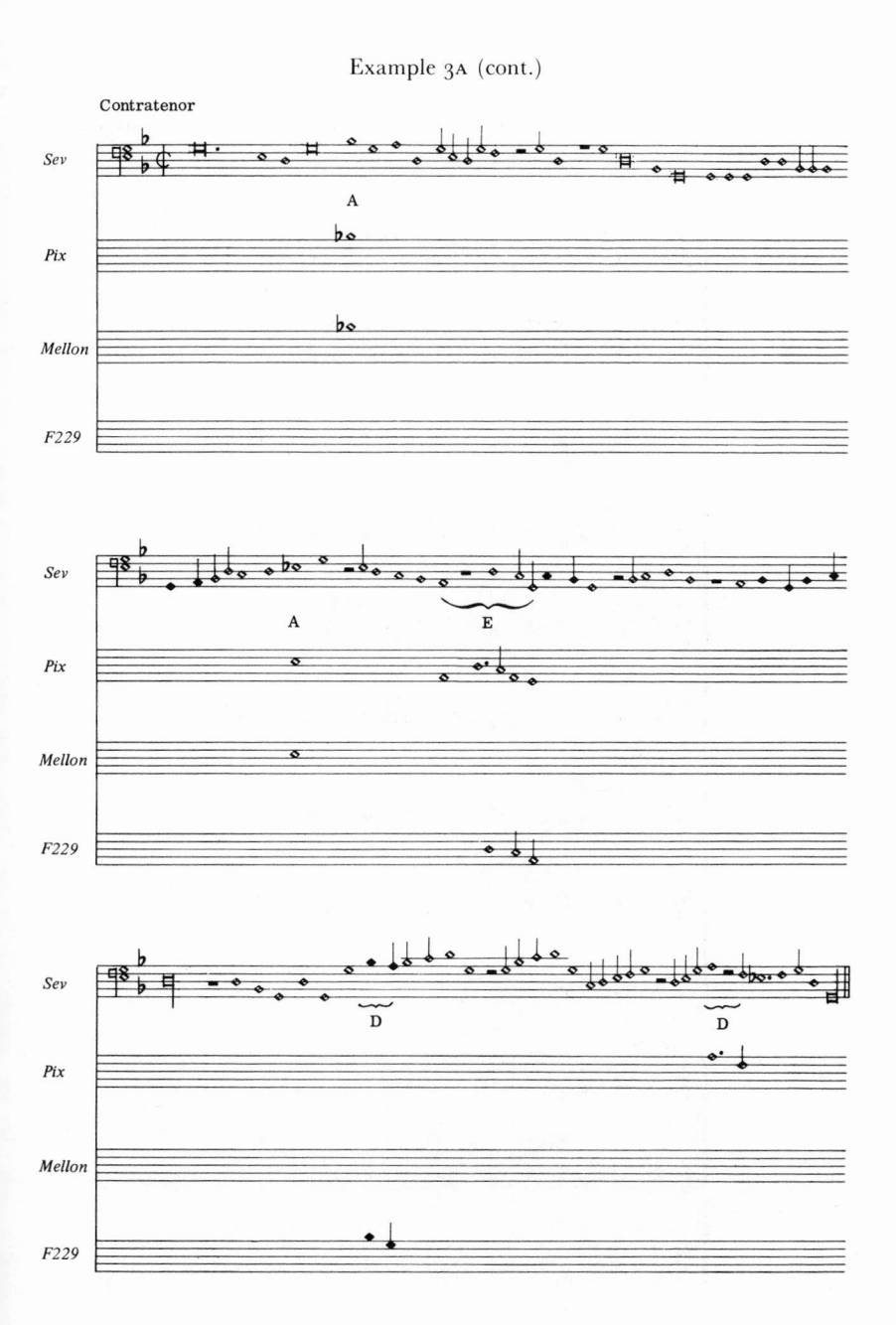

Example 3 (cont.)

B. Passage (marked E in Ex. 3A) where *Sev* (superius) and *Pix* appear to have a different origin from that of the other two sources

example shows the extent to which the lower voices conform to the readings of the three other surviving sources, *Pix*, *Mellon*, [37] and *F229*. The superius, however, breaks away from this close relationship, as the number of variants shows. Clearly *Mellon* and *F229* carry effectively the same version, particularly at the point shown in score, while *Sev* and *Pix* are also related. I believe that these last two had, at some recent point, a common ancestor for the superius, linked closely to an ancestor for *F229* and *Mellon*. For the lower voices, however, it would seem that *Sev* belongs with the two latter sources. The normal paleographical situation would have been for Scribe I to have copied the superius from the last sheet of a gathering of the work of Scribe II (intending to discard the relevant folio), but the evidence of the variants argues against this in the present case, once due allowance is made for the range of variants which Scribe I might have adopted.[38]

By this method, then, one can make some assessment of the extent to which a known scribe (known through sources he copied) might have adapted his exemplars. Indeed, this presents a manner of explaining the origin of some of the variants surviving today.[39]

I believe, therefore, that the three problems in stemmatic theory that are held to be peculiar to musical sources turn out to be blessings in disguise, providing the only means available for getting behind the sources to their exemplars, and allowing sources to be associated more closely, despite differences in their versions of the individual pieces concerned.

Atlas has argued that *Sev* belongs to the Neapolitan tradition,[40]

---

[37] New Haven, Yale University Library, M S 91. A detailed discussion of the source, including a facsimile, an edition and a concordance, has recently appeared: *The Mellon Chansonnier*, ed. Leeman L. Perkins and Howard Garey (New Haven, 1979). I am grateful to Professor Perkins for allowing me to read parts of his text in advance of its publication.

[38] Even if one wished to postulate that the superius had been copied by Scribe I from the work of Scribe II, it is significant that the variants – once allowance is made for the scribe's habits – do not step beyond the limits of the readings of *Pix*. The evidence at point *E* argues against I copying from II. As a result, there is a suggestion of two lines of movement for this chanson from the Neapolitan orbit to the Florentine – a not unlikely situation.

[39] This is only possible *because* our sources have been copied from more than one exemplar. That this is not unique to music has already been mentioned, and studies in other fields are of some value in discussing the detailed ramifications of the technique: see note 5, above.

[40] Bibliography 44, p. 257. He adds, in a footnote, that 'Naples must be favored on

basing his case on a series of individual stemmatic studies and on the statistical basis of counting up 'significant' agreements and dis-agreements. This ignores the fact that the manuscript (apart from being written by three hands over a period of time) is necessarily constructed from several distinct and lost sources, not all of which need have had the same place of origin. Indeed, even a simple analysis of the readings in *Sev* shows that some layers lie much closer to the Florentine than to the Neapolitan tradition. Further, the study of scribal habit outlined above provides a much clearer, albeit more detailed, picture of the sources of the music for the chansonnier, and one that is in closer accord with the paleographical structure.

Atlas's conclusion is based on five cases of 'significant disagree-ment' with his own Florentine source, as opposed to only two cases of agreement, both the work of Scribe I. However, even in the case of a manuscript copied entirely within one group of sources, one should hope to find some evidence of different origins for some of the music, and a re-examination of the variants here in the light of what we can deduce about scribal behaviour shows clearly that such a conclusion is too simple. In the present case, the conclusions suggest that Scribes II and III were certainly working within the tradition of Neapolitan readings, but that Scribe I copied from sources that had Florentine bases for their versions. In each case, there is some evidence of the different fascicles in each of these layers, although it is not sufficient to reach any firm conclusions.[41]

It is not possible to say, of course, that any of these readings were certainly copied from a source prepared in either Florence or Naples. For one thing, no extant chansonnier shows evidence of having been largely copied from any other surviving sources; and, for another, the pattern of transmission of many of the chansons found in Neapolitan sources requires that they were carried from Naples to Florence at some stage in their history, alongside others found in Florentine sources but without relation to Neapolitan sources.[42] *Sev*

the grounds that SevP is bound mainly in sexterns'. However, it is noteworthy that only one gathering initiated by Scribe I is not in quinterns.

I propose to use the words 'Neapolitan' and 'Florentine' in much the same sense as does Atlas, to refer to the group of sources that he has shown, in each case, to be related to each other and associated with the cities in question.

[41] The most clear-cut case is gathering *h*, mentioned above.

[42] Atlas, Bibliography 44, p. 258, remarks that the earlier Florentine group 'betrays some traces of Neapolitan influence with respect to its repertoire and its readings'.

seems to lie, as far as Scribes II and III are concerned, at a strategic point in this northward movement, in so far as much of their work shows clear influences of the Neapolitan sources, and seems to lie in a line from them to the Florentine. A stemma for many of these chansons would show *Sev* lying after those in the Neapolitan repertoire and alongside or before the earliest of the Florentine.

The work of Scribe I does not fit into this pattern: stemmata for his pieces typically show *Sev* closer to Florentine versions, on the same branch or even later than them, in readings if not in time.[43] A simple example will show this in practice: Caron's *O vie fortune*, copied by Scribe I in *Sev*, also appears in *Pix, F229* and *C.G.XIII.27*.[44] This piece is discussed by Atlas, who regards it (as far as the present sources are concerned) as surviving in two sub-traditions, citing five places of variation (shown in Example 4).[45] Each of these, except one, fulfils the pattern of scribal activity that I have outlined: thus the first two cadences are simpler in *Sev*, while the last is more ornate, and the bass figuration (Example 4D) represents the filling-in of a leap of a fifth. The case of the tenor variant is slightly more interesting, though it is not conclusive. As Example 4 shows, it is *Sev* which

He particularly mentions *Pix*, which he associates with the Neapolitan group, in part (I suspect) because of its place as sometimes 'earlier' and sometimes 'later' than *Sev* in its readings. The tacit assumption that sources are homogeneous has here led him into a more complex position than necessary with regard to *Pix*. Although it does indeed often stand close to Neapolitan versions, the situation is not difficult to understand when it is perceived that those *Sev* versions that seem to lie later than *Pix*'s readings are mostly the work of Scribe I.

[43] I believe that there was, in fact, a material lapse of time between the work of Scribes II and III on the one hand, and that of Scribe I on the other.

[44] Rome, Biblioteca Apostolica Vaticana, MS Cappella Giulia XIII.27. A study of the manuscript and its contents, with an inventory and partial edition, has been made by Allan Atlas (Bibliography 44 below). The chanson *O vie fortune* appears in the three sources as follows: *Sev*, fols. c9v–10, *Vive fortune; Pix*, fols. 78v–79; *F229*, fols. 74v–73; *C.G.XIII.27*, fols. 113v–114.

[45] The chanson also survives in Rome, Biblioteca Casanatense, MS 2856 (*Cas2856*), fols. 15v–16, and in Berlin, Staatsbibliothek Preussischer Kulturbesitz, Mus. MS 40098 (the Glogauer Liederbuch). Atlas, Bibliography 44, pp. 228–9, regards these as a separate sub-tradition, a third branch of the family. For *Cas2856*, see José Llorens, 'El Códice Casanatense 2.856 identificado como el Cancionero do Isabelle d'Este (Ferrara), esposa de Francesco Gonzaga (Mantua)', *Anuario Musical*, 20 (1965), pp. 161–78, and Arthur Wolff, 'The Chansonnier Biblioteca Casanatense 2856: Its History, Purpose and Music', Ph.D. diss., North Texas State University, 1970. An inventory and partial edition of the Glogauer Liederbuch, the work of Herbert Ringmann, appeared as vols. 4 and 8 of *Das Erbe deutscher Musik*, erste Reihe.

Example 4. Each brace gives the version in *Sev* above that in Florentine sources

A. Superius, bars 18–21
B. Superius, bars 31–3
C. Superius, bars 45–7
D. Contratenor, bars 33–5
E. Tenor, bars 21–3 (followed by the point in the other voices)

follows the imitated entry in the other voices: either Scribe I is correct and the others wrong, or, as an editing copyist, he noticed the imitation and adapted the tenor.

It is clear, therefore, that these variants do nothing to remove the piece from the Florentine sub-family: indeed, as I have suggested, they bring it nearer. In this case there is not enough evidence to show whether *Sev* was copied from a Florentine version or vice versa, although it seems possible that in other cases the source for *Sev* was from the Florentine orbit.[46] Thus scribal habit, once discovered, can reform our view of the nature, origin and function of variants, and can adapt our detailed construction of a stemma.

One other point is worth making about this chansonnier, which seems to lie in an important position in the whole Italian tradition. Atlas, in his study, drew attention to a north Italian group,[47] and the present source has frequent very close associations with the (later) readings preserved in these sources. Any analysis of the north Italian sources will come up with two lines of transmission, one coming from beyond the Alps (in the absence of related sources from Italy) and the other from further south, combining the Florentine and Neapolitan patterns in complex ways. This latter transmission seems to be intimately connected with the readings of a number of chansons in *Sev*, and furthermore of chansons drawn from the work of all the scribes. These readings (though not necessarily the source itself) seem to stand at a crucial point: they appear to represent the versions of the chansons that were transmitted up through Italy from wherever *Sev* was copied (and thus indirectly from their Neapolitan and Florentine forebears) towards the layers of north Italian sources that do not appear to have transalpine origins.[48] In this connection, it is of interest to remember that *Sev*, whose genesis is not known, first appears in public in 1515 in Rome.[49]

[46] Few of the adjacent chansons in *Sev* have more than a single concordance. Those that do have other sources tend to be related to the Florentine group of sources, and the readings also tend to follow their versions.

[47] The sources for this group are listed in Bibliography 44, p. 258.

[48] This pattern again could not be apparent so long as one is concerned merely to place sources in groups, rather than to attempt stemmata for each individual piece. The stemmatic pattern for chansons of this period is complicated – in point of fact, it is one of the few musical repertoires where I am prepared to accept the possibility of conflation – yet it is only through such stemmata that we will make sense of the position of the individual source.

[49] It was bought by Colon in Rome in 1515, according to his catalogue. See Plamenac, *op. cit.*, pp. 502–5.

BRIEF BIBLIOGRAPHY ON STEMMATIC THEORY

For a note on the coverage of and omissions from this bibliography, see note 1 on p. 319, above.

A. NON-MUSICAL STUDIES

1 Barbi, Michele. *La nuova filologia e l'edizione dei nostri scrittori da Dante al Manzoni*, 2nd edn. Florence: Sansoni, 1973.

   Has a valuable preface, stressing the rigidity of Maas and the unsatisfactory nature of Bédier. Touches on sources with multiple exemplars.

2 Bédier, Joseph. *Le lai de l'Ombre par Jean Renart*. Paris: Société des Anciens Textes Françaises, 1913; repr. 1966.

   States his position in favour of the use of a 'best text' for editing, because the pattern of variants made several stemmata equally feasible.

3 Bédier, Joseph. 'La tradition manuscript du *Lai de l'Ombre*: réflexions sur l'art d'éditer les anciens textes', *Romania*, 54 (1928), pp. 161–96 and 321–56; repr. 1970.

   A full exposition of his 'best-text' position, a discussion of the problem of two-branched stemmata, and a response to criticism.

4 Bévenot, Maurice. *The Tradition of Manuscripts: A Study in the Transmission of St Cyprian's Treatises*. Oxford: Clarendon, 1961.

   Discusses a situation involving a great deal of conflation, and in which copies are prepared from more than one exemplar. An excellent closely reasoned demonstration.

5 Böhler, W. 'Gibt es einen gemeinsame Archetypus der beiden Über-lieferungsstränge um Tertullians Apologeticum?', *Philologus*, 109 (1965), pp. 121–33.

   An example of two early traditions, both apparently good enough to be considered 'authentic'.

6 Brambilla Ageno, Franca. *L'edizione critica dei testi volgari*. Medioevo e Umanesimo 22. Padua: Antenore, 1975.

   An excellent guide to present-day methods, well illustrated with demonstrations. Leans towards the Urtext approach, but does discuss the possibility of more than one authentic version and the reason for changes in sources. (See also the note to no. 26, below).

7 Brown, Arthur. 'The Transmission of the Text', *Medieval and Renaissance Studies*, ed. John Lievesay. Medieval and Renaissance Series 2. Durham, N.C.: Durham University Press, 1968, pp. 3–20.

A brief introduction to the problem. Discusses the need to evaluate the compositor or scribe before assessing variants.

8 Collomp, Paul. *La critique des textes*. Paris: Publications de la Faculté des Lettres de l'Université de Strasbourg, 1931.

Perceptive on the pervasiveness of the 'best-text' approach in editing, and on its limitations. Not good on conflation.

9 Colwell, Ernest. *Studies in Methodology in Textual Criticism of the New Testament*. New Testament Tools and Studies 9. Leiden: Brill, 1969.

An important collection of reprinted articles on many aspects of the subject, including nos. 10 and 11, below.

10 Colwell, Ernest. 'Genealogical Method: Its Achievements and Its Limitations', *Journal of Biblical Literature*, 66 (1947), pp. 109–33; repr. in 9 above, pp. 63–84.

Useful general discussion, including comment on the various statistical methods then available.

11 Colwell, Ernest. 'Scribal Habits in Early Papyri: A Study in the Corruption of the Text', *The Bible in Modern Scholarship*, ed. J. Philip Hyatt. Nashville, 1965, pp. 370–89; repr. in 9 above, pp. 106–24, as 'Method in Evaluating Scribal Habits'.

Excellent in its manner of differentiating scribal habit and failings. Implies the connection with the stemma through assessing readings.

12 Dain, A. *Les manuscrits*. Collection d'Etudes Anciennes. Paris: Société d'Edition 'Les belles-lettres', 2nd edn, 1964.

Presents (pp.40–55) a classic statement of the copying process.

13 Dearing, Vinton. *Principles and Practice of Textual Analysis*. Berkeley: University of California Press, 1974.

Not primarily concerned with stemmatics, but an important statement of editorial method and principles.

14 Dearing, Vinton. 'Some Notes on Genealogical Methods in Textual Criticism', *Novum Testamentum*, 9 (1967), pp. 278–97.

Demonstration of the use of variants in constructing a stemma.

15 Foulet, Alfred, and Mary Speer. *On Editing Old French Texts*. Lawrence: The Regents Press of Kansas, *c.* 1979.

Contains (pp. 1–39) an excellent survey of the main positions on method, stressing their degree of effectiveness at reconstructing original and scribal versions. Discusses scribal emendation.

16 Fourquet, Jean. 'Fautes communes ou innovations communes?', *Romania*, 70 (1948), pp. 85–95.

Points out that in textual analysis faults are merely immediately perceptible changes. Argues that the presence of a tripartite stemma cannot be demonstrated beyond doubt.

17 Froger, Jean. *La critique des textes et son automisation*. Initiation aux Nouveautés de la Science 7. Paris: Dunod, 1968.
Derives his method, which uses set theory, from Quentin.

18 Greg, Walter, *The Calculus of Variants: An Essay on Textual Criticism*. Oxford: Clarendon, 1927.
Demonstrates a logical (almost statistical) technique for relating sources, using traditional methods.

19 Griffith, John. 'A Taxonomic Study of the Manuscript Tradition of Juvenal', *Museum Helveticum*, 25 (1968), pp. 101–38.
Uses statistical methods in assessing and weighing variants.

20 Hill, Archibald. 'Some Postulates for Distributional Study of Texts', *Studies in Bibliography*, 3 (1950–1), pp. 63–95.
Argues that the contents of a source reflect its origin and its associations. Produces families of sources, without internal arrangement.

21 Hill, T. 'Spelling and the Bibliographer', *The Library*, 5th ser., vol. 18 (1963), pp. 1–20.
A straightforward statement of the importance of 'accidentals' and 'non-significant' variants for source studies.

22 Housman, Alfred. 'The Application of Thought to Textual Criticism', *Proceedings of the Classical Association*, 18 (1921), pp. 67–84; repr. in *Art and Error: Modern Textual Editing*, ed. Ronald Gottesman and Scott Bennett (London: Methuen, 1970), pp. 1–16, and in *The Classical Papers of A. E. Housman*, 3 vols., ed. J. Diggle and F. R. D. Goodyear (Cambridge, 1972), III, pp. 1058–69.
A brilliant discussion of the nature of error in sources and of its detection.

23 Irigoin, Jean. 'Stemma bifides et états des manuscrits', *Revue de Philologie*, 80 (1954), pp. 211–17.
Discusses the implications of alterations in sources.

24 Kane, George. *Piers Plowman: The A Version* . . . London: Athlone, 1960.
Discusses (pp. 53–173) the limitations of a study of variants as a method for producing a recension of the readings, and the benefits of a study of scribal behaviour.

25 Kennedy, Elspeth. 'The Scribe as Editor', *Mélanges de langue et de littérature du moyen age et de la renaissance, offerts à Jean Frappier*. Geneva: Droz, 1970, I, pp. 523–31.

26 Kleinhenz, Christopher (ed.). *Medieval Manuscripts and Textual Criticism*. University of North Carolina at Chapel Hill, Department of Romance Languages, Symposia 4. Chapel Hill, 1976.
Contains several useful articles on method, some reprinted from elsewhere. A review of the collection, by Mary Speer, appears as

'In Defence of Philology: Two New Guides to Textual Criticism', *Romance Philology*, 32 (1979), pp. 335–44, discussing it with no. 6, above.

27 Maas, Paul. *Textual Criticism*. Transl. Barbara Flower from the 3rd edn, 1957, of *Textkritik*. Oxford: Clarendon, 1958.

A straightforward statement of Classical techniques, which avoids any discussion of conflation. Now rather dated.

28 Manly, John, and Edith Rickert. *The Text of the Canterbury Tales: Studies on the Basis of All Known Manuscripts*, 8 vols. Chicago: University of Chicago Press, 1940.

Vol. II is concerned with 'Classification of the manuscripts'.

29 Metzger, Bruce. *The Text of the New Testament: Its Transmission, Corruption and Restoration*. Oxford: Clarendon, 1964; 2nd edn, 1968.

Part III contains a good discussion of techniques and of reasons for deliberate and accidental changes in readings.

30 Pasquali, Giorgio. *Storia della tradizione e critica del testo*, 2nd edn. Florence: Le Monnier, 1952; repr. Florence: Mondadori, 1974.

A standard work, complementing, supplementing and updating Maas. It includes both conflation and the postulation *recentiores non deteriores*.

31 Quentin, Henri. *Essaie de critique textuelle (ecdotique)*. Paris: Picard, 1926.

Response to attacks on no. 32, below, and a modification and clarification of his theory.

32 Quentin, Henri. *Mémoire sur l'établissement du texte de la Vulgate*. Rome: Desclée, 1922.

Replaced the concept of 'error' with that of 'variant'. Attempted to develop a statistical method of comparing variants and of assessing the degree of agreement between sources, to avoid subjective decisions. Compared sources in groups of three. Generally the method has not been widely accepted outside France.

33 Rand, E. K. 'Dom Quentin's Memoir on the Text of the Vulgate', *Harvard Theological Review*, 17 (1924), pp. 197–264.

A valuable critique of no. 32, above.

34 Severs, J. Burke. 'Quentin's Theory of Textual Criticism', *English Institute Annual, 1941* (1942), pp. 65–93.

Covers Quentin's modified version, and other views. Perceptive.

35 Streeter, Burnett. *The Four Gospels: A Study of Origins*. New York: Macmillan, 1924.

Important discussions of the theory of local texts and of the reasons for change in readings.

36 Thorpe, James. *Principles of Textual Criticism*. San Marino: The Huntington Library, 1972.

343

Thorpe is a 'best-text' man, although he allows considerable freedom of emendation from other sources.

37 Timpanaro, Sebastiano. 'Ancora su stemmi bipartiti e contaminazione', *Maia*, 17 (1965), pp. 392–9.

Demonstration of the problems inherent in two-branched stemmata.

38 Timpanaro, Sebastiano. *La genesi del metodo del Lachmann*. Bibliotechina del Saggiatore 18. Florence: Le Monnier, 1963.

39 Vinaver, Eugène. 'Principles of Textual Emendation', *Studies in French Language and Medieval Literature Presented to Professor Mildred K. Pope*. Manchester: Manchester University Press, 1939, pp. 351–60; repr. in no. 26, above, pp. 139–66.

Important discussion of scribal process and habits of change.

40 West, Martin. *Textual Criticism and Editorial Technique Applied to Greek and Latin Texts*. Stuttgart: Teubner, 1973.

Intended as a replacement for no. 27, above, though adopting a rather different approach. Good discussions of emendation and of open recensions.

41 Whitehead, Frederick. 'The Textual Criticism of the *Chanson de Roland*: An Historical Review', *Studies in Medieval French Presented to Alfred Ewert in Honour of His Seventieth Birthday*. Oxford: Clarendon, 1961, pp. 76–89.

Discussion of the special circumstances in which Bédier's method can work satisfactorily.

42 Willis, James. *Latin Textual Criticism*. Illinois Studies in Language and Literature 61. Urbana: University of Illinois Press, 1972.

Principally concerned with types of scribal error and change.

43 Zuntz, G. 'A Textual Criticism of Some Passages of the Acts of the Apostles', *Classica et Mediaevalia*, 3 (1940), pp. 20–46.

Shows that the more widespread contamination is, the less likely is it that an early reading can have been lost.

B. MUSIC

44 Atlas, Allan. *The Cappella Giulia Chansonnier (Rome, Biblioteca Apostolica Vaticana, C.G.XIII.27)*, 2 vols., Musicological Studies 27. Brooklyn: The Institute of Medieval Music, [1975–6].

Uses Classical processes to group sources for each piece into families, and then to group whole sources. Tends to relate dates of readings to dates of sources, and to regard sources as homogeneous.

45 Van Benthem, Jaap. 'Die chanson *Entré je suis* à 4 von Josquin des Prez

und ihre Überlieferung', *Tijdschrift der Vereeniging voor Nederlandsche Muziekgeschiedenis*, 21 (1968–70), pp. 203–10.

Discusses readings and variants, with a commitment to the search for an authentic version.

46 Blackburn, Bonnie. 'Josquin's Chansons: Ignored and Lost Sources', *Journal of the American Musicological Society*, 29 (1976), pp. 30–76.

Discusses scribal habit. Plays down the significance of the contrafactum in understanding the relationship of sources.

47 Boorman, Stanley. 'Petrucci's Type-Setters and the Process of Stemmatics', to be published in the proceedings of the Kolloquium über Formen und Probleme der Überlieferung mehrstimmiger Musik im Zeitalter Josquins Desprez, Wolfenbüttel, 1976.

Demonstrates how the habits of individual type-setters can be deduced, and how that helps in the construction of a stemma.

48 Cook, James. 'Manuscript Transmission of Thirteenth-Century Motets'. Ph.D. diss., University of Texas, 1978.

Straightforward introduction to his method. Many of the stemmata are weak, particularly through confusing the dates of sources and of readings.

49 Dömling, Wolfgang. 'Zur Überlieferung der musikalischen Werke Guillaume de Machauts', *Die Musikforschung*, 22 (1969), pp. 189–95.

Discusses the diverse transmission patterns of individual pieces.

50 Fellin, Eugene. 'The Notation-Types of Trecento Music', *L'Ars nova italiana del Trecento*, IV, ed. Agostino Ziino. Certaldo: Edizioni Centro di Studi sull'Ars Nova Italiana del Trecento, 1978, pp. 211–23.

Gives examples of changes in notation, suggesting that they are the result of deliberate scribal change.

51 *Le Graduel Romain, édition critique par les moines de Solesmes*, IV: *Le texte neumatique* (vol. I, Le groupement des manuscrits; vol. II, Les relations généalogiques des manuscrits). Solesmes: Abbaye Saint-Pierre de Solesmes, [1960] and 1962.

A large-scale attempt at relating sources by content.

52 Hoffmann-Erbrecht, Lothar. 'Problems in the Interdependence of Josquin Sources', *Josquin des Prez*, ed. Edward E. Lowinsky and Bonnie J. Blackburn. London: Oxford University Press, 1976, pp. 285–93.

Takes an authoritarian line, based heavily on the work of Maas, to evaluating readings and relating sources.

53 Hughes, David. 'Further Notes on the Grouping of Aquitanian Tropers', *Journal of the American Musicological Society*, 19 (1966), pp. 3–12.

Relates sources by the number and order of items they have in common, and argues that a study of variants would not assist in grouping them.

54 Hughes, David. 'The Sources of *Christus manens*', *Aspects of Medieval and Renaissance Music*, ed. Jan LaRue. London: Oxford University Press, 1967, pp. 423–34.
   Discusses methods for building a stemma.

55 Karp, Theodore. 'The Trouvère MS Tradition', *The Twenty-Fifth Anniversary Festschrift (1937–1962): Queens College of the City University of New York Department of Music*. New York: Queens College, 1964, pp. 25–52.
   Uses both single pieces and groups of them to build families of sources.

56 Mendel, Arthur. [Comments in] 'Problems in Editing the Music of Josquin des Prez: A Critique of the First Edition and Proposals for the Second Edition', *Josquin des Prez*, ed. Edward E. Lowinsky and Bonnie J. Blackburn. London: Oxford University Press, 1976, pp. 723–30.
   A rare musical discussion of *recentiores non deteriores*.

57 Mužík, František. *Úvod do kritiky hudebního zápisu*. Acta Universitatis Carolinae, Philosophica et Historica 3. Prague: Universita Karlova, 1961. (English summary, pp. 97–100.)
   A demonstration of traditional procedures of textual criticism, including discussion of lost exemplars. Attempts to ascertain which version is closest to the original.

58 Räkel, Hans-Herbert. *Die musikalische Erscheinungsform der Trouvèrepoesie*. Publikationen der Schweizerischen Musikforschenden Gesellschaft, ser. 2, vol. 27. Bonn: Haupt, 1977.
   Arranges the sources in families, placing stress on the significance of contrafacta.

59 Weiss, Günther. 'Zum Problem der Gruppierung südfranzösischer Tropars', *Archiv für Musikwissenschaft*, 12 (1964), pp. 163–71.
   Groups sources on the basis of different musical settings of the same texts.

60 van der Werf, Hendrik. *The Chansons of the Troubadours and Trouvères*. Utrecht: Oosthoek, 1972.
   Discusses (pp. 26–34) problems of sources within a partly oral tradition. Accepts that scribes could make performance changes to the text unconsciously.

16

THE TRANSMISSION OF MEDIEVAL CHANT

ALEJANDRO ENRIQUE PLANCHART

THIS paper is intended essentially as a complement to that presented by Professor Bent, and thus, rather than dealing with methodological matters, it concentrates on presenting some areas where the transmission of chant differs from that of medieval or Renaissance polyphony. Many of these differences are a consequence of fundamental differences in the nature of the repertories themselves. The most obvious is that chant has nothing comparable to the vertical relationships between the parts of a polyphonic work, which often serve as a stylistic guide that permits one to ferret out certain kinds of corruption in the transmission process. Similarly, the rhythmic dislocation of a melody, which in polyphony would automatically result in stylistically unacceptable harmonic sonorities, would remain virtually untraceable in those chant repertories that survive in some form of rhythmic notation. In fact, except in very few cases it would be difficult to detect what could be called 'wrong notes' in any piece of chant,[1] since the number of stylistically plausible variants is far

---

[1] Even the seemingly obvious cases of the wholesale transposition of a phrase of chant cannot be considered as stylistically out of the question in late-medieval chant, since many of the sequences have precisely such a drastic change of ambitus in the middle verses. Occasionally in the repertory of troubadour and trouvère melodies we do encounter a case of apparent transposition that seems to destroy the modal coherence of the melody, as in the well-known case of *A l'entrada del tens clar*, where the second half of the melody was apparently copied one note too low – a suggestion that is given force by the presence of the melody without the transposed ending as a tenor of the Notre Dame conductus *Veris ad imperia* in Florence, Biblioteca Mediceo-Laurenziana, MS Pluteus 29.1, fol. 228v (facs. of the latter MS in *Firenze, Biblioteca Medicea-Laurenziana, Pluteo 29,1*, Publications of Mediaeval Musical Manuscripts 10–11 (Brooklyn, n.d.); facs. of the unique source of *A l'entrada*, Paris, Bibliothèque Nationale, f.fr. 20050 (see fol. 79v), in *Le chansonnier français de Saint-Germain-des-Prés*, Société des Anciens Textes Français 31 (Paris, 1892)). But even in this case Hendrik van der Werf, in *The Chansons of the*

greater at any given point in a chant melody than in a polyphonic voice.

Similarly, there is a considerable difference between chant and polyphony in the matter of literary texts. Text variants are less numerous and less crucial in the polyphonic repertory than they are in chant, and perhaps a distinction should be made not only between polyphony and chant but also between several of the chant repertories as well. In the layers that are generally called Gregorian chant, particularly in the texts and melodies used in the Mass, there is a remarkable degree of uniformity and stability in the literary texts;[2] but little of that stability appears in the later layers, particularly those of tropes, proses, prosulae, and the numerous combinations of these forms found in the sources. The same may apply to the yet uncharted territory of late votive chants and rhythmic offices.[3]

This view of the transmission of the late chant repertories is obscured and often obliterated by two pervasive elements. The first is the tendency of scribes to use a number of different exemplars for their manuscripts, often selecting, seemingly at random, pieces from here and there. The other is the equally prevalent tendency during the tenth and early eleventh centuries for scribes (or the cantors who oversaw their work) to change, recast, expand, or entirely recompose the musical and literary texts received from an exemplar. These changes, which are clearly deliberate, range from the omission of a line in a trope or sequence, its deliberate replacement by another, the dismembering of an otherwise stable group of trope verses, or the conflation of lines from different poems, to wholesale recomposition of the music for a set of tropes, or the thinly veiled parodying of the

---

Troubadours and the Trouvères (Utrecht, 1972), pp. 96–9, seems unwilling to regard the chaotic transposition of the melody as stylistically beyond the pale.

[2] The obvious reasons for the textual stability of the texts of the Mass propers are that they are for the most part scriptural, and that any monastic scribe had come to learn them through singing the office before he became a scribe. The texts of the Office chants, particularly the great responsories, which are often less scripturally based, are not so stable as those of the Mass chants. Outside the Gregorian repertory, we have either no coherent picture of the transmission, as is the case with the Ambrosian and Mozarabic rites, or so few sources as to make any attempt at a coherent picture hopeless, as is the case with the Old Roman and Old Beneventan chant repertories.

[3] Andrew Hughes is preparing a detailed study of the rhythmic offices, but nothing has yet appeared in print.

words of a received work in a completely new composition.[4] But despite this the transmission of chant, both melody and text, remains closer than does polyphony to the kinds of transformation and variants found in the transmission of literary texts, albeit presenting often insoluble problems to the construction of any plausible stemma for its sources.

The principles of manuscript filiation and classification of variants that were proposed by Paul Maas in 1927[5] were devised specifically to make possible a scientifically accurate recovery of the literature of Classical Antiquity. They have served this purpose admirably and have shown their influence also in clarifying the complex lines of transmission of the patristic and medieval literatures. For liturgical texts they have also contributed to the new studies on the evolution of the Sacramentary and the Missal. But the underlying assumption of these principles is the importance of the written text, not only in the sense that it is a text but in that it is written. The difficulty with such an assumption when dealing with the Gregorian and medieval melodies is obvious. The melodies were transmitted by oral tradition for some two hundred years before they began to be written down, and, even more important, when they began to be notated the symbols used were not as precise as the different letters that make up a word or the different words that make up a sentence. In non-diastematic chant notation there is virtually nothing that would clearly warn a scribe that something is wrong with what he has set down unless he knew the melody quite accurately by memory. This can be extended even to the writing of accurately heightened neums on an open field or on a field provided with a single line as a frame of reference.

One of the simplest and most widespread variants in the chant repertory may serve as an example, namely, the fairly systematic employment of F or C instead of E or B in certain melodic patterns – as in Example 1A and 1B. Both of these can be expressed in neumatic notation as in Example 1C.[6] It is significant that B is geographically

---

[4] See Heinrich Husmann, 'Sinn und Wesen der Tropen, Veranschaulicht an den Introitustropen des Weihnachtsfestes', *Archiv für Musikwissenschaft*, 16 (1959), pp. 135–47; Alejandro Enrique Planchart, *The Repertory of Tropes at Winchester*, 2 vols. (Princeton, 1977), I, pp. 150–3 and 207–10.

[5] *Textual Criticism*, transl. Barbara Flower (Oxford, 1958).

[6] Planchart, *Repertory*, II, pp. 253–4, gives all of the earliest sources for the Kyrie. A case could be made that version A, which could be extrapolated back to Ivrea,

Stemmatics and music sources

Example 1

restricted to sources from the East Frankish region or from the places where both the East and West Frankish traditions met (such as Paris and the northeast of France), but it cannot be traced definitely much further back than the thirteenth century because until then the East Frankish sources show neither heightening nor a staff. The question that the editor is faced with is whether, given a manuscript with cheironomic neums from the East Frankish region, he should extrapolate back the F or C of the Eastern sources. A corollary question is: Is there a way of telling when the two traditions split or which was the primary tradition? Neither question can be answered by stemmatics, and yet they are both of central importance if one wants to recover the oldest 'Gregorian' tradition.

I have chosen such a simple and well-known example as that of the 'Germanic chant dialect' because it is typical of the category of problems that do not admit a single solution. Indeed, in this case it is quite likely that the split in the tradition occurred before the advent of the earliest neumatic notation. Under such circumstances we are then limited to extrapolating back from the versions in staff notation or in heightened neums and placing the non-diastematic sources in one or another of the traditions on independent bibliographic or paleographic grounds.

Biblioteca Capitolare, MS LX, fol. 71, or Verona, Biblioteca Capitolare, MS CVII, fol. 31, is as old as or older than version B, which can be extrapolated back to Berlin, Deutsche Staatsbibliothek, MS theol. IV° 11, fol. 79, Munich, Bayerische Staatsbibliothek, Cod. lat. 14083, fol. 102, and *idem*, Cod. lat. 14322, fol. 101. In this, as in many other instances, the Vatican edition has given more weight to the German sources. (On Ivrea MS LX, cf. *Le Graduel romain*, II: *Les sources* (Solesmes, 1957), p. 54; on the Verona and Berlin sources, cf. H. Husmann, *Tropen- und Sequenzenhandschriften*, RISM B/V/1 (Munich and Duisburg, 1964), pp. 187 and 62 respectively. On the Munich MSS, see note 11 below.)

Version A: Graduale Sarisburiense, ed. Walter Howard Frere (London, 1894), plate s. Version B: *Die Graduale der St Thomaskirche zu Leipzig (14. Jahrhundert)*, ed. Peter Wagner (Leipzig, 1930–2), II, p. 190. Version C, in neums, is from St Gall, Stiftsbibliothek, MS 339, in *Paléographie musicale*, I (Solesmes, 1889), p. 26. On the geographic distribution of this and other variants of the so-called 'Germanic chant dialect', see Wagner, *Die Graduale*, II, pp. v–xxiv, and *idem*, *Einführung in die Gregorianischen Melodien*, II: *Neumenkunde* (Leipzig, 1905), pp. 280–6.

Some chants, particularly those for the Ordinary of the Mass as well as some of the sequences, sometimes present a different picture in that the distribution of the earliest sources permits a reasonable guess as to their place of origin, either in the East or the West, and so it is possible, faced with the variant described above, to assume the primacy of one or another of the versions. This is precisely what the monks of Solesmes have done in the case of the relatively late *Kyrie Lux et origo*, whose earliest sources are East French and German, and which in the Vatican edition begins on G-A-C, even though the earliest readable versions of the melody, all from the West and Italy, read G-A-B.

A further category of problems that does not always admit clear stemmatic solutions is posed by the literary texts and their contexts. As noted above, the chant repertories show a wide divergence in the nature of their text transmission, from the relatively stable texts of the Gradual to the bewildering variety of the tropers. But even within the Gradual there are a number of important variants that may or may not be the result of transmission. The order of the pieces, particularly in the series of Sundays after Pentecost, the Masses of Easter week, and several other segments, was dependent in a large number of cases upon matters of local liturgical usage. It is quite possible that a scribe copying from a book that did not conform to the local custom would have altered what he copied as necessary. This is all the more possible since the texts of the Mass propers, because they are psalmodic, and because of their constant repetition throughout years of attending and singing the liturgy, were completely familar to the scribe, who could then devote most of his concentration to the reordering of the Masses demanded by local custom. In the trope collections the possibilities for reordering and transposition of pieces from one liturgy to another are even wider, and the instability of the repertory itself may reflect the lack of an old tradition sanctioned by Papal legend and Imperial authority. This instability of the repertory served as a further spur to the liberties that cantors and scribes felt they could take with the received versions of both the melodies and the texts of the tropes.

At this point it may be well to call attention to a specific problem of transmission that the trope collections seem to have in common with the polyphonic anthologies of the later middle ages and the early Renaissance, namely that, as David Hughes has pointed out, 'Not one of the extant tropers served directly and consistently as a model for any of the others. In short, all extant sources are terminal.'[7] The major trope collections are by now well known, and in many instances there is independent evidence – liturgical, calendric, and bibliographic – that permits the establishment of a chronology for most of them as well as locating them geographically with a fair degree of exactitude. Günther Weiss, Hughes,[8] and several other scholars have grouped them in a number of families, the most obvious of which are:

(1) The Aquitanian Tropers, including as a subgroup those produced at the Abbey of St Martial de Limoges. This subgroup includes Paris, BN, lat. 1240, 1834, 1120, 1121, 909, 1119, and parts of 1084.[9]

(2) The St Gall Tropers, including a subgroup formed by St Gall 381 and 484, two manuscripts that show an unusual number of common features.[10]

(3) The St Emmeram Tropers, Munich, clm. 14083, 14322.[11]

(4) The Nonantolan Tropers, Bologna, BU 2824, Rome, BC 1741, and BN 1343.[12]

(5) The Winchester Tropers, Cambridge, CC 473, and Oxford, Bodley 775.[13]

---

[7] David G. Hughes, 'Further Notes on the Grouping of the Aquitanian Tropers', *Journal of the American Musicological Society*, 19 (1966), pp. 163–71.

[8] Günther Weiss, 'Zum Problem der Gruppierung südfranzösischer Tropare', *Archiv für Musikwissenschaft*, 19 (1964), pp. 163–71, and Hughes, *op. cit.*

[9] Paris, Bibliothèque Nationale, MS lat. 1240: cf. RISM B/v/I, p. 137. *Idem*, MS lat. 1834: cf. J. A. Emerson, 'Fragments of a Troper from Saint-Martial de Limoges', *Scriptorium*, 16 (1962), pp. 369–72. *Idem*, MS lat. 1120: RISM B/v/I, p. 128. *Idem*, MS lat. 1121: RISM B/v/I, p. 130; tropes transcribed in P. Evans, *The Early Trope Repertory of Saint Martial de Limoges* (Princeton, 1970). *Idem*, MS lat. 909: RISM B/v/I, p. 118. *Idem*, MS lat. 1119: RISM B/v/I, p. 126. *Idem*, MS lat. 1084: RISM B/v/I, p. 120.

[10] St Gall, Stiftsbibliothek, MSS 381 and 484: cf. RISM B/v/I, pp. 42 and 47 respectively.

[11] Munich, Bayerische Staatsbibliothek, Cod. lat. 14083 and Cod. lat. 14322: cf. RISM B/v/I, pp. 74 and 78 respectively.

[12] Bologna, Biblioteca Universitaria, MS 2824: RISM B/v/I, p. 170. Rome, Biblioteca Casanatense, MS 1741 (C.IV.2): RISM B/v/I, p. 182, facs. in G. Vecchi, *Troparium Sequentiarium Nonantulanum*, Monumenta Lyrica Medii Aevi Italica, I: Latina, i (Rome, 1955). Rome, Biblioteca Nazionale, MS 1343 (Sessorianus 62): RISM B/v/I, p. 185; H. Pfaff, *Die Tropen und Sequenzen der Hs. Rom, Naz. 1343* (diss., Munich, 1948).

[13] Cambridge, Corpus Christi College, Library, MS 473: RISM B/v/I, p. 150.

(6) The Nevers Tropers, Paris, BN lat. 9449 and n. a. lat. 1235.[14]

(7) The Beneventan Graduals, Benevento, Biblioteca Capitolare, VI.34, 35, 38, 39, and 40.[15]

In an earlier study I offered a detailed analysis of the trope fascicles of Cambridge, CC 473, and Oxford, Bodley 775, in order to show how both manuscripts went back to an exemplar copied between 978 and 986. Bodley 775 seems to be an atypically faithful copy of that exemplar to the point of transmitting the wrong date for the feast of the Dedication of the Church, while CC 473 appears as the more usual copy in the sense that it is a selective copy of the exemplar with a considerable number of revisions, additions and deletions to the material contained in the model. The only element that made CC 473 exceptional in this case was the extreme care and planning that the additions and revisions of the model show.[16]

There may be, however, an instance of two tropers that can be shown to be directly related – or, rather, as directly related as we can find two tropers to be. These are Paris, BN lat. 1120 and lat. 1121. The trope fascicles of BN lat. 1121 contain not a single piece not present in BN lat. 1120, except in the Christmas series where the older manuscript is now missing several folios. Paul Evans has also pointed out some small details that indicate that BN lat. 1121 was indeed copied from BN lat. 1120, the most striking of which concerns the trope *Expurgans populos* for Easter Tuesday. In BN lat. 1120 the large decorated initial at the start of the text includes not only the 'E' but also the 'x' of 'Expurgans'. The scribe of BN lat. 1121 thus copied simply what he saw as normal text, i.e. 'purgans'. The copyist who supplied the capitals for BN lat. 1121 did the work on his own and failed to notice the absence of the 'x', so that the first word in BN lat. 1121 now reads 'Epurgans'.[17]

But even if BN lat. 1120 was the basic exemplar for the trope fascicles of BN lat. 1121, the later source is only a selective copy of

Oxford, Bodleian Library, MS Bodley 775: RISM B/v/I, p. 158. Complete edn of tropes in Planchart, *Repertory*, II; inventories *ibid.*, II, pp. 1–10 and 11–20 respectively; cf. A. Holschneider, *Die Organa von Winchester* (Hildesheim, 1968), pp. 14–27.

[14] Paris, Bibliothèque Nationale, MS lat. 9449: RISM B/v/I, p. 140. *Idem*, nouv.acq.lat. 1235: *Le Graduel romain*, II, p. 111.

[15] See *Le Graduel romain*, II, pp. 32–3; introductions to *Paléographie musicale*, XIV and XV (1931 and 1953). Facs. of MS VI.34 in *ibid.*, XV.

[16] Planchart, *Repertory*, I, pp. 78–125.

[17] Evans, *Early Trope Repertory*, p. 48.

the exemplar, and one done by two and possibly three scribes working on the same material who apparently collated this material with other manuscripts. The entire process of the production of the trope fascicles of B N lat. 1120 and 1121 may be described as follows. The trope fascicles of B N lat. 1120 seem to be a copy of an exemplar (or exemplars) originating outside St Martial and possibly outside Aquitaine. The manuscript shows the work of two and possibly three scribes: Scribe I copied the text, Scribe II provided it with music in unheightened Aquitanian neums, and Scribe III (who could be the same as either I or II) copied the ornamental capitals and the rubrics. While it is reasonably clear that Scribe I used a written exemplar that he followed with some consistency, it is by no means certain that Scribes II and III did so. In a few instances B N lat. 1120 has texts that follow the north French tradition for those tropes, and invariably all of the melodies in the manuscript belong solidly not only in the Aquitanian tradition, but in what could be called the central St Martial tradition.[18] In addition, texts that were essentially foreign to the Aquitanian repertory were left for the most part without music. Scribe III needed not an exemplar, but only the small guide letters provided in the margin and his own knowledge of the liturgy in order to set down the ornamented capitals and the rubrics.

B N lat. 1121 follows lat. 1120 exactly in matters of text and melodic version, and in a large number of notational details such as specific ornaments and the use of liquescent neums – details that would be by no means self-evident to a scribe copying a different exemplar. The changes in the younger source, however, are both typical and quite telling. First of all, virtually all of the tropes left without music in B N lat. 1120 are eliminated by the text scribe of B N lat. 1121. Occasionally the scribe of B N lat. 1120 provided music for a trope that did not belong to the normal St Martial repertory, such as *Hodie regi archangelorum* (fol. 58v). The text scribe of

---

[18] Cf., for example, the case of the Introit trope *Quem creditis super astra*, published in Günther Weiss (ed.), *Introitus-Tropen*, I: *Das Repertoire der südfranzösischen Tropare des 10. und 11. Jahrhunderts*, Monumenta Monodica Medii Aevi 3 (Kassel, 1970), no. 303. The piece, which is most likely an Aquitanian trope originating *c.* 950, survives with two melodies, one in the large Aquitanian anthologies and all manuscripts from outside Aquitaine, and the other, whose earliest sources are B N lat. 1834 and B N lat. 1120, found only in the manuscripts copied at St Martial.

BN lat. 1121 thus mechanically entered the words in his copy, but the notator did not take the trouble of adding the neums. In a similar case, that of *Caelestem Christe largire* in BN lat. 1121 (fol. 37), even the notator began to enter the music for the piece before realising that it was also not part of the normal trope repertory of the abbey, whereupon he aborted the copy after the first verse. It is also likely that Scribe III of BN lat. 1121 did not have BN lat. 1120 in front of him when he executed the initials and the rubrics. Not only the mistake cited above for *Expurgans populos* but also the great variation between the two sources in the common rubrics suggest independent work by Scribe III.

All the foregoing would suggest that BN lat. 1121 is the perfect candidate for elimination as a witness at least as far as the text and the music if not the rubrics are concerned, even if the scribe did show the strange initiative of rendering the transliterated Greek tropes of BN lat. 1120 in actual Greek characters. But the music scribe of BN lat. 1121 has added a significant element to his copy of the exemplar in that his neums are carefully heightened in order to show the precise intervallic relationship between the notes. This is an element that the neumatic text of BN lat. 1120 did not really provide, and one that represents a conflation of the oral tradition with the received written text, a conflation that renders the resultant semiology more precise.

The scribe of BN lat. 1121 also added or deleted ornamental notes, mostly liquescences, to the melodies that he copied from BN lat. 1120. These do not seem to be contaminations from other written exemplars, but rather symptoms of the oral tradition, most likely influenced by the manner in which the scribe himself or the cantors at St Martial performed the pieces.[19] In this case we have a derivative source that does give us essential information about aspects of the performance of the music that are not always indicated in the exemplar.[20]

In the case of the liquescences, however, the tradition of singing such ornamental notes, tied as it was to the presence of certain final

---

[19] There is some evidence that the notators of the tropers were occasionally the cantors themselves; see Evans, *Early Trope Repertory*, p. 34, and Planchart, *Repertory*, I, pp. 32–3.

[20] Cf. M. Bent, 'Some Criteria for Establishing Relationships between Sources of Late-Medieval Polyphony', this volume, pp. 295–317.

consonants in the syllables to be sung,[21] gives an impression of consistency in a large number of sources; but in a more restricted field it should also be noted that the liquescences, particularly when they appear in conjunction with a relatively large leap, show also a considerable number of irrational variants in terms of the manuscript tradition, suggesting that in a number of cases they were not written out but yet they were sung. This is thus another case of contamination from an oral tradition interfering with our view of the filiation of the written sources, for these variants cannot be dismissed as insignificant until we understand considerably more than we do today about the performance indications in the chant manuscripts.[22]

There are also occasional 'wrong notes' in BN lat. 1121, but these can be detected only through an exhaustive comparison with all of the other Aquitanian sources. The wrong notes, however, do not seem to affect the written tradition quite as drastically as they do in, let us say, the polyphony of the fourteenth and fifteenth centuries. They may be present in BN lat. 1121, but absent in manuscripts that, like BN lat. 909, 1119, or even 1084c, may represent partial copies or derived sources based on BN lat. 1121 among other exemplars. The crux of the matter here is not that they might have been corrected in later sources, but rather that they were not even perceived as wrong notes in BN lat. 1121. A case in point occurs in the Offertory trope *Munere namque tuo Stephanum* (fol. 6v), where the neum group on the last syllable of 'munere' begins G-A-D, rather than the G-A-C found in every other source.[23] The version of later St Martial manuscripts such as BN lat. 909 and 1119 does not necessarily represent a correction. Instead I suspect that cantors, who knew the melody anyway, stared time and again at the mis-heightened dot in BN lat. 1121 and sang C nevertheless. Not until there was the fixed and continuous frame of reference of a staff did this kind of 'wrong

---

[21] This practice, although relatively widespread, is seldom found with the extreme consistency that it shows in the Beneventan Gradual–Tropers now at the Biblioteca Capitolare in Benevento.

[22] The nature and extent of the kinds of small variants found in the Aquitanian Tropers may be seen in the synoptic edition of the opening verse of *Discipulis flammas* in Weiss, *Introitus-Tropen*, pp. xxvi–xxvii, or in the edition of *Ecce dies magni meritis* in Planchart, *Repertory*, I, pp. 349–60.

[23] Evans, *Early Trope Repertory*, p. 140, tacitly corrects the pitch of the manuscript, although again it may be that the 'wrong note' was as 'invisible' to him as to the medieval cantors.

note' become perceptible enough to be perpetuated in successive copies. The same may be applied to the curiously slanted heightening found in a manuscript such as Benevento, Biblioteca Capitolare, VI.40, which, if taken literally, would suggest a gradual rise of the pitch across the line. In this source, as in several other manuscripts with open-field notation, the frame of reference will shift tacitly with each new verse of a trope, and curiously enough, the sense of when to make such an adjustment becomes extremely accurate in a very short time.

Given the present state of knowledge of the trope repertory, in terms of both its text transmission and its melodic styles, significant variants in the melodies do not occur until completely different tunes are set over the same words in two different sources; but, by the same token, a large number of seemingly superficial variants cannot yet be dismissed as insignificant, so that the problems have to be approached from two directions at once. One method is to begin separating and classifying the repertories according to the solid evidence presented by the major variants such as completely new melodies for a text, or recombinations of the text lines of a set of tropes; the other is to begin charting in a rational and easily retrievable manner the myriad of minute differences encountered when comparing virtually any two versions of a trope melody, or indeed any two versions of a considerable number of the seemingly more stable melodies of the older layers of Gregorian chant.

Work on the first of these possible ways of dealing with the problems has been carried on sporadically and piecemeal by a number of scholars. Günther Weiss was apparently the first to call attention to the tropes with multiple melodic traditions in the Aquitanian sources, and to the way in which such tropes could be used to clarify the relationships between the manuscripts.[24] David Hughes later set out to demonstrate that trope repertories and the order in which the pieces were copied within a single feast could also be used to separate these many terminal sources into related families.[25] The example that he chose to illustrate his method, the Introit tropes for the Ascension, has proved to be a singularly felicitous one on account of the existence of a source that Hughes did

---

[24] Weiss, 'Zum Problem', as well as the introduction of *Introitus-Tropen*, pp. v–xxv, provided the earliest discussion of the multiple melodic traditions of the Aquitanian repertories.   [25] Hughes, 'Further Notes', pp. 5–6.

not take into account, a fragmentary Troper from St Martial, Paris,
BN lat. 1834,[26] that comes close to being an intermediate source in
that it shows the scribe in the process of putting two traditions
together and reordering the repertory. Thus the case of the Ascension tropes may be worth examining in some detail here.

The oldest Aquitanian troper, BN lat. 1240, which shows the state
of the repertory at St Martial about 936, has only two pieces,
Terrigenis summis and *Hodie redemptor mundi*. Both pieces belong to the
oldest layers of the trope repertory and are relatively widespread
throughout Europe. *Terrigenis summis* is, if anything, older than *Hodie
redemptor*, and this may account for its position at the head of the
series despite the tendency shown time and again by scribes to place
'Hodie' tropes at the head of the series on account of the clearly
introductory nature of their texts.

The next two Aquitanian sources, neither of which stems from St
Martial, are BN lat. 1084b,[27] which shows the state of the repertory
around 950, and BN lat. 1118, a highly conflationary manuscript
that gives the repertory of *c.* 980–96. Their trope series are:

BN lat. 1084b	BN lat. 1118
	(1) *Quem creditis*
(1) *Hodie redemptor*	(2) *Hodie redemptor*
(2) *Dum patris*	(3) *Dum patris*
(3) *Terrigenis*	(4) *Terrigenis*
	(5) *Celsa potestas*
	(6) *Quem verbum*
(4) *Montis oliviferi*	(7) *Montis oliviferi*

The two additions to the series of BN lat. 1240 found in BN lat.
1084b are Aquitanian pieces that must have originated between 936
and 950. They appear only in the Aquitanian sources or in manuscripts heavily dependent upon them, Apt 18 (*Dum patris* and *Montis*)
and Vich 105 and 106 (*Montis*).[28] The three further additions found
in BN lat. 1118 present a different picture. *Quem creditis* is probably

---

[26] Described and inventoried in Emerson, 'Fragments from a Troper from Saint
Martial de Limoges', pp. 369–72 and plate 30.

[27] BN lat. 1084 contains three series of tropes: the first (fols. 39–51) I shall call
1084a; the second and principal series (fols. 53v–90) 1084b; and the third (fols.
124–142v) 1084c.

[28] Apt, Cathédrale Sainte Anne, Bibliothèque du Chapitre, MS 18: G. Björkvall,
'Les deux tropaires d'Apt', diss., Stockholm, in preparation. Vich, Biblioteca

an Aquitanian trope composed after 950, and one that achieved a
certain popularity throughout the West. *Celsa potestas* is a piece
probably imported from northern France, which may go back to the
middle of the tenth century, even though its earliest sources are all
around 990–1000. *Quem verbum* is apparently an Aquitanian trope
made relatively recently, one that did not receive a wide diffusion
even within the region.

Interestingly enough, these three pieces turn up in BN lat. 1084c,
a supplement to BN lat. 1084b that was compiled before 1000. Two
things are worth noting in the series as it appears in BN lat. 1084b
and 1118. First, in BN lat. 1084b the normal scribal tendency to
place the 'Hodie' trope at the start has caused the displacement of
Terrigenis. The insertion of a new piece between the two also suggests
that this tradition is not dependent upon that of St Martial. Secondly, the only kind of piece that could displace one of the old
'Hodie' tropes from its position at the head of a series – namely,
a large-scale piece that borrowed the prestige of the famous
Easter trope – has now appeared in BN lat. 1118 at the start of the
series.

The way these tropes were copied at St Martial is not known until
the final decade of the tenth century, when we encounter three
important sources in close succession: BN lat. 1834 and lat. 1120,
both from *c.* 990–1000, and BN lat. 1121, from *c.* 1000 or slightly
later. The trope series in these three manuscripts present an
extremely interesting picture:

BN lat. 1834	BN lat. 1120	BN lat. 1121 (909, 1119)
	(1) *Quem creditis*	(1) *Quem creditis*
(1) *Hodie redemptor*	(2) *Hodie redemptor*	(2) *Hodie redemptor*
		(3) *Dum patris*
(2) *Terrigenis*	(3) *Terrigenis*	(4) *Terrigenis*
(3)*Montis oliviferi*	(4)*Montis oliviferi*	(5) *Montis oliviferi*
(4) *Dum patris*	(5) *Dum patris*	
(1) *Quem creditis*[29]		
(2) *Celsa potestas*[30]	(6) *Celsa potestas*[31]	

Capitular, MS 105 (cx) (Ripoli no. 111; inventory no. 7614): RISM b/v/1, p. 97.
Idem, MS 106 (Ripoli no. 31; inventory no. 7613): RISM b/v/1, p. 96.
[29] Added after the Introit series with the rubric 'Isti sunt primi tropi'.
[30] Added after the Offertory and Communion tropes; copied without music.
[31] Added after the Offertory and Communion tropes; copied without music.

359

The main series of BN lat. 1834 shows what the situation probably was at St Martial around 950. It involves the reordering of the two pieces found in BN lat. 1240 and the addition of the two Aquitanian pieces of *c*. 950, although not in the same order as in BN lat. 1084. The scribe then entered (from another exemplar?) the *Quem creditis* at the end of the series and added the rubric 'Isti sunt primi tropi'. *Celsa potestas*, which could not be fitted into the space available, was then squeezed in at the end of the communion tropes.

As can be seen from the table, the series in BN lat. 1120 is simply a 'fair copy' of that in BN lat. 1834, whose rubrics have been followed; and *Quem creditis*, capitalising on its borrowed pedigree, has been given the pride of place.

BN lat. 1121, copied from BN lat. 1120, follows its readings quite exactly, but the order of the pieces has been disturbed, and the source of the disturbance is not very difficult to find. It is a source that transmits the order found in BN lat. 1084, and indeed it may well be BN lat. 1084, which must have reached St Martial around the time when BN lat. 1121 was being copied. Note, however, that none of the additions in the supplement of BN lat. 1084 was accepted into the St Martial repertory except for *Quem creditis*, which carried a cachet all of its own, and which nevertheless was only half-accepted at St Martial, for the scribes took the words but not the music. Indeed, *Quem creditis* survives with two distinct tunes, one found in the northern manuscripts and in the Aquitanian sources from centres other than St Martial, and the other restricted entirely to the St Martial manuscripts.[32]

The contamination of the sources goes both ways, however, for not only did the presence of BN lat. 1084 affect the way the scribe of BN lat. 1121 ordered a repertory that he was copying from BN lat. 1120, but BN lat. 1084 was altered here and there to make it conform with the use of St Martial. The most extensive alteration, and one readily perceivable, is the addition of a second supplement (fols. 39–51). This section, BN lat. 1084a, has often incomplete tropings with cues that refer not only to the chant being troped but to trope verses already found in BN lat. 1084b. In addition, at the start of the entire manuscript *Quem creditis* is copied in full, but this time with the St Martial melody (fol. 1).

[32] The two melodies appear in Weiss, *Introitus-Tropen*, no. 303.

The situation outside St Martial is more complex. Apt 17, a manuscript that often transmits idiosyncratic versions of the texts and unique melodies, has here a duplication of the series of BN lat. 1118 with the omission of one piece and the characteristic addition of a trope found nowhere else in the Aquitanian sources. BN n.a. 1871 also duplicates the series of BN lat. 1118, but in a manner that suggests a mid-point between BN lat. 1084b and 1084c. That is, it shows the series of BN lat. 1084b with the *Quem creditis* placed naturally at the beginning, and then the two other additions of BN lat. 1084c at the end of the series.

Finally, BN lat. 887, 779, and 903[33] reflect a different situation. They have a restricted repertory taken from one or another of the large anthologies that preceded them. BN lat. 779, copied in close proximity to St Martial, reflects the ordering of the sources from the abbey; the other two manuscripts transmit the ordering of the non-St-Martial manuscripts.

If these relationships are complex when dealing simply with the order of the repertory, they become increasingly so when one proceeds further. The case of *Celsa potestas*, the northern import into this repertory, is particularly instructive. The oldest version, which I shall call A, is a constellation of three verses that was known in England by 978 and in Italy by 1000. It has a stable tradition in both places as well as in the north of France. This version appears in Apt 17 with music, and in BN lat. 1118, 1834, and 1120 without. But this is not quite the same piece that is listed in BN lat. 1118 on p. 358 above, for version A was copied in this manuscript out of place, mixed with the tropes for the Dedication of the Church. A second version, B, consists of the first and last verses of A with two completely new verses in between. Furthermore, the first verse of A has been subjected here to an extensive revision and also has a new melody. This is the version found within the series of BN lat. 1118 and n.a. 1871, and in the second of these sources the scribe left out the music for verse two. Finally, a third version consists of B without verse two. This is what appears in BN lat 1084c and in BN lat. 903; it is also the version that the singer would have to perform if he was reading from BN n.a. 1871.

---

[33] Paris, Bibliothèque Nationale, MS lat. 887: RISM B/v/1, p. 117. *Idem*, MS lat. 779: RISM B/v/1, p. 115. *Idem*, MS lat. 903: *Le Graduel romain*, II, p. 96; facs. of fols. 1–147 (i.e. excluding tropes and proses) in *Paléographie musicale*, XIII (1925–30).

The presence of A in BN lat. 1118 does suggest that *Celsa potestas* may have reached Aquitaine through sources outside St Martial, and that the reworking of the piece took place after about 950. Its rejection from the St Martial repertory once more underscores the relatively conservative and local tradition that the abbey's sources appear to represent.

A comparison of the northern melody found in BN lat. 13252 and in the Anglo-Saxon Tropers with the version found in Aquitaine or with the rewriting of version B would have to proceed syllable by syllable and, within each syllable, neum by neum in the case of extended melismata. In the case of *Celsa potestas* there are only three versions and some fifteen sources, so the problems are more or less manageable. This is simply not the case with many of the other tropes, particularly the 'international pieces'. In my study of the Winchester Tropers I edited the opening verse of one of them from twenty-five sources. The text tradition is in this case mercifully simple, with only two major versions, but the melodic tradition is completely incoherent, with seven major variants. Thus a first investigation of the melodic tradition, if it is to include not just the major variants but also the small ornamental changes that may or may not be significant for the manuscript tradition, would have to take account of thirteen more manuscripts known to me, and possibly others that I have not yet examined such as the Kassel Tropers and the Volterra fragments.[34] In any case, a stemma has to be made for every syllable of the text or, rather, for the music above each syllable of the text, a problem compounded by one or two cases of horizontal displacement of the melody. Already at the simple level available from the synoptic edition one can see that the melodic tradition often flatly contradicts the textual one and also the relationships that it may be possible to establish between sources on independent bibliographic grounds. The only continental source that shows the same text as the English tropers, Cambrai 75,[35] has a completely different melody.

Given the practice of rewriting and recomposing the melodies and

[34] Kassel, Murhardsche Bibliothek der Stadt Kassel und Landesbibliothek, MS theol. IV° 15: *Le Graduel romain*, II, p. 42 *Idem*, MS theol. IV° 25: *Analecta hymnica*, XLVII (Leipzig, 1905), p. 23. Volterra, Biblioteca Guarnacci, MS L.3.39: RISM B/V/I, p. 187.

[35] Cambrai, Bibliothèque Municipale, MS 75 (76): *Le Graduel romain*, II, p. 39.

the texts from one centre to another, and the addition or deletion of ornaments to the chant, variants that seem to be independent of a written tradition, there is always the risk of seeing agreement where there is only coincidence or, conversely, of becoming hopelessly mired in a bog of small variants that may not indeed be significant or even signs of anything more than the local style of a given cantor.

The collation of melodic variants in these chants cannot be done properly without the help of computers. Already Jacques Froger has arrived at this conclusion regarding the chants for the Mass, and René-Jean Hesbert has published in the fifth volume of the *Corpus antiphonalium officii* the first results of a computerised concordance for the office chants. In the case of the tropes David Hughes developed a useful system of matrices to collate and detect relationships between variants, and this process is now being put into a form that can be translated into a remarkably simple computer language by Joseph Diamond. The first results of Diamond's program[36] again reveal surprising contradictions between the melodic traditions and what one would normally expect from bibliographic knowledge about when and where the manuscripts were copied.

A clear view of the manuscript traditions (perhaps filiation is simply beyond our reach in the case of chant sources) is crucial if we are going to attempt to recover the notated melodies in their earliest forms, those found in the sources written in staffless unheightened neums. At this stage I still regard the detailed study of local repertories as the most important step that needs to be taken in the field of medieval chant. It is here also that manuscript filiation can be not only useful but a possible avenue of investigation. Only when the different repertories are sufficiently well known will it be possible to see beyond them and attempt to recover the melodic substratum that may or may not underlie all of them.[37]

[36] 'Straight Talk on Cursive Neumes: The Melodic Tradition of a Family of Tenth Century Agnus Verses', unpublished paper, Harvard University, 1979. I am particularly grateful to Mr Diamond for access not only to his paper but also to the computer program and printouts that he used.

[37] For assistance in several consultations of sources and the checking of materials that were unavailable to me at the time of writing, I am most indebted to two of my students, Christine Brain and Elizabeth Sack.

17

THE PROBLEM OF CHRONOLOGY IN THE TRANSMISSION OF ORGANUM DUPLUM

Edward H. Roesner

THE repertory of organa, conducti, and incipient motets created for the most part in Paris during the second half of the twelfth century and the first decades of the thirteenth may constitute the earliest body of polyphony conceived primarily in writing. It is certainly the first to have enjoyed a stable transmission, perhaps exclusively in written form. The extant sources originated in places as diverse as the British Isles, Paris itself, and Poland, and in institutions as different in character as the secular cathedral, the mendicant house, and the royal chapel. All of the manuscripts are late; the earliest, LoA and F, were not copied before the late 1220s and the mid thirteenth century, respectively – several decades after the creation of the repertory they contain.[1] For the music of Paris those decades were not merely a time of recopying from earlier exemplars, however. The readings that have come down to us offer telling evidence that the repertory was subjected to recasting on a massive scale for perhaps the greater part of its history.

The organa dupla reveal the most striking variations from source to source, perhaps because their idiom placed fewer constraints on the *organista* than did the poetic texts and multi-voice fabric of the

---

[1] *Sigla*: Ber = Berlin, Staatsbibliothek der Stiftung Preussischer Kulturbesitz, MS lat. 4° 523; F = Florence, Biblioteca Medicea-Laurenziana, MS plut. 29.1; LoA = London, British Library, MS Egerton 2615; Mo = Montpellier, Faculté de Médecine, MS H.196; MüA = Berlin, Bibliothek Johannes Wolf, unnumbered fragment (destroyed); StV = Paris, Bibliothèque Nationale, MS lat. 15139; W_1 = Wolfenbüttel, Herzog August Bibliothek, Cod. Guelf. 628 Helmst.; W_2 = Wolfenbüttel, Cod. Guelf. 1099 Helmst. References to the organa and clausulae follow the system in Friedrich Ludwig, *Repertorium organorum recentioris et motetorum vetustissimi stili*, 2nd, complete edn, ed. Luther A. Dittmer, 2 vols. in 3 (Brooklyn, 1964–78), to which the reader is referred for bibliographical information about the works discussed in this paper.

other genres. One manuscript may provide a new setting for the repeat of a Respond or for the Gloria Patri, while another requires the singer to re-use the music of the first Respond or to underlay the doxology text to the polyphony for the Verse. Two sources may contain altogether different settings of the same plainchant, or some sections may agree while others differ. A segment of chant cast in organum purum in one source may appear in discant in another, or in a different sustained-tone setting. W_1 includes two separate collections of clausulae, and F provides six, so that the *cantores* could introduce still further changes into the music. Variations in detail are equally numerous, if not more so, and include differences in intonation and cadential figures, variations in the length of melismas and in the melodic or rhythmic profile of a line, alternative forms of notation for a melodic figure, and – less tangible – different rhythmic interpretations for the same notational design owing to changes in the musical context.

The table opposite illustrates two aspects of this state of affairs as found in the different states of *Alleluia, Veni electa mea* (M 54): large-scale variations in musical substance and variations in the cadence formulas that characteristically articulate both sustained-tone and discant clausulae. The organum is extant in W_1, F, W_2, MüA (fragmentary), and Ber (fragmentary), and is provided with seven independent clausulae in F (one each in the first cycle and the supplementary second cycle, three in the third cycle, and two in the fifth).[2] There is agreement among all extant sources of the organum at 'Alleluia' and at the beginning of the Verse, 'Veni electa', and nowhere else. These are also the only sections set in organum purum in all sources. Where sources transmit different material, W_1 and MüA tend to agree against F, W_2, and Ber. The latter group proceeds entirely in discant after the beginning of the Verse, the former in organum purum for much of the work. (It is puzzling that W_1 and

---

[2] Cf. Luther A. Dittmer, *A Central Source of Notre-Dame Polyphony* (Brooklyn, 1959), pp. 100–7. As the table indicates, this work shares material with several other organa. This larger complex of relationships is discussed in Norman E. Smith, 'Interrelationships among the Alleluias of the *Magnus liber organi*', *Journal of the American Musicological Society*, 25 (1972), pp. 179–202. For additional information on the relationships and variations among the organa, see *idem*, 'Interrelationships among the Graduals of the Magnus Liber Organi', *Acta Musicologica*, 45 (1973), pp. 73–97, and Rudolf Flotzinger, *Der Discantussatz im Magnus Liber und seiner Nachfolge* (Vienna, 1969), pp. 17–55.

Large-scale variations in Alleluia, Veni electa mea

Section	Concordance[a]	Cadential formulas[b]
'Alleluia'	W₁, F, W₂	
'Veni'	W₁, F, W₂, Ber (inc.): F–288, F–434	F: F–288, F–434: *all others
'electa'	W₁, F, W₂, Ber	W₁, F: *W₂, Ber
'mea'	W₁, MüA (inc., '-a' only survives), F–224 ('-a' portion): F, W₂, Ber, F–203: F–224 ('me-' portion): F–286	W₁, MüA, W₂, F–203: F, F–224, F–286: *Ber
'et ponam te'	W₁, MüA: F, W₂, Ber, F–203	*Ber: all others
'in thronum'	W₁, MüA (inc.):ᶜ F, W₂, Ber, F–203: F–435	W₁: MüA: F, F–203: W₂: *Ber, F–435
'meum'	W₁, MüA, Ber: F (part 1 only), W₂, Ber, F–203: F (part 2 only)	W₁: MüA, F–203: F, W₂: *Ber
'quia concupivit'	W₁, MüA: F, W₂, Ber	W₁, MüA: *F, W₂, Ber
'rex'	W₁, MüA⁴: F, W₂, Ber, F–287	W₁: MüA: F: W₂, Ber: *F–287

The setting of 'Veni' (W₁, F, W₂, Ber) = 'Herodes' (M 8 *Laus tua deus, Herodes iratus*) in W₁, F, W₂ = 'Paraclitus' (M 26 *All. Paraclitus*) in F, W₂ = 'Justi' (M 43 *All. Justi epulentur*) in F. Music from '-a' in 'mea' (W₁, MüA, F–224) recurs in '-lo-' of 'angelorum' (M 39 *All. In conspectu*) in W₁, F, W₂.
Music from 'meum' (W₁, MüA, Ber) recurs in 'viscera' (M 32 *Benedicta, Virgo dei*) in W₁ and in the setting a 3 in W₁ and F.

ᵃ Italic indicates sections in organum purum; different settings are separated by :
ᵇ The absence of a cadential formula is indicated by *.
ᶜ The MüA setting at 'in thro–' is uncertain owing to a gap in the manuscript. The surviving part agrees with W₁, but the size of the gap suggests that the setting was longer.
ᵈ At 'rex' MüA has a gap between the penultimate tenor note and the very end of the work large enough to admit another setting of this clausula.

MüA disagree only at places where a gap appears in MüA. It may be that this fragment is being interpreted incorrectly.)[3] At 'meum' Ber agrees with W_1 and MüA against F and W_2, breaking the pattern of concordance. The cadence formulas vary independently of the clausulae they articulate, with F and W_2 agreeing only once against W_1 and MüA, and once against W_1 alone. Cadence formulas appearing in the independent clausulae may or may not agree with those in the corresponding places within the organum proper. Thus, although F and F-203 are in substantial agreement, they concur in their choice of cadence formulas at 'et ponam te' and 'in thronum', but not at 'mea' or 'meum'. Although the table does not indicate it, cadence formulas may recur from clausula to clausula within the work. In F, for example, 'Veni', 'mea', 'in thronum', and 'rex' all conclude with the same formula (see below, Example 4A). Ber stands alone in providing a cadence formula only for the end of the organum as a whole.

The first – and, to date, the only – comprehensive explanation of the developments taking place in organum duplum was offered seventy years ago by Friedrich Ludwig in his *Repertorium*. Ludwig saw the states in the three major collections as standing in the chronological order W_1–F–W_2. W_1, according to Ludwig, preserves a state close to Leonin's original *magnus liber*; F transmits the activity of Perotin and his generation in all its richness; and W_2, drawn partly from the Perotinian tradition but also retaining material that Perotin had replaced, preserves the organa at the end of their life. The assumption behind this chronology is that an early style, organum purum, gave way to a later, more developed one with the emergence of the discant clausula. From the latter sprang a new genre, the motet, and the old genre of organum passed out of existence. This evolution in style involved several interrelated developments, including the shortening or elimination of sustained-tone melismas, the replacement of organum purum with discant and the replacement of 'less advanced' discant with more sophisticated, tightly structured writing, a movement away from free, open-ended, improvisatory writing to controlled, closed, composed work, and a move-

---

[3] Cf. Luther A. Dittmer, 'The Lost Fragments of a Notre Dame Manuscript in Johannes Wolf's Library', Jan La Rue *et al.* (eds.), *Aspects of Medieval and Renaissance Music: A Birthday Offering to Gustave Reese* (New York, 1966), plates 13–14 and pp. 127–8.

ment away from free rhythm to strictly measured, regularly modal patterns. The W_1 organa, which include significantly more organum purum than the texts in F and W_2, offer an early state of the repertory. Supporting this appraisal is the fact that the W_1 discant sections – and, indeed, the entire manuscript, apart from its 'more advanced' independent clausulae – have virtually no ties with the new genre of the motet. Conversely, the discant in the F and W_2 organa was frequently drawn upon by motet-composers. F, moreover, includes an important collection of early motets, and W_2 has a large repertory of clearly younger French motets. W_2, furthermore, includes few discant sections that are not found in F or W_1 as well, and it has no independent clausulae, a signal to Ludwig that the process of revision 'ist hier zum Stillstand gekommen',[4] and a confirmation of the youth of the W_2 repertory suggested by the nature of its motet collection.

It is now generally agreed that Ludwig's hypothesis is too simple. The sources do not each contain a distinct stage in an organic process of growth, development, and decline. Whatever the nature of the development that the organa underwent, each manuscript transmits a mixture of earlier and later material in combinations that are likely to vary from work to work. Clearly a process of recasting and, very probably, conflation took place that involved numbers of musicians and many centres of activity. The surviving manuscripts preserve only a sample of this work, and without exception the discovery of a new source has added new variations to those already known. Despite these reservations, however, the criteria on which Ludwig based his hypothesis are still generally accepted.[5] They remain today the principal guidelines for examining the chronological relationships among the different states of the organa, and they are applied equally to large-scale variations and to all kinds of disagreements in melodic and rhythmic detail. I suggest, however, that none of these criteria is as secure as the research based on it would imply, and that some are wholly invalid.

The presence or absence of motets, early or late, in an organum

[4] Ludwig, *Repertorium*, I/1, p. 175.

[5] Recent distinguished examples may be found in Flotzinger, *Discantussatz*; in Fritz Reckow, 'Das Organum', Wulf Arlt *et al.* (eds.), *Gattungen der Musik in Einzeldarstellungen: Gedenkschrift Leo Schrade*, 1 (Berne, 1973), pp. 434–96; and in Kenneth Levy, 'A Dominican Organum Duplum', *Journal of the American Musicological Society*, 27 (1974), pp. 203–11.

source need not concern us, since it has no bearing on the age of the organa in that manuscript. Equally insignificant, I would argue, is the aloofness of the W_1 discant sections from the motet, a situation that can be explained simply as a result of the lack of interest by the W_1 branch of the Paris tradition in the motet idiom. (Indeed, some of the W_1 discant sections show signs of being distinctly modern. A case in point is the setting of 'mea' in *Alleluia, Veni electa mea*, which uses hocket in a way that suggests the prior existence of a full-dress modal system.) I shall concentrate here on two of Ludwig's most influential criteria for determining chronology: the extent of the sustained-tone writing and the character of the rhythmic style. They will be discussed individually, but of course they are fundamentally and inextricably interrelated.

When Parisian organum passed out of existence, organum purum as a style died with it while discant lived on in the motet and a host of other genres. It does not follow from this, however, that discant grew out of organum purum, that sustained-tone writing contracted into discant, or that settings in discant were used always to replace others in organum purum. It is well known that most of the independent clausulae replace sections already in discant style. And many sections in organum purum are among the most stable in the entire repertory, as the transmission of *Alleluia, Veni electa mea* attests (the setting of 'Veni' is found in no fewer than ten redactions, with four different texts). When a section exists in organum purum in one source and in discant in another, one clausula may indeed have been introduced as a replacement for the other one, but this does not mean that the replacement was necessarily composed specifically for that purpose. The two clausulae could have been composed without reference to one another, as parts of independent organum settings of the same plainchant. Independent origin appears to account, for example, for the two states of *Descendit de caelis* (O 2), preserved in W_1 and F. The Respond is the same in both states, but the Verses are entirely different. The reason is clear: the two versions are based on different forms of the plainchant, each intended for a different service, even though the compilers of W_1 and F undoubtedly intended them to be used for the same feast. In *Alleluia, Video celos* (M 4), similarly, the discant clausula on 'Video' in F appears not to have been composed to replace the setting in organum purum in W_2, for the two are based on variant forms of the chant. They may have originated in different places, but at the very least their tenors were drawn from books that reflect different liturgical traditions.[6] Despite their presumed disparate origins, the two clausulae end with the same cadence formula – evidence that an act of conflation brought an independently conceived composition into the organum as a replacement for part of the setting. Strictly speaking, however, it is misleading to regard such clausulae as standing in a direct chronological relationship to each other.

In *Alleluia, Veni electa mea* W_1 and MüA have organum purum at 'et ponam te in thronum', while the other three sources have a discant setting. Despite their different musical substance, the two versions use the same cadence formula at 'te', the only instance of complete agreement among the five sources with regard to cadence formula in the entire organum (Example 1). This unanimity is enough to indicate that one setting replaced another, but it does not tell us which – the organum purum or the discant – was the replacement.

Example 1. Cadence formulas in 'te' in *Alleluia, Veni electa mea*

A. After W_1, fol. 41

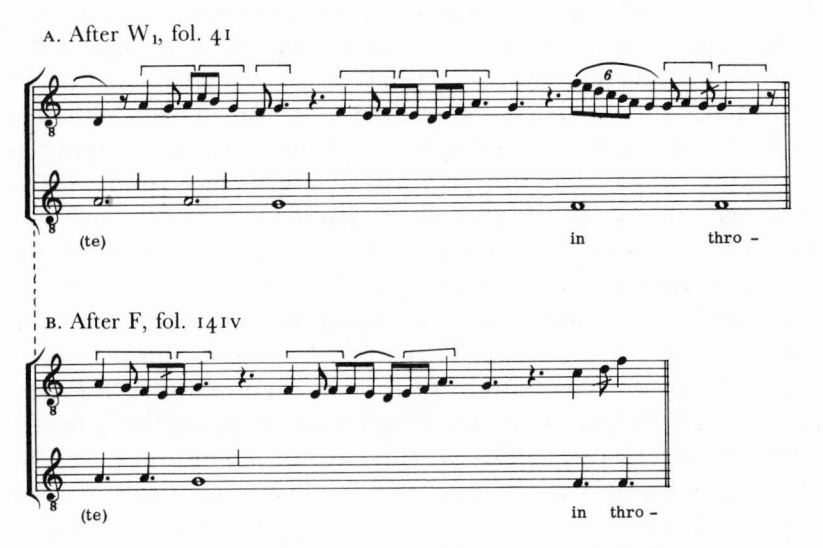

B. After F, fol. 141v

---

[6] See Norman E. Smith, 'Some Exceptional Clausulae of the Florence Manuscript', *Music and Letters*, 54 (1973), pp. 407–10, and *idem*, 'Interrelationships among the Alleluias', p. 178. Both of these cases, along with many other problems surrounding the origins of individual organa and clausulae, await clarification from a thorough study of the Parisian liturgical sources and those of related traditions.

There is evidence that the process of recomposition could have involved replacing discant with organum purum. The peripheral setting of *Propter veritatem* (M 37) appended to the W₁ *liber organi* is undoubtedly a recomposition of some form of the Parisian organum found in different states in F, W₂, and W₁ itself. This is evident from its use not of the *Propter veritatem* plainchant melody proper, but of the somewhat synthetic version of it that was apparently fashioned specifically for the Parisian setting.[7] The composer responsible for the unique version in W₁ stripped away the original – Parisian – duplum, leaving only the discant clausula on 'aurem tuam' and a few cadence formulas, and then reworked some of the Parisian melodic material while he provided new polyphony for most of the setting. In so doing he turned the section on 'veritatem', treated as a discant clausula in all Parisian versions of the organum, into a setting in organum purum.

Sustained-tone composition appears to have continued to be cultivated, not only in some peripheral organa, but also in seemingly late settings by *organistae* active at or near the centre of the tradition. F, a source with strong claims to a Parisian origin, transmits two settings of *Crucifixum in carne* (O 9), the second one found also in W₂, and the first one unique to F. The *unica* in F are often regarded as being among the youngest organa in the repertory. Their circulation in Paris during the second quarter of the thirteenth century is attested to by F, but they do not appear to have been widely disseminated, unlike the core of the Parisian repertory, probably because they came into being later than the time during which the organum tradition spread from Paris. The unique *Crucifixum in carne* organum in F uses sustained-tone writing throughout, music cast in often irregular or unpatterned rhythmic designs. In this respect its organum purum differs strikingly from that in the peripheral *Propter veritatem*, which tends to follow the patterns of the rhythmic modes with almost textbook regularity. It is worthy of note that it was the Parisian musician who used the rhythmic language freely, not the peripheral one.

[7] Regarding this tenor see Heinrich Husmann, 'The Origin and Destination of the *Magnus liber organi*', *Musical Quarterly*, 49 (1963), pp. 327–8. The StV clausula on *Propter veritatem*, in discant, is also based on the tenor of the organum rather than on the plainchant; see Jürg Stenzl, *Die vierzig Clausulae der Handschrift Paris, Bibliothèque nationale latin 15139 (Saint Victor-Clausulae)* (Berne, 1970), pp. 72–3.

There are many examples in which melismas in organum purum vary in length from source to source. These are generally viewed as instances of abbreviation, and in many cases there can be little doubt that they were indeed shortened. Perhaps the most clear-cut examples of such reduction are found in the mensural redactions of the organa tripla in Mo; a few others may be found in W$_2$. All too often, however, such an explanation is unsatisfactory. Let us consider two examples of 'abbreviation' offered by Fritz Reckow. Example 2 presents the beginnings of the first and second Responds in the F version of *Propter veritatem*. Reckow explains the shortness of the second Respond as 'eine bezeichnende Auslassung von Organum per se-Gliedern, in denen das gleiche Motiv dem Bearbeiter wohl

Example 2. The openings of the first and second Responds of *Propter veritatem* in F

A. Respond 1, fol. 128

B. Respond 2, fol. 129

373

allzuoft sequenziert erschien . . .'[8] The material in question is a standard formula used dozens of times in the organa, varied in accordance with slight deviations in the tenor and its place in the work as a whole. The omitted tenor note proves conclusively that the second Respond has been shortened. However, the abbreviation resulted not from an attempt to improve the composition, but from a functional consideration – the placement of the Respond after the Verse, a position that in F is usually occupied by a brief setting. (Cf. the treatment of the three Responds provided for *Viderunt omnes* (M I) in F, all three based on the same formula as *Propter veritatem*.) Otherwise, why would the first Respond not have been shortened as well?

The different readings of the opening of the Verse of *Ex eius tumba* (O 25), shown in Example 3, represent a different situation. Reckow

Example 3. Variant openings of the Verse of *Ex eius tumba*
A. After F, fol. 81   W$_2$:

B. After W$_1$, fol. 21

Ca -   ter - va -   tim

suggests that 'die Melismen über den drei ersten Tenor-a erschienen dem Bearbeiter offenbar allzu monoton . . .: von der langen Halteton-Partie in W_1 bleibt in F and W_2 nur eine Art K "Klanggerüst"; über den anschliessenden, in der Tonhöhe wechselnden Tenortönen sind die Fassungen F und W_2 gegenüber W_1 dann sogar umfänglicher und motivisch beziehungsreicher gestaltet'.[9] In fact, however, these would appear to be different formulas, each of which has its own textual history. The F–W$_2$ design is also found in the Verse of *Concede* (O 24) in W$_1$, F, W$_2$, and Ber. The W$_1$ line, slightly varied because of differences in the tenor, appears in the Gloria Patri of *Te sanctum* (O 22) in F and W$_2$. A third formula, not entirely unrelated to these two, is used in the Gloria Patri of the F and W$_2$ versions of *Ex eius tumba* and *Concede*. There is, then, no reason to regard Example

[8] Reckow, 'Das Organum', p. 471.   [9] *Ibid.*, pp. 471–2.

3A as a modernisation of Example 3B, or, in fact, to suppose that
either derived directly from the other. This holds true for the
remainder of the Verse of *Ex eius tumba*, in which W_1 stands apart in
large measure from F and W_2.

In numerous instances, variations in the length of melismas in
organum purum might be explained as resulting from a process of
expansion, rather than from one of reduction. The style of organum
purum is characterised by the development and variation of small
melodic cells and larger melodic sequences, among other things;
these elements, together with the loose syntax permitted by the
sustained-tone texture and the overall flamboyance of the idiom,
combine to make expansion by a zealous *organista* as plausible as
pruning by a tidy-minded editor. Most instances of the shortening or
elimination of sustained-tone material involve stereotyped cadential
flourishes that, as we have seen, circulated independently of the
clausulae to which they are affixed. The formula at the end of 'Veni'
in the F version of *Alleluia, Veni electa mea* is without doubt an
accretion to the text: none of the nine concordances for this clausula
includes it, and the figure is found at three other points in the F copy
of the organum, but not at all in the other states (see Example 4A). At
two places where the formula appears in F, the version in W_2 has
different, much longer figures, one found also in W_1, MüA, and
F-203 (Example 4B) and the other unique to W_2 (Example 4C).
Although we lack substantial data regarding these cadence formulas,[10] it appears likely that many details of their melodic,
rhythmic, and notational style reflect the house style of a particular
institution or *cantor*, or – to phrase it slightly differently – of the
editor–compiler of the manuscript. Because of their separate existence, of course, the notation of these figures must often be read
differently from that of the material surrounding them, and it often
suggests a sudden if brief change of mode (as in the F formula in
Example 4A).[11] The disjunct way in which these formulas may be

---

[10] See Flotzinger, *Discantussatz*, pp. 178–87, and Smith, 'Interrelationships among
the Graduals', pp. 82–5 and 93–6, passim.

[11] Anonymus IV seems to allude to this phenomenon when, in his discussion of
the use of decorative *colores* at important points in an organum, he mentions *organistae* 'qui ponunt ante illam paenultimam [in the duplum voice] unam, duas vel
tres vel plures, prout melius competit vel competierit de uno modo vel pluribus
modis . . .': Fritz Reckow (ed.), *Der Musiktraktat des Anonymus 4*, 2 vols. (Wiesbaden, 1967), I, p. 88.

Example 4. Some cadence formulas in *Alleluia, Veni electa mea*

A. F, fol. 141v, at 'Veni', 'mea', 'thronum', and 'rex'

B. At 'mea' in W₁, MüA, W₂, and F–203 (after W₂, fol. 85)

C. At 'thronum' in W₂, fol. 85

fitted to their context is particularly evident in some of the insular chant settings in W₁, fascicle XI, where an abrupt change in mode is often accompanied by a sudden shift in tessitura – so much so that these formulas have occasionally been mistaken for the addition of a third voice. They seem clearly to be the work of local musicians influenced by Parisian models. (For two clear-cut examples from W₁, XI, see the Offertories *O vere beata* and *Ave regina caelorum*, fols. 210v and 211.)

The fragmentary state of the Parisian *liber organi* in Ber represents the organa dupla in the shortest form known. The reduction in scale is accomplished, however, primarily through the omission of cadence figures, not by cutting into the body of the music, as a comparison of the organum purum setting of *Concede* in Ber with the readings in W₁, F, and W₂ will make clear. The virtual absence of cadence formulas from the Ber text of *Alleluia, Veni electa mea* is certainly a sign that the state is a late one, or at least that it stands at some distance from the centre of the organum tradition, for cadence formulas are basic to the organum idiom and to music influenced by it. Their omission has a somewhat negative effect on the Ber text, weakening the articulation and the internal cohesiveness of the individual discant sections of which it is largely comprised, and causing the music to appear less like a representative of the central tradition and more like a modest peripheral setting influenced by that tradition, such as one of the organa in StV. (In contrast, the fourth and fifth clausula collections in F, which are the only clausulae that in large part provide shortened versions of sections in organum purum, generally shorten the organum purum itself, while retaining often extended cadence flourishes.)

One piece of theoretical evidence appears explicitly to support the theory that organa were modernised by curtailing their organum purum: the remark of Anonymus IV that 'magister Leoninus, secundum quod dicebatur, fuit optimus organista, qui fecit magnum librum organi de gradali et antifonario pro servitio divino multiplicando. Et fuit in usu usque ad tempus Perotini Magni, qui abbreviavit eundem et fecit clausulas sive puncta plurima meliora, quoniam optimus discantor erat, et melior [at discant] quam Leoninus erat. Sed hoc non est dicendum de subtilitate organi.'[12] This statement is not without its problems of interpretation, however. 'Better clausulae or puncta' undoubtedly are to be understood as discant settings, probably the sophisticated and often lengthy clausulae composed to replace other discant sections and often transmitted in the collections of independent clausulae. These works would not shorten the organa in any sense. By 'abbreviavit eundem' Anonymus IV could have meant that Perotin abridged Leonin's *liber*, leaving out some organa, but this appears improbable and would scarcely have elicited a comment in this context. It has been suggested that evidence of the 'shortening' is to be found among the 154 snippets of polyphony that make up the fourth and fifth clausula collections in F, most of them music for passages set in organum purum in the organa themselves.[13] Many of these terse alternatives to the 'subtleties of organum' are, in fact, severely shortened versions

[12] *Ibid.*, p. 46.
[13] William G. Waite, 'The Abbreviation of the *Magnus Liber*', *Journal of the American Musicological Society*, 14 (1961), pp. 144–58. See also Ernest H. Sanders, 'The Question of Perotin's Oeuvre and Dates', Ludwig Finscher *et al.* (eds.), *Festschrift für Walter Wiora zum 30. Dezember 1966* (Kassel, 1967), pp. 241–9.

of the very organum purum they replace. But once again, I question whether they are what Anonymus IV had in mind. Unlike the 'better' clausulae, only a handful of them can be found worked into the organa in one or another source, and, unlike both the known works of Perotin and the 'better' clausulae, their circulation appears to have been extremely limited. Finally, most of them do not share the concern manifest in Perotin's works and in the 'better' clausulae with structure, rhythmic architecture, and expansiveness of design. One can, of course, postulate that they represent a different phase of Perotin's career, but I wonder whether these snippets, which are individually rather insignificant and which together fill a mere six folios in F, represent activity that Anonymus IV would have considered a significant aspect of Perotin's work. I would feel equally uneasy about a suggestion that he was referring to the kind of abbreviation found in Ber. Although these reservations are merely nagging doubts, not ironclad arguments, they nevertheless prompt one to ask whether Anonymus IV could have had something else in mind by 'abbreviate'.

Abbreviare means 'to shorten, reduce, abridge', but in the thirteenth century it also meant 'to write down, record', with *componere* as a cognate.[14] Anonymus IV uses *abbreviatio* in the sense of 'a writing, treatise'.[15] Given the writer's rather loose treatment of vocabulary generally, *abbreviare* in the passage under consideration could easily be read as meaning 'to write down'. That is, Perotin could have 'made a redaction' of Leonin's *liber organi*, editing a version of the repertory and imposing on it his own preferences regarding notation and rhythm, adjusting or replacing the cadence formulas to his own taste, and providing 'many better clausulae or puncta', either in the organa themselves or in a separate collection. Abbreviation as such is not ruled out by this interpretation, but Anonymus IV's remark would fit any of the extant sources, W₁ included.[16]

---

[14] *Mittellateinisches Wörterbuch*, fasc. I/I (Berlin and Munich, 1959), cols. 15–16; R. H. Latham (ed.), *Dictionary of Medieval Latin from British Sources*, I (Oxford, 1975), p. 3.

[15] Reckow, *Anonymus 4*, I, p. 50.

[16] It is conceivable that Anonymus IV had in mind a redaction in mensural notation, which he claims was well developed by the time of Perotin (see Reckow, *Anonymus 4*, I, pp. 46 and 50). Since Perotin's works were almost certainly conceived in modal notation, however, doubts must linger concerning this point and, indeed, concerning the reliability of this English writer dealing with developments in a different country a half-century or more earlier.

I suggest, then, that a passage in sustained-tone writing is not necessarily earlier than one setting the same chant segment in discant, and that the course taken by a particular organum could include either expansion or reduction in the size of melismas, and the addition or removal of cadence figuration. But the problem involves much more than mere differences in texture or scale; above all, it involves the character of the rhythm. This factor raises the complex issue of rhythm in organum purum, to which we must briefly turn our attention.

In a treatise of seminal importance for both thirteenth- and twentieth-century interpretations of modal rhythm, Johannes de Garlandia, writing probably in the second quarter of the thirteenth century, distinguishes between two rhythmic styles: *modus rectus* – used in discant, some organum purum (writing called 'copula' by Garlandia), and music for more than two voices – and *modus non rectus* – used in other passages of organum purum. The former style, *modus rectus*, adheres closely to the patterns of the six rhythmic modes. *Modus non rectus*, on the other hand, departs from 'alicuius rectae [mensurae], quia longae et breves rectae sumuntur debito modo primo et principaliter. In non recta [mensura] vero sumitur longa et brevis non primo modo, sed ex contingenti.'[17] (That is, in proper measure, used in *modus rectus*, proper longs and breves are identified primarily by means of mode; but in improper measure, used in *modus non rectus*, the values are to be inferred not from a mode but from the context as circumstances provide.) This is an apt description of the situation obtaining in organum duplum: some sustained-tone passages, like most discant, are cast in the regular chains of ligatures that connote the modes, while others present successions of ligatures so irregular and unpatterned that they bear little resemblance to any modal design. In numerous instances, moreover, lines written in irregular ligatures in one manuscript appear in another source cast in strictly modal configurations. Many scholars, most recently and persuasively Fritz Reckow, have suggested an evolutionary progression from the free, 'un-modal' *modus non rectus* to the orderly, strictly measured patterns of *modus rectus*.[18]

Now, the 'rhythmic modes' are theoretical constructs abstracted from a musical language that had been in existence for a half-century

---

[17] Erich Reimer (ed.), *Johannes de Garlandia: De mensurabili musica*, 2 vols. (Wiesbaden, 1972), I, pp. 88–9.   [18] Reckow, 'Das Organum', pp. 457–65.

or more. They are skeleton outlines of the 'ways' (*modi*) in which one
can deduce the intended rhythm from an inherently non-rhythmic
notation. In *sine littera* writing, which is our concern here, 'mode 1' is
a synthesis of many ligature configurations that are all read in a
similar way, as Examples 5A and 5B illustrate. All end on the ternary
'beat' and begin before it, perhaps on the preceding beat, if the
context requires. The 'first rhythmic mode' expresses this 'way' of
reading ligatures in outline form. This 'mode' will produce both the
flexible designs of Example 5A and the strictly 'modal' patterns of
Example 5B, depending on such variables as the character of the line,
the degree of melodic activity, and so on. The other modes derive
from the same rhythmic language as mode 1, synthesising their
material in a similar way.

Example 5

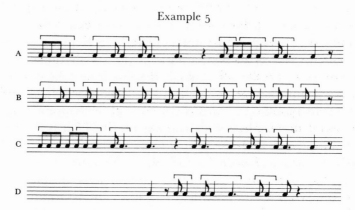

Modus rectus and *non rectus* are opposite extremes in this theoretical
construct, notions formulated to relate the modal outlines more
closely to the realities of musical practice. If, owing to the nature of
the line, the music is written in ligatures that conform to the modal
outline, the rhythm observes *modus rectus*. If the ligatures are so
irregular that an underlying pattern is impossible to discern or infer,
it observes *modus non rectus*. The rhythm of such passages cannot be
identified by using a modal outline as a guide, but must be deduced
from those elements of the music that shaped the rhythmic language
in the first place: the harmonic context, and the position of the
gesture within the larger line. In practice, of course, most music
would fall somewhere between these two theoretical extremes.

Modal rhythm is a flexible language. The irregular ligatures in

Example 5A could be read as in Example 5C without departing from the first mode. Or the end of the example could be read as in Example 5D, in the second mode. The ambiguity inherent in irregular ligatures would produce chaos in discant or organum triplum, where two or more moving parts must coordinate. Such music requires the relatively unambiguous ligature designs that approach the extreme of *modus rectus*. In organum purum, on the other hand, the sustained tenor imposes no such constraint, and the *organista* was free, if he chose, to use the more varied designs that approach *modus non rectus*, designs that are inherently multiform in their rhythmic connotations. Indeed, the potential for florid display in organum purum would tend to elicit flexible rhythms of this kind. (This explains why voices were seldom added to organa dupla to create three-voice compositions, a common procedure in other Parisian genres, and why the few examples that do survive involve discant sections exclusively.)

Garlandia formulated his classification of *modus rectus* and *non rectus* from observation of early-thirteenth-century practice. There is, I suggest, no chronological relationship implicit in the distinction between these two styles. How, then, does one explain variations in notation from source to source?

Reckow has offered the music shown in Example 6 as an illustration of how a passage in free-flowing *modus non rectus* was modernised into one in *rectus*.[19] (The rhythmic interpretations shown on the staff are Reckow's; the ones above the staff are mine and will be discussed shortly.) It is possible, however, that the movement was in the opposite direction, from greater notational clarity to lesser. Modal notation is something of a makeshift, imposing rhythmic implications on figures that were first and foremost expressions of melodic gesture. As often as not, perhaps, the imposition of a rhythmic dimension forced the ligatures to be used in ways that ran counter to their normal deployment in the melodic design. This inherently unstable orthographic situation resulted in an ever-present tendency for the notation to revert to a more natural state, for the scribe to express the musical substance, as he perceived it, in more efficient and effective notation than he found in his exemplar. This potential for decay of the notational design is a basic element in the transmission of *sine littera* writing prior to the development of a mensural

[19] *Ibid.*, pp. 469–70.

Example 6. Variant readings at 'super aquas multas' in *In columbe* (o 4)

A. W₁, fol. 18

super

B. F, fol. 67v

super

C. W₂, fol. 48

super

a - quas

a - quas

a - quas

Example 6 (cont.)

orthography. In Example 6 the possibility that a first-mode ligature pattern suffered debasement at the hands of a scribe appears no weaker than the suggestion that an originally non-modal line had modal rhythm superimposed on it.

At the close of 'super' F has a brief cadential figure, pointing up the fact that 'super' and 'aquas multas' are actually two distinct clausulae. W_1, its notation at 'super' thoroughly debased, ends this clausula with a mere statement of the melodic sequence that the scribe has adopted to express the musical substance found in the other two readings. The result is a different kind of break between the two clausulae than the ones found in F and W_2. The independence of the two clausulae from each other becomes still more evident when the descending figure returns at 'multas' and all three sources cast the figure in an 'un-modal' form. Significantly, it is almost exclusively the descending figure alone that sustained decay; the remainder of the clausula has melodic material that provided less of a temptation to uninformed or heedless scribes, and retained its clear modal profile.

Decay in ligature design does not mean that the notation would have continued to be read according to its original intent (and therefore in some arbitrary way, as Reckow's transcription of the F text of 'super' implies), or that it would have lost all rhythmic meaning and been read in a 'free' rhythm. The *cantor* would have been unaware that decay had set in, and would have read the new figures according to the same principles as he would the old, generating in Example 6 a series of simple two-beat 'progressions' (placed above the staff as noted). Short-winded progressions of this kind are especially common in such modest chant settings as the peripheral works in W_1, fascicle XI and the organa in StV.

Alterations in ligature design could have come about for a variety of reasons other than mere relapse to a simpler form of notation. An editor might have eliminated one or more alternative interpretations in a passage that admitted several different ones. (That is, he could have converted *modus non rectus* into *rectus*; cf. the openings of *Alleluia, Assumpta est Maria* (M 33) in W_1 and W_2.) An extended passage in sequence could have tempted an *organista* to introduce variations in rhythmic or melodic detail. Conversely, a sequential passage that had been notated inconsistently for some reason, or that included some variation, could have been made consistent by a tidy editor. A passage originally in *modus rectus* could have served as a point of departure for a florid display by a local *organista*. Or an elastic rhythmic design could have been brought into line with newer tastes. The last-named possibility is less a matter of variations between *modus non rectus* and *modus rectus* than of mensural redactions, such as those in Ber and Mo, where the musical fabric has sometimes been forced into rhythms that are the products of a later age, that are foreign to the style of the organa, and that could not even have been expressed in modal notation.

I have suggested that there are alternative explanations for variations that are customarily viewed according to an evolutionary hypothesis. My point is not that one interpretation will always be right and the other wrong, but rather that the nature of the music often makes it impossible to arrive at a decision. Ludwig's view of the developments in the organum repertory seems less appropriate for variations within organum duplum itself than for the relationship of organum to other genres – for example, peripheral chant settings or, in the other stylistic direction, the motet. Within the organa, material appears to have been reworked in ways that could be either traditional or forward-looking, depending on the individual *organista* or other circumstances.

Let us turn from a discussion of filiation in the organum repertory considered on the broadest level to an examination of a single composition that achieved an unusually wide circulation, the clausula in organum purum on 'Veni' from *Alleluia, Veni electa mea*.[20] As is shown on p. 367, this setting is extant in ten readings in four organa (four for M 54, three for M 8, two for M 26, and one for M 43: facsimiles of all ten appear in Plates 1–4, below). Four of these states are in F, three in W_2, and two in W_1, enabling us to compare variations within individual manuscripts as well as those within each organum and from work to work. (The mensural version of M 54 in Ber will be of only limited value in this discussion because of the fragmentary state of its 'Veni' clausula and the extensive alterations made in the notation. It will not be considered in most of the examination to follow.)

The clausulae fall into two groups: M 26 on the one hand, and M 8, 43, and 54 on the other. M 26 concludes with the tenor notes D-C-D-D while the other three clausulae have only D-D – a variation that is reflected in different yet related dupla (see Example 7). The conclusion of M 26 is an extended cadence formula that occurs in several organa, always above the tenor pitches C-D. (One of these is in the W_1 state of M 54, where it rounds off the final discant clausula, on 'rex'.) The other formula appears to be found only in the versions of our clausula in M 8, 43, and 54. Although it differs from the M 26 figure in important ways, it shares with the latter a strong orientation towards C, a note present in the M 26 tenor but not in the others. This suggests that some form of the M 26 design may have been the point of departure for the other formula. This C orientation is stronger in some readings than in others: in the two W_1 clausulae and in the F text of M 54 at point *a* in Example 7, and in W_1 (again) and the W_2 copy of M 54 at point *c*. The variations group themselves at least partly by manuscript: the two W_1 states are consistent at both points *a* and *c*, the two W_2 states at *a*, and the three F states at *c*. When readings in other sources agree with W_1 at *a* or *c*, those readings are from M 54. (The F and W_1 readings of M 54 agree in another detail, the presence of a seemingly superfluous *tractus* after

---

[20] Cf. Flotzinger, *Discantussatz*, pp. 86–8, and Smith, 'Interrelationships among the Alleluias', pp. 190–1.

Example 7. Variant readings in the cadence formula of 'Veni' and related clausulae
A. From M 26, after F fol. 118
B. From M 54, after W₁ fol. 40v
C. Readings for M 8, 43, and 54 that depart from W₁ M 54

the three longs G-E-D.) The relative closeness of W₁ to the M 26 cadence formula can also be seen at point *b* in Example 7, where F, in contrast, characteristically turns to a second-mode pattern in all three states, and where the W₂ states read *simplex-ternaria*, a typical element in the notational dialect of this source.

The readings in the body of the clausula present two kinds of variations: disagreements in duplum ligature formation and variations in the alignment of the parts. The duplum consists of two passages in sequence, labelled *a* and *b* in the transcription offered in Example 8. The collation in this example shows virtual unanimity in the treatment of the numerous descending five-note figures in sequence *a*. The first one appears as a *coniunctura* in all readings, while each of the three following five-note figures is written as a *clivis* with three appended *currentes*, a design that is not varied in any of its twenty-seven appearances in Example 8. The extraordinary stability of these figures may derive from the fact that the notation serves both the melodic and the rhythmic content equally well, minimising the chances of decay. The other ligatures, by comparison, vary considerably from source to source, and within the same source. The variation in bar 3 offers alternative ways to express the same rhythm. Coincidentally, perhaps, the W_1 and W_2 readings of M 8 agree against the W_2 copy of M 26 (where the notation once again reflects the W_2 dialect), and against the other states. Elsewhere in the clausula variations in ligatures would seem to imply different rhythms, as I have suggested in Example 8. The W_1 readings of M 8 and M 54 agree with each other, but are not internally consistent in sequence *a*, where each of the three statements of the pattern has a different ligature design. The readings in W_2 differ from those in W_1 in both sequences *a* and *b*. Its readings for M 26 and M 54 agree, and they are internally consistent, but in its text of M 8 the ligatures in sequence *a* depart from those in the other two W_2 states. (At sequence *b*, unlike the situation in Example 6, above, it is W_1 that has the 'more modal' ligatures, not W_2.) In F all four states agree with W_1 in their readings for sequence *b* (the single exception, in M 54, is probably a momentary scribal lapse). The readings in sequence *a*, on the other hand, tend to agree with those in the W_2 text of M 8. Thus there are three variants in sequence *a*: W_1 (both texts), F (all four texts) and the W_2 text of M 8, the W_2 texts of M 26 and 54. In sequence *b* the readings in W_1 and F agree against those in W_2.

Variations in the alignment of parts suggested in the different copies of our clausula are summarised in Example 9. (Cf. Figures 1–3, below, for the alignment as it actually appears in the sources. A variety of paleographic and other factors make it impossible and misleading to duplicate this underlay exactly.) Although often accorded little credence because of its seeming inconsistency, tenor–duplum alignment can be of considerable interest. In the Respond of *Propter veritatem* (M 37), for example, W_1 and W_2 agree in their alignment, while F appears explicitly to call for something quite different. That the alignment in F is not fortuitous is confirmed by the fact that it occurs twice, in each of the two Responds that F provides for *Propter veritatem*. (See Example 2, above, where the openings of both F Responds are transcribed, but with the alignment

Example 8. Variant readings in the duplum of 'Veni' and related clausulae (The uppermost staff presents 'Veni' after W₁, fol. 40v. Departures from this reading are aligned beneath it.)

Example 8 (cont.)

Example 9. Variations in the alignment of voices in 'Veni' and related clausulae
(The duplum is taken from the W₁ text of 'Veni'.)

Example 9 (cont.)

taken from Reckow's edition rather than from the manuscript itself.
In F the first tenor note appears beneath the repeated C at the close
of the second duplum *ordo*; in W_1 and W_2 it appears at the beginning
of the work as in the example, while the *second* tenor note (like the
first, an F) is placed beneath the two Cs.)[21] In the 'Veni' clausula
under discussion, similarly, the alignment seems to have been indicated in the manuscripts with some care, as the way in which the
readings tend to group, once again, by source makes clear. The two
states in W_1 appear to be in overall agreement, except for some
indecision over where to place the tenor E in sequence *a* and one
variation in sequence *b*. (The latter may be more apparent than real;
it is possible that the alignment in M 8 was also intended for M 54.)
The four states in F are also in near agreement, apart from the askew
alignment of three tenor notes in M 8, and, in M 43, an error and some
superfluous strokes. (The latter may suggest that M 43 derived from
yet another organum using this clausula, a state that has not survived.) The treatment of sequence *a* is less internally consistent and
symmetrical in W_1 than in F, and the different alignments – which
may suggest differing rhythmic interpretations of the duplum ligatures – in sequence *b* are worthy of note. The three states in W_2
disagree at three points: the seemingly misplaced G in M 26; the
alignment at the beginning of sequence *b* in M 54, which agrees with
W_1 rather than with F or the other W_2 readings; and the missing F in
M 8, which probably resulted from an attempt to impose the same
alignment on all statements of the sequence pattern. (In its treatment of duplum ligatures in sequence *a*, on the other hand, M 8 is the
only one of the W_2 readings of this passage that is *not* internally
consistent: see Example 8.) Otherwise, the W_2 readings tend to agree
with those in F.

It is clear both from manuscript alignment and from the sense of
the music that changes in tenor notes do not necessarily coincide
with the beginnings or ends of duplum phrases. The clausula consists of two pre-existent elements, a segment of plainchant and a pair
of duplum formulas extended in sequence. The way in which these
elements are combined seems reminiscent of the examples in the
Vatican Treatise, but on a larger scale, involving groups of five and

---

[21] The practice of singing several duplum notes before the entrance of the tenor is
described by Anonymus IV; see Reckow, *Anonymus 4*, I, p. 88.

four tenor notes, not one or two.[22] It would appear likely that, in joining these two disparate elements together, the composer modified the endings of the duplum formulas so that they would fit with the tenor, but that he – or the editors responsible for the states in which the work survives – did not necessarily have a firm idea about how they were to line up at other points in the clausula. The solutions implied by manuscript alignment vary considerably. At the beginning of sequence *b* the W_1 texts opt for establishing a regular tenor pattern in duplex longs. In M 54, if the underlay in the manuscript is accepted, this creates a dissonant clash at the beginning of the second statement of the duplum sequence. In the W_1 text of M 8, on the other hand, the offending clash is avoided by a different alignment, one that agrees with all other readings of the passage. In the W_2 copy of M 54, the removal of the tenor G from the end of sequence *a* to the beginning of sequence *b* would seem to represent something of a lapse in editorial or scribal judgement after the composer had gone to the length of modifying the duplum pattern in sequence *a* so that it would accommodate a cadence with tenor G. Thus the readings in F and in the W_2 text of M 8 (provided that the apparently excised tenor F is restored) appear to have achieved the most satisfactory solutions. These happen also to be states that agree in their duplum ligature designs in sequence *a*. It remains uncertain, however, whether these readings represent the work of the composer or of a careful editor.

As we have seen, the readings in the 'Veni' complex tend to group themselves according to source, a sign that the 'house style' of the manuscript – reflecting local usage or the predilections of one or more redactors – played a crucial role in shaping the states of the organa that have come down to us. House style is a factor that must be borne in mind when readings from one source are used to clarify ambiguous ligatures in another. Beneath this local overlay the patterns of variation among different states for one organum or among the different organa can be discerned only fleetingly. In the cadence formula the W_1 readings are closer to their presumed prototype, M 26, than are the others; and the states of M 54 tend both to agree among themselves more closely, and to reflect the relationship with

[22] See Frieder Zaminer, *Der Vatikanische Organum-Traktat (Ottob. lat. 3025)*, Münchner Veröffentlichungen zur Musikgeschichte 2 (Tutzing, 1959), pp. 52–71 and *passim*.

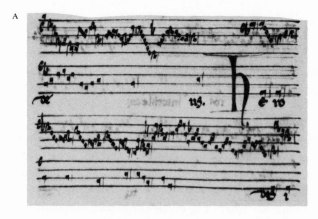

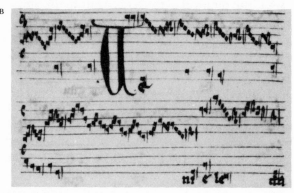

Figure 1. 'Veni' and related clausulae in W₁: (A) M 8 'Herodes', fol. 28; (B) M 54 'Veni', fol. 40v

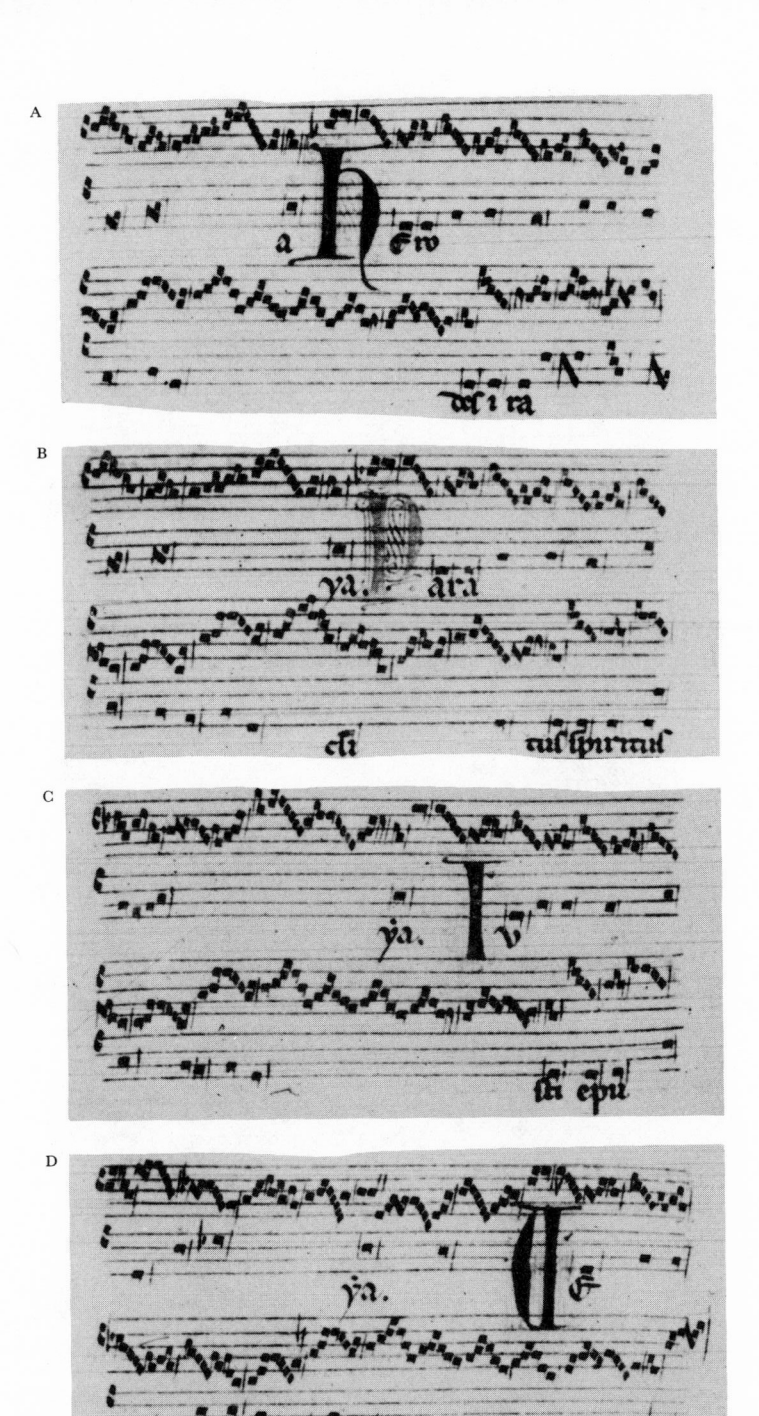

Figure 2. 'Veni' and related clausulae in F: (A) M 8 'Herodes', fol. 104v; (B) M 26 'Paraclitus', fol. 118; (C) M 43 'Justi', fol. 133v; (D) M 54 'Veni', fol. 141v

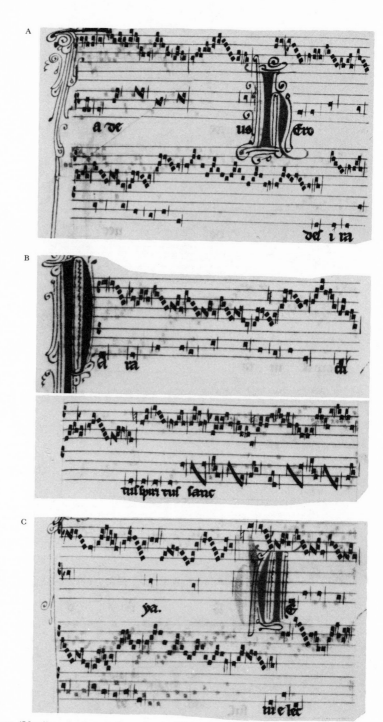

Figure 3. 'Veni' and related clausulae in W₂: (A) M 8 'Herodes', fol. 67v; (B) M 26 'Paraclitus', fols. 74v–75; (C) M 54 'Veni', fol. 85

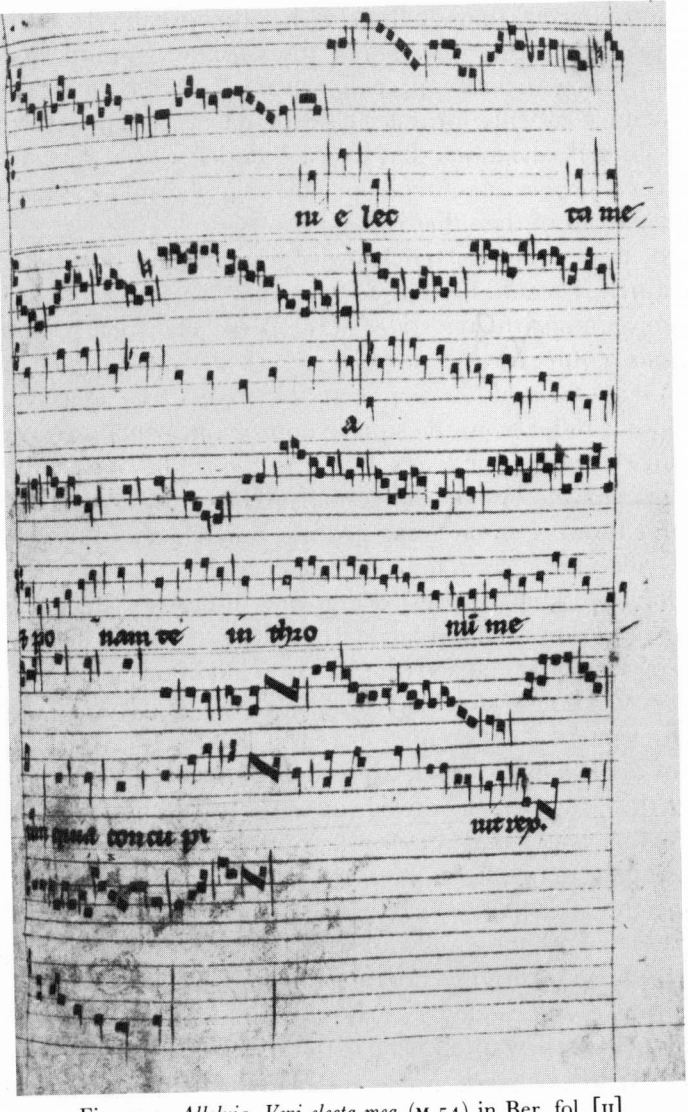

Figure 4. *Alleluia, Veni electa mea* (M 54) in Ber, fol. [II]

M 26 more sharply, than do those of the other organa. In the body of the clausula, on the other hand, the variations group somewhat differently, as we would expect after seeing the behaviour of similar if less extended cadence formulas elsewhere in M 54. There seem to be no directional variations that might identify M 8, 26, 43, or 54, in whatever state, as the source from which the clausula was taken over into one or all of the other organa.[23]

In the present state of our knowledge about how the organa were transmitted, I would hesitate to construct a stemma to explain the variations among the ten states of the 'Veni' clausula. A number of questions require clarification before such a stemma can be attempted. In what form of notation were the organa first conceived, and how does it differ from the square notation in which they survive? The answer may provide a solution to the riddle of why the Paris repertory survives in late sources only. The creation of an organum was something of an on-going process, and the act of transmission itself would almost seem to have been enough to stimulate recomposition or reworking. In view of this fact, liturgical, paleographical, and stylistic tools need a great deal of sharpening to aid in identifying layers of compositional activity. Partly to aid in this task, we need to analyse the 'house style' in each source in much greater detail. Which elements in the notation reflect local or personal tastes in rhythm and melody, which are primarily orthographic in nature, and, of the latter, which derive from the habits of individual scribes? The organa tripla and quadrupla, and the conducti in the same manuscripts, may offer some measure of outside control in investigating this problem. Which elements in the duplum – cadential flourishes and other figures – are local products? Inextricably linked to the problems of original notation and house style is the question of the nature of the melodic content itself. Much of it consists of stereotyped gestures; these need to be identified, and their behaviour studied. Which elements are fixed, and which are variable? Within what limits, and in what contexts does variation occur? Are the melodic components in organum purum, which often seems to be more formulaic than discant, more or less stable than those in discant?

Like the readers of *Piers Plowman* we have several versions of our

[23] For examples of directional variations involving other portions of M 8, 26, and 43, see Smith, 'Interrelationships among the Alleluias', pp. 188–90 and 197–9.

text, each worthy of study in its own right. Unlike the students of Langland's allegory, however, we have not proceeded far towards determining the nature of the relationship among these versions. We cannot yet penetrate much beyond the extant sources in the search for the *libri organorum* of Leonin and Perotin.

GENERAL INDEX

Accolti, Bernardo, 173n
Agricola, Alexander, 86n, 87, 122, 251n, 254, 261, 266, 267, 271–2, 275, 276, 291
Agricola, Jannes, 291
Agricola, Martin, 62, 63, 68–9, 71
Agricola, Rudolph, 235–6
Alamanni, Luigi, 178n, 191n
alphabet in verse, 113
Ana, Francesco D', 34
Anglo-Saxon Tropers, 362
Animuccia, Giovanni, 179n
Anonymus IV, 377–8
Anselmi, Giorgio, 33n
Anthony of Padua, St, 29
Antico, Andrea, 79, 167, 176n, 211
Aquilano, Serafino, 173
Aquitanian tropes, 352, 357–62
Arcadelt, Jacob, 167, 170, 171, 172, 174n, 178, 180, 184n, 214n
Arena, Antoine, 144–5
Arndt von Aich, 67n, 134, 135, 140, 141, 148–61 passim
Aron, Pietro, 279, 280, 283, 289
Aston, Hugh, 106–7
astronomy, Merton school of, 95
Attaingnant, Pierre, 52, 137, 138, 142, 143, 148–61 passim, 211, 218
Augustinian order, 7

Barbingnant, 269, 272, 291
Barle, 291
barzellette, 175
Basin, 269, 271, 291
Bedford, John, Duke of, 9
Bedingham, John, 268, 291
Bell, Alexander, 11
Bembo, Pietro, 165, 174, 175–6, 177, 179
Benedictine order, 7, 33–4, 35
Beneventan Gradual–Tropers, 353, 356n
Berchem, Jachet, 179n, 209, 212, 215, 217, 218, 223
Beringen brothers, 211
Bernardo, 168

Binchois, Gilles, 268, 269, 291
biscantare treatment of plainsong, 22–3, 29, 36
Bologna, Bartolomeo da, 26, 34
Bonifazio, Dragonetto, 179, 181, 182–3
Boris, 279, 291
Bourdon, 291
Braxatoris, W., 291
Brebis, 243
Bridlington Priory, 7
Bruges, 235
Brumel, Antoine, 48–9, 51–2, 53, 54–5, 56, 267, 274, 291
Brynstone, John, 100, 111
Buglhat, Johannes, 213–15
Buriton, John, 99–100, 111
Burzio, Nicola, 33n
Busnois, Antoine, 254, 255, 256, 260, 264, 265, 273, 274, 276, 291
Buus, Jacques, 129n, 216, 221, 222, 272
Buxheim Organ Book, 79

cadence figures in organum, 366–8, 371, 375–6, 376–7, 379
Cambio, Perissone, 216–17, 223, 224
canons (of the Church), 22, 37, 38, 41, 55
canons (musical), 107–8, 116
cantus-firmus treatments, 81, 82, 83, 87–8, 139
canzone, 128–9, 167
Capirola, Vincenzo, 144
Capone, Neri, 210, 223
cappelle, 126; *see also* Este, Duke Ercole I d'; Sforza, Galeazzo Maria
Capretto, Pietro, 36
Cara, Marchetto, 31, 127n, 166n, 173n, 180
Carmen, Johannes, 27, 29
carols, 16, 17
Caron, 242, 254, 264, 273, 291, 337–8
Carpentras (Elzéar Genet), 167, 168n, 172n, 176
Casale, Rolando da, 33–4

General Index

INDEX OF MANUSCRIPTS

Index of Manuscripts

Segovia, Catedral, MS without number:
252n, 261, 263, 265, 278, 279, 280,
281, 282, 283, 284, 290
Seville, Biblioteca Colombina
5-1-43: 261, 270, 271, 281, 283, 285,
326–7
7-1-28: 279, 290
Sutton Coldfield, Oscott College, B.4:
165n, 170

Tournai, Bibliothèque de la Ville, 94:
134, 136, 141, 145, 148–61 passim
Trent, Biblioteca Capitolare, 93: 297,
298, 299, 314, 317n
Trent, Castello del Buoconsiglio
88: 86n
89: 261, 262, 278, 290
90: 284, 290
91: 261, 290
Trent, Museo Provinciale d'Arte
87: 303n, 317n
88: 317n
89: 317n
90: 297–8, 299, 311, 314, 317n
91: 317n
92: 317n
Turin, Biblioteca Nazionale, Riserva
musicale, I.27: 263, 290

Vatican City, Biblioteca Apostolica
Vaticana
Archivio della Cappella Giulia, XIII.27:
85, 90n, 126n, 128n, 251n, 252n,
259, 261, 263, 265, 267, 272, 273,
278, 279, 280, 281, 282, 286–7, 299n,
337
Archivio della Cappella Sistina, 14: 27
Archivio di San Pietro, B.80: 308, 317n
Chigiana I.I.4: 230n
Vat. Lat. 11953: 282, 290
Vat. Mus. 571: 170n
Vatican City: see also under Rome
Venice, Archivio di Stato
Consiglio dei Dieci, Registro 13: 196n
Consiglio dei Dieci, Registro 14: 206
Consiglio dei Dieci, Registro 16: 206
Senato, Terra, Registro 34: 217n
Scuola di San Giovanni Evangelista,
Registro 140: 205–6
Scuola di San Giovanni Evangelista,
Registro 141: 198n

Scuola di San Marco, Busta 82: 206–7
Scuola di San Marco, Registro 16bis:
200n, 206
Scuola di San Marco, Registro 17:
193n, 201n
Scuola di San Marco, Registro 18: 207
Scuola di San Rocco, Seconda
Consegna, Registro 44: 197n
Scuola di San Rocco, Seconda
Consegna, Registro 45: 202n, 207
Scuola di San Rocco, Seconda
Consegna, Registro 46: 198n
Scuola di Santa Maria della Carità,
Registro 253: 207, 208
Scuola di Santa Maria della
Misericordia, Registro 166: 207–8
Venice, Biblioteca Nazionale Marciana
ital. IX.145: 27n, 35
ital. Cl. IV. 1795–8: 169n, 201n
Verona, Biblioteca Capitolare
CVII: 350n
757: 261, 283, 288
Vich, Biblioteca Capitular
105 (CX): 358–9n
106: 359n
Vienna, Österreichische National-
bibliothek
1783: 86n
18810: 281, 282, 290
Volterra, Biblioteca Guarnacci, L.3.39:
362

Warsaw, Uniwersitiet Muziekolowskiego
Institut, mf. 2016: 279, 290
Washington, Library of Congress
M 2.1 L 25 Case: 251n, 254n, 266, 268,
270–1, 279, 281, 290
M 2.1 M 6 Case: 90n, 287
Wolfenbüttel, Herzog August Bibliothek
Cod. Guelf. extravag. 287: 270–1, 290
Cod. Guelf. 628 Helmst. (W₁): 365,
366, 367, 368, 369, 370, 371, 372,
374, 375, 376, 382, 383, 384, 385,
386, 387, 388–93, 394, 398
Cod. Guelf. 1099 Helmst. (W₂): 365,
366, 367, 368, 369, 372, 373, 374,
375, 376, 382, 384, 385, 386, 388–93,
396

Zwickau, Ratsschulbibliothek, 12: 283,
290